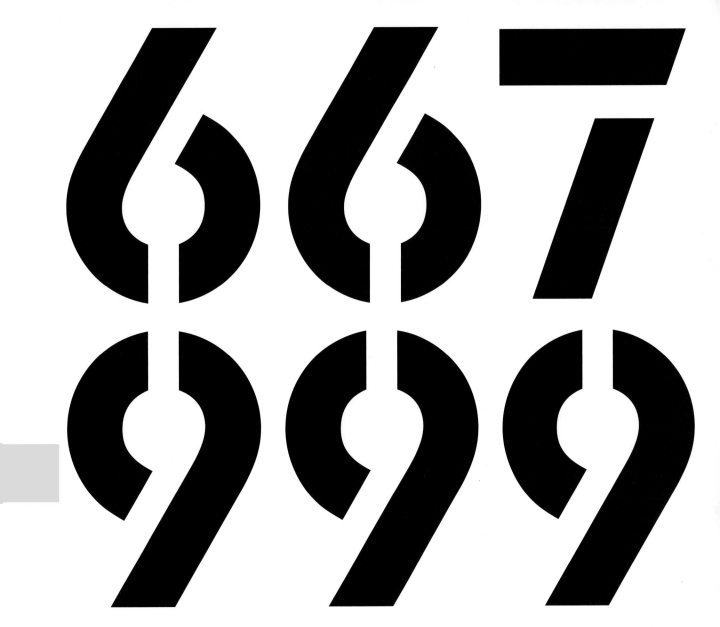

PHAIDON DESIGN CLASSICS **VOLUME THREE**

The 999 design classics included in this book have been chosen in consultation with a wide range of international design-world insiders. Academics, critics, historians, curators, journalists, designers and architects were asked to select industrially-manufactured objects that conform to our definition of a Phaidon Design Classic, as specified on the cover. Every object selected meets at least one of the criteria within our overall definition and many of them meet more than one.

The final choice of objects illustrated in this three-volume set is the result of a rigorous selection process and meticulous research. The collection includes a huge variety of consumer products, ranging from chairs to aeroplanes, which date from the Industrial Revolution to the present day. Garments, fashion accessories and objects that have been designed for highly specialist use, are not included.

Most of the objects are still in production and the majority of them are available to buy. When something is no longer manufactured, it is not usually because the design itself has become obsolete, but rather because the technology it was designed for has since become outdated.

To make the book as contemporary as possible we have also included objects created more recently. It is, of course, more difficult to judge which of the products created in more recent decades will eventually be regarded as classics, but we have included those we consider to be the 'classics of tomorrow' according, once again, to our definition.

736 Spirale Ashtray *Achille Castiglioni*	**759** Rotaro Floor Sweeper *Leifheit Design Team*	**783** Papillona Lamp *Afra Scarpa, Tobia Scarpa*
737 KV1 *Arne Jacobsen*	**760** 06LC Seiko Quartz Watch *Seiko Epson Design Team*	**784** Tratto Pen *Design Group Italia*
738 Parentesi *Achille Castiglioni, Pio Manzù*	**761** SS 750 Desmo *Fabio Taglioni*	**785** Uni-Tray *Riki Watanabe*
739 Laser Sailing Dinghy *Bruce Kirby*	**762** Sommeliers Range *Claus Josef Riedel*	**786** Suomi Table Service *Timo Sarpaneva*
740 Box Chair *Enzo Mari*	**763** Togo *Michel Ducaroy*	**787** Kryptonite K4 *Michael Zane, Peter Zane*
741 Trac II - Safety Razor Division *Gillette Design Team*	**764** Sciangai *Gionatan De Pas, Donato D'Urbino, Paolo Lomazzi*	**788** Ashtray *Anna Castelli Ferrieri*
742 Tizio *Richard Sapper*	**765** Salt and Pepper Rasps *Johnny Sørensen, Rud Thygesen*	**789** Sonora *Vico Magistretti*
743 Pollo Vase *Tapio Wirkkala*	**766** Bic ® lighter *Flaminaire Design Team*	**790** Glass Chair & Collection *Shiro Kuramata*
744 Programma 8 *Eija Helander, Franco Sargiani*	**767** Ariette 1/2/3 *Afra Scarpa, Tobia Scarpa*	**791** Nuvola Rossa *Vico Magistretti*
745 Minitimer *Richard Sapper*	**768** Pony *Eero Aarnio*	**792** Cricket Maxi Lighter *Cricket Design Team*
746 Omstack Chair *Rodney Kinsman*	**769** Playmobil *Hans Beck*	**793** Vacuum Jug *Erik Magnussen*
747 Honda Civic *Honda Design Team*	**770** Servomuto *Achille Castiglioni*	**794** Atollo 233/D *Vico Magistretti*
748 Cuboluce *Franco Bettonica, Mario Melocchi*	**771** Input Ice Bucket *Conrad Associates, Martin Roberts*	**795** Telephone Model F78 *Henning Andreasen*
749 SX-70 Polaroid Folding Camera *Henry Dreyfuss, Henry Dreyfuss Associates*	**772** Tennis Racket *Howard Head*	**796** Cab *Mario Bellini*
750 Wiggle Chair *Frank Gehry*	**773** Cucciolo Toilet Brush *Makio Hasuike*	**797** Atari Joystick CX40 *Atari Design Team*
751 Divisumma 18 *Mario Bellini*	**774** Corkscrew *Peter Holmblad*	**798** 9090 Espresso Coffee Maker *Richard Sapper*
752 Beogram 4000 *Jacob Jensen*	**775** 4875 Chair *Carlo Bartoli*	**799** Proust Chair *Alessandro Mendini*
753 Porsche Design Chronograph *Ferdinand Porsche*	**776** Rubik's Cube® *Ernö Rubik*	**800** Billy Shelf *IKEA*
754 Noce *Achille Castiglioni*	**777** Banco Catalano *Óscar Tusquets Blanca, Lluís Clotet*	**801** ET 44 Pocket Calculator *Dieter Rams, Dietrich Lubs*
755 Tripp Trapp Child's Chair *Peter Opsvik*	**778** VW Golf A1 *Giorgetto Giugiaro*	**802** A'dammer *Aldo van den Nieuwelaar*
756 Sinclair Executive Calculator *Sir Clive Marles Sinclair*	**779** Chambord Coffee Maker *Carsten Jørgensen*	**803** Mattia Esse *Enrico Contreas*
757 SL-1200 Turntable *Technics Research and Development Team*	**780** Vertebra Chair *Emilio Ambasz, Giancarlo Piretti*	**804** Frisbi *Achille Castiglioni*
758 Kurve Flatware *Tapio Wirkkala*	**781** Kickstool *Wedo Design Team*	**805** 5070 Condiment Set *Ettore Sottsass*
	782 Brompton Folding Bicycle *Andrew Ritchie*	**806** Gacela (part of Clásica collection) *Joan Casas y Ortínez*

The Timor is one of a series of perpetual calendars that Enzo Mari designed for Danese in the 1960s. Its shape was inspired by the old train information signals that Mari remembers from his childhood in the 1940s. Despite its distinctive form, Mari has stated that his primary interest was in the precision of the graphics. This use of a strong graphic language is evident in Mari's other plastic products for Danese, such as the Colleoni Pencil Holder, Hawaii Egg Cups, Borneo Ashtray and Tongareva Salad Bowl. Together with his printed posters, these works clearly demonstrate his affection for linear graphics. Mari's choice of ABS plastic as the primary material, rather than alternatives such as painted metal, was due to its durability and ease of assembly as well its low cost, given the complexity and number of parts involved. Mari felt these factors were more important than issues of taste, although the smooth, glossy surface and precision of the moulded ABS undoubtedly adds to the timeless appeal of the product. Timor is one of Mari's best-known products, partly due to its unusual shape but also because of the memorable promotional photograph, which presented it in a fan format. The name Timor has no particular significance, other than that, at the time, all Danese products were named after islands. When asked about the practicalities of Timor, his response was very honest: 'There are substantial problems with all perpetual calendars. You have to remember to change them every day; you have to interact with them. Other problems are that you cannot write on them and there are no holidays or festivals shown'. For these reasons he does not use a Timor himself saying, 'I don't want to have to remember to change the date every single day!' Despite this, the calendar is a beautiful object that is still in production today.

A marvellous vehicle, and from an era when Britain's motor industry was at such a low point, make the story behind the Range Rover a particularly intriguing one. It was developed over many years as a 4x4 vehicle to sit somewhere between the more utilitarian Land Rover and the up-market-ish Rover saloon family. It used the tremendously powerful, yet lightweight, Buick designed, aluminium V8 3500cc engine, as used in the Rover SD1 saloon. The Range Rover was built on a steel box section chassis with simple, bolt-on aluminium bodywork. The look of the vehicle came about initially through the engineering design team, including Spen King and David Bache, the bodywork stylist. The same team who designed and engineered this supremely handsome and world-beating vehicle also designed the incredibly ugly and disastrous Austin Maestro, hence, the Range Rover immediately stood out as being a very different animal from the majority of the Leyland family of vehicles (excluding the Mini, of course). It was immediately very well received, as a very rugged yet also elegant four-wheel drive workhorse, as well as being considered a very stylish urban run-around, which ended up competing with the prestige estate and saloon car market. One of the most influential vehicles ever designed, it gave birth to a whole new genre of vehicle, nowadays often referred to in US terminology as SUV's or 'sports utility vehicles'. Part of its success came from the fact that it was built on the already globally successful thoroughbred technology of the Land Rover, but adding levels of comfort and sophistication not previously associated with four-wheel drive vehicles. These combined qualities of butchness and grace meant it sat happily in city streets as much as on country lanes. It was and is, still seen on country estates and council estates. It was in production in a couple of different guises for a total of thirty-two years and prompted many imitations, as well as its own replacement, which came in 2002.

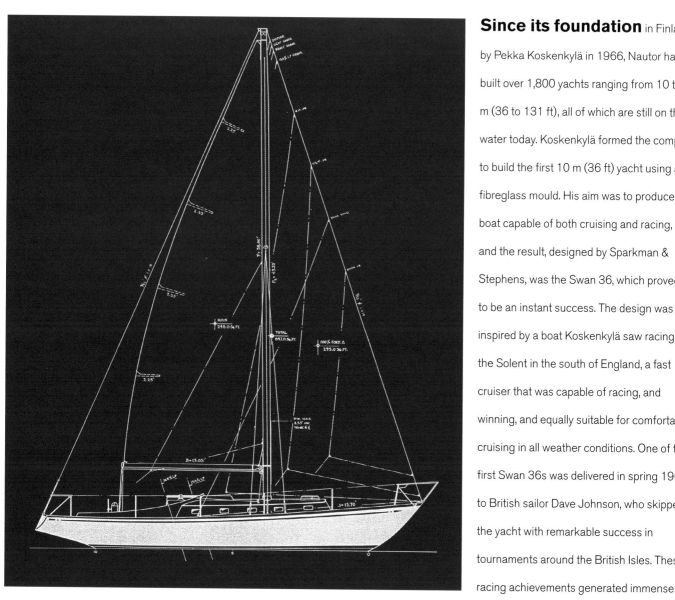

Since its foundation in Finland by Pekka Koskenkylä in 1966, Nautor has built over 1,800 yachts ranging from 10 to 40 m (36 to 131 ft), all of which are still on the water today. Koskenkylä formed the company to build the first 10 m (36 ft) yacht using a fibreglass mould. His aim was to produce a boat capable of both cruising and racing, and the result, designed by Sparkman & Stephens, was the Swan 36, which proved to be an instant success. The design was inspired by a boat Koskenkylä saw racing in the Solent in the south of England, a fast cruiser that was capable of racing, and winning, and equally suitable for comfortable cruising in all weather conditions. One of the first Swan 36s was delivered in spring 1967 to British sailor Dave Johnson, who skippered the yacht with remarkable success in tournaments around the British Isles. These racing achievements generated immense

publicity and established Nautor as a manufacturer of high-performance racing yachts. The yacht was made of fibreglass, with wood trim. The hull is moulded in one piece from two parting female moulds, as one would expect from the shape of the reverse transom and cutaway keel; the deck unit, too, is a single mould although of a sandwich construction, with a layer of foam between the two skins. The interior was designed by Ole Enderlain, one of the foremost yacht designers in the world. The cruising version of the boat was available with a choice of two or three cabins, and the cabin details were all teak. Throughout, the yacht's construction is of the highest quality. Today, Nautor, under the direction of Leonardo Ferragamo, has branched into the luxury yacht market, with German Frers as the head of design.

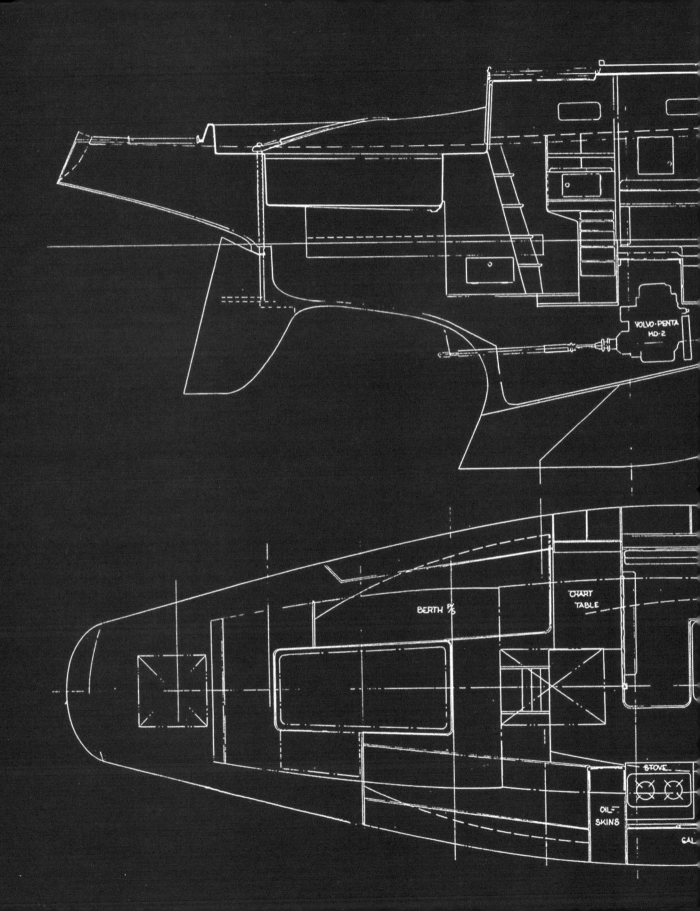

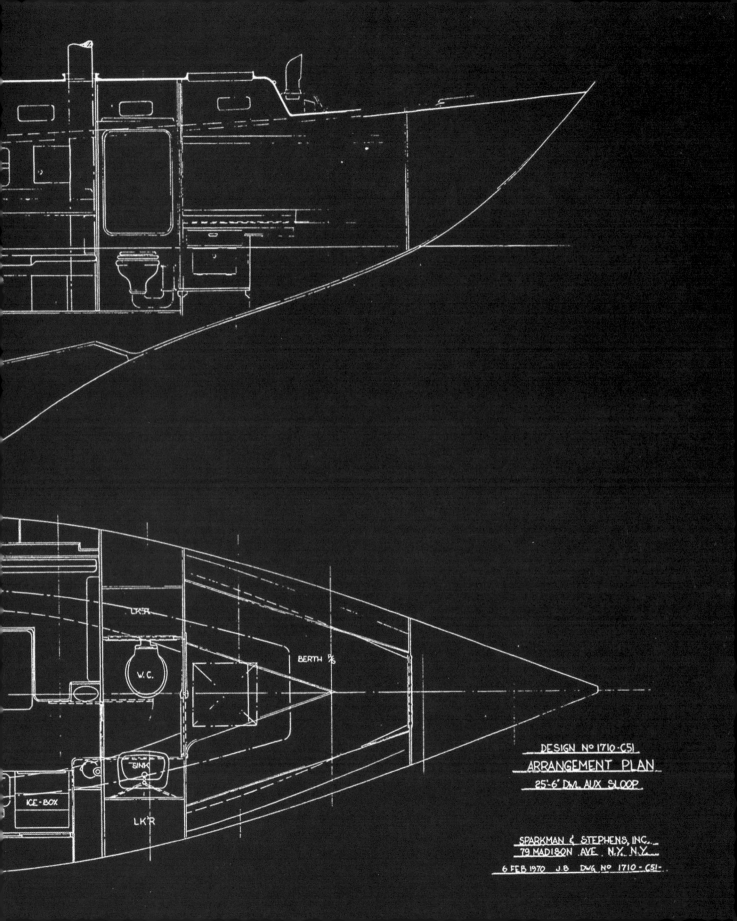

DESIGN Nº 1710-C51

ARRANGEMENT PLAN

25'-6" D.W.L. AUX. SLOOP

SPARKMAN & STEPHENS, INC.
79 MADISON AVE. N.Y. N.Y.
6 FEB 1970   J.B   DWG Nº 1710-C51-

Tongue Chair (1967)
Pierre Paulin (1927–)
Artifort 1967 to present

In the late 1950s the Dutch furniture manufacturer Artifort made an important decision. By engaging Kho Liang Ie, a visionary designer and connoisseur in art and design, and as aesthetic adviser, the company radically modernized its collection. Upholstered furniture in the traditional Dutch style was replaced by a new approach to furniture design that was at times so revolutionary that it was a step too far even for its international competitors such as Knoll International or Arflex. The Tongue Chair by Pierre Paulin is just such a piece of furniture, which is ahead of its time. Paulin originally trained as a sculptor, but his interest in furniture design grew during the early 1950s when he was working for Thonet. But it was not until Harry Wagemans invited him to join Artifort, that his own ideas for furniture were realized. The Tongue, a stackable, ultra hip, almost mattress-like piece of lounge furniture, gave new meaning to the concept of sitting, suggesting that the sitters might drape themselves over its curves rather than sit upright. Because of this unfamiliar, possibly uncomfortable concept and its peculiar shape, the chair was initially made simply as a prototype. Only after some of the company's young workers spent a night lounging on the prototypes did it become clear that the chair met the needs of a young avant-garde clientele sensitive to modern design. It is not difficult to identify the essence of the flower power in this quirky chair. The new shape was made possible by borrowing production techniques from the car industry. A metal frame was covered with webbing, rubberized canvas and a thick, comfortable layer of foam. Traditional upholstery was radically simplified by using a piece of elastic fabric with a zipper over the frame, marking the end of a long tradition of painstaking and time-consuming upholstery techniques. The slip-cover was available in a range of bright colours, making the chair easy to customize to various interiors, or become the attraction point of a room. The Tongue Chair was quite radical for its time in terms of its shape, yet its comforting form which embraces the body, has proved its success throughout the years.

Braun, creators of electrical products for domestic use, are pioneers of the minimalist aesthetic, where all superfluous features are removed. This coffee grinder has a single operation button in a contrasting colour, which blatantly identifies its function: to activate the grinder, and also clearly declares it as a design feature. Its minimal capsule shape was a dramatic development in kitchenware design and from the hand-powered grinders traditionally used. Together with Braun's other domestic electrical items, the KSM 1 followed a principle that separated essential standard forms from any superfluous detail, so creating the smooth, cylindrical shape. The slight narrowing towards the base and top made it easy to hold, the flat base ensured stability, and the size and shape of the lid made it fit easily into the palm of the hand, guaranteeing a safe and easy-to-use coffee grinder. The clean, sharp shape of the coffee grinder, along with the black lines of the Braun logo presented the austere appearance that the company was known for. Following a three-year collaboration with the Hochschule für Gestaltung in Ulm, known for pioneering modern functionalist design, Braun created a bold and recognizable corporate image that permeated every area of the company from marketing to products, including Weiss's KSM 1 design. Braun's policy was to work with cutting-edge designers and, as a leading product designer of the time, Reinhold Weiss was one of a number who worked with the company. His design, despite no longer being in production, is still admired and sought after today and can demand high prices from collectors. With the renaissance in the drinking of real coffee in the home, as opposed to the popularity of instant in the 1970s, combined with the rise in popularity of retro chic and Pop style, the demand for grinders, including the KSM 1 has grown. This has led to its being widely copied and illustrates the popularity of a functional, minimalist design aesthetic for domestic, and in particular kitchen, items. Braun continues to pioneer the use of beautifully sculptural and minimal forms for its kitchen appliances and produces grinders that visibly owe their design to the KSM 1.

Der Hoflieferant.

Warum der Volkswagen Transporter auf allen europäischen Höfen so gern gesehen wird, ist schnell erklärt.

Erstens gehört er zu den zuverlässigsten Lieferanten der Welt. (Er wird seit über 28 Jahren in über 4,7 Millionen Exemplaren gebaut.)

Zweitens liefert er auch an Höfe, die abseits von befestigten Straßen liegen. (Seine Antriebsräder bekommen durch das Gewicht des Motors sichere Bodenhaftung. Und drehen so nicht leicht durch.)

Drittens liefert er wirtschaftlich. (Eine Tonne Nutzlast schafft der Volkswagen Transporter mit dem 37 kW (50 DIN-PS) Motor, der 11,4 Liter Normalbenzin oder mit dem 51 kW (70 DIN-PS), Motor, der 11,8 Liter Normalbenzin verbraucht (DIN), 100 km weit.)

Und viertens macht der Fahrer ein freundlicheres Gesicht als viele andere Lieferanten. (Er fährt bequemer, weil der Transporter einen Arbeitsplatz hat, der nach ergonomischen Gesichtspunkten gestaltet wurde.) Hat man Ihnen je bessere Argumente für einen Eintonner geliefert?

 **Der Transporter.**

Although it may be responsible for bringing the concepts of a 'station wagon', 'microbus' and 'minivan' into the automobile world, the Volkswagen T2 began life as a rectangular box stuck on top of a Volkswagen Beetle chassis. Although it was subject to numerous refinements and modifications, the basic shape never departed very much from that. The 'design' was the work of Ben Pon, a Dutch Volkswagen importer who sketched it out while visiting the manufacturer's factory (then under the control of the British Army) in Minden, Germany, in 1947. Pon's design was based on the Plattenwagen, a small, crude, flat-bed transporter used to move heavy weights around the factory. And, by 1950, after a few aerodynamic tweaks in the wind-tunnel, Volkswagen was producing a nine-seater van (the T1) that, almost incredibly, used the same wheel-base, engine and chassis as the four-seater Beetle. Where the Beetle was marketed behind the slogan 'Think Small', the Volkswagen Bus was sold to people who could 'Think Tall'. The emphasis was on cargo space, with the driver's seat in front, and the engine behind, placing the area for cargo between the axles, which allowed the pressure on the axles to remain uniform whether or not the bus was fully loaded. The T1, or Splitscreen Bus, produced during 1950–67, was replaced by the more advanced T2 in 1967. The new version boasted a more powerful engine than its predecessor and the first-generation model's split windshield was replaced by a single pane of glass, leading to the vehicle's name, the 'bay window' bus. The swing-

open, barn-style doors on its side were replaced with a more elegant sliding door. But many of Pon's innovations, such as placing the driver above, rather than behind the front wheels, have become the basis of the majority of compact transporter vehicles that have followed in its wake. The T2 was built during August 1967 and produced until May 1979, during which time over 2.4 million were manufactured. The name T2 was the factory name; popularly it was known as the 'Type 2 Transporter', as the 'Breadloaf' in the US, or as the 'Hippie Van' in the UK. There were four generations of the bus, T1, T2, T3, and T4, but the entire line has always been known as the Type 2.

Cylinda-Line originated as a number of rough sketches on a napkin by designer Arne Jacobsen. Still in production today, the Cylinda-Line is a successful feat of design for several reasons. Launched in 1967 as a range of eighteen pieces with no preliminary market research and on a largely uncharted audience, all the individual items present a successful negotiation of Jacobsen's dual commitment to organic form and to the clean lines of Modernism. From the original sketches Cylinda-Line was developed over a three-year period, with Jacobsen and Stelton working in close collaboration. Stainless steel is an exceptionally demanding material and, when it is badly worked, irreversible tension stripes and uneven surfaces are formed. Since the technology did not yet exist to create Jacobsen's pure cylindrical forms in stainless steel, it was necessary to develop new machines and welding techniques. The resulting semi-automated equipment and current welding techniques gave a rigorous precision to the seamless

cylindrical forms, and the extremely high machine tolerances yielded sleek, brushed surfaces. However, its unique technique also made it extremely difficult to manufacture. Jacobsen's resolute demand for perfection made Cylinda-Line a successful design and enabled Stelton to broaden and extend the possibilities in the manufacture of stainless-steel homeware. Cylinda-Line was put on the market in 1967 and immediately attracted considerable international attention for its striking black nylon handles of rectangular outlines and interior arcs, which both contrast and offset the cylindrical body. The range gained early recognition that same year when awarded the inaugural ID prize, founded by the Danish Design Council. Several other prizes followed, including the International Design Award of the American Institute of Interior Designers in 1968. Jacobsen's Cylinda-Line represents the broadest and most commercially successful application of formalist principles for the domestic consumer, and the range was a triumph for neo-Functionalism as a mass-market product.

Arne Jacobsen

Hobart 'Hobie' Alter and his friend Gordon Clark, from the generation of the Beach Boys, are two surfers with a passion for trying out new ideas and taking this sport to new extremes. They used to surf off Capistrano beach in California, and it was there that they built their first surfboards in fibreglass and foam. These experiments led to the Hobie catamaran 14, 1967, which went on to become the most widely used catamaran in the world. While the Hobie Cat 14 was widely used, it was not long before the updated Hobie Cat 16 made its first appearance on the Californian beach just two years later. The idea was to design a boat that was both easy for one person to sail single-handedly, and could be launched from the beach. The Hobie catamaran 14, 4.25 m (14 ft) multi-hull catamaran, was made from fibreglass, a

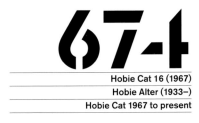

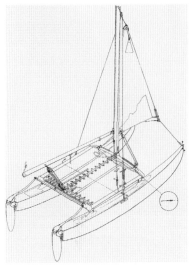

material now widely used in boat-building for its twin advantages of being lightweight and rigid. The shape is of particular interest, with its two characteristic asymmetrical hulls, giving the boat its unique V-shape. The opposing hulls have been considered as a successful alternative to the more archetypal keel of a boat. The Hobie Cat 16 is now an icon of sailing for pleasure, and more than 100,000 have been produced, and are used in schools and regattas worldwide. Sailing with a Hobie Cat 16 is an exhilarating experience; one can find oneself precariously perched on just the leeward hull when travelling at very high speeds. Because of the single mainsail and the characteristics of catamaran sailing, the Hobie Cat 16 performs best when wind meets beam and the waves are high.

Eero Aarnio

The Finnish designer Eero Aarnio rose to glory in 1966 at the Cologne Furniture Fair with the unveiling of the capsule-like Ball Chair that was made of polyester reinforced with fibreglass. The 100 cm (40 in) diameter mini-environment captured the imaginations of buyers from around the world and earned considerable press coverage, instantly elevating the young designer into the industry limelight. The manufacturer at the time, Finnish furniture company Asko, was thrilled by the success of the chair and commissioned more work from the new star. Aarnio had earned overnight success from the production of furniture that was perfectly in tune with the brash consumerist culture that was emerging at the time. His Space Age designs encapsulated a wave of optimism that was liberating society from the firm hold of tradition. During the 1950s the public needed to be convinced of the strength and durability of plastic. By the next decade these reservations had been overcome and challenging convention was the order of the day. Aarnio's overnight success had rooted him firmly in the liberal Pop era when preceding design values were being questioned, and garish colours and other-worldly plastic forms were increasingly popular home additions. Aarnio had discovered that plastic was the ideal material for the bulbous and organic shapes that were heralded at the time. His next big hit was the Pastil Chair of 1967, which won the American Industrial Design Award in 1968. This candy-coloured seating object, also referred to as the Gyro Chair, was the 1960s answer to the rocking-chair. Aarnio had essentially designed a new type of furniture that is comfortable, yet playful and suitable for use both indoors or out. Its shape was taken from the sweet, or 'pastil', further developing the space of the earlier Ball Chair, while utilizing the same diameter. Aarnio's prototype for the Pastil was made from polystyrene, so that he could work out the measurement and its potential as a rocking chair. The oil crisis of 1973 halted production of many of his polyester designs. In the 1990s a revival of interest in the design of the 1960s has since brought several pieces back into production by Adelta, and it is manufactured in moulded fibreglass-reinforced polyester. Aarnio and Adelta create these pieces in a variety of colours, allowing the consumer to choose between lime green, yellow, orange, tomato red, light and dark blue, and the more restrained black and white.

Back in 1932 Paul Ricard created a pastis, an aniseed-flavoured spirit, which he claimed was the finest in Marseille. By 1938 Ricard had taken Paris by storm and had begun an aggressive advertising campaign aimed at dominating the French spirits market. Ricard was light years ahead of the marketing game, with bold billboard advertisements and events sponsorship. Ricard's ambition was to create a strong consumer image and a very visual presence in the bars, restaurants and cafés of France. Along with the employment of a dedicated sales team, which would forcefully lobby these establishments, Ricard developed a merchandising programme that was nothing short of progressive. Ricard's pastis is a long drink, a relatively new invention back in the 1930s, and so intended to be mixed with five parts water. The company supplied stockists with Ricard-branded tableware: glasses, ashtrays and carafes for the essential water ritual. The carafes quickly became a staple addition to café tabletops across the country and, although their design has changed over the years in tandem with an ever-evolving branding exercise, the Ricard carafe has a recognizable silhouette. The angular design would have seemed very modern (as modern as the brand it was promoting) on its invention. The carafe then evolved by an ever-changing application of graphics and colour, with minor alterations to the vessel's form. Ricard recognized that the carafes would quickly become covetable, collectable and the subject of idle café chat. By the 1960s the Ricard logo had been long interwoven with French street culture. The 1967 carafe design displays a contemporary form and a new logo incorporating the company's most recent colours of blue, yellow and red. Ricard is a brand synonymous with French heritage and is a continuing champion of creative marketing. The Ricard accessories, carafes included, can still be found littering the tabletops of French cafés and restaurants, although now their varied forms are as much an encyclopedia of design through the past century as they are a note on the changing fashions and patterns of consumption.

677

Concorde (1967)
Sir Archibald E Russell (1904–95)
Pierre Satre (1909–80)
Bill Strang (1920–)
Lucien Servanty (1909–73)
British Aircraft Corporation & Sud Aviation
1967 to 2003

The great story of Concorde will be forever clouded by the tragic accident in Paris in July 2000, which led, ultimately, to the retirement of Concorde as the fastest and most recognizable passenger airliner in aviation history. While it was taking off, a tyre hit a piece of metal that had fallen from another aircraft, causing the tyre to shred and start a catastrophic fire. Minutes later the damaged Concorde crashed, leading to the deaths of all the passengers on board. The terrible end was in stark contrast to the almost heroic dream that brought Concorde into being. Supersonic flight was a military standard in the 1950s, and it seemed inevitable that supersonic passenger flight was a short step away. Boeing had a concept for an SST (Supersonic Transport) on the drawing-board when Britain's aerospace industries began a joint study for their own SST. The costs involved in creating a supersonic aircraft big enough to carry passengers, however, were daunting. Across the Channel the French aerospace industry came to the same conclusion. But the dream had taken a powerful hold on the imaginations of both the British and French authorities and in an unprecedented agreement, signed ten years before Britain joined the European Community, the two governments decided to pool their resources to produce a supersonic passenger aircraft, named, appropriately, Concorde. With factories in Filton, England, and Toulouse, France, the consortium of BAC and Sud Aviation (later Aérospatiale) began the long and arduous process of design development that took fourteen years, many thousands of hours testing and a spiralling budget before the first supersonic, transatlantic service began in 1976, run jointly by Air France and British Airways. This transatlantic service would become Concorde's mainstay for a quarter of a century. The design challenges presented by a passenger-carrying supersonic jet are enormous: engines, wing-shape, airframe, materials, all had to be radically rethought for an aircraft to break the mythical sound barrier. Concorde had a cruising speed of Mach 2, or 2,160 kph (1,350 mph), urged along by four Rolls Royce/SNECMA Olympus engines. Uniquely for a commercial aircraft, Concorde's engines had after-burners, devices that reheat the jet exhaust by injecting pure fuel into the already super-heated gas, creating a jolt of extra thrust. These were used at take-off and when going transonic, creating the orange glows that thrilled many a fan watching a Concorde departure. For almost twenty-five years of operation Concorde represented the very best of European aerospace design in an aircraft that was romantic, exciting and very sexy. That romance is no longer, as Concorde retired from commercial service after its last supersonic flight across the Atlantic from JFK, New York, to Heathrow, London, on 24 October 2003.

An enduring visual statement of the 1960s, the Blow Chair was the first inflatable design to be successfully mass-produced, although inflatable furniture had been available in Denmark as early as 1961. Its comic, bulbous shape was inspired by Bibendum, Michelin's nineteenth-century publicity character, while its technology was pure twentieth century. Its PVC cylinders, for instance, are kept together by high-frequency welding to ensure strength. The chair was the first collaboration produced by DDL Studio, started by De Pas, D'Urbino and Lomazzi in 1966 in Milan, with a focus on urban development and industrial design. All the designers shared an unconventional attitude towards design. By the 1960s mass production and the emergence of new materials had influenced a cultural trend towards prefabrication and disposable commodity. DDL's aim was to design simple and inexpensive objects for a fresh,

alternative, youthful style of living. The company also experimented with materials, looking to pneumatic architecture installations for inspiration. The studio approached practical furnishing with designs permeated with irony and lightness, characteristics that are reflected in the Blow Chair. The chair, which can be easily deflated and inflated at home, is a milestone in furniture design in its dismissal of traditional notions of high cost and permanence. It was created for indoor and outdoor use, although its plastic material made it impractical during the hot summer. The Blow's life span was expected to be short, as it got easily damaged, and even came with a repair kit, and its cheap price reflected this. When it first came out, it generated a huge amount of publicity for Zanotta. In the 1980s the company revived it as a design classic.

678

Blow Chair (1967)
Gionatan De Pas (1932–91)
Donato D'Urbino (1935–)
Paolo Lomazzi (1936–)
Carla Scolari (1930–)
Zanotta 1967 to present

Advertisement, 1968

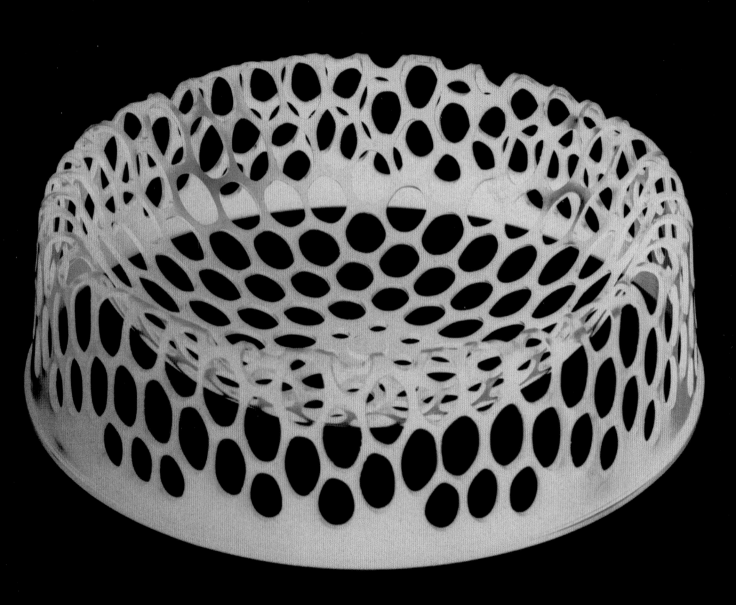

The Adal Fruit Bowl is a finely tuned container for fresh fruit, but it far exceeds this function. It is an enduring by-product of a very personal vision and heart-felt journey which persists to this day. The vacuum-moulded PVC bowl evolved from a series of investigations beginning as early as 1960 with the design of a similarly perforated metal tray. In 1965 Mari collaborated with Danese, and was researching industrial fabrication using 'poor' materials. In 1968, Adal appeared with its simplified, economical shape and obvious function. In contrast with an earlier bowl, this new design eliminated the need to finish the edging separately, by inverting the shape and controlling the initial pattern of perforations. Mari's careful investigations of materials, forms and production presuppose that design can communicate a broader social agenda. With purposeful forethought, each detail of Adal's design and fabrication sought to promote common dignity by using more accessible materials and by removing the repetitive work other objects required in their manufacturing process. Adal succeeds as a design of quality, beauty, and innovation. It also provides a timeless commentary on the once heated debate about the democratization of design, which was finally resolved with the rise of mass production. In 1997, after Alessi's acquisition of the rights to various earlier Enzo Mari designs for Danese, the Adal was again in production with only a minor modification, now using heat-formed polystyrene.

This portable record player, available in white and a reddish orange, was a precursor to the Sony Walkman of the early 1980s, without the advantage of the long playing-time or the flexibility of tape playback. A 45 rpm record was slipped into a space along the top, along similar lines as a toaster. The record could be played with the unit standing vertically or lying horizontally. The metal handle could be lifted and lowered and the whole unit be transported like a small handbag, transforming the phonograph into a fashion accessory. In this respect it was not unlike the advertising campaign for the Apple iPod, which suggests that the computer is more than just a utilitarian object, but a style statement. Mario Bellini's work during the 1960s and 1970s for electronic companies such as Olivetti, Brionvega and Minerva frequently featured a plastic sculptural shell that covered the interior electronics with little visual reference to the inner workings. This playful, sculptural quality evolved, not from function, but from the desires of the designer and his interest in inspiring a sense of fun. Like the Pop Art of the day, the final form of Bellini's designs had little to do with their utility. Another significant concern for Bellini was his desire to enhance the sensual qualities of his designs, creating a better connection between the user and object. This is expressed in the sculptural qualities of the record player. Perhaps most importantly, the Pop Record Player also reflects a response to changing cultural times, as music, dancing and partying became spontaneous and, with the portable Pop, could happen virtually anywhere. In a period when pop stars sang about 'Dancing in the Streets' the Pop Record Player was the perfect accessory.

681

Sacco (1968)
Piero Gatti (1940–)
Cesare Paolini (1937–83)
Franco Teodoro (1939–)
Zanotta 1968 to present

The 1960s saw a rise in the production of furniture that used modern, inexpensive materials such as injection-moulded plastics. Inflatable and disposable furniture became part of an evolution in interiors and furnishings, reflecting the youth-led socio-cultural upheavals of the decade. Italian manufacturer Zanotta jumped on the 'Pop furniture' bandwagon with the production of the Sacco chair designed by Piero Gatti, Cesare Paolino and Franco Teodoro, which was shown to Aurelio Zanotta in 1968. Although prototypes had been made several years earlier, the first commercially produced beanbag seat easily adapted to whatever position the sitter assumes. The designers originally proposed a fluid-filled transparent envelope, but the excessive weight and complications of filling it eventually led to the ingenious choice of using millions of tiny semi-expanded polystyrene beads. Sacco was marketed by Zanotta as the chair of the 1,001 Nights (1,000 positions by day, one position by night, and marvellously comfortable). Soon, the beanbag became the seat of choice of the fashionable jet set. However, due to the difficulties of patenting a sack of polystyrene balls and the ease of manufacturing, it was not long before the market was flooded with cheap Sacco reproductions, which also made Zanotta an internationally recognized brand as a result. Its advertising campaign for the beanbag also established a sense of lifestyle that matched what the chair represented – something fun, comfortable, cool, and of its period. Hence, what began as a high-quality designer piece of furniture quickly developed into a low-cost, mass-produced space filler. Although today beanbags are largely deemed unfashionable, the Sacco chair survives as a symbol because of its pioneering design and as a representation of the 1960s mood of optimism.

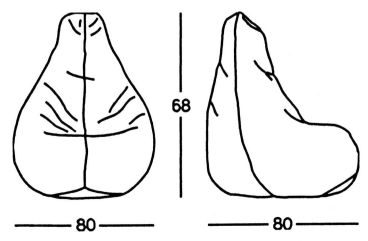

Advertisement, 1969

Launched in 1971, the melamine Clam Ashtray was a sign of the times. Measuring 14 cm (5.5 in) in diameter, the ashtray would have been a familiar sight in the trendy homes of the era. Its appeal endures even now, with examples appearing in vintage shops all over the world, as well as being recently revived by Tom Dixon for Habitat. The Clam was designed by British graphic designer Alan Fletcher, who came up with the idea while travelling on top of one of London's double-decker buses, heading towards his studio. He first pictured a shape which resembled Dutch Edam cheese – a mental image which sprang to mind, as with many of his ideas. Each Clam, as it became informally known, consists of two halves, made from a single mould; when closed, they contrast perfectly to form a graphic sculptural object. The machine cutting was so precise that even without a hinge the two halves slotted tightly together, flush along the join. When opened and turned on their backs, the separate clams become instant ashtrays, with the snaking serrated edge providing a natural resting place for a burning cigarillo. Original versions have Mebel, the name of the manufacturer, elegantly scrolled on the underside, displaying its authenticity. Italian manufacturer Mebel was enthusiastically promoting the virtues of melamine and used it to create a wide range of household goods that matched the casual entertaining preferences of a new generation getting to grips with a burgeoning design scene. Design Objectives, based in Devon, United Kingdom, made fifty editions of the pressed brass and chrome version to honour the original melamine ashtray. The Clam Ashtray's simple form, so effectively executed, has been found in all corners of the world – from banks in Buenos Aires, to bars in Bangkok – not only being used as an ashtray, but to hold paperclips, pins, stamps, buttons, keys, or spare change.

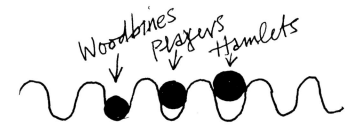

682

Clam Ashtray (1968)
Alan Fletcher (1931–)
Mebel 1972, 1992 to present
Design Objectives 1973 to 1976

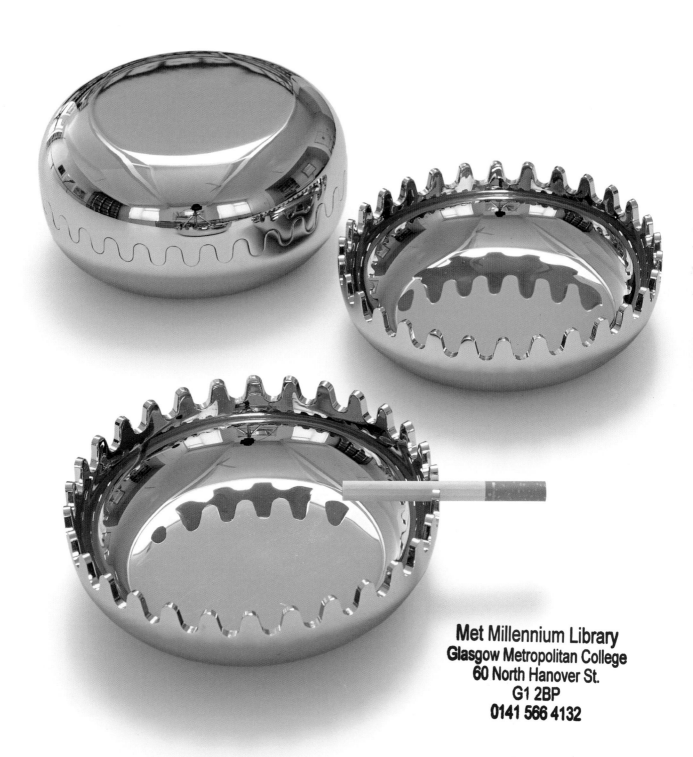

1) Set the camera to manual system
Turn the F stop ring to move the "A" mark (AUTO) off the link marked in front of view finder. The Auto system is switched to manual system. Set any one of the F numbers to the red line. The shutter can be released freely regardless of light condition.

Umschaltung der Kamera für manuelle Blendeneinstellung
Man dreht der Blendenring um den "A"-Marke weg. Damit wird die Automatik abgeschaltet und man kann die Blenden von Hand einstellen. Indem einfach der gewünschte Blendenwert gegen die rote Linie gestellt wird. Der Verschluss lässt sich dabei ohne Rücksicht auf die Lichtverhältnisse immer auslösen und belichtet 1/40".

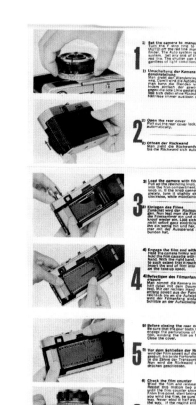

2) Open the rear cover
Pull out the rear cover lock. The cover will open automatically.

Öffnen der Rückwand
Man zieht die Rückwandverriegelung heraus, bis die Rückwand sich automatisch öffnet.

3) Load the camera with film
Fill up the rewinding knob. Put the film cassette into the film compartment. Push the rewinding knob in. If the knob cannot be pushed in completely, turn it slightly clockwise or counterclockwise, while maintaining pressure.

Einlegen des Films
Zunächst wird der Rückspulknopf herausgezogen. Nun legt man die Filmpatrone in die Filmkammer ein und drückt den Rückspulknopf wieder ein.

4) Engage the film end with the take-up spool
Hold the camera firmly with your left hand and hold the film cassette with the thumb of the left hand. With the right hand, pull out the film end to such extent that it reaches the take-up spool. Insert the end of film into any of the six slots on the take-up spool.

Befestigen des Filmanfangs an der Aufwickelspule
Man nimmt die Kamera in die linke Hand und hält sie mit dem Daumen die Filmpatrone fest.

5) Before closing the rear cover
Be sure that the gear teeth on the sprocket spool engage the perforations of the film both sides in the film, winding the film on to the take-up spool. Close the cover.

Vor dem Schließen der Rückwand
wird der Film soweit auf die Aufwickelspule aufgespult, bis die Perforationen des Films sicher in die Zähne der Transportstummel eingreifen. Nun wird die Rückwand durch einfaches Andrücken geschlossen.

6) Check the film counter
Wind the film and release the shutter button. Repeat this motion two or three times until the film counter shows the number "1". From this point start taking pictures.

Das Bildzahlwerk

7) ASA film speed setting
Rotate the ASA setting ring in front of the lens barrel until the ASA number of the film being used appears in the ASA window. When using ASA 32 film, you may set at ASA 40 dot.

Einsteuerung der Filmempfindlichkeit
Man dreht den ASA-Einstellring vor der Objektivfassung bis in dem kleinen Fenster die erforderliche ASA-Zahl sichtbar wird.

8) Set the camera to Auto system
Turn the F stop ring until the "A" mark clicks and stops at the red line.

Einstellung auf Automatik
Man dreht den Blendenring, bis die Marke "A" am roten Indexstrich einrastet.

9) Focusing
The focusing ring has distance symbols (yellow) and scales in two different colors: white (meters) and yellow (feet). Take an approximate distance between your camera and the subject, and set appropriate distance symbol to the red line by rotating the focusing ring.

Scharfeinstellung
Der Schärfering ist mit Entfernungssymbolen (gelb) und 2 Skalen markiert; die weiße Skala für m, die gelbe für feet.

10) Compose the picture and release the shutter
Hold the camera firmly. Look through the viewfinder and place the subject in the center of the frame. Press the shutter release button with the flat part of the index finger, but NOT with the tip of this finger.

Suchen und Auslösen
Man hält die Kamera fest ans Auge, blickt durch den Sucher und wählt den wirksamsten Bildausschnitt.

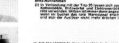

11) Rewind the film
When a roll of film is completely exposed, rewind the film. DO NOT attempt to advance the film. The film is completely exposed when the film counter indicates the number 36, 20 or 12 depending upon the length of film used. Press the rewind button on the bottom of the camera body. Lift the rewind crank and turn it in the direction of arrow.

Rückspulen des Films
Je nach der eingelegten Films ist der Film voll belichtet, wenn das Zählwerk 36, 20 oder 12 anzeigt.

Flash photography
(1) The use of either flash bulbs or an electronic flash is recommended. If red warning signal appears in the viewfinder.
We recommend you our penned style Pen Flash CL which accepts AG-1 and AG-1B for color photography or AG-3N.

Blitz-Aufnahmen
(1) In Verbindung mit der Trip 35 lassen sich sowohl Kolbenblitze, Blitzwürfel und Elektronblitzgeräte verwenden.

(2) Set the camera to manual system by turning the F stop ring (see 1) in preceding page.
The shutter speed is automatically set at 1/40 sec.

(2) Die Kamera wird auf manuelle Einstellung umgeschaltet, indem man den Blendenring um "A" wegstellt und die nötige Blende wählt.

(3) The Olympus Pen Flash CL can be connected simply by slipping its foot on to the accessory shoe.

(3) Die Trip 35 hat einen Suchereinblick mit abgebildetem Mittenkontakt.

(4) When using ordinary flash gun or electronic flash, slip the foot of the unit on to the accessory shoe and attach the flash connecting plug to the synchronising socket on the camera.

(4) Bei Verwendung von Blitzgeräten ohne Mittenkontakt wird das Verbindungskabel dieser Geräte mit dem Kontaktstecker an der Kamera verbunden.

There are some cameras that remain in the public consciousness long after they have been discontinued, and in the United Kingdom the Olympus Trip 35 is one of these, the beneficiary of a popular advertising campaign featuring David Bailey, which was first transmitted in 1977. Bailey, perhaps the best-known British photographer, still regards the camera as one of the greatest contributions to photography. The Trip 35 was a palm-sized compact camera using 35mm film. The camera's distinguishing feature was a circular panel of convex transparent cells around the main lens, which collected light for the selenium light meter. The meter automatically set the shutter and aperture and provided a red pop-up low light indicator in the viewfinder window. The camera was a logical development from Olympus's popular Pen range of half-frame cameras. Half-frame cameras had never fulfilled their potential and the Trip 35 camera offered the benefit of a full-frame negative in a camera that was not much bigger than the Pen, although it did not offer the range of features and interchangeable lenses of the advanced Pen models. It was suited to amateurs who did not need a single-lens reflex but who wanted better quality than a simple fixed box camera could provide. The Trip 35 was backed by a television and press campaign that was extremely effective and popular. This, coupled with the camera's reliability, ensured a rare longevity and the camera was only discontinued when electronics started to offer greater flexibility than the Trip's mechanics could. Its successor, the Trip AF series, was a Trip in name only and adopted electronics and auto-focus to compete in a modern way with a new generation of automatic cameras.

As one of the world's best-known industrial designers, Dieter Rams has shaped the products of one of Germany's most famous companies, Braun. During his forty-year career with the company he developed his signature style of neutral colours and pared-down functionalism, a vision that was inspired by the Bauhaus tradition. The T2 Cylindrical Cigarette Lighter, designed by Rams in 1968, shows the continuation of this approach. Its simple, clean lines are the essence of minimalism. As with all of Rams's products, ease of use is a strong factor in the design. During Rams's career at Braun black began to replace the earlier, lighter neutrals, such as beige, and would be the chosen colour for all electronic goods for the next thirty years. The T2 was no exception. The lighter was also

inspired by the new developments in magnetic ignition technology. The featured element of the design, and the part which Rams struggled with most, was where to place the indentation for the thumb to apply the most pressure to the magnetic ignition pad. As a smoker himself, Rams preferred to treat accessories such as lighters as sculptural objects. The T2 was clearly one of these sculptural forms, available in either black or chrome-plated steel, and with a sturdy, authoritative presence. At a time when many industrial designers were creating products that looked like contemporary furniture, Rams sought to design pieces that were honest in their use of materials and stripped of extraneous styling, even in the most humble of items, such as the T2 Lighter.

Although Joseph Sutter led the Boeing design team on the 747 Jumbo Jet, the man generally credited with the creation of the world's biggest, and perhaps most successful, commercial airliner did not even work for Boeing – he was Juan Trippe, legendary founder of Pan Am. Trippe started the first transatlantic air service with Pan Am and foresaw the global mobility that we now take for granted. In 1965 no aircraft had the range or capacity to take advantage of the new demand for long-distance travel. Pan Am's own 707s were flying at full capacity and Trippe urged Boeing to make a much bigger plane which could fulfil his grand ambitions and vision. The result was the 747. Dubbed the 'Jumbo Jet' by the British press when it was introduced by Pan Am in 1970 on the New York-London route, the 747 became instantly recognizable by its enormous size and the characteristic bulge over the nose. This bulge was the design team's response to one of Trippe's specifications. Hedging his bets, Trippe wanted a nose that could be converted to cargo doors should there not be enough passengers to fill such a big aircraft. The pilots sat above the nose and the space behind the cockpit, envisaged by the designers as a crew rest area, was commandeered by Trippe for the coolest lounge

Boeing 747 (1968)	
Joseph Sutter (1921–)	
Juan Trippe (1899–1981)	
Boeing Design Team	
Boeing 1968 to present	

in international travel. And so it became, for a generation of what Virgin Atlantic now calls 'Upper Class' passengers. Trippe's commitment to the 747 was a huge gamble for both Pan Am and Boeing. The disastrous oil crisis of 1973 was a severe blow to the international travel business and placed Pan Am, with its huge fleet of 747s, under an impossible financial burden which would ultimately lead to bankruptcy. The Boeing 747, in all its variations, is a marvel of aviation design. Any one of its high-bypass turbofan engines produces more power than all four engines of the old 707 put together. In a turbofan only part of the large fan forces air into the jet engine, while a large outer section of the fan simply blows air at high speed out of the back, adding 'found' thrust to the propulsion of the jet itself. The Jumbo's range and carrying capacity have been unmatched since its introduction. Although more than 1,200 747s have been delivered since 1968, it is now under threat from more fuel-efficient, extended-range twin-engine aircraft (ETOPS), including Boeing's own 767 and 777. And with the launch of the Airbus A380 in 2005, the 747's position as the biggest aeroplane of them all has finally ended.

Charles Hollis Jones

The thin layer of acrylic that stretches from the front part of the steel frame to the rear joins, forming an elegant sling-shape in between, is so technically adept it almost defies belief. At times, depending on your perspective and the light in which it is observed, the seat seems to disappear, leaving behind only the crisp shape of the bent steel-frame as proof of its existence. When the chair's designer, Charles Hollis Jones, was at his most prolific during the 1960s and 1970s, he gained international recognition as a pioneer of acrylic furniture, lighting and accessories. Jones's Sling Chair now forms part of the Getty Collection and is widely recognized as one of his most important pieces, illustrating both his considerable skill and the exciting potential for acrylic as a medium. Historically, acrylic – or Lucite, as it was branded – had been given short shrift as a material suitable for bespoke furniture design. Jones had himself previously been drawn to the qualities of glass, a material perfect for fulfilling the stylistic expectations of his glamorous Hollywood Hills clientele. Yet glass was technically limited, shattering under stress and impossible to use for weight-bearing furniture. When Jones was commissioned to design a beautiful showcase chair, which could be set up and dismantled in five minutes and be possible to fit into a limited storage space, he had already produced a wide range of work in acrylic. However, none of his previous pieces had required the material to be stretched to the degree that was needed here. For assistance Jones turned to the aircraft industry, where acrylic had long been used in the manufacture of aircraft windows. Once it had been stretched and left to cool, the newly moulded acrylic was considerably strengthened; the resulting chair could support 230 kg (507 lb). By omitting the cross members that were usually needed for support, the chair was able to showcase an uninterrupted sweep of acrylic as never before achieved. Like all of Jones's furniture, the chair was a highly limited model, with only 250 produced between 1968 and 1991. Thus, in 2002, Charles Hollis Jones reissued another 250 sling chairs, content in the knowledge that not only are his original designs proving highly collectable, but they still remain in use as had always been intended. The Sling Chair represents a moment in furniture design history: the point at which technology and an undervalued material combined to take a bold step forward.

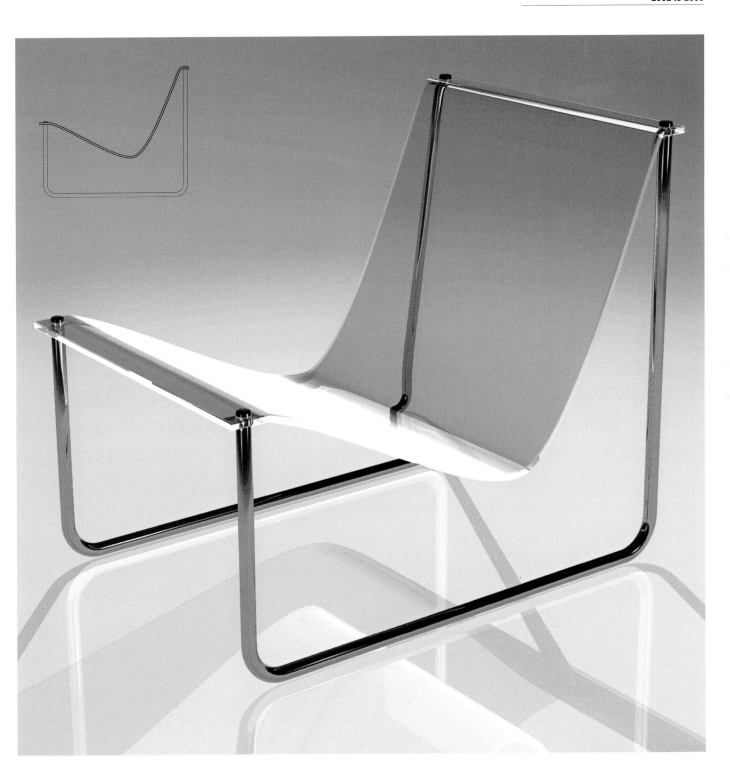

Shiro Kuramata remains one of the most audacious and innovative designers of the mid- to late twentieth century. His work varied in both style and use, but all his designs were products of his approach to materials. The Pyramid of 1968 is a transparent acrylic set of drawers mounted on castors with seventeen graduated drawers in contrasting black. The inclusion of drawers in his designs was one of Kuramata's signatures, because he always hoped to find what he did not put in them. Kuramata's preoccupation with form and shape is an enduring theme in his work. His obsession with the square, for example, was explored in a series of designs for drawers executed between 1967 and 1970. The most dramatic of his designs during this period is the Pyramid Furniture, with its architectural form and stacked drawers decreasing in size. The traditional feet have been replaced by castors, cleverly incorporating both movement and versatility. Pyramid was symbolic of Kuramata's design ideology and reflects the confidence and creativity of design that grew out of postwar Japan. Kuramata's work broke new ground through the use of innovative materials. With its unconventional form, Pyramid clearly illustrates the designer's passion for the unusual, the sensual and the ephemeral. Kuramata reconsidered the relationships between form and function and in doing so created new designs that in turn imposed his own surrealist, minimalist ideas on to everyday objects.

Verner Panton

688

Living Tower (1968)
Verner Panton (1926–98)
Herman Miller 1969 to 1970
Fritz Hansen 1970 to 1975
Stega 1997
Vitra Design Museum 1999 to present

Verner Panton designed modern furniture with personality. While always elegant, his designs show a remarkable diversity, and nowhere is this more pronounced than in his Living Tower, or 'Pantower' as it sometimes called, which was shown as part of the 1970 Cologne Furniture Fair. A novel, almost impertinent design, it embodies the spirit of the 1960s. In fact, it almost defies definition, as it falls between categories of being a seating unit, storage area or a work of art. No single term suffices, but all who see it fall in love with its friendly curves. The frame is made of birch plywood, padded with foam and covered in Kvadrat wool upholstery. Today it is available in three colours: orange, red and dark blue. This piece of furniture, which comes in two sections, forms a square when pushed together. The Living Tower brings out the child in all of us – it seems to invite the user to sit on the highest curve, with feet dangling off the side in glee, which is exactly what Panton would have liked. He once said he wanted 'to encourage people to use their fantasy and make their surroundings more exciting'. It is fitting that such a piece of furniture should have been designed by a man who travelled round Europe in a VW camper van, making contacts with manufacturers, and indeed, someone who worked at Arne Jacobsen's architectural office from 1950–52. Panton was born in 1926 in Gamtofte, Denmark, and trained at a technical college in Odense, before going on to the Royal Danish Academy of Fine Arts in Copenhagen. In 1955 he set up his own design office and by 1958 he had already caused uproar at the Fredericia Furniture Fair with his novel chair designs, hanging them from the ceiling of his stand like the works of art they indubitably were. Some critics went so far as to say that they should not be called chairs at all because they had none of the usual elements a chair should have, such as legs or backs. But the success of the Living Tower lives on as an example of a work of art, combining the features of a chair into a sculptural form.

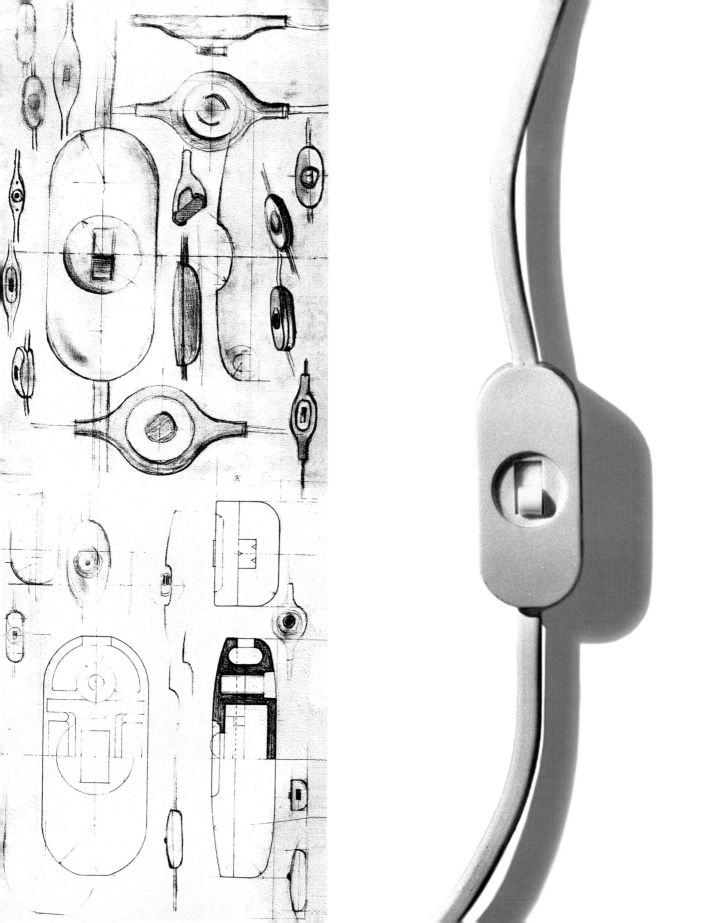

689

VLM Switch 'Interruttore Rompitratta' (1968)
Achille Castiglioni (1918–2002)
Pier Giacomo Castiglioni (1913–68)
VLM 1968 to present

The occasion of Achille Castiglioni's seventieth birthday prompted his Milanese studio to have a cake specially ordered from the local patisserie. The cake was a clever over-sized replica of the VLM Switch, or Interruttore Rompitratta. Castiglioni had designed the switch in 1968, with his brother Pier Giacomo, who died later that November, ending their long and productive partnership. This was not the first switch designed by the Castiglionis, nor even their first in-line switch, and was hardly surprising for a partnership whose modern reputation has strictly industrial roots. During the years preceding their work for VLM, they had created press button floor switches for Flos, and had already designed over two-dozen lights for commercial production. What may be more surprising, however, was Achille Castiglioni's insistence that the VLM Switch was the single design out of all his work of which he was most proud. In 1967, VLM had just opened its second factory, an automated and modern plant for producing accessories for lights. The company was growing rapidly and had aspirations to extend its reach far beyond Italy. It was with this background that VLM approached the Castiglioni studio seeking a newly designed switch. Strongly championed by VLM engineer Orthmann, the Castiglioni brothers designed a simple, anonymous switch that has sold well in excess of 15 million and continues to be sold today. Its softly curved underside thoughtfully anticipates the surfaces it may come to rest on as well as allowing it to sit comfortably in the palm of the hand. If grappling in the dark, the sharper edges of the top casing identify the correct orientation with only the slightest touch. The switch itself rests neatly within a middle indentation and slides securely on or off with an audible click – the sound of a hidden half-bearing snapping into place, held taut by a cleverly concealed spring placed between it and a metal strip used either to complete or break the electric current. Thousands of people across thirty countries use this switch daily without any awareness of the design or the designers, a testament to the absolute triumph of this product.

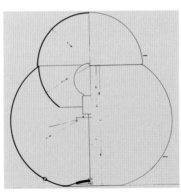

In the late 1960s Western designers became newly fascinated with Japanese culture. Many designers were inspired by the technological advances that were transforming industries ranging from watches to consumer electronics. This led to interest in the Japanese psyche, with particular reference to Zen Buddhism and its role in Japan's recovery after World War II. For Italy's design vanguard, this phenomenon presented both challenges and inspiration. Sergio Asti, one of Italy's most prolific designers throughout the second half of the twentieth century, worked in furniture, electronics, lighting and accessories and transformed his interests into multiple expressions of a renewed Italian commitment to innovation, quality and detail. For Asti these interests find eloquent articulation in the refinement and simplicity of his Daruma lamp, which was manufactured by Candle in 1968. According to legend, during the fifth or sixth century the Indian sage Bohidharma, also known as Daruma, travelled to China's Middle Kingdom and introduced a form of Buddhism that would come to be known as Zen when it took hold in Japan. Different legends explain how Daruma attained enlightenment: one story relates how it occurred after years of meditation in a cave without blinking or moving his eyes. Another version contends that during his years of meditation his arms and legs atrophied and fell off. He was so infuriated by falling asleep during meditation that he, somehow, cut off his eyelids. Centuries later this story came to be embodied in the armless, legless, eyeless Daruma or tumbler doll that can be found throughout Japan, and Daruma has become a symbol of undaunted spirit, resilience and determination. These three characteristics are key ingredients in the Japanese formula for success. The design for the Daruma lamp was based upon a collection of white porcelain canisters of the same name that Asti designed for the Japanese manufacturer Aura in 1967. The Daruma lamp combines a spherical base of opaque glass and a smaller translucent globe into a single eye-like form that balances like a traditional Daruma doll. Lacking of all other surface details, it is a reinterpretation of the various stories that constitute the Daruma myth. Legless, armless and without a shading lid, it provides pervasive illumination. Daruma symbolizes an aspect of the postmodern sensibility that relished the opportunity to create a pan-cultural interpretation of an archetype.

691

Garden Egg Chair (1968)
Peter Ghyczy (1940–)
Reuter 1968 to 1973
VEB Schwarzheide DDR 1973 to 1980
Ghyczy NOVO 2001 to present

Peter Ghyczy

If the purpose of garden furniture is to bring something of a domestic interior to an outside space, then Peter Ghyczy's Garden Egg Chair is perhaps the perfect design. Housed in an egg-like shell made of fibreglass-reinforced polyester, the flip-top chair back folds down to create a waterproof seal so that, regardless of the weather, it can be left outside, although it is equally suitable indoors. In complete contrast to this hard, impervious exterior, the shell opens up to reveal a soft, plush, fabric-lined detachable seat that has many of the qualities of an old-fashioned armchair (and, because you have to open the Egg up to sit on it, a very real sense of interior comfort). In this way the Egg fuses classic ideas of comfort with modern materials and methods of fabrication. While Ghyczy remains silent about the inspiration behind his design, the fusion of natural form and contemporary craftsmanship may suggest some connections with the Art Deco movement, while the overall style is instantly recognizable as pure 1960s Pop. These days, however, the Garden Egg Chair looks most like some sort of giant precursor of the flip-top mobile phone. Ghyczy, originally from Hungary, left after the Revolution of 1956 and moved to West Germany, where he studied architecture. Following his studies, he joined Reuter, a company that produced plastic products, and shortly afterwards became the head of the design department. It was here that he wanted to create specifically unique pieces of furniture and the Garden Egg is one of the products that emerged from this. He left in 1972 because of the rather conventional approach of Reuter, and eventually the chair was reissued by the designer's own firm, Ghyczy NOVO, in 2001. While the design remains the same, the new model is made of recyclable plastic and incorporates an optional swivel base.

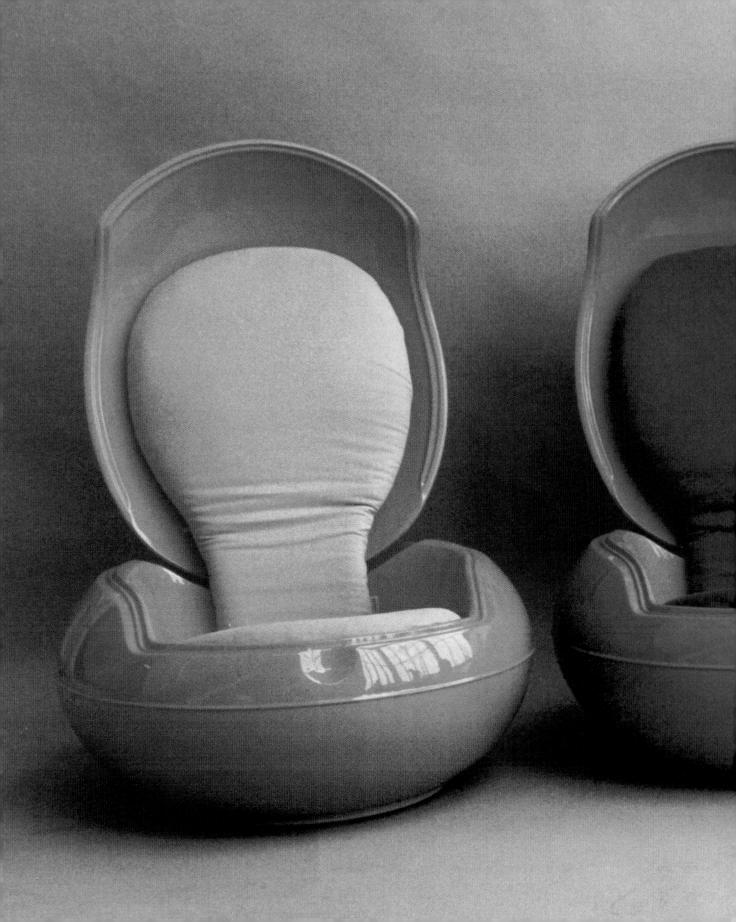

692

Tam Tam (1968)
Henry Massonnet (1924−)
STAMP 1968 to present
Branex Design 2002 to present

Also known as the Diabolo Stool, because its shape – two cones that appear to 'float' along a piece of string – is similar to the Diabolo toy, the Tam Tam was born out of the new production possibilities presented by the 1960s plastics boom. Henry Massonnet's company, STAMP, produced plastic iceboxes for fishermen, but in 1968 Massonnet decided to harness the potential of his injection-moulded production process and apply it to the manufacture of tough, portable and economic stools. Yet while its materials and manufacture were new, the Tam Tam appeared to have been designed to look like an extremely stunted and simplified classical column. It came in a variety of colours and split into two identical pieces so that it might be more easily transported or stowed away. And once Brigitte Bardot was photographed seated on one, the Tam Tam quickly became a fashion icon, a status that was enhanced by the fact that Tam Tam owners could disassemble one stool and combine it with a half in another colour to create their own individual looks. The Tam Tam was a huge success and more than 12 million were sold. However, following the oil crisis of 1973 and its consequent effect on the plastics industry, production of the Tam Tam slowed down. However, after Sacha Baron Cohen (aka Ali G), a collector of 1970s furniture, discovered one in a car boot sale, he contacted Massonnet and the Tam Tam was relaunched through a new manufacturer, Branex, in 2002. The stool continues to be produced in the same factory, using the same mould, but now comes in a greater variety of colours (thirteen, seven of which are translucent) and patterns. The Tam Tam has enjoyed an afterlife in other ways as well. Its qualities of cheapness, adaptability and the ease with which it can be moved around have made it an important inspiration for later designs such as Philippe Starck's Bubu Stool.

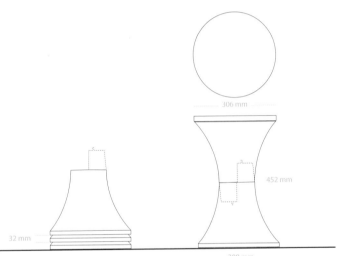

306 mm

32 mm

452 mm

300 mm

Enzo Mari's Pago-Pago design counters all our accepted ideas about vases. The design is neither elegant, as we usually expect vases to be, nor is it precious. Instead it is a strange, irregular shape, formed from a particularly durable form of plastic. The fact that the Pago-Pago shatters all stereotypes about the vase is unsurprising, given the preoccupations of its designer. Enzo Mari, brought up in Novara, Italy, with little formal education, is one of today's most original and rigorous thinkers on the subject of design. 'If everybody likes a product that I have designed,' he once said, 'it means that I have affirmed reality as it exists, which is precisely what I do not want to do.' Mari's insistence on looking at a problem from every possible angle and ignoring any preconceptions he may have has led him to some unlikely designs, and the Pago-Pago is chief among them. Perhaps the most remarkable thing about the Pago-Pago is that it is essentially two vases in one. Standing one way up it offers a narrow, circular mouth, suitable for small flowers, while the other way up it becomes a wide-mouthed vase, able to hold far larger bouquets. The two cavities share an interior wall, enabling the vase to be manufactured economically in a simple two-part mould. The vase is made from ABS (acrylonitrile butadiene styrene) plastic, the material that is also used to manufacture Lego bricks. ABS is a tough material that comes in a range of strong colours and gives objects a gleaming finish, a fact that particularly pleased Mari. Although best known as a cerebral designer, even Mari is not immune to the allure of the shiny.

Tapio Wirkkala's multicoloured free-blown Bolle vases were designed for the Italian company Venini, who commissioned him during the mid-1960s to create new glass pieces using traditional methods. These vases are remarkable for the subtle sense of static equilibrium Wirkkala achieved by appearing to balance coloured bands of different thicknesses within both the encased volume and its carefully delineated profile. In style and technique they are also very different from Wirkkala's work for Finnish glass-making firm iittala. His work for them was often in clear glass, blown or thickly moulded to evoke natural forms such as fungi, leaves or ice. The Bolle vases were a departure for Wirkkala, who made use of *incalmo*, the sixteenth-century glass-making technique and speciality of the Murano-based glass industry, in which two flaming masses of glass vessels, usually of different colours, are grafted on to one another to create one piece. The differences between Wirkkala's Italian and Finnish work can be accounted for in two ways. In Italy, he was able to leave behind much of his need to say something about Finland or Finnish nature. He was also able to work within a different glass-making tradition, one that had different recipes for glass and a different set of manufacturing skills. During his time working with Venini, Wirkkala set out to exploit these differences, using a range of colours and a thinness of glass unavailable in Finland. Wirkkala's Finnish work was often driven by a desire to evoke feelings about his homeland, hence the feeling of weightiness and apparent coldness. His output for Venini, on the other hand, was abstract, usually far more thinly blown, and much more colourful. Despite this, paradoxically, it often seems more restrained. The Bolle vases have been, almost since their inception, one of the company's more popular lines.

The Marcuso Dining Table's sleek lines, glass top and stainless-steel legs make it a cult classic today. Its position within Italian design history is unusual, however, both for its 'casual' conception and for the complex technological research that made its production possible. Historically, the design of glass and metal tables had illustrious precedents. They had been developed by Marcel Breuer, the Bauhaus metal workshop and even Le Corbusier. Yet the joining of the two materials had never been truly resolved and always required an incredible amount of effort in designing the supporting frame. It was while observing a vent window of a car that Marco Zanuso was inspired to create a glass and stainless-steel table devoid of any heavy structure. Between 1968 and 1970 he initiated a research programme with Zanotta into ways of joining glass and stainless steel directly. Once again, manufacturer Zanotta relinquished any quick commercial payback in favour of experimentation and promotion of new developments. Zanotta and Zanuso invented and patented a special gluing method that, under the influence of a 'cold' light reacted to glass and steel in a way that invisibly held them together. The end result is a glass surface that appears barely placed on the stainless-steel legs. In reality it is very firmly stuck, as the legs are screwed on to stainless-steel discs fixed to the glass top. The technological achievement of the Marcuso Dining Table was a first for the 1960s and mass production ensured it became an immediate commercial success. Its conception has often been compared to that of a piece of modern architecture: like a building it is made of glass and steel, with its structure and construction voluntarily exposed. These qualities have ensured it is still in production by Zanotta today.

Sony Press Conference, 1968

Founded in 1946 by engineer Masura Ibuka and physicist Akio Morita, the Japanese electronics manufacturer Sony had developed a reputation for innovative technological solutions, creating the world's first pocket-sized transistor radio and portable colour television. But in October 1968 Sony launched arguably its most significant product to date in the form of the first Trinitron colour television, the KV-1310. History was made as the company incorporated its unique Trinitron cathode ray tube (CRT), a single-gun, three-beam aperture grille with a cylindrical flat screen, which eliminated the problems of horizontal crossbars encountered by rival companies and created a striking flat screen. This produced a comprehensively brighter, more detailed and richer picture performance than its competitors. The KV-1310 was created by a team under the direct supervision of Ibuka. He believed that the reign of radio was ending, and that the future lay in manufacturing televisions so Sony entered into a collaborative partnership with Hollywood's Paramount Pictures to create a colour

television. The new colour television was named Trinitron, a compound derived from trinity, meaning the union of three, and 'tron', from electron tube. The first model had a 33 cm (13 in) screen, and the product line swiftly expanded to include larger domestic screens and portable micro-televisions. Sony's achievement was recognized with the award of a technical Emmy for the development of the Trinitron picture tube. Thanks to its unique CRT technology, Sony began receiving enquiries from computer manu-facturers who required bright, ultra-high-resolution screens to display small characters and fonts. The Trinitron screen was fitted to a number of early personal computers, before Sony developed a specialist graphical display monitor based on the three-beam aperture grille system, thus enabling software manufacturers to create the first viable computer-aided design software. Sony has continued to maintain a leading technological edge, and remains a market leader in audio-visual displays.

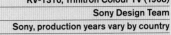

It is impossible to look at the success of the BMW 2002, with its black-painted stainless-steel grille, in isolation, as, like many successful designs, it was the result of the evolution of older models. During the 1960s, BMW was facing both the postwar economy and a general lack of popularity and, while it continued to produce practical and luxury models, the company's sporting image from the 1930s had been lost. The Neue Klasse or New Class, a four-door model, was the structure on which a two-door was developed to improve road handling, with a lighter body and, of course, a sportier appearance. The result came in a number of models, including the 1500, the 1600 and then the 1600-2, so named because it used the1600 engine, but had two doors. The 1600-2 was immediately compared to the likes of sports cars by Alfa Romeo. Following the design of the 1600-2, Alex von Falkenhausen and Helmet Werner Bönsch, the planning director, separately experimented with placing a 2-litre engine into a two-door model, and discovered each other's efforts by chance. They both felt this was an uncanny but marvellous solution and collaborated on putting the car into production. The sportier two-door 1600-2 (later renamed 1602) had a twin-carburettor 1600 engine that did not pass American federal exhaust emission regulations, and therefore could not be imported into this vital market. But the 100 hp 2-litre four-cylinder engine in the 2000 coupé met the regulations, and, aware of the importance of the US market, US importer Max Hoffmann and sales director Paul Hahnemann encouraged the proposal for the two-door. There was opposition from the company's engineers, as the engine was considered quite large for these dimensions, but the sales potential was too lucrative to miss, and led to the launch of the 2002. During its eight-and-a-half year production, which ceased in 1976, three generations of the BMW 2002 were manufactured, each with their own subdivisions within the various models. The models built between 1968 and 1973 had larger bumpers specifically for the US market, and there were other differences between the 80,000 models built for the US, and the 745,000 sold throughout Europe. But regardless of the slight differences, the wide expanses of glass and thin roof pillars of the 2002 conveyed lightness, elegance and speed.

Sergio Mazza

When it was introduced in 1968, Sergio Mazza's Toga was a ground-breaking design on a number of levels. Not only did its single-moulded form reject the traditional armchair concept of a seat with four legs, but it was also boldly experimental in its exploration of the latest advances in plastics and how these could be applied to new production methods. Toga was the product of a time when Artemide, the company founded by Mazza and Ernesto Gismondi in 1959, was experimenting with new materials for furniture and accessories. Architect and designer Mazza developed the chair following initial trials made by Artemide designers such as Angelo Mangiarotti, Vico Magistretti with his Demetrio forty-five stackable plastic tables, and Mazza himself with the Mida armchair. The original model for the Toga was built in wood, and the few prototypes that were produced using this

model were realized in fibreglass coating, then soaked in polyester resin, the same procedure used for boat, caravan or car bodywork. The Toga mass-production model was, however, created using a steel mould and the chair was produced via an injection-moulding system finished with a strong, durable and colourful thermoplastic ABS resin. The most distinctive feature of the Toga was that it did not follow a classic armchair design but instead comprised a single structure, produced in a single-moulded and ergonomically tailored piece. Its compact volume meant that it could be packaged in an almost cubic pack, and its form also meant that it was easily stackable. The Toga is possibly one of Artemide's key pieces in terms of its technical experimentalism and boundary-pushing design. It formed an outstanding contribution to the aesthetics of plastic of that period, in its harmonious unification of material, shape and colour.

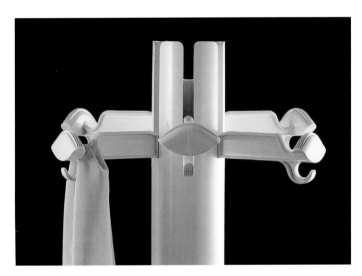

At first sight Planta appears to be a simple, sleek cylinder, but when all the components are folded out, it becomes a coat and umbrella rack. This witty product is made in black or white ABS plastic and measures 170 cm (67 in) tall. The upper part of Planta features six fold-down arms; each has two different hooks at its end. These two hooks allow two items to be hung separately from each arm. In the lower part, there are two C-shaped elements that can be swivelled out to hold umbrellas. Each of these C-shaped parts lines up with an indentation in the base; this secures the umbrella in place and catches the water that drains from it. The umbrella holder is an optional feature. The base of the stand is heavy enough to support the potential weight when the piece when fully laden. The product has been out of production for a period of time, but has been reissued on occasion, as a limited edition. Piretti has worked for the Bologna-based furniture manufacturer Castelli since 1960. This product was designed as part of a series of innovative plastic furniture, known as the PL series, the best-known item of which is the Plia Folding Chair. The common element in the series, apart from all items being made of plastic, is that they are all foldable or convertible into a smaller form. Piretti developed various inventive design solutions using prefabricated parts and modular systems, which were easy to mass-produce. Planta is both a product of 1960s Italian design, and has the timeless qualities of other products from the PL series.

With a pop of the cap and a twist of the base, a tube of solid glue rises, ready for use. The branding reads loud and clear: the 'Pritt' logo is picked out in simple sans-serif lettering on the plastic tube-shaped container, with its red cap and body, and black twisting base. The humble Pritt Glue Stick, now omnipresent in home and office, was the result of a 'Eureka!' moment on board an aircraft in 1967 and went on to enjoy huge commercial success. While this case study in branding has spawned many copycat products, its ubiquity has rendered it almost invisible and its distinctive identity may go unnoticed by the average home or office worker. Pritt stick manufacturers Henkel of Germany must celebrate the day they sent Dr Wolfgang Dierichs on that business trip. On board the aircraft en route, Dierichs absent-mindedly observed a young women applying lipstick. It occurred to him that a firmly set glue with a consistency rather like a lipstick would be much more convenient to use than the runny glue generally available at the time. Back at Henkel and together with Dr Janos Arnos Muszik, inventor of solvent-free glue, Dierichs formulated a solid glue and Henkel launched it on to the stationery market. It was an instant hit. No other brand has outsold Pritt since its introduction and annual sales today register at 130 million. Dierichs' story is the stuff of dreams, where a moment's inspiration leads to monumental commercial success. The Pritt Glue Stick represents the ingenuity of simple convenience, and it is a product that does not require any improvement.

Harley-Davidson Easy Rider Chopper (1969)
Harley-Davidson Design Team
Harley-Davidson 1969

Peter Fonda and Dennis Hopper in *Easy Rider* (1969), directed by Dennis Hopper

Dennis Hopper's cult film, *Easy Rider* (1969), had several stars, including Hopper himself, Peter Fonda and Jack Nicholson in his breakout role. In design terms, however, the iconic object of the film is Fonda's heavily customized Harley-Davidson Panhead, nicknamed 'Captain America'. The *Easy Rider* Harley-Davidson is probably the most famous individual motorcycle in the world. And its design history is interesting, since it is not a design object per se. Rather it is the pivotal moment in a fifty-year movement of personalizing, or customizing,

motorcycles (and automobiles) that began arguably in World War II, and is undergoing a huge renaissance today. GIs returning from the Pacific theatre of World War II found themselves in southern California, where ex-War Department Harley-Davidsons and Indian Chiefs were easy to find and cheap to build. Taking cues from the bomber nose art that was the preserve of the US Army Air Force, the impulse was to paint the tanks as a personal statement, and to 'chop' or 'bob' the excess weight from these lumbering old bikes. Tuning the engines was the next and obvious step.

From there it was natural that young outlaws would race their bikes up the wide highways and on the desert flats of California. That, incidentally, is where the elongated forks come from, for ease of steering in a straight line. By the time Hopper and Fonda made their film, the chopper movement had become a form of 'outsider' art. Fonda himself styled the bikes, of which four were made; two for him and two for Hopper, nicknamed the 'Billy' bike. Or perhaps 'styled' is too strong a word, for the desire was simply to have a local customizer turn four ordinary, and very used, Harley-Davidsons into extravagantly chromed and stretched choppers for a film. With this simple wish, coupled with the starring role in *Easy Rider*, a film that turned out to be a counterculture classic, Fonda's Captain America had an impact along with the inherent design qualities it possessed.

The Boalum lamp is an experimental in both its form and its technology. The light is flexible and can be arranged in different configurations to create strikingly sculptural effects. It is made from industrial translucent PVC tubing lined with metal rings, with each section housing four low-watt bulbs. PVC, a soft and pliable plastic skin developed in the 1930s and originally used for cable and wire insulation, was one of the iconic materials of the 1960s, especially in its use for inflatable furniture. In the Boalum lamp each unit can be plugged into another, creating what *Domus* magazine described in 1969 as 'an endless snake of light'. The lamp can be coiled or left straight, hung on the wall, or draped on furniture or the floor. It can be used singly, or can be connected together to create a light eight metres long. The Boalum lamp embodies the Pop sensibility in design, which questioned the conventions of product types with wit and ingenuity and ushered in a generation of lively and irreverent domestic objects. The lamp's modularity was typical of 1960s experimentation, and was seen in everything from seating to 'plug-in' fantastical architecture. The light's capacity for extension meant it was seen as an ideal product for the informal 1960s home, where sitting was to be replaced with lounging and where the uses of furniture were to be interchangeable and adaptable to alternative social situations. Boalum was the ideal lighting product for these soft, inflatable, pliable and fluid furniture forms that resulted from this change in attitude. Livio Castiglioni was the eldest of three brothers, all of whom led influential careers in postwar Italian design. In the early years they worked together, but Livio left the practice in 1952. He continued to work in a similar vein to his brothers, designing the Boalum lamp with Gianfranco Frattini for Artemide, who first produced the lamp from 1970 to 1983 and reissued it with some adaptations in 1999. Boalum is also included in several design museum collections, including the Philadelphia Museum of Art and the Museo del Design Italiano, Milan.

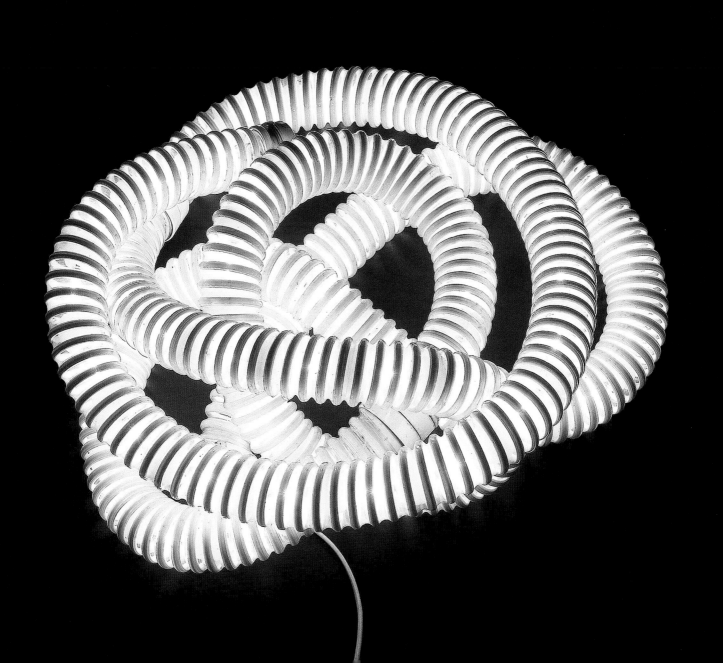

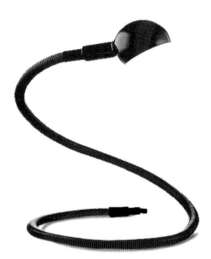

This small table lamp is comprised of a flexible metal tube covered in PVC, with an enamelled aluminium shade. The Hebi, which means 'snake', is a task light, and with its fully adjustable arm and rotating shade can be twisted to provide localized lighting. The metal tube can be twisted to lie flat so that the lamp can stand on a table. The lamp also comes in a shorter version, which can be inserted into a clamp fixed to a table edge or shelf. The lamp has an in-line switch, the casing for which was designed by Achille Castiglioni. The Hebi is a sophisticated example of design combined with engineering. It offers both the flexibility and personality of other Italian products of the late 1960s, such as Livio Castiglioni's Boalum lamp, which also uses PVC-covered tubing. However, Hosoe's light is tailored to the work environment, despite its pop affiliations. He found the simple, flexible tube in a store near the Columns of Saint Lorenzo in Milan, which cost a mere fifty cents for fifty metres. It was fusing this so-called precious material that he collaborated with Valenti to create a lamp that could support itself by folding the tube to form a base. This is a product in which the concept lay in the movement of the material. With its soft curves, it rolls along and is crowned by a small diffuser. The key behind this lamp is that there is no base, simplifying the design, making it unique and allowing for immediate interaction with the user. Hosoe was born in Japan in 1942, where he trained in aerospace engineering at Nihon University, graduating in 1967. In the same year he moved to Italy, working as a designer with Alberto Rosselli until the mid 1970s, then setting up the Design Research Centre in 1981, followed by his own studio, Isao Hosoe Design, in 1985. The Hebi is still in production since it was first introduced by Valenti, an industrial lighting company founded in 1929 that became associated with experimental and technically innovative products in the 1960s. The Hebi Lamp was one of Valenti's most successful products of the period, capturing the futuristic and quirky spirit of the 1960s. Hosoe has won many awards for his work in the fields of transport, furniture and product design. His work has had a particular emphasis on the design of electronic and telecommunications products, which mirrors his technical background.

Uten.Silo encapsulates the spirit of adventure and experimentation in 1960s plastics design. Moulded in a single piece of ABS, it represents all that plastics is capable of and demonstrates perfectly its qualities and capabilities. With its bright, shiny colours of black, white, orange and red and molten surface, it simply could not have been made out of any other material. Uten.Silo became an immediate best seller, partly because it reflected so successfully the changing lifestyles of the times. The idea of displaying life's trivia and necessities in a playful yet highly choreographed manner among the thirty-two slots, pouches, hooks and clips appealed especially to the new generation of young homeowners. Dorothée Becker, who was neither a trained designer nor an artist, first had the idea for a toy consisting of a large piece of wood with geometrically shaped notches and matching elements. Becker recalls, 'The aim was for children to develop a feeling for the characteristics of geometric shapes in play.' But Becker abandoned the idea of a toy when her own children showed no interest in it. The inspiration behind the final design of Uten.Silo also owed much to Becker's childhood memories: 'My father owned a drugstore and photo shop in Aschaffenburg. When I was a child there were countless drawers there full of fascinating things waiting to be discovered, including a hang-up toilet bag made of waxed cloth full of pockets for the various toiletries. The bag held items that would normally have been stored vertically in a horizontal position. I never forgot this practical idea and later used it in Uten.Silo.' Uten.Silo was originally called 'Wall-All' and was first put into production by Ingo Maurer, (formerly known as Design M), the company founded by Becker's husband, the designer Ingo Maurer. Maurer invested 250,000DM of his company's money in a metal injection mould weighing over three tons: 'an incredible amount of money for our young company'. Following its initial overwhelming success, production of Uten.Silo was halted in 1974 as plastics fell out of favour following the oil crisis. A smaller version, Uten.Silo II, was manufactured in 1970 by Ingo Maurer, but that too was discontinued in 1980. In 2002 Vitra Design Museum reissued Uten.Silo, and also reintroduced the smaller model, as well as a version in chromed plastic.

Dorothée Becker

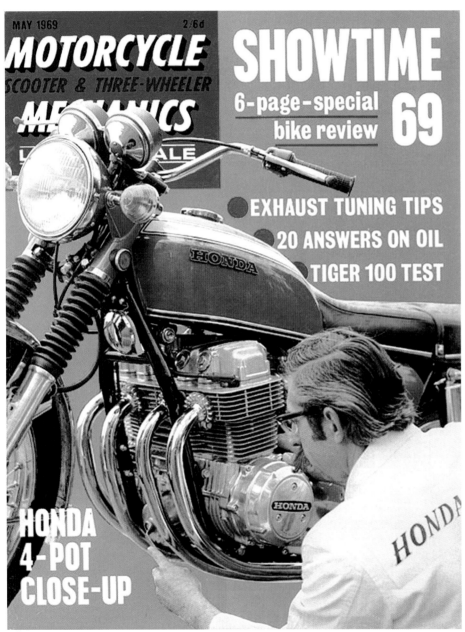

MAY 1969   2/6d

MOTORCYCLE
SCOOTER & THREE-WHEELER
MECHANICS

SHOWTIME
6-page-special
bike review
69

- **EXHAUST TUNING TIPS**
- **20 ANSWERS ON OIL**
- **TIGER 100 TEST**

HONDA
4-POT
CLOSE-UP

Motorcycle Mechanics, May 1969

As the 1960s came to their swinging conclusion, the world of motorcycle design was in a state of some confusion. For several years Honda and MV Agusta had dominated Grand Prix racing with a series of multi-cylinder bikes, including glorious three-, four- and six-cylinder machines ridden by legends such as Mike Hailwood and Giacomo Agostini, and motorcycle racing was enjoying a golden age. And yet road-going motorcycle design was in the doldrums. The great British marques, Triumph, BSA and Norton, were all on their last legs, victims of bad management, bad manufacturing practices and chronic lack of investment. In the United States Harley-Davidson had not yet found its modern voice. Only the Japanese seemed to be looking forward with any vision, but their collective stock-in-trade were small-capacity runarounds and lightweight machines. Then in 1969, drawing on a decade of Grand Prix success, Honda introduced the CB750 and the landscape was suddenly and dramatically changed forever. Here was a powerful, large-displacement bike with a transverse, four-cylinder engine, complete with a disc brake and electric starter as standard. Not one of these attributes was unique; indeed, four-cylinder motorcycles had been manufactured since the early part of the century. But the overall design was of an elegance and coherence that had simply not been seen before. With its four upswept exhaust pipes and its lustrous finish, the Honda Four, as it became known, demanded to be looked at and admired, if grudgingly at first, particularly by diehard rough-trade biker fans. What bike fans saw along with the evident quality of the engineering was outstanding attention to detail. Leaking bike oil had been the curse of all motorcycles for seventy years; this one did not leak. The Honda CB750, outstandingly successful and continuing in production in various guises until 1982, was the gold standard by which all other large-capacity sporting motorcycles came to be judged.

Honda CB750 (1969)
Honda Project Design Team
Honda 1969 to 1982

For all its apparent radicalism, the design of the Raleigh Chopper was actually the culmination of a long period of evolution and a refinement of many other earlier designs. But this is not to undermine its lasting importance; on the contrary, it is proof of how the right design emerged at the right time and in the right place. The story of the Chopper begins in the motorcycle counterculture of 1960s California. To those bikers, 'chopping' meant the customization of their machines. Famously, these bikers had younger brothers who adapted their pushbikes in imitation of their elders' alterations. Popular alterations then began to appear in US production-line bikes as the two main manufacturers, Schwinn and Raleigh, got involved, and these alterations then passed into the 'DNA' of the Chopper, notably the high ape-hanging handlebars, the long seat and the raised back. Meanwhile, the United Kingdom was lagging behind in bike design innovation, so Raleigh flew its chief designer, Alan Oakley, to the West Coast of the United States to investigate. It is claimed that he sketched the design of the Chopper on the back of an envelope on his return flight; a story that is, however, disputed by other designers, including Tom Karen of Ogle Design who at the time worked on concept designs for the eventual Chopper. But however the design appeared, the Chopper Mk1 was launched in the United States in 1969 and in selected locations in the United Kingdom the next year. Although it had relatives and predecessors in the United States, the Chopper was a radical departure for the English and proved instantly popular. There are many causes of this success, and many reasons the bike embedded itself so firmly as the symbol of a 1970s childhood. For a start, the launch, by chance, coincided with the release in England of the film *Easy Rider*, which glamorized and popularized the biker culture of the United States, and the Chopper resembled the low-riding 'hogs' in the film. Also, its pure difference was alluring; its geometric frame, wheel ratio, seat and handlebars were completely distinctive. But perhaps the most important factor was that it looked and felt tough. It looked as though it had been designed with more grown-up priorities than most bikes, a product of motorcycle and car design. The gearstick was an important part of this; advertising played on how it made the Chopper more like a racing car than a bike. It felt as though it treated kids like adults. And for that, it won the hearts of a generation, and has made its comeback in the 2004 reproduction.

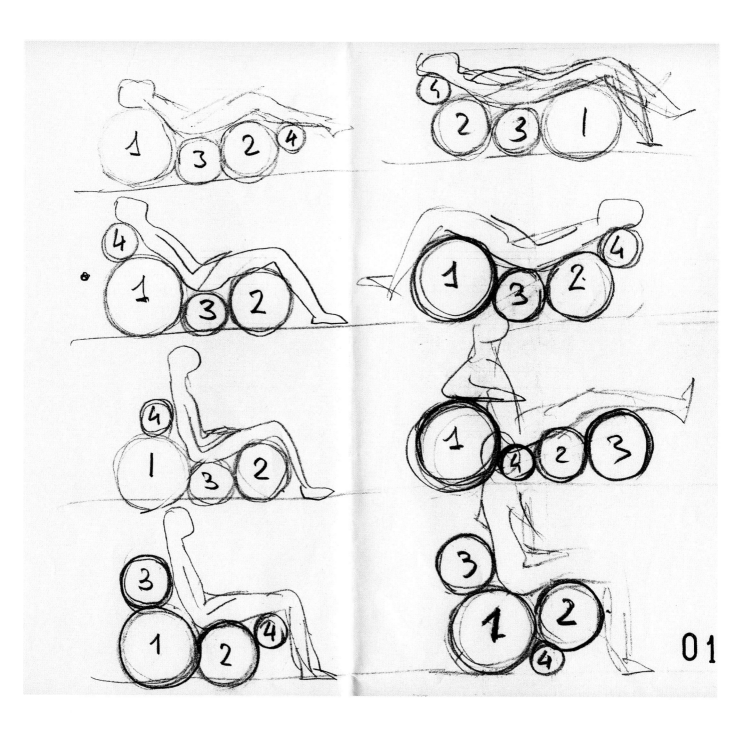

01

Apart from being the first-ever seating system that came in a drawstring bag, Joe Colombo's Tube Chair is an enduring example of the Italian designer's pioneering Pop explorations. Four plastic tubes of varying sizes covered in polyurethane foam and upholstered with vinyl came concentrically nested; once unpacked, the buyer was able to combine them in any sequence via tubular steel and rubber connecting joints. From task chair to chaise longue to a full-on couch (when two sets were joined), Colombo's machine for living was decidedly different from those proposed by earlier designers like Le Corbusier, whose visions were predicated on one-size-fits-all Modernism. Open-ended options that suited a range of sizes, shapes and attitudes were the rule of the day in the mid- to late 1960s, which saw unprecedented change in material culture and social mores. Rather than follow accepted definitions of what a chair – or any design object – was, Colombo created products that were embedded with recombinant possibility out of materials that were strange and unfamiliar to the majority of Italians. The Tube Chair fell into a category of design that Colombo termed 'structural seriality', or single objects that could multitask in a number of ways. He created other seating systems at the time that echoed the Tube's metamorphic nature, including his 1968 Additional System, a seating kit made of interchangeable polyurethane blocks that could be adjusted according to task and taste, and his 1970 Multichair, a cloth-covered polyurethane creature whose tripartite structure could be creatively configured. Colombo's penchant for polymorphism was manifest in his early years, first in a childhood obsession with constructing cities of the future out of Meccano, and then as a painter in the free-flowing, sensual Arte nucleare movement that was popular when he was an art student in the 1950s. His natural aversion to rectilinear lines was turned into a design aesthetic when he began experimenting with production processes using plastics in the electrical conductor factory that he and his brother Gianni took over from their father in 1958, and again when he started collaborating with adventuresome Italian manufacturers like Flexform, which produced the Tube until 1979.

Tube Chair (1969)
Joe Colombo (1930–71)
Flexform 1970 to 1979
Vitra Design Museum 2006 to present

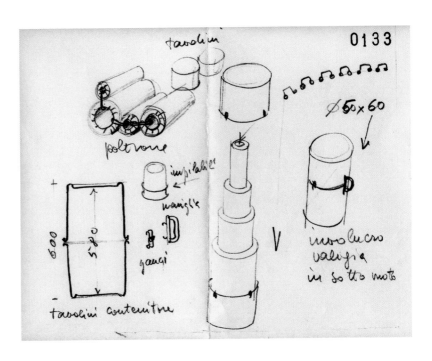

The apparently simple and utilitarian form of Anna Castelli Ferrieri's storage units proved highly influential at the time of their design. The bright and integrally coloured units exploited the progressive technology of injection-moulded ABS plastic, while the clean lines and functional design offered a low-cost storage solution. The materials, simplicity and modularity of the design allowed for enormous flexibility. Any quantity of units could be stacked, providing a wide range of opportunities for use, whether in the bathroom, bedroom, kitchen or living areas. A landscape of units in various vibrant colours was adopted by an ever-adventurous consumer market. Add-on features such as castors or doors supplemented the appeal and the design rapidly found favour with the design- and style-conscious. Ferrieri trained in architecture and worked alongside Franco Albini before establishing her own architectural office. In 1943 she married chemical engineer, Giulio Castelli, who later founded the renowned plastic furniture manufacturer, Kartell. In the mid-1960s Ferrieri turned to product and furniture design and was soon appointed as a design consultant and later as design director at Kartell. In this role she has been highly influential in the growth and status of Kartell as an international leader in design-led plastic products and furniture. Using advanced technologies pioneered by Kartell, Ferrieri's understanding of the capabilities of this new material and its production processes, combined with her strong design sensibilities, resulted in this highly successful product. They are still produced by Kartell although now only in silver and white, and the storage units continue to compete in price within a crowded market-place, while the design proves to be timeless.

708

Cylindrical Storage (1969)
Anna Castelli Ferrieri (1918–)
Kartell 1969 to present

Walter Gropius

Walter Gropius was one of the great enforcers of principles in twentieth-century architecture and industrial design. Through the founding of the Bauhaus in 1919, architecturally trained Gropius implemented a new schooling approach in which crafts-men, artists and businessmen would co-exist under the same roof. His aim was to break down the arrogant class divisions that had previously fractured these groups. His skill as the director lay in his ability to successfully pool together a diverse and international staff for the school, resulting in a cosmopolitan mélange of talent at the Bauhaus in Weimar from 1919.

Several decades later, having left the Bauhaus and worked in England for a few years, Gropius emigrated to the United States in 1937 and founded The Architects' Collaborative (TAC) in 1945. His architectural practice was made up of individuals of varying talents that reinforced Gropius's belief that teamwork formed a more imaginative design base. Some might argue that he was just continuing his founding principles of the Bauhaus education system within his own private enterprise. While his architecture and design were important, Gropius had a significant influence on the promotion of the Modernist movement

and spent considerable time sharing his lessons of the Bauhaus through lectures, writing, and teaching. His practice in the USA unveiled a few notable projects such as the designing of the Harvard Graduate Center between 1948 and 1950, and the Pan-Am building in New York in 1963. Meanwhile, after the war, the German ceramics firm Rosenthal was actively seeking an intelligent policy towards international design. They commiss-ioned Beate Kuhn's free-forming, organic and sculptural ceramics in the 1950s, while also taking on America's streamlining master Raymond Loewy for a coffee service in 1954. Gropius's

TAC Tableware for Rosenthal managed to merge Kuhn's and Loewy's design tendencies with its own distinct bulbous form that was characterized by its emphasis on the curve. The hemispherical elevation of the teapot, for example, made was reminiscent of the elementary shapes adopted in the Bauhaus, while the streamlining of the handle in relation to the spout made references to the styling of that period. The tableware appeared in Rosenthal's Studio-Line collection in 1969 and has remained in production ever since.

A rare example of office equipment as fashion accessory, the Valentine Typewriter has become semantic shorthand for the perceived Pop values of the 1960s: fun, bold, bright, independent and plastic. While the Valentine's internal mechanics were nothing particularly new, its housing and configuration were very unusual. In redefining the look and feel of this familiar object, the Italian/British design team responsible continued in a long tradition of ground-breaking products by Olivetti. Certain typewriters had been described as 'portable' since the 1930s, although their heavy-cast chassis and bulky forms meant that they were really anything but. The Valentine, however, had a low-profile design, all-plastic body, came with a matching slip-on cover and even had a handle. Everything, in fact, that would encourage people to take it with them, and not be afraid to use it in unusual places. Sottsass particularly wanted the Valentine to facilitate communication and to remove the formality of writing a typewritten letter. One early iteration (which was later abandoned) even did away with the ability to type both upper and lower case, thus further reducing the machine's weight as well as pre-empting the informality of texting and emails. Sottsass described the machine as being 'for use any place except an office, so as not to remind anyone of monotonous working hours but rather to keep amateur poets company on quiet Sundays in the country or to provide a highly coloured object on a table in a studio apartment.' This links it closely to the Apple iBook, whose creators espoused a similar philosophy thirty years later. It is not known whether the Valentine was owned predominantly by poets or It-girls, but several made their way into museum collections (including the Design Museum, London, and The Museum of Modern Art), and it did not escape the notice of the judges of the prestigious Compasso d'Oro. The original version remained in production until 2001.

Four Florentine architects, Andrea Branzi, Gilberto Corretti, Paolo Deganello and Massimo Morozzi, founded Archizoom in 1966 during a period when international designers were seriously examining the values of modern design in relation to the political ideologies of the time. These designers were concerned with the conventional attitudes that were being applied to the built environment and set out to challenge and strip away design's functional subservience and self-conscious role as a status symbol in society. The group claimed that the rationalist ideals exercised by their modernist predecessors would, if taken to extremes, breed sterile, artificial and illogical trading domains for humans, as they demonstrated in several conceptual architectural presentations, notably the 'No-Stop-City' project of 1970. Around the same time Archizoom created the Mies Chair, a distinctly rationalist chair in its structural rigidity and simple use of materials. As the name implies, the group were making distinct references to the pioneer, Ludwig Mies van der Rohe, whose similar considered use of materials and geometry they were mimicking. The designers exaggerated the constructive elements of the two triangular chrome supports, between which they stretched a taught rubber sheet to obscure the obvious function of the chair. Their primary concern was to prompt ironic comment but, equally ironically, in doing so they had created an entirely functional chair. The steeply angled rubber seat comfortably gives way when sat upon. Despite the addition of a head cushion and footstool, however, its appearance remains uninviting and threatens traditional notions of comfort and relaxation. The chair attracted considerable attention when introduced at the Milan Salone del Mobile in 1969, at a time when innovative and provocative design were high on the Italian agenda. A major contribution to the Radical Design movement spanning 1968 to 1978, the work of Archizoom symbolized the antithesis of 'good design' pretensions. Despite the break-up of the group in 1974, their work continued to prove influential in the Anti-Design movement of Studio Alchimia and Memphis, and the Mies Chair remains in production.

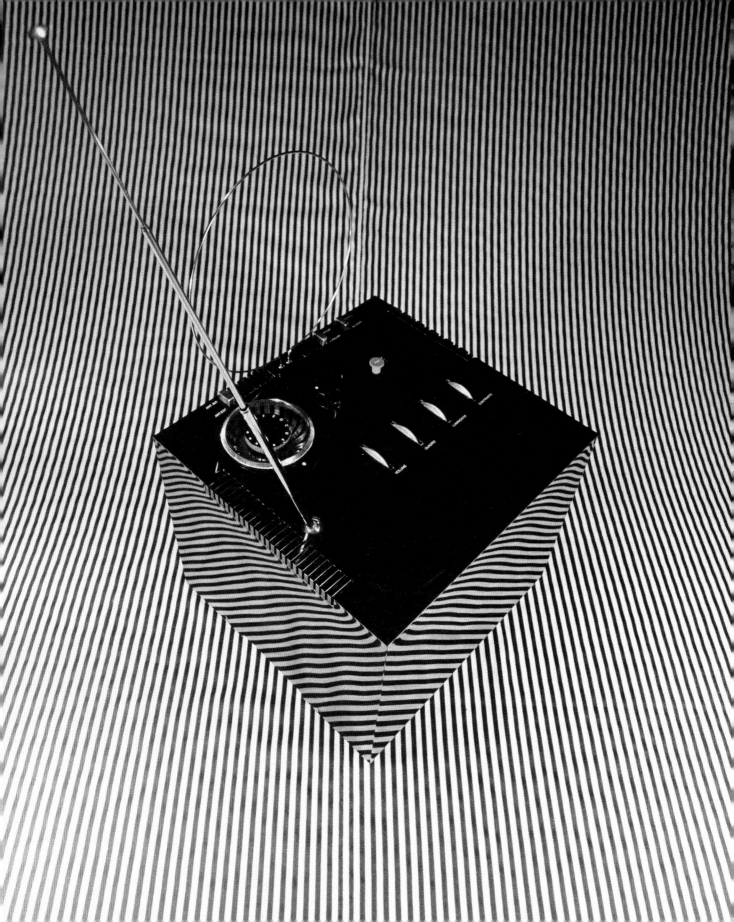

712

Brionvega Black ST/201 (1969)
Marco Zanuso (1916–2001)
Richard Sapper (1932–)
Brionvega 1969 to 1970s

This black cube designed by Marco Zanuso and Richard Sapper looks nothing like a traditional television. It is not a framed cathode-ray tube but a mysterious cube that reveals its true meaning only when it is turned on, revealing itself as a 30.5 cm (12 in) 'tube'. Although small and handy, this television is more of an interior object than a portable technological apparatus. The television appears as a floating black cube, with seventeen grooves on each side, which work like a speaker. The draw-out antenna, operation buttons, and tuning knobs are visible on the top. By putting these buttons on top of the set and by making the cathode-ray tube visible only when the set is turned on the designers emphasize the technological mystique of the machine. The black box stands for the highest degree of abstraction, as an almost surrealistic object, which alternately appears when on and disappears when off. Brionvega was founded in 1945 as a producer of radios and other audio products, and originally operated under the name BPM. The company

expanded in 1952 by introducing televisions. As part of its commitment to high standards, the company always insisted on its products being easy to use and long-lasting. Brionvega's motto is 'technique in its purest shape', and their products are design classics from the very moment they are put on the market, which is why they never lose their appeal even after decades. Their ethos is evident in the manufacture of this technically advanced product, which combines an elegant and stylish formal solution. Brionvega hired Zanuso and Sapper as design consultants in 1959 in order to compete with electronic products being made in Japan and Germany. Their aesthetic style became known as 'techno-functionalism', and by collaborating with these top designers the company was able to create products of a timeless appearance that responded to a new, modern style of living. The ST/201 was the precursor to an even 'blacker' cube, the Cuboglass made in 1992, produced out of crystal. However, it is the latter design from the 1960s which today resides in The Museum of Modern Art's permanent collection.

Steve McQueen in *Le Mans* (1971), directed by Lee H Katzin

One icon helped to create another when Steve McQueen took the wheel of his Porsche in the 1971 movie *Le Mans,* conspicuously wearing the new Heuer Monaco watch. It was deliberately styled to appeal to a motor-racing clientele and its bold design did enough to catch McQueen's eye and so seal its immortality as the ultimate accessory. Today it is still referred to by collectors as the 'Steve McQueen'. But McQueen was not the first driver to wear this distinctive timepiece. That honour fell to the Swiss, Jo Siffert, who bore Heuer logos on his overalls and car as Heuer became the first sponsor of Formula One racing, which was not connected at that time with the sport. Sadly, Siffert died in 1971 and Heuer explored other opportunities, of which the Le Mans tie-in must surely have been the most successful early triumph. But the Monaco was far more than a celebrity trinket. It was one of the first chronograph watches with an automatic movement, a holy grail watchmakers had been striving for throughout the 1960s. Such was the pressure to get to market that Heuer teamed up with fellow Swiss companies Breitling, Buren and Dubois Depraz to develop the micro-rotor 'Chronomatic' movement, and beat international competition to the punch. Aside from its highly distinctive blue face and orange hands, the Monaco had the added distinction of being the first chronograph with a square waterproof case. The Monaco was ultimately taken off the market in 1978, but returned twenty years later in a slightly different form, with its crown winder located at 3 o'clock, instead of at 9 o'clock as the Steve McQueen model had been. TAG Heuer (so named since the 1985 merger with the TAG group) has also rung the changes since then, most ambitiously in 2003 with the Monaco 69, which combined analogue and digital chronograph faces in the same double-sided case. The watch's chunkiness did not stop the company releasing two ladies' versions in 2004.

71-4

Designer Gaetano Pesce

established his reputation as one of the most unconventional designers of the Italian design scene of the 1960s with his UP Series of anthropomorphic armchairs for the company then called C&B Italia. Premiered at the 1969 Milan Furniture Show, the series was made up of a set of seven chairs for different needs, such as seating for children, for adults or for more than one or two people. The organic shapes of the set itself have lent the design a simple but comfortable appeal, but the real innovation was found in the packaging. The chairs were moulded out of polyurethane foam, compressed under a vacuum until they were flat and then packaged in PVC envelopes. The expanded polyurethane took on the volume specified in the design only when the envelopes were opened and the materials came into contact with air. This inventive and technologically advanced use of materials allowed Pesce to engage

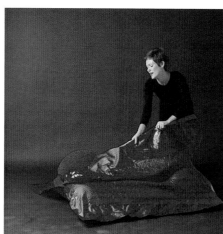

the purchaser as an active participant in the final phase of the product's creation. At the time Pesce described his UP Series as 'transformation' furniture, intended to turn the act of purchasing into a 'happening'. Pesce named the curvaceous UP 5, 'Donna' (Woman), and declared: 'In that design I was expressing my own view of women; they have always been, against their own wills, prisoners of themselves.' With Pesce the difference between art and a design is blurred. For him, production is a means of reaching a wider audience, for the expression of political thought and reflections on the condition of man in contemporary society. Throughout his career he has straddled the realms of design, art and architecture. The UP Series also included the UP 7, a giant foot, like a fragment of a colossal statue. But it is the UP 5, reissued by B&B Italia in 2000, that has enjoyed a successful revival.

INSTRUCTIONS

1. Grab the handle so the knot is free.
2. Move hand in an up & down motion.

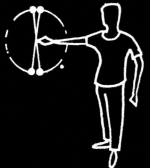

THE FIRST STEP

HAND - OFF

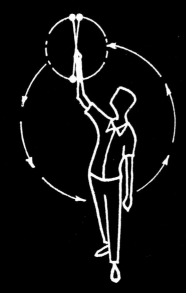

EARTH ORBIT

DOUBLE FEATURE

UNDERPASS

SUPER -PRO

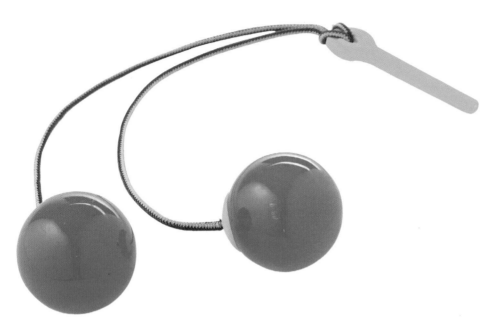

The Clackers craze that swept the US and the UK in the early 1970s fizzled out almost as fast as it hit the schools and streets. Clackers, otherwise known as Klackers, Click Clacks and Whackers, and a myriad of other onomatopoeic names, are a simply designed toy: two lengths of chord, each with a ball attached to one end, are joined at the other end by a ring attachment. Clackers were in effect similar to a miniature version of the 'bola' – a rope with weights at the end used by South American gauchos to capture wild horses and cattle. But unlike the 'bola', the Clackers had no particular use. The main purpose was to get the balls tapping, or clacking, against each other by lightly pulling on the ring attachment. The challenge was then to make the Clackers go faster and faster until they were smacking against each other at a high speed, above and below the hand. The Clackers phenomenon reached its peak in 1971, when a Clacker cacophony filled every school playground at break-time. Rumour has it that the craze originally started when a high school pupil created Clackers for a science project and then started selling them to all his friends. Bruised and swollen knuckles, broken wrists and eye injuries caused by stray balls and shrapnel ensured the fad's swift demise. Plastic was the most popular choice for Clacker balls, although a mix of real and anecdotal evidence suggests that early models were, alarmingly, made from ceramic or glass. The Consumer Product Safety Commission (CPSC) in the US is reported to have abruptly pulled these hazardous Clackers from the shelves soon after their release. In the 1990s novelty companies produced a safer but perhaps more boring version of Clackers with lightweight plastic balls connected by plastic rods. In 1993 NASA sent these Clackers into space in the space shuttle as part of a research project testing various popular toys in a gravity-free environment. The result of the experiment was that owing to the lack of gravity the balls lacked the momentum they required to work effectively. Currently, Clackers are a staple 'fad' feature of nostalgia websites.

Magistretti was not the first designer to attempt

a single-moulded plastic chair, but the Selene chair is one of the most

elegant expressions of this particular design paradigm. It succeeds

mostly because it exploits rather than resists the material from which it

is made and the technology used to make it. Magistretti was already a

highly experienced architect and designer of furniture, lighting and

other products by the 1960s when he began experimenting with

plastics. The decade preceding this design saw huge advances in

plastics technology and many new synthetic materials became viable

for mass production. The Selene chair is made of injection-moulded

polyester reinforced with fibreglass. The manufacturer was Artemide, a

technologically advanced company who proposed the material to

Magistretti. Chairs made in a single moulding offer manufacturers

huge advantages because their production is so much faster than that

of chairs made using traditional techniques. Yet the chairs are

technically very complex and tooling for their production is a huge

investment. The manufacturer's risk, therefore, is very great if the chair

fails to sell. The most striking feature about the Selene chair is the

innovative S-shape of the legs. They are effectively thin planes of

plastic without a solid core. The S-shape gives the legs structural

solidity while reducing the weight of the chair. The form also means

the legs can be moulded integrally with the seat and back. As if this

were not advantageous enough, the Selene chair is also stackable.

716

Selene (1969)
Vico Magistretti (1920–)
Artemide 1969 to 1972
Heller 2002 to present

717

Hawker Siddeley Harrier (1969)
Sir Sidney Camm (1893–1966)
Hawker Siddeley Design Team
Hawker Siddeley Aviation 1969 to present

Following the remarkable advancements in jet engine and airframe technology in the 1940s and 1950s, many countries began to investigate the idea of a vertical take-off, fixed-wing aircraft that would ultimately reduce the need for large, costly aircraft carriers and vulnerable airfields and air force bases. In the late 1950s the UK began development of the Harrier jump-jet, a model that would revolutionize aircraft design. The Harrier jump-jet was originally designed for the Royal Air Force as a research aircraft to explore the possibilities of vertical take-off and landing, and to be used as a reconnaissance and tactical strike fighter in support of land forces. Central to the Harrier jet's design is the innovative Rolls-Royce 'Pegasus' turbofan engine. Conceived by Rolls-Royce chief scientist, Dr A Griffith, the Pegasus was a specialized lift engine with a series of thrust nozzles that are required to vector the engine's thrust. Because it can harness this considerable thrust, the Harrier jump-jet has exceptional stability when hovering and is highly manoeuvrable in flight. At Hawker Siddeley Aviation, Sir Sydney Camm and his team of designers created the original Harrier P1127 aircraft around this new engine in 1957 and continued developing the Harrier design thereafter. The principal design features of the craft include a single crew cockpit of minimal weight that maintains the centre of gravity, allowing a bigger proportion of the aircraft to be used for fuel and equipment. The 7.7 m (25 ft) wing-span is relatively narrow because the provision of vectored thrust for take-off and landing has reduced the importance of wing lift, and this in turn saves weight and drag. The overall length of the jump jet is 14.27 m (47 ft), its height is 3.43 m (11 ft) and it weighs 11,793 kg (11.6 tons). Maximum speed is approximately 1,186 kph (737 mph). The Royal Navy Sea Harrier, as a variant model, is virtually identical except that it boasts a Blue Fox radar nose and raised cockpit for improved pilot visibility. Often described as the most effective single-seat strike aircraft in the world, and the first warplane of the future, the fully developed Harrier jump-jet combat craft entered regular service with the RAF in early 1969. Modified versions of the aircraft still feature in active military service around the world today.

Isao Hosoe never set out to design an ashtray. At the time the Japanese designer had been experimenting with forming plastics into a distinctive wave shape. When he curved the rippled plastic into a circle he realized the resulting form would make a perfect ashtray. The striking product of this exercise was seized upon by former Kartell CEO Giulio Castelli, who immediately decided to put it into production. It is not surprising that the cheap, fun, plastic ashtray appealed to the Italian design company, Kartell, which is renowned for its innovative use of plastic to produce bold and light-hearted objects and furniture. Hosoe's ashtray fits in perfectly with this house style, with its brightly coloured and perfectly round form. The striking object seems to echo a clown's red nose or the circle at the bottom of an exclamation mark. And although the ashtray, available in white, black and red, may have been created by chance, its form was actually highly functional. The curving ridges provide a place to rest a cigarette and melamine, the material used, is incredibly hard and durable, so the bright colours do not fade or mark under the burning cigarettes. Most of all, the ashtray, itself a product of playing with different plastics, turns smoking into a form of play. Hosoe, who has never smoked except for one or two cigars a year, liked the idea that the smoker has to decide where on the wave form to extinguish the cigarette: the convex male side or the concave female side. The ashtray is also double-sided, with the ridges offering a choice of sides to use. The ashtray has been out of production since 1996, but there is still a thriving collectors' market for the product.

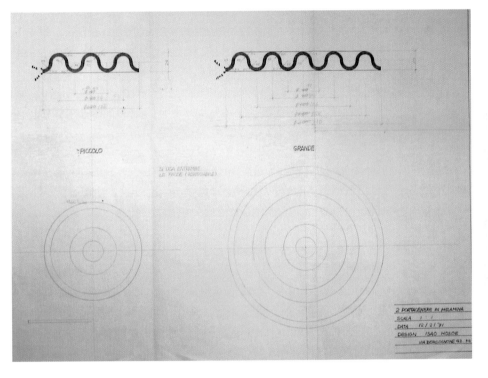

Many of Achille Castiglioni's designs reflect his interest in solving old problems in new and original ways. His Primate stool approaches the act of sitting from a new direction, and disregards the idea of the seat as something that demands you sit upright with your feet on the floor. Castiglioni instead provides a support for the sitter's knees, with a cantilevered stool raised above, forcing the sitter to assume a position similar to praying or kneeling at an altar. This way of sitting was inspired by yoga and Zen meditation, as well as studies in ergonomics popular in Scandinavian countries. Such a posture seems counter-intuitive, yet it works with the form of the body, keeping the torso erect without putting any strain on the back. At the same time, the pose creates a less formal style of sitting, one which feels and appears less permanent and is thus perhaps more closely in tune with our hurried modern lifestyles. It also takes up less room than traditional seating, and is easier to move, making it more compatible with the small living spaces common in urban environments. For all these reasons the stool promotes the casualness of interaction that was so sought after in the late 1960s and early 1970s. The stool is made of a firm black polystyrene base, with a stainless steel tubular stem supporting the polyurethane foam cushion, covered in either leather or pleather. The choice of colours, of orange, black or white, reflected the taste for strong, graphic colours in the late 1960s and early 1970s. The Primate stool is another example of how eclectic Castiglioni's designs were. Throughout his career he was rarely beholden to one overriding style. In terms of form, this stool is most closely allied to some of his 'ready-made' objects. Working from ideas borrowed from Marcel Duchamp, Castiglioni produced a number of designs in which he used existing pieces and parts from other sources and adapted them for a new function. The car-like seat cushions used in the Primate, for example, suggest a new adaptation of a previous technology. The stool caused controversy when it was first produced, with one letter to the Italian newspaper *Paese Sera*, in February 1977, questioning who could design such a 'contraption' and equating the piece with the corruption of the 'good taste' the public expected from contemporary design. Most recently the Primate stool was exhibited at a fair in Cologne in 1999 as part of the Zanotta archive, proof that an object that was once subversive has now been accepted into the design pantheon.

The term 'tensegrity' was coined by American architect Buckminster Fuller to refer to large structures that exist in a state of perfect tensional equilibrium, or the stake in which the forces pushing outwards from the structure are cancelled out by circumferential forces banding the structure. Pressure applied anywhere to the structure is distributed evenly through it. Fuller's renowned geodesic domes are an obvious example of tensegrity, but the principle is so elegant that not only are these domes theoretically unlimited in size, they also have applications in nanotechnology and have been assembled on a molecular level. Whatever the scale, the same rules apply. Fuller himself said that tensegrity shared characteristics with pneumatically inflated structures. With this in mind, it is hardly surprising that Adidas turned to geodesics when designing the Telstar Football, which was first used in the 1970 World Cup. The Telstar consists of thirty-two panels: twenty white hexagons and twelve black pentagons. These panels tessellate in three dimensions, forming a geodesic sphere. The ball was a big success. It was much lighter than other balls (making it less painful to kick), far closer to being a perfect sphere and less likely to deform or split. Where its predecessors had mostly been simply brown, the Telstar's black-and-white pattern was not only distinctive but helped players determine if a ball was spinning in flight and has become the archetype of what a football should look like. Ask a child to draw a football, and they will probably draw a white circle filled with black dots, the Telstar, and its successors. These balls are one of the most unique fusions of geometry and sport.

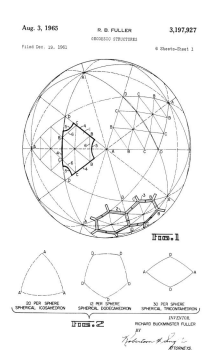

Aug. 3, 1965   R. B. FULLER   3,197,927
GEODESIC STRUCTURES
Filed Dec. 19, 1961   6 Sheets—Sheet 1

FIG. 1

20 PER SPHERE
SPHERICAL ICOSAHEDRON

12 PER SPHERE
SPHERICAL DODECAHEDRON

30 PER SPHERE
SPHERICAL TRICONTAHEDRON

FIG. 2

INVENTOR.
RICHARD BUCKMINSTER FULLER
BY
Robertson & Smythe
ATTORNEYS.

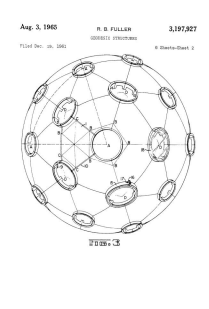

Aug. 3, 1965   R. B. FULLER   3,197,927
GEODESIC STRUCTURES
Filed Dec. 19, 1961   6 Sheets—Sheet 2

FIG. 3

INVENTOR.
RICHARD BUCKMINSTER FULLER
BY
Robertson & Smythe
ATTORNEYS.

INVENTOR.
RICHARD BUCKMINSTER FULLER
BY
Robertson & Smythe
ATTORNEYS.

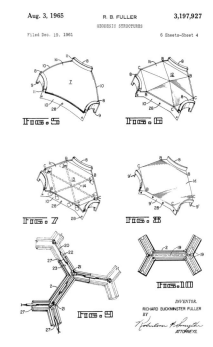

FIG. 5

FIG. 6

FIG. 7

FIG. 8

FIG. 9

FIG. 10

INVENTOR.
RICHARD BUCKMINSTER FULLER
BY
Robertson & Smythe
ATTORNEYS.

The In Attesa, meaning 'waiting' in Italian, is a waste-paper bin of beguilingly simple design. At first glance it appears to be a simple cylinder, gently canted towards the user like a liner's funnel for an easier 'shot'; closer inspection reveals a more complex form that integrates subtle and ingenious details. The bin is not in fact a pure cylinder. It tapers gradually outwards towards its top to free it easily from its moulding tool and to allow stacking. The sides flare elegantly outwards as they approach the lip of the bin, which is both smooth and satisfyingly thick. Inside the bottom of the bin are three concentric rings formed from ridges on the surface of the plastic. These create the impression of a target, but rather than being pure decoration they enable the bull's-eye to hide the blemish made by the plastic injection point on the reverse. Looking into the bin, the base and the rings of the target appear circular but, because the base cuts through the tube of the body at an angle, they are all in fact ellipses, carefully dimensioned to trick the eye. In Attesa was designed by Enzo Mari, perhaps the most committed explorer of product design as a language. The piece is a testimony to the designer's ability to add useful function to mundane archetypal forms, his method hiding skilful geometry behind outward

visual simplicity. In 1971 the bin was released simultaneously by the Italian company, Danese, and the US company, Heller. It is one of many products Mari has designed for Danese since their relationship began in 1957, a year after Mari left college, and which still continues today. Curiously, in 1977 a straight-sided version named Koro was produced, and in 2001, to celebrate the product's thirtieth birthday, Danese (now the sole manufacturer of In Attesa) released Scomparto In Attesa, a semi-circular compartment that sits inside the bin to allow waste to be separated.

721

In Attesa (1970)
Enzo Mari (1932–)
Danese 1971 to present

The Bocca Sofa, often referred to as the 'Marilyn' in homage to Marilyn Monroe, is a reworking of Salvador Dali's Mae West Lip Sofa of 1936, made for the English collector of Surrealist Art Edward James. Dali's original also formed part of a *trompe-l'oeil* room composition of Mae West's face that he created for his home in Figueras, Spain. The version by Studio 65 is covered in a red stretch fabric, matching Monroe's famous lips, rather than Elsa Schiaparelli's 'Shocking Pink', the colour originally used by Dali. Its designers named the sofa 'Bocca', the Italian word meaning 'lips', but it was also christened 'Marilyn' by Eleanore Stendig when it was first introduced to the USA. The sofa represents an early attempt at 'redesign' – one strategy of the Italian Anti-Design movement – by the Turin-based collective Studio 65. Anti-Design proposed that design had reached an impasse, and the only alternative and valid route forward was to simply to redesign iconic pieces from the past. Linked to Surrealism in the 1930s, the sofa easily translated to the Pop Art of the 1960s, using a much reproduced and iconic image from pop culture and presenting it isolated, exaggerated, and out of

context. The sofa was made from expanded polyurethane foam, a material hitherto only found in the military and automotive industries. While only five of Dali's sofa are known to have been made, the later reworking by Studio 65 was put into limited production by the Italian company Gufram as part of their Multiples Series of 1967–76. Gufram invited a number of radical artists and designers to contribute designs where creative freedom to experiment took precedence over function. Other sofa designs in the series included Piero Gilardi's Sassi (The Rocks) of 1968, and Gruppo Sturm's humorous Pratone (Giant Grass) of 1971. Designs from the Multiples Series are still produced in limited numbers.

722

Bocca Sofa ('Marilyn') (1970)
Studio 65
Gufram 1972 to 1989
Studio 65 1989 to 1995
Edra 1995 to present

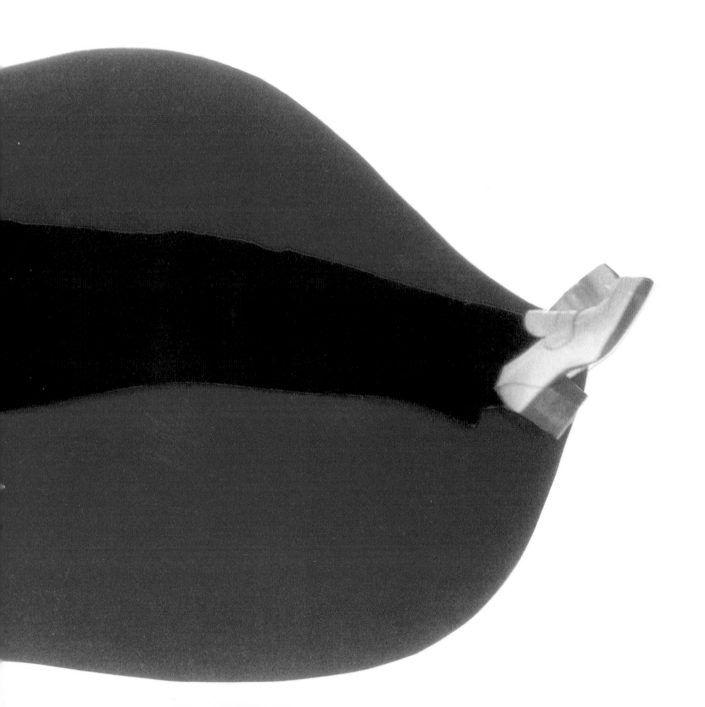

Paris Motor Show, 1970

Since its commercial introduction in 1970, the Citroën SM, or Série Maserati, has represented a pinnacle in luxury car design, leading one *Motor Trend* writer to enthuse, 'I feel this tremendous compulsion to tell you uncategorically that the Citroën SM is the best car in the world.' Playfully dubbed 'Sa Majesté' (Her Majesty) by SM lovers the world over, the car was the result of eight years of collaboration between Citroën's in-house design team, led by Robert Opron, and Giulio Alfieri, creator of the Maserati C114 engine used in the SM. While the car bore a familial resemblance to the Citroëns that preceded it, notably the revolutionary DS model, with its hallmark low-slung, scarab-like chassis, hydro-pneumatic suspension and road-hugging front-wheel drive, the SM included some unusual design details that had drivers and critics alike raving, including subtle streamlined fins, rack-and-pinion power steering and a self-centring steering wheel that activated the directional headlights. The car's

popular front headlamp arrangement, with its glassed-in line-up of three bulbs flanking a centrally located licence plate, was replaced in the United States with a more conventional layout for safety, much to the chagrin of American enthusiasts. A wraparound windscreen and low-slung profile gave it a sleek appearance that started showing up on TV and in the movies as well as in the personal collection of such unlikely enthusiasts as the writer Graham Greene, the Soviet premier Leonid Brezhnev, the Ethiopian emperor Haile Selassie, and the Ugandan dictator Idi Amin. Although the car was widely admired during its five-year run, selling in excess of 12,900 models to connoisseurs in Europe and North America, the energy crisis of the mid-1970s put an end to the gas-guzzling car's viability in the face of an emerging recession, and the appearance of smaller-bodied, more economical cars coming out of Japan.

Giancarlo Pirett

Since it first went into production in 1970, over 4 million examples of Giancarlo Piretti's Plia folding chair have been sold by Bologna-based furniture manufacturer Castelli. This modern translation of the traditional wooden folding chair – consisting of a polished aluminium frame and a transparent, moulded perspex seat and back, effortlessly collapsing by means of an efficient folding mechanism – was revolutionary in postwar furniture design. Its key feature is a three-metal disc hinge component. The backrest and front support, as well as the seat and rear support, are constructed within two rectangular frames and one U-shaped hoop. Together with the clearly visible hinge mechanism, the Plia's folding form is reduced to a single compact unit thickness of five centimetres. The chair's

transparent, concave-moulded plastic seat and back would have been considered highly appropriate manufacturing details. Although furniture designers were soon to be faced with economically restrictive remits, the development of plastics technology in the late 1960s was eased by low world oil prices. Piretti produced both domestic and contract furniture for Castelli in his role as in-house designer. His design ethos for the company – functional, inexpensive, space-saving and geared to large-scale production – was embodied in the Plia chair. With its rounded edges and corners, and intended for both indoor and outdoor use, it quickly became popular for its lightness and flexibility. Within the economic and Pop-cultural context of the late 1960s it reflected the industry's move towards a

youth-based, anti-materialist socialist attitude, and the avant-garde preference for low-cost and unpretentious design. Stackable when folded either out or flat,

sleek, functional and structurally elegant, the Plia chair continues to hold its own. Piretti went on to become Castelli's director of research design, a post he held until 1972.

The humble double-circuit metal key-ring is a modern marvel, a tiny masterpiece of engineering and utility that nearly all of us carry and few appreciate. The underlying concept of the key-ring is hundreds of years old, but its present refined state is the product of modern precision manufacturing and metallurgy. It was only introduced in the early 1970s, replacing the older bead-chain. Its essential design is simplicity itself, which is the foundation of its extraordinary usefulness, and the reason that it is almost impossible to imagine it being replaced as long as we need to carry keys with us. It consists of a tight spiral of steel, which coils over on itself to complete two circuits. These orbits are so closely pressed to each other that at first glance the ring appears to be a closed metal loop. However, the end of the spiral can be pulled away from the loop and then slipped into the hole at the end of a key. Once the key is pushed back between the two orbits of metal, the loop snaps shut again and the ring, now closed, passes securely through the hole at the top of the key. There are no mechanisms or moving parts; it is simply a tight coil of slightly springy metal. But once the key is on the ring, there is

little chance of it coming off again by accident. And when not being carried, the ring makes storage in a prominent place easy by dangling from a hook. Of course, more than one key can be carried on a keyring. A standard size loop can take about half a dozen before it becomes tricky to add and remove keys. But the name 'key-ring' is simply a reflection of the design's most common use. Effectively, the ring can group and carry anything of an appropriate size with an appropriate hole, from whistles to watches, from penknives to torches, from bottle openers to Bibles. This almost limitless flexibility has led to a whole industry of promotional, souvenir and advertising key chains, all designed for the simple metal loop, and most often coming with one attached, such is the minimal cost of its manufacture. It is not an exaggeration to say that this prosaic little ring holds a good deal of our lives – access to homes, workplaces and vehicles – together. And in honour of that small but important role, we reward the little ring with unlimited customization, going so far as to imprint our personalities on it. It is one of the most intimate design objects we can ever own, and one of the cheapest and least regarded.

Istogrammi d'architettura con riferimento a un reticolo trasponibile in aree o scale diverse per l'edificazione di una natura serena e immobile in cui riconoscersi. Superstudio 1969

SUPERSTUDIO

Adolfo Natalini, architetto
Cristiano Toraldo di Francia, architetto
Piero Frassinelli, architetto
Roberto Magris, industrial designer

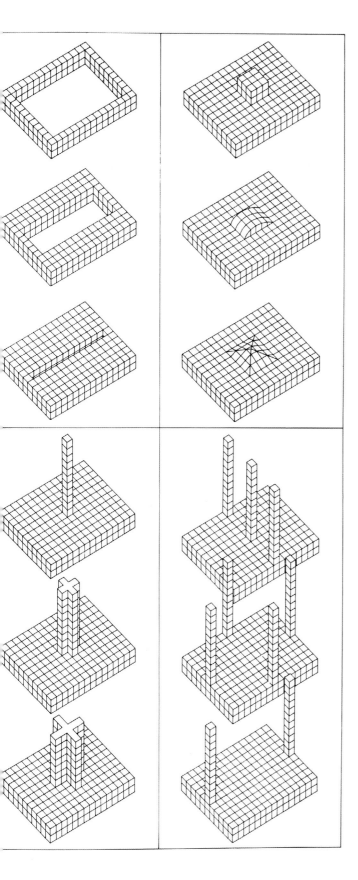

The rigorously spartan appearance of the Quaderna Table, with its stern, geometric form and grid-patterned plastic laminate top, recalling the cheap laminates found in 1950s cafés and coffee bars, presented a stark contrast to the lush curves and rich colour of Italian Pop design of the 1960s. The Quaderna range, which included tables, benches and seats, was a comment on the excesses of Pop design and represented a return to a more rational approach to design. It also marked the genesis of the radical Italian Anti-Design movement. Superstudio was founded in 1966 in Florence by Adolfo Natalini and Cristiano Toraldo di Francia, who were later joined by Alessandro and Roberto Magris and Gian Piero Frassinelli. Alongside other radical groups such as Archizoom, a fellow Florentine group founded in the same year, Superstudio was born out of the restless political climate of the 1960s. The group set out to undermine the certainties of the modernist movement and its tool was polemical criticism. Yet, unlike its British contemporaries Archigram, who viewed architecture and design as a positive force to embrace a hedonistic future, Superstudio came to see architecture as malevolent and blamed it for the bland, faceless nature of many modern cities. The name Quaderna refers to the grid pattern silk-screened on to the table's plastic laminate. The grid was a recurring theme in Superstudio's work. It represented the strict, regimented nature of modernist architecture and design and was used as a metaphor for the way an unthinking globalization was swamping the world. The grid first appeared as Il Monumento Continuo, a proposal for a gridded superstructure that would wrap around the world in a parody of contemporary urban planning. Superstudio wrote that ultimately the grid would form 'a single continuous environment, the world rendered uniform by technology, culture, and all the other inevitable forms of imperialism'. Superstudio was disbanded in 1978. During its existence the Quaderna range was one of the few items that it actually produced; the group's work was conceptual and theoretical, rather than being concerned with building or production. Quaderna Table is still in production today, while Superstudio's collages and drawings have been acquired for the Centre Georges Pompidou in Paris and The Museum of Modern Art in New York.

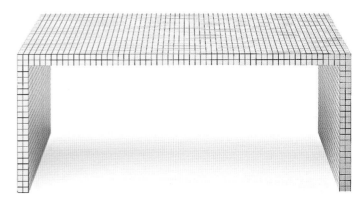

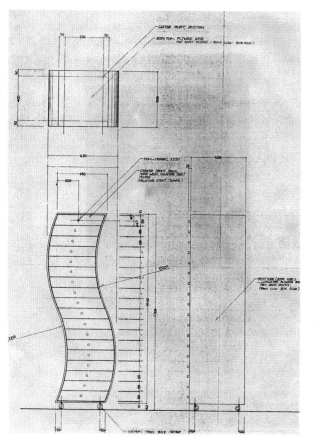

Shiro Kuramata combined the Japanese concept of the unity of the arts and invented a new design vocabulary: the sensation of floating lines and release from gravity, transparency and the construction of light. His furniture pieces are realized in a process of meticulous craftsmanship and a painstaking attention to detail. The project officially titled 'Furniture in Irregular Forms Side 2', (but titled 'Side 1' by Cappellini) designed in 1970, consists of chests of drawers of eighteen slightly different drawers moving on four simple rollers, with a wave-like shape along the sides. One of the pieces has a running curve along both sides, and is accompanied by another piece, this time with a frontal wave. It is an early example of his significant differentiation between shape and function. This design has a figurative approach and can be looked at and associated with a swinging body. Its minimalist structure and reduced means create a strong impression, making it highly recognizable, and giving it a strong identity. The piece can also be seen as a predecessor of the philosophy espoused by the Memphis group of the early 1980s. Shiro Kuramata was a great admirer of Ettore Sottsass and Memphis, with its playful spirit and love of bright colours, and he joined Sottsass's collective ten years later. Even today, the chest of drawers still embodies an extraordinary combination of a minimalist functional sculpture with lightness of form. The pieces stem from Kuramata's pursuit of experimenting with drawers during the late 1960s. When Cappellini reissued them in 1986, there was a renewed interest in Kuramata, due to his postmodernism approach, during a period when he was already revered for his conceptual approach to furniture and interior design.

Furniture in Irregular Forms Side 1 (1970)
Shiro Kuramata (1934–91)
Fujiko 1970 to 1971
Aoshima Shoten 1972 to 1998
Cappellini 1986 to present

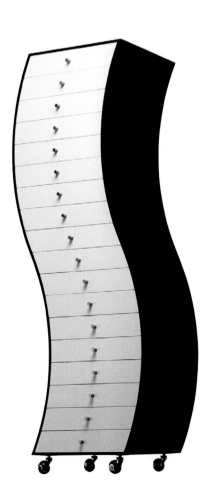

Committed to imagining the environment of the future, Italian architect and designer Joe Colombo was one of the definers of the Pop era interior. His space age 'living units' were barometers of the latest production methods and synthetic materials, whose streamlined plastic efficiency influenced many a sci-fi movie set. By the late 1960s he had more or less abandoned freestanding furniture to focus on seamless, convertible interiors. Designed in 1970, a year before his early death at the age of forty-one, the Optic Clock is one of Colombo's enduring classics. As stylized as Colombo's aesthetic was, it was always driven by practicality. In this instance the clock's casing, which is made of red or white ABS plastic, projects out over the clock face like the rim of a camera lens to prevent light reflections. The casing also projects at the back so that it can be tilted upwards as well as placed flat, while there is a hole in the top to hang the clock on a wall. The graphic treatment of the numbers plays on the clock's inherent roundness, but the traditional hierarchy is inverted so that the minutes and seconds are numbered rather than the hours. In this way, the fat hour hand, with its circular eye, can frame the dots that people know at a glance, while the slender minute and second hands make the precise time much easier to read. The Optic Clock was produced in the same year as the first digital watch, and it aims at the same precision as the digital clocks that would start to replace the analogue variety in the coming decade.

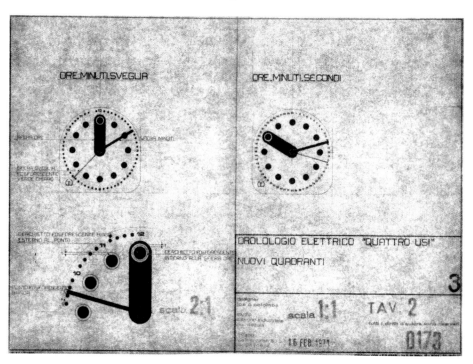

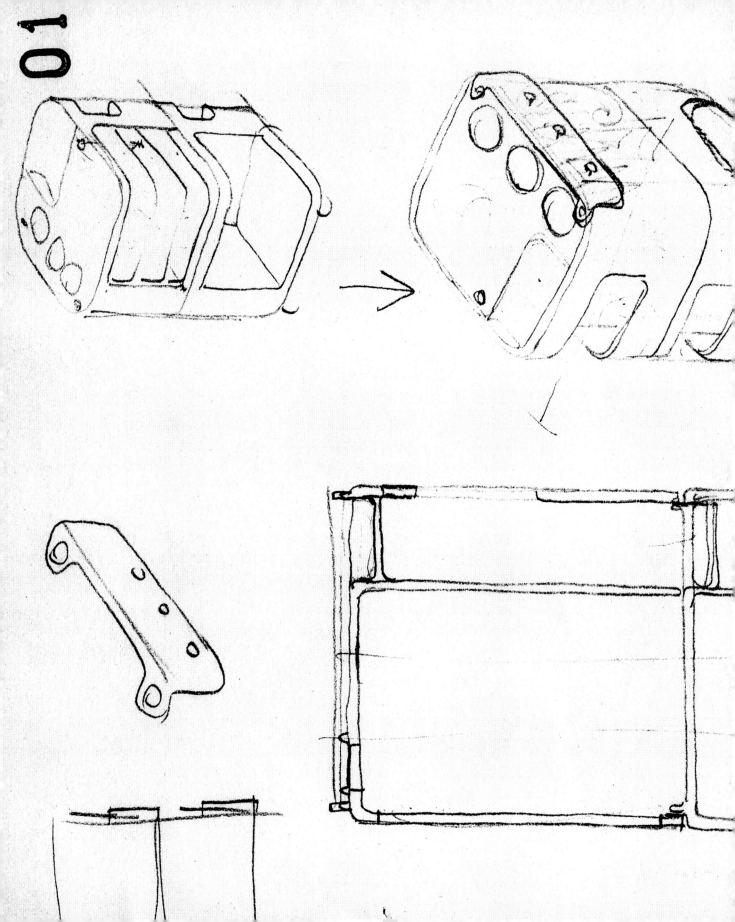

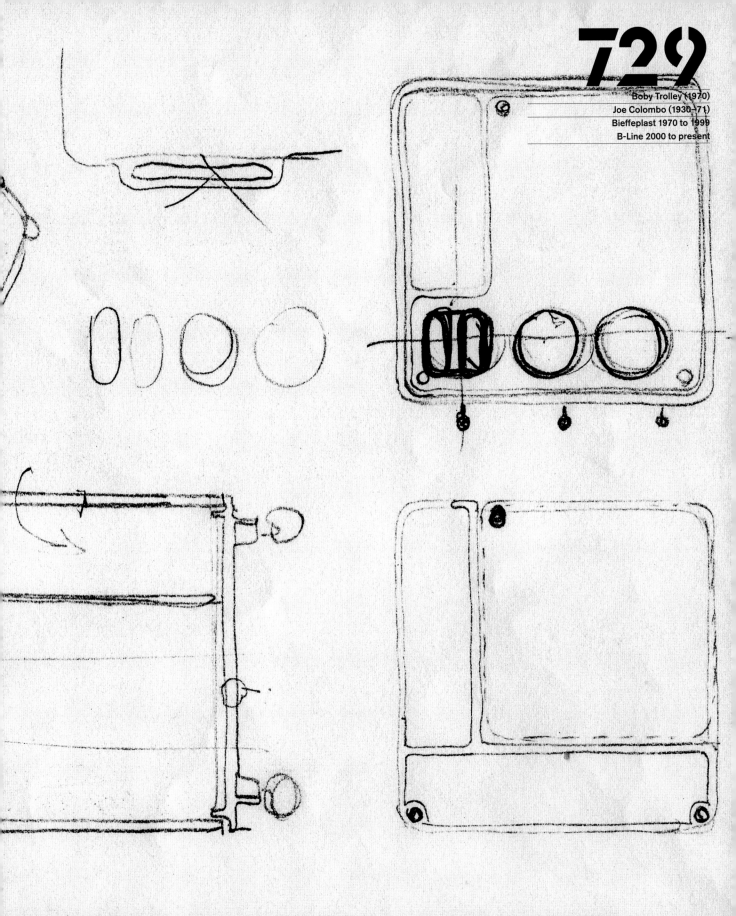

Boby Trolley (1970)

Joe Colombo (1930–71)

Bieffeplast 1970 to 1999

B-Line 2000 to present

The Boby Trolley typifies Joe Colombo's approach to designing multifunctional solutions for the home and office. His philosophy was often to identify a problem first, with the solution following as a reflection of his understanding of the needs of contemporary culture. The Boby Trolley was designed to satisfy the storage requirements of a draughtsman, although it demonstrated a multifunctional purpose within both the home and the office. It is a modular design of injection-moulded ABS plastic, available in a host of colours. A series of sections can be added to suit the user's needs. Set within the height of the trolley are revolving drawer units, drop-in trays and open storage. Its flexibility of use is enhanced by the addition of three castors. The bright colours and practicality immediately found favour in design-conscious homes and offices. The design achieved iconic status through its individualistic profile and inherent practicality as a mobile storage unit. The sinuous cut-away shelves break the overall volume, while the shelves cantilever elegantly and the drawers almost demand to be pushed open, rotating outwards via the hidden spindle. Colombo's design is softened through a finely balanced mix of radii. The appealing curves of what is essentially a box are sensitively designed to the point of brilliance, revealed when one examines the 'wheel arches' of the trolley. The Boby Trolley remains important as it forms part of the assimilation of plastic as a valid material in the home and office. The design could have been realized economically only in plastic and its impact on the cultural use of that material is significant. Beyond stand-alone designs for lighting, seating and homewares, Colombo pursued an intellectual quest for multifunctional units creating highly progressive designs. He explained, 'Given the increasingly rapid evolution of the human race', he aimed to design 'equipment for living that is autonomous and flexible and that can be coordinated, converted and utilized in different ways, so it always adapts itself to its user'. The Boby Trolley endures as an accessible piece of design that encapsulates the Colombo philosophy of use of materials and technology. Bieffeplast continues to supply a demand for the design, despite technological and user changes within the contemporary design studio. The storage capabilities and flexibility of the Boby Trolley outweigh the reality of the conceptual, paper-free design office.

'Good design is as little design as possible,' Dieter Rams, Braun's former and legendary head of design. Ultimately the HLD 4 was just one of a huge number of products Rams designed for Braun and other manufacturers. With the HLD 4 Hair Dryer he designed for the company in 1970 he was as good as his word. The hair dryer had originally been created in the 1920s, and by the 70s an aesthetic consensus appear to have been reached by manufacturers – it should have a handle and a snout both attached to the motor and air ingress in the middle. Rams rebelled against this. Anything considered remotely unnecessary was stripped away. Instead, you have a curvaceous oblong-shaped piece of plastic with a power socket at the base and the airways on the front. It made the hair dryer appear more compact and had the added bonus of looking like nothing else on the market. Apparently Rams took his inspiration for the HLD 4 from some of the early fan heaters by other designers working with Braun, such as Reinhold Weiss. Where the HLD 4 differed from its predecessors, was that the slots which pull the air in are at the front of the dryer rather than the back. This meant that the user's hand was no longer able to block the flow of air and the dryer could work much more efficiently and effectively. Its long-term influence is, however, debatable. The consuming public, it seems, would still rather dry their hair with a product that follows a more traditional form, rather than the modernist, strict shape of the design by the legendary Dieter Rams.

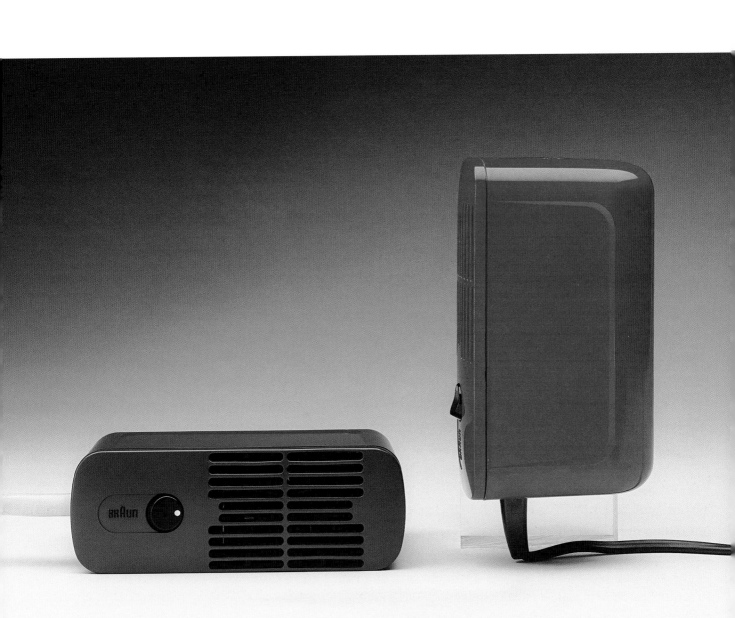

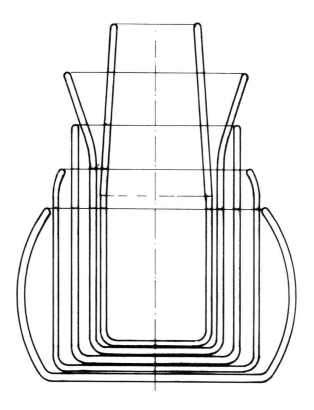

Objects that stack are traditionally associated with a degree of uniformity, but not when they are designed by Cesare 'Joe' Colombo. Each of the five hand-blown crystal glasses in his 5 in 1 set is different, ranging from a short tumbler to a long water glass. And while the stack itself has a functional logic as a space-saving device, it is also the product of Colombo's personal sense of beauty, designed to be a stylized, sculptural flower bud, which unfurls as each glass is removed. Before Colombo set up his design studio in 1962 he had been an avant-garde artist and he maintained a strong sculptural sensibility through all his design work. He died in 1971, but in the nine years of his studio's existence it produced over 300 works and cemented Colombo's reputation as one of the most important postwar Italian designers. The creation of flexible systems for the home was one of Colombo's long-standing concerns: 'If the elements necessary to human existence could be planned with the sole requirements of manoeuvrability and flexibility,' he said, 'then we would create an inhabitable system that could be adapted to any situation in space and time.' In 1969 he had created the Tube Chair, consisting of four cylinders that could be arranged in a number of different combinations or disassembled and stacked one inside the other; the 5 in 1 extends this idea by providing a single object that can adapt to all its user's drinking needs. The set was designed just one year before Colombo's death, and the manufacturer, Progetti, has been producing it since 1989, following his precise drawings. The singular block of glasses includes a tall spirit glass, a wide-rimmed sherry glass, a wine glass, a water glass and a short, squat brandy glass.

731

5 in 1 Stacking Glasses (c.1970)
Joe Colombo (1930–71)
Progetti 1989 to present

Giotto Stoppino

The Magazine Rack was an important piece within Italy's exciting early-1970s climate of design and production. Architect and designer Giotto Stoppino first developed the idea for the Magazine Rack in 1970. Made of plastic in a variety of colours, its essential construction was of two pocket elements bridged by another, smaller element that also functioned as a handle. Its synthetic, moulded and usefully flexible form, which can be stacked easily, fit the design and production mandate of its Milan-based firm, Kartell, to produce durable yet interesting objects for the home and office that exploited new technologies and the ideologies of Pop design. In Italy, Stoppino was one of a few high-profile 'consultant designers'. These Italian super-stars of design advised large mainstream manufacturing companies, like Kartell, and moved them forwards, throughout the 1960s and early 1970s, from elite design towards an avant-garde, Pop and culturally democratic aesthetic. The intent was rational, production oriented and technologically creative. Throughout this period, Kartell worked with plastics technology to become an industry leader; designers such as Stoppino helped to define Kartell as a firm committed to experimen-tation with new synthetic combinations. Domestic objects such as the Magazine Rack were the result of new plastics such as polypropylene, which allowed for a limitless range of cast forms and colours. After 1968, Stoppino moved away from architecture and concentrated on interior and industrial design, utilizing the materials and techniques of mass production as his chief inspiration, and translating the influences of 1960s student movements, Pop Art, music, design, and film, onto domestic products. The Magazine Rack is a manufactured object representative of Italy's reputation as a centre of design innovation and experimentation at the turn of the decade. It now is most recognizable in its adapted form, a semi-transparent and coloured four-pocket version, introduced in 1994 as a unique variation on the original design. This reinterpretation is still produced by Kartell. A silver, semi-transparent finish was introduced to the line in 2000.

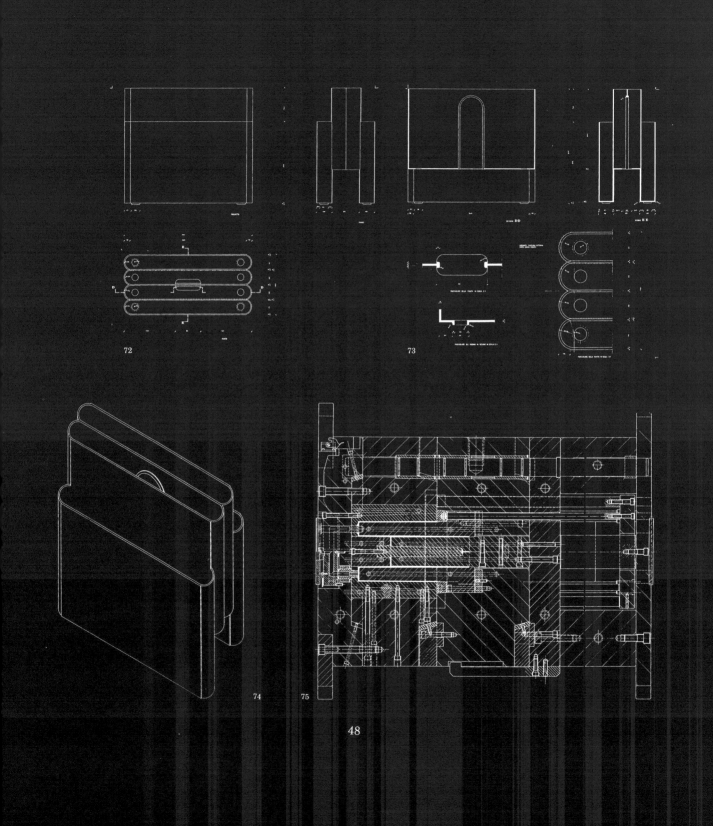

72

73

74   75

48

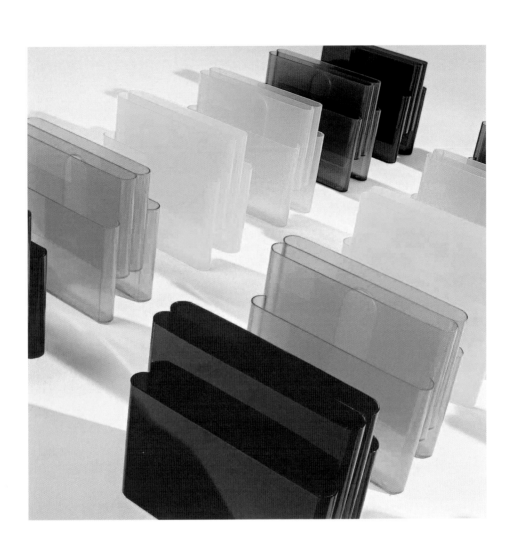

The distinctive green-barrelled Ball Pentel R50 is one of the most successful pens in the world, with over 5 million produced each year. First launched in 1970, the Ball Pentel introduced the world to rollerball technology – an evolved version of the ubiquitous ballpoint – and a disposable pen that could offer something to match the refined writing finish of a traditional fountain pen. Unlike ballpoint pens, which use a viscous oil-based ink, rollerballs use a thinner, water-based ink that on the one hand allows them to write more smoothly and dry more quickly, and on the other gives that fountain-pen-like finish, which is one of the primary reasons for the Ball Pentel's success. Within the green barrel, the ink is held in a fibre cylinder, which, while wet to the touch, does not leak or spill ink everywhere. The cylinder is pressed down, by the colour-coded base of the pen, onto a fibre 'spike' that transfers the ink by capillary action to a hard alloy tip. Crucially, this ink storage and transfer method, developed in Japan, from where Pentel originates, does not rely on gravity, allowing the pen to continue functioning regardless of the angle it is being used at. In keeping with a product that is essentially halfway between the old (a fountain pen) and the new (a Bic-style ballpoint pen) the body of the Ball Pentel borrows the traditional outer shape and feel of the former – albeit formed out of plastic – while delivering the splatter-free ease of use that had led to the success of the latter.

writing is the knife and fork of the mind.

Ball Pentel Fine Point R50 JAPAN

Kitchen scales have historically involved two elements: the display, normally a round dial with a hand, and the receptacle for food. These elements tended to be kept distinct, with most attention being given to the measuring display. However, Terraillon was the first to approach a scale as a holistic product, in some ways almost suppressing the display in favour of the activity of cooking itself. The scale encloses its mechanistic system, and is made into a simple-to-use domestic tool. When designing products to be manufactured, Marco Zanuso, a noted architect, did not alter his process. In architecture he reconfigured space to achieve a desired flow; in products he reconfigured their components to achieve a desired use. For the Terraillon scale the architectural logic is quite beautiful: the lid can be used either with food on top of it, or reversed and used as a container for liquids or grains, a versatility previously not possible. For the display the wheel is hidden and appears less mechanical. With the clever use of magnification and angle, the display is visible when the countertop is lower than eye-level – a similar dynamic also used for Zanuso's Algol Television of 1964, where the screen was tilted upwards. This product is not flawless, though. The scale's moving platform is inside the outer shell, which means that food or liquid can fall into the surrounding gap. It is clear that Zanuso's ideas about what forms good design prevail. The Terraillon Kitchen Scale is a superior example of converting complexity into simplicity, and at a modest price. Its continued and unbroken production is testament to this, even with the influx of modern digital pressure pads on the market.

The Rolls-Royce Phantom VI embodies a very particular type
of Britishness. While many iconic cars are celebrated for their cutting-edge
technology and aesthetics, the Phantom VI seems to sum up the end of an era.
The Phantom was first created in 1925, becoming the car of choice for royalty
and heads of state. Produced in 1971, the Phantom VI was the largest, most
expensive, and, arguably, most luxurious car Rolls-Royce ever made, with a
wheelbase of 3,683 mm (145 in). The exterior (or coachwork) was created by
Mulliner Park Ward Design, and it came with a V8 engine and drum brakes.
It gained iconic status when the company built a special version for Queen
Elizabeth II to celebrate her Silver Jubilee in 1977. This version was manufactured with an even higher, perspex roof over the rear compartment to allow
greater visibility of its occupants. Production of the car lasted until 1992; the
last ever Phantom VI was apparently delivered to the Sultan of Brunei, at that
time the richest man in the world. This opulent car owes as big a debt to the
crafts movement of the beginning of the century as it does to industrialization
and despite its dimensions, it retains a certain elegance. However, it speaks for a
Britain that is long gone; a time of deference, when the monarchy was cherished
and leaders respected. Rolls-Royce itself seemed to agree and the company did
not make another variation on the Phantom until it was purchased by BMW in
1998. Ironically, it took a German company to revive a quintessentially British
design. At 6 m (19 ft) long, the New Phantom is a shade smaller than its
predecessor and although it uses contemporary materials allied to a BMW V12
engine, it manages to retain a sense of Rolls-Royce heritage.

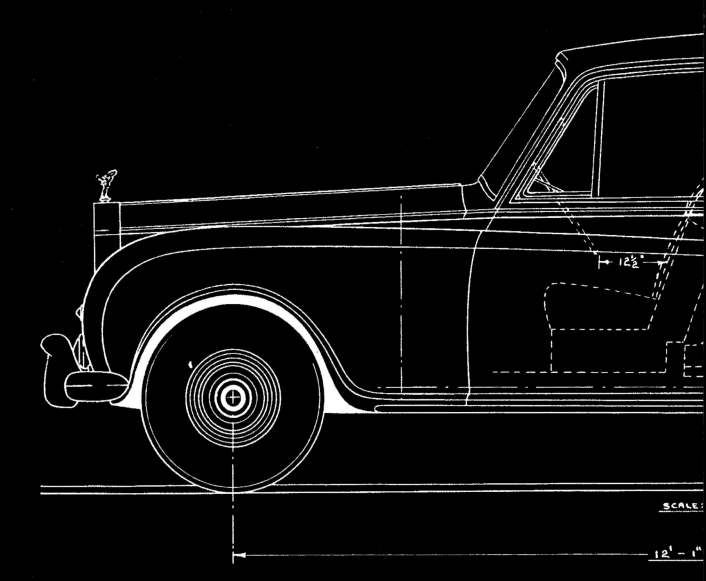

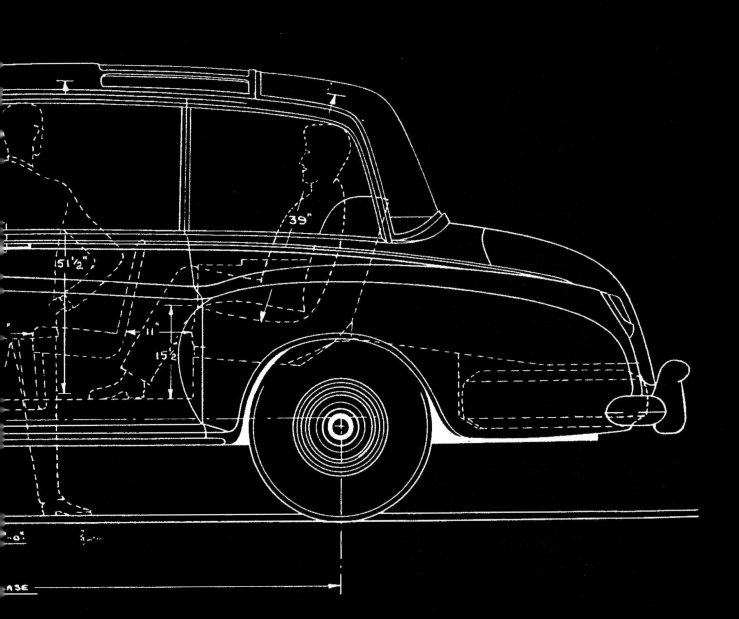

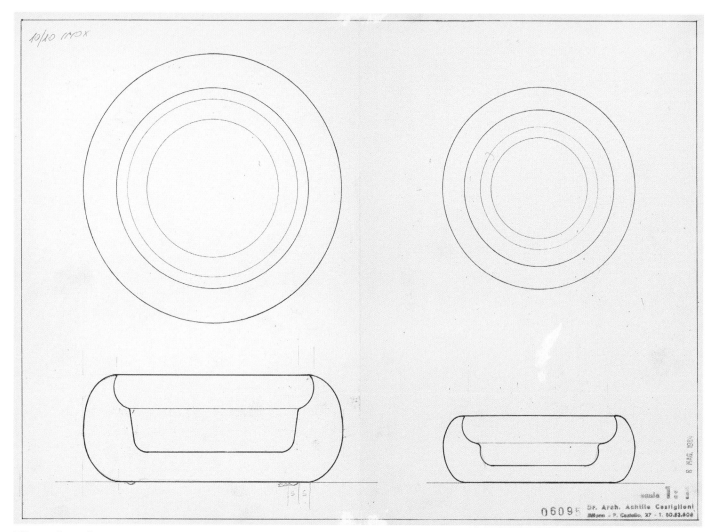

The simple yet elegant design of the Spirale Ashtray belies its ingenuity. Such an apparently effortless solution is the mark of an archetype, and is typical of Achille Castiglioni's approach to design, where familiar objects are subtly improved and redefined by a careful attention to practical detail and an appreciation of everyday human behaviour. This is the language of rationalism tempered with ironic humour and sculptural form. A lifelong smoker himself, Castiglioni designed the Spirale Ashtray in response to the dilemma of the absent-minded smoker who leaves cigarettes smouldering in the ashtray. A spring coil holds the cigarette over the bowl and prevents it from falling as it burns down. The spring is removable, making a messy and unpleasant cleaning task easy. When Alberto Alessi joined the family firm in 1970, Castiglioni was one of the first industrial designers he commissioned to make a variety of products. The best way to persuade Castiglioni to accept a commission, according to Alessi, was to 'bring him an idea that tickles him'. Originally made by the Italian company, Bacci, in 1971, the ashtray was produced in both white and black marble, and in silver plate. The ashtray was transferred to Alessi in 1986, where it was made in 18/10 stainless steel (the figure 18/10 refers to the proportion of chromium to nickel in the stainless steel alloy). Alessi now produces the ashtray in polished steel mirror in two diameters: 12 cm (4.7 in) and 16 cm (6.3 in). Amongst the collections of design aficionados, whether smokers or not, this ashtray is one of those rare pieces whose proportion and uncomplicated combination of elements speak to all.

Spirale Ashtray (1971)
Achille Castiglioni (1918–2002)
Bacci 1971 to c.1973
Alessi 1986 to present

Water taps and bathroom fittings remained untouched by the vision of the designer until surprisingly late in the twentieth century. Whilst many designers, for instance Le Corbusier, had clearly noticed such things and were very careful about which ones they included in their buildings (Le Corbusier preferred English examples because they worked best), they did not seem to think that they needed altering or improving in any way. The KV1 mixer tap, part of a series of fittings in a range called Vola, is probably the world's first commercially successful designer tap. Most of the design work was carried out by Teit Weylandt, working under Arne Jacobsen's supervision in his design office. However, the basic idea, including the underlying mechanism which operates in a different way from the conventional screw tap, had already been worked through by engineer and industrialist Verner Overgaard, the owner of the company IP Lund (which is now called Vola). On the basis of Overgaard's preparatory work, Jacobsen quickly recognized the potential for the visual rationalization of the unit. Interestingly, Weylandt's solution to the design problem of the KV1 has much in common with the way Jacobsen worked in designing his Egg and Swan chairs, that is, in terms of the fusion into an aesthetic whole of different functional parts. By restricting the vocabulary of forms used in the design to a range of cylinders, by minimizing the number of these, and by cleverly combining the lever controlling the force of water with the rotating knob that governs its temperature – dispensing with separate hot and cold taps – Weylandt managed to produce an object that seemed an improbable simplification of and improvement on existing models. Like many of the designs from Arne Jacobsen's office, it seems to have been created for a time that has yet to come.

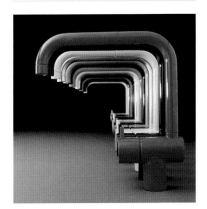

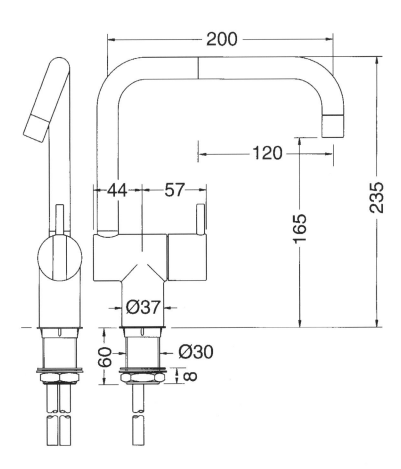

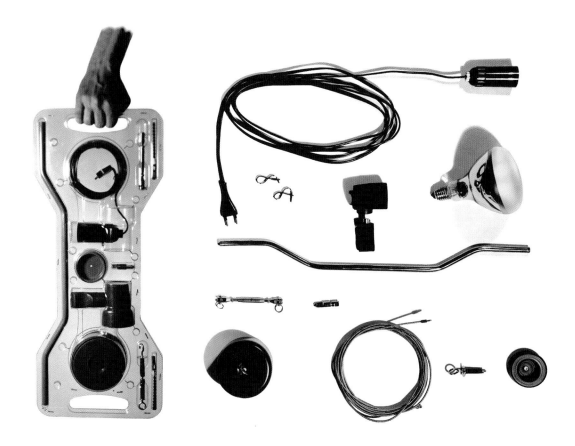

Achille Castiglioni always respectfully acknowledged Pio Manzù as the originator of the Parentesi lamp. Manzù imagined a fixed vertical rod with a cylindrical box that would slide up and down it, with a slit for the light and the chosen position held in place with a screw. When Manzù died prematurely in 1969, Castiglioni continued to develop the idea based on a simple sketch. Looking at this inherited concept with fresh eyes, Castiglioni replaced the rod with metal cable that is hung from a hook in the ceiling and kept taut by a rubber-coated iron weight, which barely touches the floor. A chromed or enamelled stainless-steel tube, shaped like a bracket (on which the product name was based), slides up and down the cable and supports a rotating rubber joint, to which is fixed the lamp-holder with electric lead and 150-watt spotlight bulb. So why doesn't the weight of the tube and lighting fixture cause it to simply slide to the bottom of the cable? The shape of the steel tube creates enough friction with the taut wire to prevent the spotlight from moving once it is in position, but it can be slid up or down effortlessly by hand. The light fixture and bulb have total freedom to point in any direction – and are able to swivel 360 degrees on the vertical and horizontal axes. Most of the components used in the lamp are widely manufactured items, packaged and sold like a kit to be easily assembled by the customer. The shape of the transparent pressed-plastic pack was determined by the lines of the bracket-shaped tube and incorporates handles at both ends for easy carrying. The visual declaration of the 'kit' contents and the standard appearance of its 'off-the-shelf' packaging placed no inflated importance on the 'design' worthiness of the light itself. Nevertheless, in 1979, the Parentesi earned Castiglioni one of the highest accolades awarded in the design industry – the prestigious Compasso d'Oro award. The fixture is also part of the permanent collection in The Museum of Modern Art in New York.

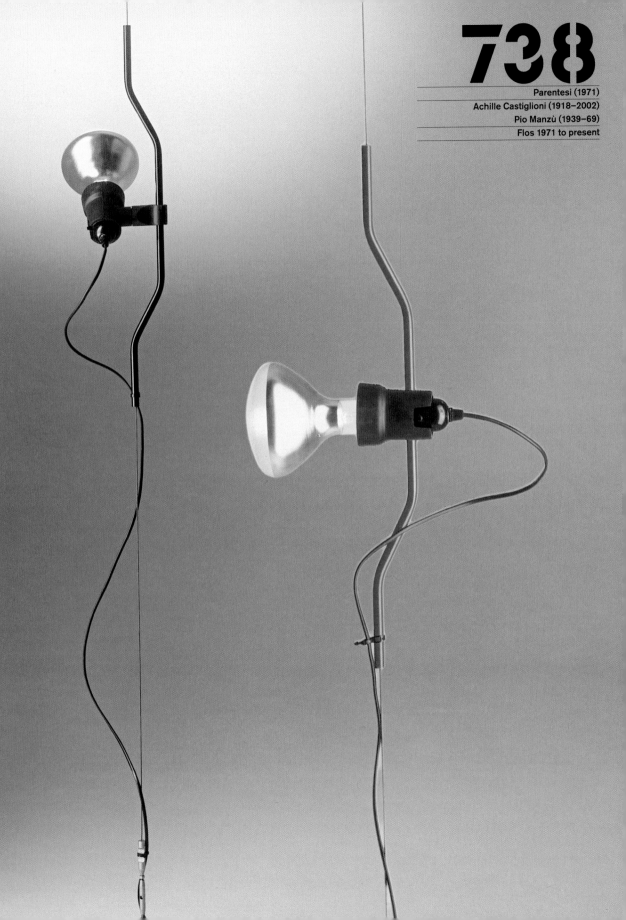

738

Parentesi (1971)
Achille Castiglioni (1918–2002)
Pio Manzù (1939–69)
Flos 1971 to present

The story of the Dinghy begins in 1913, when George Cockshott won a boat-designing competition. The idea behind the competition was to produce a tender for big yachts, that yacht-owners could race in fashionable bays across the world. The only rule for the competing boat-builders was to follow the brief with extreme precision. The great surprise was that Cockshott, the winning designer, was neither boat designer nor architect; he was just a passionate sailor. Because Cockshott's boat was fast, easy to sail and cheap, it was immediately successful, especially in Britain and southern Europe. In 1919 the Dinghy was chosen by the International Yacht Race Union as the first International Class, and in 1920 and 1928 it achieved Olympic recognition in the *en solitaire* class. From the 1930s the Dinghy appeared on seas around the world, always with its wood thoroughly polished and a well-dressed owner at the helm. The Dinghy was 'clinker-built', a technique whereby the hull is constructed so that each wooden plank overlaps the one below. A transom stern, low freeboard and a fractionated mast were also employed to ensure maximum stability and strength in this comparatively small vessel. The Dinghy is one of the first racing boats and now is probably the only one with a fractionated mast. Two little benches are used to stiffen the hull, and when it is racing, two special stools are needed to make the boat more rigid. Most of today's dinghies are made in fibreglass, with only a few boat-builders following traditional methods. There are separate racing classes for the classic and the modern, and surprisingly little difference in performance. They are widely used in southern Europe, particularly Italy, and also in Turkey, with the most important dinghy race taking place annually in Portofino, organized by the Italian Yacht Club.

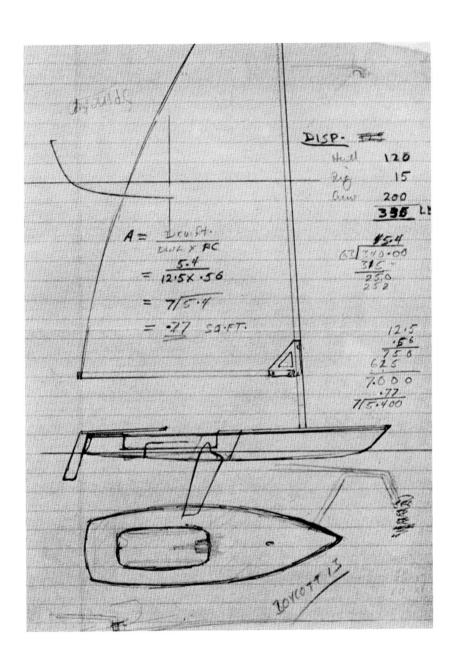

DISP. ~~115~~

Hull   120

Rig   15

Crew   200

335 LB

$$A = \frac{1 \text{ cu.ft.}}{DWL \times AC}$$

$$= \frac{5.4}{12.5 \times .56}$$

$$= 7\overline{)5.4}$$

$$= .77 \text{ SQ.FT.}$$

$$\begin{array}{r} 5.4 \\ 63\overline{)340.00} \\ 315 \\ \hline 250 \\ 252 \end{array}$$

$$\begin{array}{r} 12.5 \\ .56 \\ \hline 750 \\ 625 \\ \hline 7.000 \\ .77 \\ \hline 7\overline{)5.400} \end{array}$$

BOYCOTT 13

The Box Chair is an ingenious self-assembly chair consisting of a perforated injection-moulded polypropylene seat and collapsible tubular metal frame. All the parts come apart to fit in a box which, in turn, fits into its own plastic bag or box. To some degree the design reflects Mari's love of puzzles, and its chunky, no-nonsense appearance, combined with its vibrant colours, including an acid yellow, bright orange and cobalt blue, show how Mari was master of producing fashionable and highly desirable objects that were also intelligent, thoughtful and, above all, rational. The Box Chair was an instant success, coinciding neatly with the 1970s initiative for easily transportable flat-pack furniture. An artist and theoretician, Enzo Mari was not trained as a designer, but had studied classics and literature at the Academia di Belle Arti di Brera in Milan during the 1950s. Naturally drawn to the intellectual activity surrounding the contemporary design scene in Italy, he soon began to design products himself. He first worked with the Italian plastics product manufacturer Danese, where he learned to be a master plastics technician. Not surprisingly, many of Mari's designs have an underlying concern with the theoretical, especially with the role of design in contemporary culture and the relationship between the object and the user. Mari's approach to design was, and continues to be, rigorously rational. He himself describes his work as being 'elaborated or constructed in a way that corresponds entirely to the purpose or function.' Mari turned his hand to furniture in the 1970s. His skill with plastics combined with his rational approach to design meant he could produce wonderfully dynamic pieces that had an underlying simplicity, lifting them above the merely fashionable. Some of his earliest chair designs share with the Box Chair a pared down quality with a supremely functional aspect. No longer in production today, the Box Chair was briefly reissued in 1996 by Driade.

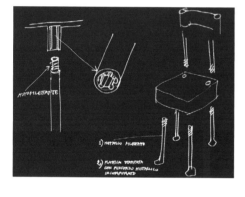

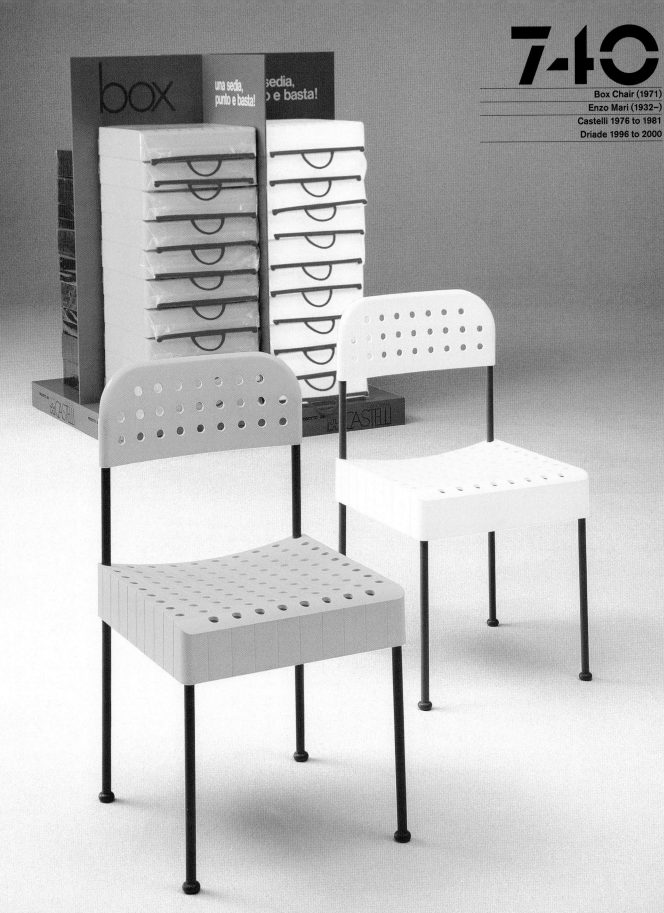

Box Chair (1971)
Enzo Mari (1932–)
Castelli 1976 to 1981
Driade 1996 to 2000

box

una sedia,
punto e basta!

> We'll stop making razor blades when we can't keep making them better.
>
> ~King C. Gillette

The company founded by King Camp Gillette in 1901 has been responsible for many shaving innovations during its hundred-year history. This began with the safety razor first marketed in 1903, a milestone in razor design because before that all razors had to be resharpened, which was a skilled and laborious process. In an attempt to further improve the design, various means to simplify the blade-changing mechanism were developed, including one-piece models that twisted open, and the Techmatic (also by Gillette), which incorporated a wind-on blade strip. The most significant breakthrough, though, from both a performance and marketing point of view came in 1971 with the introduction of the first fixed twin-blade cartridge razor, the Trac II. Developed in house, this had a slide-on element to which the user fixed the blade cartridge, which was sold separately in multi-packs. Gillette later launched the first disposable razor in 1976, but the Trac II was the first to have replaceable cartridges. At the time there was much debate concerning the value of two blades over one, but the marketing campaign 'Two blades shave better than one,' proved extremely persuasive. The Trac II helped the company to further increase its market share (already 55 per cent before the Trac II was introduced). The marketing device of selling the razor kit relatively cheaply and then charging a premium for blade refills proved so effective that it was soon copied by all other manufacturers. By 1973 the Trac II was being sold successfully outside the United States, which in turn established the company's reputation for research and helped the development of premium products that would make further innovations easier for the market to accept. The Trac II is still available and popular over thirty years later, despite subsequent innovations such as pivoting heads, lubricating strips and, more recently, both three-, and four-blade interchangeable heads. Through constant innovation and research, Gillette remains the key player in the razor market, and continues to outsell other manufacturers by almost five products to one.

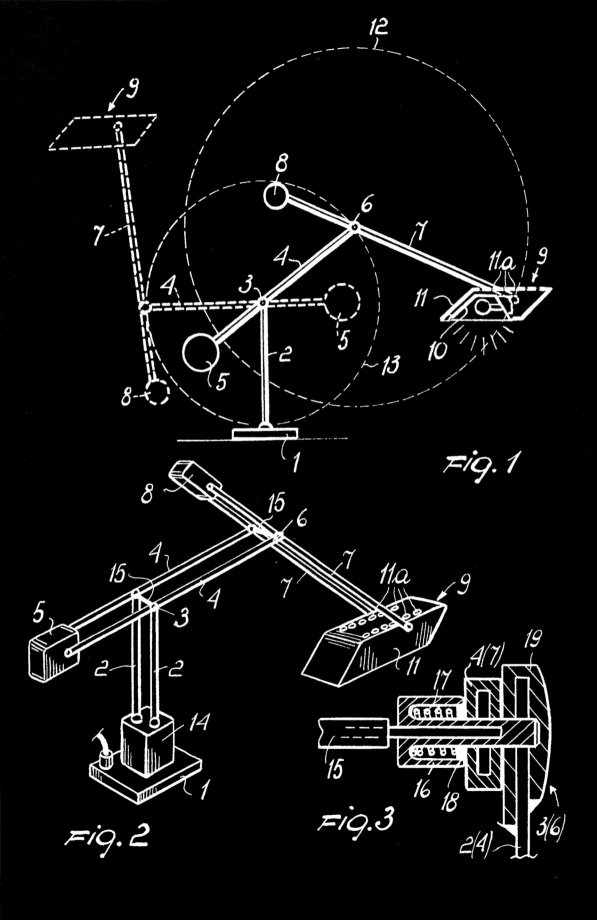

Fig. 1

Fig. 2

Fig. 3

The Tizio lamp has become emblematic of both extreme functionalism in design and an aspirational designer lifestyle. Although developed as a work lamp it has also achieved popularity as a designer object for domestic interiors, as much at home in the 1990s loft apartment as in the 1970s high-tech studio. Richard Sapper decided on a profession as a product designer after a varied educational background in engineering and philosophy. In the early 1970s he collaborated with Italian designer Marco Zanuso, with whom he created several audio-visual products for Brionvega. His work demonstrates a concern for re-thinking the basic principles of objects. The Tizio lamp developed following a conversation with Ernesto Gismondi, an aeronautical engineer who founded lighting company Artemide with architect Sergio Mazza in 1959. In 1970, Gismondi suggested that Sapper design a work lamp for Artemide, and when Sapper responded in 1971, it was with a product that mirrored his own needs when working. 'I wanted a work lamp with a wide range of movement but one that, despite its ability, would claim only a small amount of space,' Sapper said. He also preferred a lamp that would shine directly on the surface below, but without a cumbersome reflector positioned too closely to the head. The result was a lamp that combined appropriate new technology (halogen light) with a carefully engineered and flexible structure. The Tizio lamp uses a system of counterweights to hold the bearing arm in position, so that with the touch of a finger, the height and extension of the lamp can be adjusted with precision. The bearing arm can rotate through 360 degrees on its heavy base, and the small reflector turned to face in any direction. Furthermore, the bearing arm also works as a low-voltage conductor, so there is no need for wires to run from base to bulb. The lamp is made of metal with a strong but lightweight fibreglass-reinforced nylon coating. The joints are not screwed together, but fixed with a form of snap fastening, so that if the lamp falls, the joints snap apart rather than break, and can be snapped back together. In totality (it is made of over 100 components), it is a remarkable combination of engineering and ingenuity in a spare and elegant form.

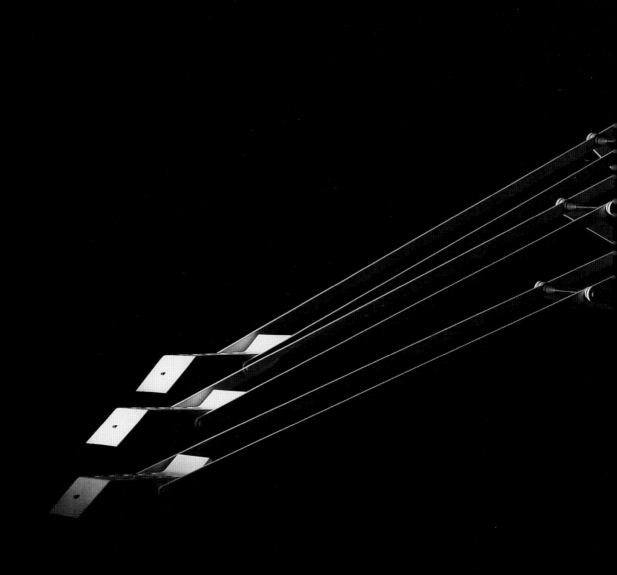

Tapio Wirkkala was on a short visit to the United States in 1955, working in the office of Raymond Loewy, when he first encountered Philip Rosenthal. Loewy had been commissioned by Philip Rosenthal to design a number of dinner services for Rosenthal Porzellan, which the company hoped would help to improve its market share in North America. Before he returned to Finland, Wirkkala worked on one of the services. Although it was completed by another designer, Philip Rosenthal was impressed enough with Wirkkala's work to ask him to continue working for him. The result was a highly regarded dinner service called Finlandia and subsequently, between 1956 and 1985, nearly twenty other table services, plus about 200 different vases and art objects. Included in this output are the unglazed porcelain Pollo Vases of 1971. Although these are rather enigmatically shaped and rock gently when pushed because of their curved bases, the form of the vases, in common with a major part of Wirkkala's output, was inspired by the natural world of Finland. It is no coincidence that an individual Pollo Vase closely resembles the shape of a wading bird, or something like a duck standing asleep with its head tucked under a wing. Around the rims of the vases are a number of raised spots arranged in concentric circles. These help to give some relief to the otherwise undecorated surface, but also form a tactile element. Probably the most noteworthy feature of the design, and something that generally concerned Wirkkala throughout his collaboration with Rosenthal, is the surface texture of the porcelain, which in this case is inspired by stones and rocks that have been polished smooth by the action of wind and water.

Pollo Vase (1971)
Tapio Wirkkala (1915–1985)
Rosenthal 1971 to present

The Programma 8 range of tableware represents an important phase in the history of Alessi production. In the early 1970s Alberto Alessi invited his architect friend, Franco Sargiani, and the Finnish graphic designer, Eija Helander, to work on the design of a new range of stainless-steel tableware that began with a brief for an oil jug. The initial project expanded into a revolutionary series of adaptable and flexible forms that would enhance the food they contained and that would use table space more efficiently. The two architects carried out international research, examining how tableware was used and how people dined in different countries. The result was Programma 8, a large-scale assortment of trays and containers based on a modular system of squares and rectangles. The system represented an international innovation in household objects and was backed by a major advertising campaign. Programma 8 was radical for a number of reasons: it used steel in its own right and not as a substitute for more expensive materials, its shape was unlike any other and it acknowledged that younger professional consumers were living in flats and small houses where space was at a premium. The collection satisfied the key aims of making the food visible, and was equally suitable for dining alone or with large groups. Programma 8 led the way in new concepts regarding domestic tools, offering practicality, not only in its idea of allowing several items to co-exist simultaneously, unifying to create a whole, but also because the collection was stackable. The collaboration with Sargiani extended to graphic design, packaging and exhibition stand design and continued until the end of the 1970s. The modular set has been reissued by Alessi in 2005, and now includes ceramic containers with polypropylene covers, along with the original containers for oil, vinegar, salt and pepper, as well as various trays and cutting boards.

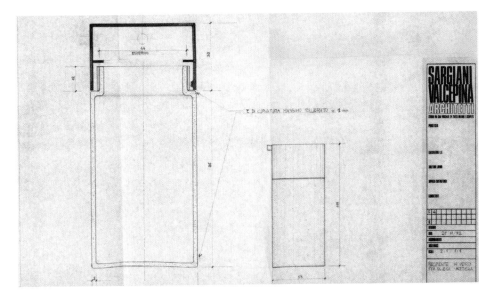

Programma 8 (1971)
Eija Helander (1944–)
Franco Sargiani (1940–)
Alessi 1971 to 1992, 2005 to present

The circular kitchen Minitimer is characteristic of product designer Richard Sapper's intelligent fusion of technology and style. The design is understated and pragmatic; the mechanism revolves inside the outer casing so that the remaining time is visible from above and the side in the small circular window. The 7 cm (2.75 in) diameter, discreetly small timer, is produced in black, white or red, and is loosely reminiscent of scientific or car instruments. With one turn, the timer can be set to up to sixty minutes, after which it rings when the target time is reached. The success of the design has been recognized since its initial production. Ritz-Italora, based near Milan, is the original manufacturer, and the French company, Terraillon, has produced it under licence since its debut in 1971. Terraillon, established in 1942, has produced bathroom and kitchen scales since it began, and is now the European market leader for these items. The company has successfully combined design with technology, due in no small part to the fact its designers have always worked closely with its research departments. Sapper's creative approach to engineering is apparent in his most familiar designs. While he became a specialist in electronic products, such as radios, televisions and lighting, Sapper became known for his designs for the casing of such products. This may explain the success of the timer, as its casing cleverly sandwiches the middle section. The Minitimer is an elegant and discreet object, but with a lengthy and dedicated following, as well as being part of the permanent collections at The Museum of Modern Art in New York and the Pompidou Centre in Paris.

Rodney Kinsman

Overtly expressing the high-tech style of the 1970s, British designer Rodney Kinsman's

Omstack Chair is one of the most elegant evocations of the decade's furniture manufacturing mandate to produce high-quality, low-cost objects of beauty and practicality on a large scale, utilizing industrial materials and systems of production. Available in a number of coloured paint finishes, the chair is composed of an epoxy-coated, stamped sheet-steel seat and back, attached to a tubular steel frame. Its design allows it to be stacked, or clipped in rows, thus making it a popular choice both with cost- and fashion-conscious buyers as well as with institutions, in particular art and design colleges. A graduate of London's Central School of Art and Crafts, Kinsman recognized early on in his career that only low-cost and multi-purpose products would capture a market in times of economic uncertainty. As younger consumers were an important demographic within his projected buyer profile, the chair needed to satisfy economic, as well as stylistic demands. To that end, his consultancy practice, OMK Design, utilized industrial materials and inexpensive methods of production. Furniture design of the 1970s was characterized by rationalist manufacturing principles that highlighted, by way of materials, those associated with heavy industry (such as pressed or stamped metal, steel scaffolding and rubber flooring), and in production terms, the use of advanced technology. Ideally, furniture designers attempted to eschew ornament for forms that signalled a confidence in industrial rationalism. Design often articulated this belief by being sold disassembled and off the shelf. Intended for use both indoors and out, the Omstack Chair, in form and use of materials, is reminiscent of Hans Coray's 1938 Landi chair, although this prewar modernist classic is constructed of bent and pressed aluminium. Kinsman's Omstack remains in production to this day.

Omstack Chair (1971)
Rodney Kinsman (1943–)
Kinsman Associates/OMK Design 1971 to
present

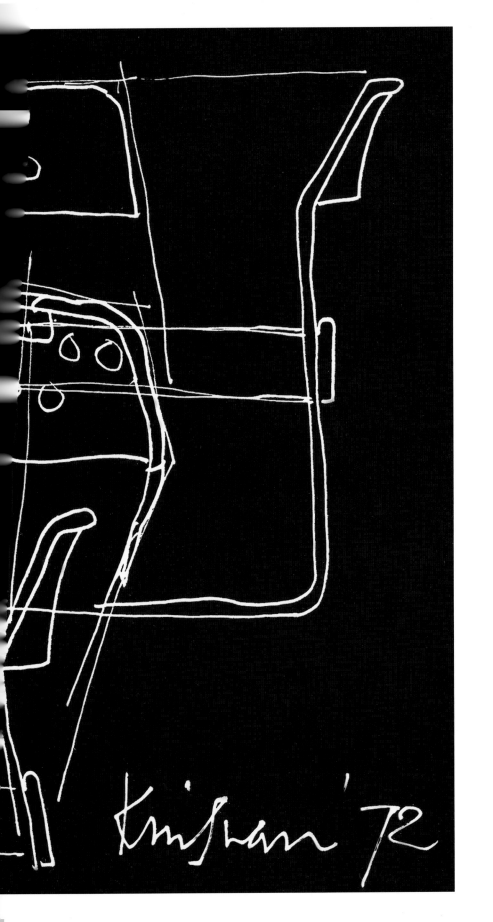

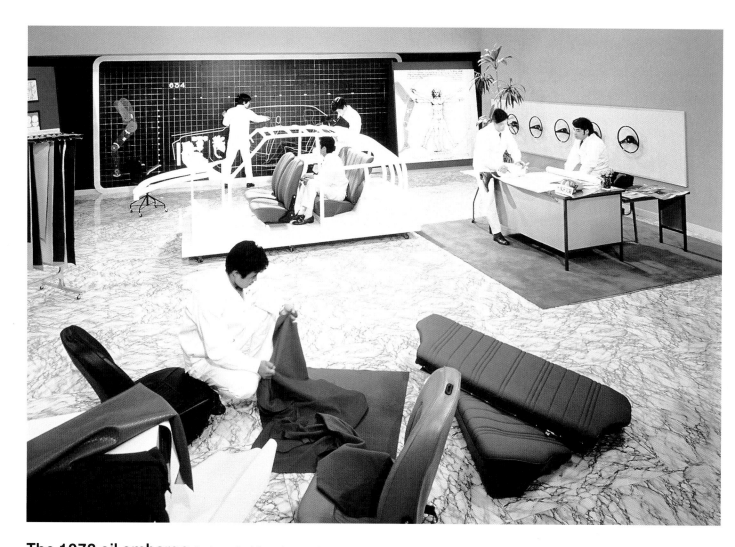

The 1973 oil embargo that resulted from America's support of Israel during the Yom Kippur War had a devastating impact on the country's automotive industry but provided Japanese makers and their energy-efficient smaller cars easy entry. Honda, which had been making cars for only eleven years, imported its first Honda Civic into the United States in 1972 and met with overwhelming success from a population that was previously renowned for its fondness for oversized vehicles. With a wheelbase of only 216.5 cm (86.6 in) and a length of 349.5 cm (140 in), the Civic was much smaller than the average American car, although its transversely mounted engine and front-wheel drive arrangement allowed for four passengers. The rear seat could be folded down to accommodate more than 20 cubic feet of space in the hatchback, as much, Honda claimed, as any average-sized car on the market. In addition to rocketing fuel prices, the early 1970s saw a rise in environmental consciousness that would result in the founding of the Environmental Protection Agency (EPA) and the commitment to reduce automotive emissions by 90 per cent by 1975. In the light of this increased awareness, in December 1972 the Japanese company released a new model Civic that came with a CVCC (Controlled Vortex Combustion Chamber) engine that eliminated the need for a catalytic converter and unleaded fuel, a feature that further cemented Honda's success in the United States. Subsequently, the Civic was recognized by the EPA as the most fuel-efficient car during 1974 and 1978. Now in its thirty-third consecutive year of production, the eighth generation of Civic is due to be released at the end of 2006 and the car continues to be a highly successful product for the Honda company.

7-17
Honda Civic (1972)
Honda Design Team
Honda 1972 to present

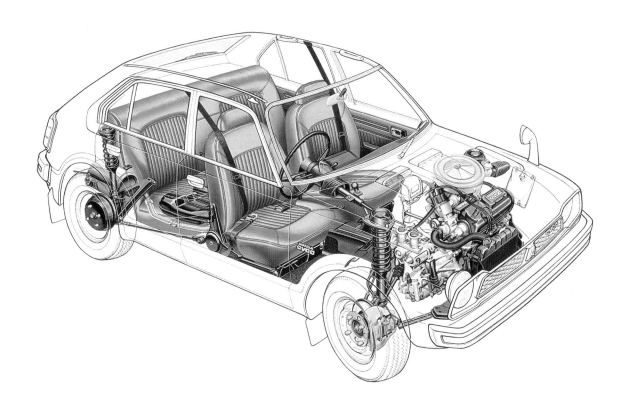

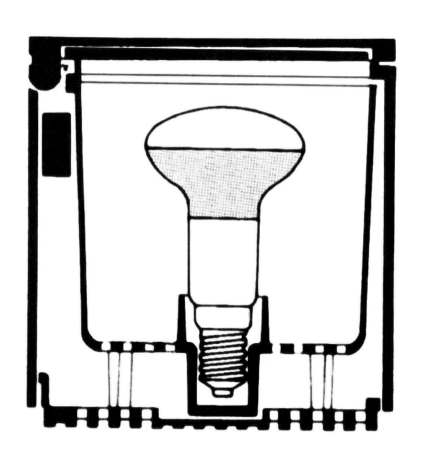

11
4" 11/32

10 x 10
4" x 4"

The Cuboluce is literally a box of light lit with a single 40-watt bulb housed in an ABS plastic (acrylonitrile-butadiene-styrene) container. The action of opening the lid switches on the light, while the angle of the lid determines the brightness. Highly characteristic of Italian product design of the early 1970s, the Cuboluce shows a sophisticated use of high-quality plastics and a desire to create a smooth and minimalist housing for electrical components. The light can be used as a bedside or table light, and its discreet and inviting form makes it an object of fascination even when switched off. ABS was developed from experiments in the manufacture of synthetic rubber during World War II. Its exceptional toughness and rigidity has meant that it is commonly used in the automotive industry and for cased products such as computers. Designed by Franco Bettonica and Mario Melocchi (as Studio Opi), the Cuboluce is one of a range of products based on cuboid and cylindrical forms created by the designers for the Milanese company Cini&Nils. Others include an ashtray, magazine rack, ice bucket and flower vase, all made of melamine or ABS plastics. The Cuboluce and other Cini&Nils products are now part of the permanent design collection of The Museum of Modern Art in New York.

The SX-70 Polaroid Folding Camera reputedly cost $750 million to design and introduced one-step instant photography that required no peeling or subsequent coating on the photographic print. The SX-70 name came from a project number assigned to the original self-processing camera and film in 1943. Physically, the camera was a pocket-sized single-lens reflex camera but it was expensive, with an initial retail price that put it beyond the reach of most consumers. During the first full year of production 415,000 cameras were produced. The SX-70 was designed by Henry Dreyfuss Associates of New York and was a high point of Polaroid's technical capabilities. The designers helped to make Polaroid's technical innovations accessible to users. Polaroid's founder, Edwin Land, liked Dreyfuss because, he explained, 'He didn't know what couldn't be done.' Land specified that the new camera had to fit inside a suit jacket pocket, with prints which must be self-contained and develop in daylight without human intervention. The film packs produced ten prints, which were 7.8 x 8 cm. The camera's iconic status was recognized at once: Charles and Ray Eames made a short film about it and Laurence Olivier chose it as his only product endorsement. The camera demanded new technologies, which Polaroid scientists, chemists and designers were able to come up with: automatic exposure, auto-focusing, flat batteries to be contained within the film packs, and chemicals in the new film packs that worked for a designated time, stopping once development was complete. The camera's distinctive collapsing shape was unlike any camera of the previous seventy years. The original model in chrome and leather was virtually handmade. It was joined by models with sonar auto-focus, and a simplified viewfinder as well as a gold limited-edition commemorative camera. Polaroid stopped producing the SX-70 in 1982. Since that time the company has established its instant-picture cameras in niche markets such as passport and ID photographs, as digital technologies have eroded its traditional markets. The photographs produced by the SX-70 on the new film packs attracted a roster of artists such as Ansel Adams, Helmut Newton, Mary Ellen Mark and Andy Warhol. Polaroid encouraged this interest and, as prints could be altered during development by physical manipulation or the application of heat, SX-70 photography evolved into an art form in its own right.

7-49

SX-70 Polaroid Folding Camera (1972)
Henry Dreyfuss (1904–72)
Henry Dreyfuss Associates
Polaroid 1972 to 1977

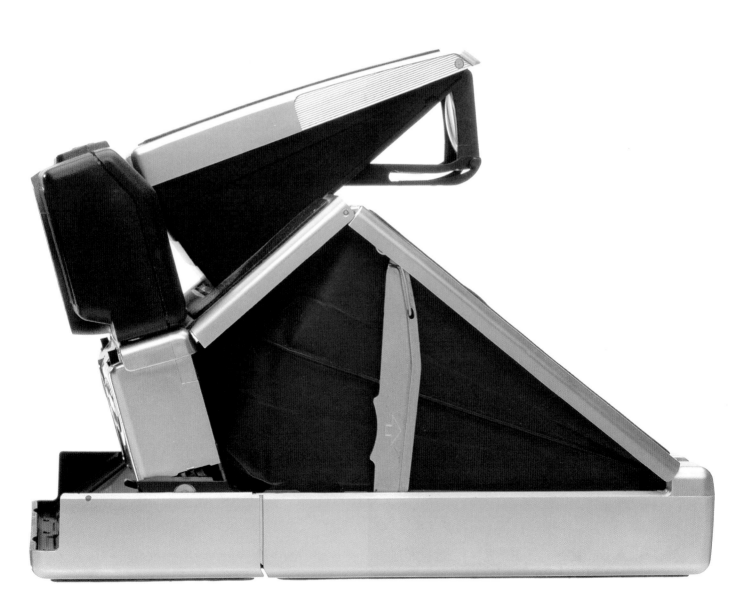

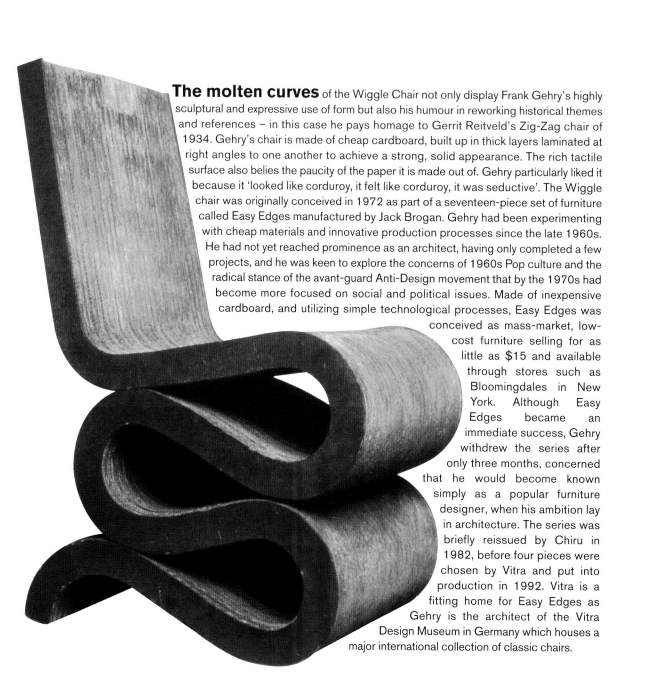

The molten curves of the Wiggle Chair not only display Frank Gehry's highly sculptural and expressive use of form but also his humour in reworking historical themes and references – in this case he pays homage to Gerrit Reitveld's Zig-Zag chair of 1934. Gehry's chair is made of cheap cardboard, built up in thick layers laminated at right angles to one another to achieve a strong, solid appearance. The rich tactile surface also belies the paucity of the paper it is made out of. Gehry particularly liked it because it 'looked like corduroy, it felt like corduroy, it was seductive'. The Wiggle chair was originally conceived in 1972 as part of a seventeen-piece set of furniture called Easy Edges manufactured by Jack Brogan. Gehry had been experimenting with cheap materials and innovative production processes since the late 1960s. He had not yet reached prominence as an architect, having only completed a few projects, and he was keen to explore the concerns of 1960s Pop culture and the radical stance of the avant-guard Anti-Design movement that by the 1970s had become more focused on social and political issues. Made of inexpensive cardboard, and utilizing simple technological processes, Easy Edges was conceived as mass-market, low-cost furniture selling for as little as $15 and available through stores such as Bloomingdales in New York. Although Easy Edges became an immediate success, Gehry withdrew the series after only three months, concerned that he would become known simply as a popular furniture designer, when his ambition lay in architecture. The series was briefly reissued by Chiru in 1982, before four pieces were chosen by Vitra and put into production in 1992. Vitra is a fitting home for Easy Edges as Gehry is the architect of the Vitra Design Museum in Germany which houses a major international collection of classic chairs.

750

Wiggle Chair (1972)
Frank Gehry (1930–)
Jack Brogan 1972 to 1973
Chiru 1982
Vitra 1992 to present

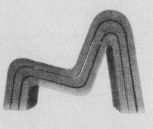

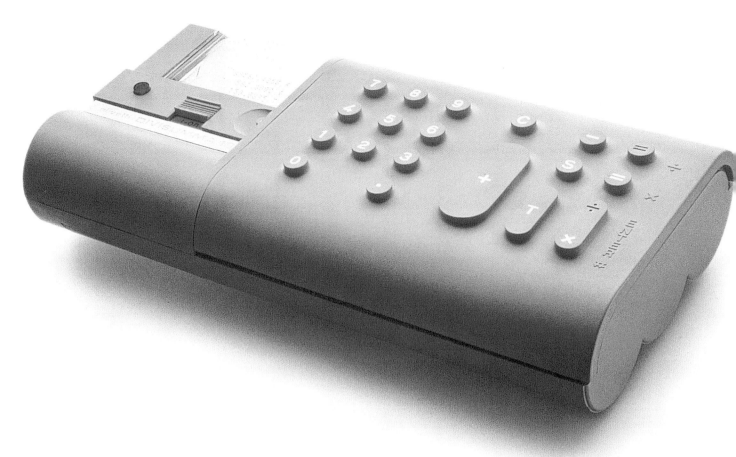

The bright, rubberized Divisumma 18 calculator marked a radical development both for Olivetti and Mario Bellini in the early 1970s. It coupled simplicity with playfunessl, producing a machine unlike any made before. The introduction of new technologies, such as micro-electronics and plastics, had a significant impact on designers at this time. The heavy, metal enclosures of postwar machines were inevitably being replaced by smaller, cheaper plastic designs. Injection-moulding techniques also brought opportunities for new shapes, with fewer limitations on the forms that could be moulded. Interesting then, that Bellini at Olivetti, along with Ettore Sottsass, heralded an age of architectonic designs based on slab-sided forms. Architecture was a common starting point for Italian designers in the mid-twentieth century and Bellini had studied it at the Milano Politecnico, graduating in 1959. Perhaps also, the traditional production of technical 2-D drawings had a more limiting (and subconscious) influence than is often recognized. Industrial designers, along with architects and engineers, were trained to think, design and realize in front-, side- and plan-view elevations, and the box-shaped designs ultimately reflected these particular viewpoints. As a hand-held electronic printing unit with no display, the key differentiator of the Divisumma 18 was its bright yellow ABS plastic 'skin'. Olivetti clearly intended to market it to a new breed of consumer; an advertising image showed one being held by a hip young businessman walking under a blue sky, implying freedom. However, its radical design appealed to only a small segment of the population and the production of the rubberized keyboard proved too costly to ensure mass success. Regardless of this, through his affiliation with Olivetti, Bellini created a calculator that was the aesthetic pinnacle of consumer electronics in the early 1970s. The Divisumma 18 can justifiably claim to have been the source of numerous tactile and emotive 'soft-tech' electronics products that followed in the late twentieth century.

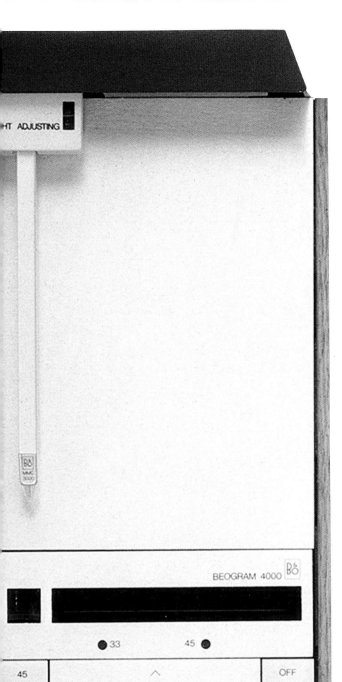

HT ADJUSTING

BEOGRAM 4000

33   45

45   ∧   OFF

<   >

33   ∨   ON

The distinctive flat, integrated design of the Beogram 4000 was a revelation to hi-fi consumers when launched in 1972. Inspired by the Bauhaus architectural style of Mies van de Rohe, the modernist design created a radical aesthetic by placing the controls on the top of the appliance, rather than on the front. Available in teak, rosewood, oak or white trim to complement the sleek aluminium and tinted perspex of the lid, the record player's design featured linear slides rather than the traditional rotary knobs used by Bang & Olufsen's competitors. Designed by Jacob Jensen, Chief Designer with Bang & Olufsen between 1964 and 1985, the Beogram 4000 marked the development of a design approach to create clean, simple and intuitive products that have placed him amongst the most recognized designers in the world with more than 100 international design awards. The record player featured an electronic tangential pick-up arm which, by moving in a straight line towards the centre of the record, placed the pick-up precisely in the record's groove, avoiding the sound distortion caused by the arc movement of traditional arms. One of the design's most striking features was the record player's second arm which, through the use of a photocell, could determine the size of a record. The almost magical quality of the automatic selection between an LP, EP or Single and automatic play mesmerized consumers of the day. When matched with its twin, Beocenter 4000, it created the Beosystem 4000, elegantly combining a 2 × 40 watt amplifier, record player, AM/FM radio, high-quality cassette deck and speakers to create the first lifestyle audio system. Regularly updated for many years, the design was widely copied during the 1970s as other hi-fi manufacturers developed 'music systems', but Bang & Olufsen's lifestyle-orientated strategy, aimed at design-conscious consumers placing taste and quality before price, ensured a market leadership in design that continues to the present day.

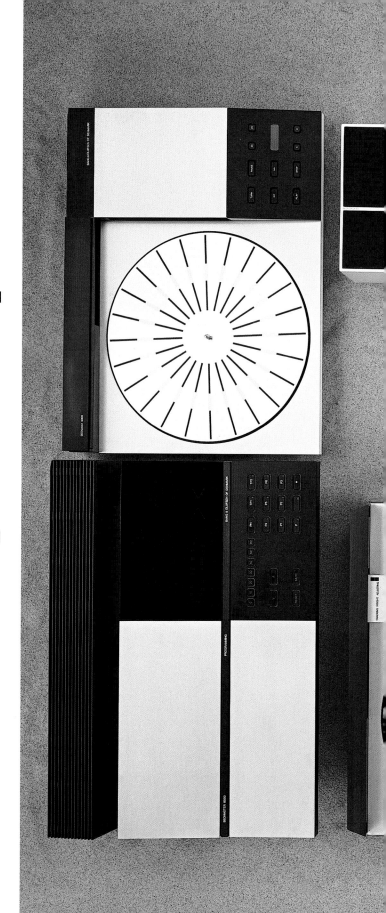

The Porsche Design Chronograph is a perfect union of engineering innovation and refined product design, a combination synonymous with its famous creator, Ferdinand 'Butzi' Porsche, designer of the bodywork for the legendary Porsche 911. The Chronograph was the very first to feature a mechanical movement, immediately setting it apart from other chronographs on the market, which still had to be rewound manually. To achieve this breakthrough Butzi worked closely with the watch manufacturer Orfina, a Swiss company founded in 1922 and renowned for its precision watch-making. In addition to its key mechanical advancement and crafted accuracy, the Chronograph was designed to last. To achieve this the watch face was initially hardened by a sintering process, which was later updated to a method called 'plasma coating'. In this new procedure a specific atmosphere was created in a vacuum that encouraged the precipitation of titanium oxide particles on to the watch surface, making it extremely durable. However, although the Chronograph was developed to be a high-performance watch it was always designed with the consumer market in mind, specifically a fashion-conscious public interested in the kudos of engineering technology. Accordingly, the striking black face of the watch is derived from the cockpit instruments of planes and racing cars. It succeeds in displaying a lot of information, counters for date/day, and seconds, minutes and hours, for measuring time and speed while maintaining a simple and strong design. The matt black face contrasts with the time markers and dials, which are in bright white. The monochrome design is then punctuated by a bold scarlet second hand. The Porsche Design Studio was founded in 1972 in Stuttgart after 'Butzi' left Porsche. The firm moved to Zell am See in Austria two years later, from where it continues to make luxury watches and sunglasses. The Porsche Design Chronograph was the studio's first product and, although production of the watch ceased in 1986, thanks to Butzi's design and its long-lasting qualities it remains much sought after.

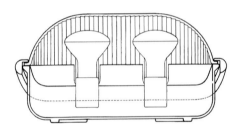 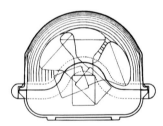 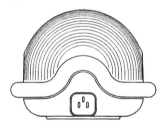

Noce was designed by Achille Castiglioni as a tough and durable light of industrial appearance, capable of being used outdoors and kicked or knocked without damage. The name 'noce', meaning walnut, refers to the outer casing of two halves, one of toughened safety glass, the other of die-cast metal, which makes it literally 'a hard nut to crack'. Inside the shell are two adjustable bulbs, which can be swivelled on their axes to direct the beam and so avoid glare. The bulbs are housed in the metal base shell, and the glass shell, either frosted or transparent, is fixed over them by a die-cast collar, sealed with a neoprene joint to make it weatherproof. By placing the light on the ground, interesting light effects can be created in the outdoor environment, lighting objects and foliage from beneath. Castiglioni stated that, in designing Noce, his intention was to create a form of lighting that could come from the ground. He said, 'Natural light comes from the sky. Since electric light is artificial, it should come from the floor.' He also described his approach as 'doing less' rather than doing more, so that designing is a process of deletion rather than addition, eliminating the superfluous to achieve a synthesis of pragmatic and stylistic needs. In the case of Noce, the product takes a subordinate role in its surroundings, and so its form is correspondingly discreet. When switched on, its purpose is to cast light on other objects, not upon its own form. Its durability, expressed in the choice of tough materials and solid forms, suggests that this is a product with a job to do, rather than an object of contemplation. Despite its industrial appearance, it has an organic quality to it, and when switched on looks like a glowing stone or shell. The Noce lamp can be used indoors, and also comes in an alternative wall-mounted model. It continues to be manufactured by the Italian company Flos, a long-term manufacturer and collaborator of Castiglioni.

The Tripp Trapp Child's Chair was the first chair developed specifically with the needs of children in mind. Deceptively simple in design, it is the most versatile of chairs, adapting with the child as it grows. It gives the best support while at the same time allowing the child enough freedom of movement 'to explore the world in comfort and safety'. The Tripp Trapp was designed in 1972 by the Norwegian designer, Peter Opsvik, after seeing his two-year-old son, who had outgrown his high chair, sitting uncomfortably at the table with his feet dangling and his arms unable to reach up to the table top. Opsvik's response was to create a chair that allows children from the age of two to sit at the family table in comfort and at the same height as adults, so they can interact with the rest of the family. As the child grows, the seat and the footrest can be adjusted in height as well as depth, enabling children of all ages to sit in the correct posture at the right height with their feet well supported. Peter Opsvik is one of Norway's best-known designers, celebrated for his work in ergonomic and sustainable design. This chair, too, was developed according to Opsvik's ergonomic principles, giving children a good start in life by providing balance, support and control. While Opsvik's designs for adults encourage movement within the sitting position, for safety reasons the Tripp Trapp is more static. The Tripp Trapp chair is made of cultivated beech and can be bought either untreated or varnished and in a number of different colours. Over 4 million Tripp Trapp chairs have been sold worldwide since their launch in 1972. Although there have been copies, the Tripp Trapp's main rival is said to be second-hand Tripp Trapp chairs, usually inherited and passed down within families.

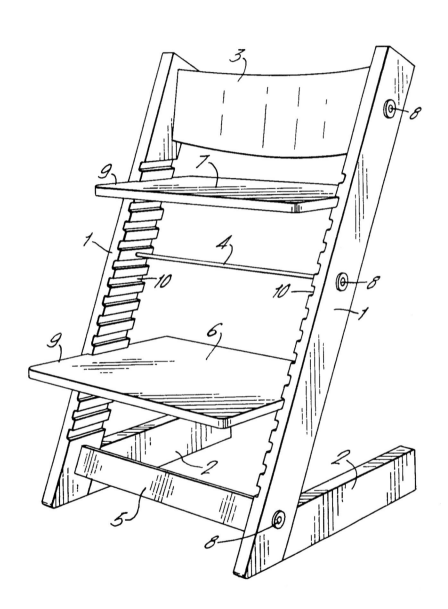

Clive Sinclair was a great innovator who had a profound influence on products that we now take for granted. He is best known for the Sinclair Executive Calculator. Sinclair had been interested in the idea of miniaturizing electronics, such as radios, from an early age. After leaving school at eighteen, he founded his own company, Sinclair Radionics, in 1961. By using catchy advertisements, he sold kits to make small-sized radios, and finally turned his attention to calculators in 1972. The result was the Sinclair Executive Calculator. When it was introduced in 1972, it was the slimmest calculator in the world by some distance, measuring only 56 mm × 138 mm × 9 mm (2.2 in × 5.4 in × 0.35 in) and able to fit into a shirt pocket without creating an unseemly bulge. The secret of the Executive was in the battery. While most calculators of the era used normal AA battery sizes, the Sinclair model used button cells. To achieve this, rather than providing power to the calculator's chip continuously, Sinclair discovered it could be pulsed and the internal capacitance of the chip would store enough charge to keep it working until the next pulse was required. It reduced power consumption dramatically and allowed the use of the smaller cell, providing twenty hours of continuous use from only three mercury button cells. The small keyboard was the result of the innovative design, with rubber pips that would press down upon the beryllium-copper contacts. Sinclair followed the Executive with more calculators, including the Cambridge and the Sovereign, but came under pressure from Japanese manufacturers. He changed direction, and a generation grew up learning to use computers at home. He later became obsessed with miniaturizing the television. A brave, and occasionally misguided, risk-taker, he deserves to be remembered for the Executive.

Until the late 1960s turntables had used a belt drive to spin vinyl records, which over time would stretch and wear, causing records to turn in a warped rotation and thus cause mechanical noise to infiltrate the stylus, creating unwanted acoustic interference. In 1969 Technics introduced the first direct-drive turntable, the SP-10. A series of technical improvements led to the introduction of the first SL-1200 in 1972. On a direct-drive turntable the motor is directly coupled to the record platter and turns at the same rate as the record. Since there is no need for additional parts to transfer the motor's torque to the spinning platter, the turntable suffers from lower mechanical rumble and flutter, while benefiting from greater rotational stability and a far longer service life, a fact amply demonstrated by the large number of original decks still in active service today. In 1979 the seminal Mk2 version was released, which added quartz direct-drive accuracy, a feather-touch start/stop button, heavier aluminium platter, lighter tone arm and, crucially, a slide pitch control. Its utilitarian appearance has been hugely influential in modern consumer electronic design, with over three million sold since its introduction. The ability to start the turntable at any speed allowed a DJ to have far more control over the delivery of the music than with common consumer turntables, which suffered from a delayed start. While most belt-driven consumer turntables did not naturally spin backwards, the Technics SL-1200 spun backwards to accommodate the DJ who needed to spin the record forwards and backwards to hear the cue point through a set of headphones. This mechanical ability was imaginatively used by DJs who moved the record rapidly forwards and back, creating a scratching sound that became a staple of the rap music emerging from New York in the late 1970s. Through the use of the pitch control and the slip mat on the platter, DJs began to explore the ability to alter a record's speed, mixing seamlessly between two separate tracks by synchronizing their beats per minute. This enabled DJs to play continuous sets, responding to their audiences' demands from the dance floor. Through the emphasis on dance beats, rather than lyrical melodies, DJs created modern dance music and culture.

■ EXPLODED VIEWS

- Cabinet and Chassis Parts

Note: For the set with serial number sheet change mark $\boxed{E}$, the power transformer is fitted as shown below.

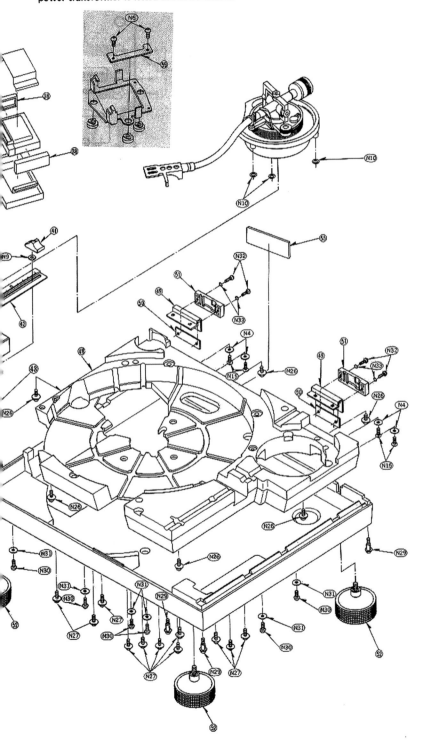

The Kurve cutlery range is among the defining designs to come out of the long and prolific association between Finnish-born designer Tapio Wirkkala and Rosenthal, the established yet experimental homeware design company based in Upper Franconia. One of the most versatile, imaginative and successful figures of postwar Scandinavian design, Wirkkala worked across a wide spectrum of disciplines from glass, ceramic, metalware and jewellery to furniture, industrial design and even packaging. Initially working as a sculptor and graphic designer and winning first prize in a competition to design new Finnish banknotes, Wirkkala established his reputation as a homeware designer in 1946 with a winning entry in a glassware competition organized by the Finnish glass company iittala. The matt-finish stainless-steel Kurve Flatware range of cutlery, which was produced posthumously by Rosenthal in 1990, draws on Finland's Arctic landscape and traditions, and particularly the domestic designs of the region's indigenous Sami people. The pared-down ergonomics of the Kurve forms recall the simple cutlery of the Sami. Wirkkala shared their ancient craft sensibility, always carving his cutlery patterns and prototypes from wood in the early stages, and would only authorize production when he was satisfied with the 'grip' of the wooden model. Wirkkala believed passionately in the idea of the creator as artisan and that the intrinsic quality of the materials should dictate the design, very much in the Scandinavian humanist tradition. Yet a sculptural beauty and poetry permeate the sensual curves of the Kurve range. From 1957 on Rosenthal gave free rein to Wirkkala's design vision, a collaboration which yielded a collection of elegant homeware products, the Kurve being one of the most enduringly popular among them.

Tapio Wirkkala carving wooden prototypes

The modern carpet sweeper is essentially a mechanical version of the dustpan and brush,

something halfway along the evolutionary scale that runs from bristles on a stick to the modern vacuum cleaner,

both in terms of what it does and how it looks. Although the first carpet sweeper was patented in 1811, by

James Hume in England, and mass-produced versions (most notably those designed by Melville Reuben

Bissell) were developed in the USA during the second half of the nineteenth century, it was in Günter Leifheit

and Hans-Erich Slany's productions that the device achieved its most celebrated and perfect form. Leifheit set

up the manufacturing company Günter Leifheit KG in Nassau in 1959. By 1960 he was producing his first

carpet sweepers and by 1970 he was doing so at a rate of 2 million per year. Although he had been inspired by

carpet sweepers he had seen in the United States in 1957, Leifheit designed an improved version that was

slimmer and incorporated a retractable handle, thus allowing it to be more easily pushed under large items of

furniture such as wardrobes and beds, as well as a top-removing dustpan. In its design the 1973 Rotaro merges

the clean lines and strong geometry of German Modernism of the 1930s, with a touch of the more recent

American modern style in such details as the prominent dial. The sweeper itself runs on six wheels that drive

three rotating brushes, two of which are at the side and have a spring suspension. Their purpose is to displace

dirt and debris that are then swept up by a central brush roller into the removable dustpan. The brushes are

height adjustable, with four settings, in order to accommodate various types of carpet or flooring. In addition to

these design features, the Rotaro is composed of a sheet-metal housing, a wooden axle and strong natural

pig bristles, making it one of the most enduring sweepers on the market; more hardy, in fact, than many

subsequent versions.

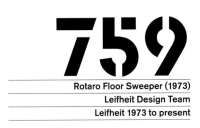

759

Rotaro Floor Sweeper (1973)
Leifheit Design Team
Leifheit 1973 to present

P.A. 025 711 ★ 16. 1. 65

Dipl. Ing. Ludewig
Dipl. Phys. Buse
Patentanwälte
Wuppertal-Barmen
Unterdörnen 114

FIG.1

FIG.2

FIG.3

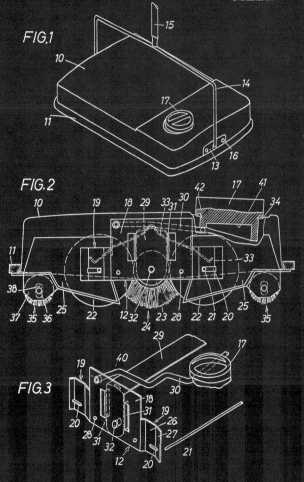

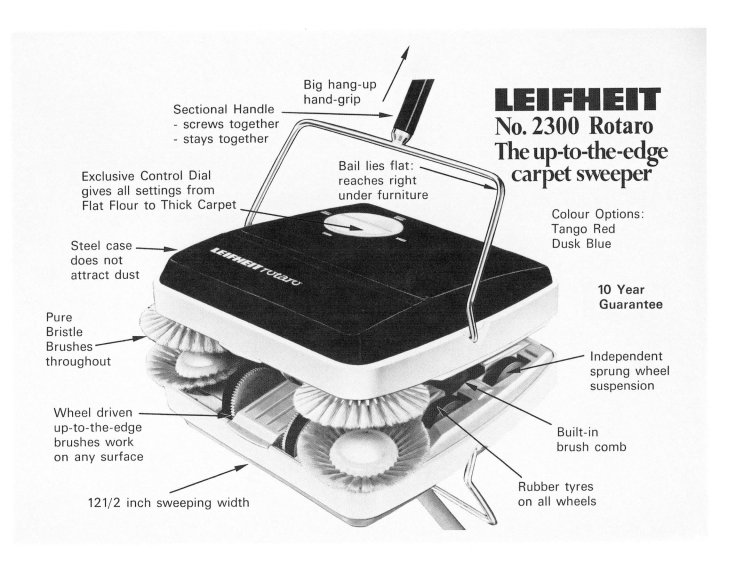

Big hang-up
hand-grip

Sectional Handle
- screws together
- stays together

Exclusive Control Dial
gives all settings from
Flat Flour to Thick Carpet

Bail lies flat:
reaches right
under furniture

Steel case
does not
attract dust

Pure
Bristle
Brushes
throughout

Wheel driven
up-to-the-edge
brushes work
on any surface

121/2 inch sweeping width

LEIFHEIT
No. 2300 Rotaro
The up-to-the-edge
carpet sweeper

Colour Options:
Tango Red
Dusk Blue

**10 Year
Guarantee**

Independent
sprung wheel
suspension

Built-in
brush comb

Rubber tyres
on all wheels

腕時計の新しい歴史をひらく液晶表示式の水晶発振式デジタル腕時計

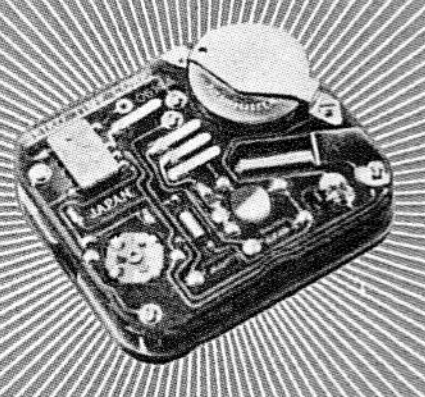

06LC機械体

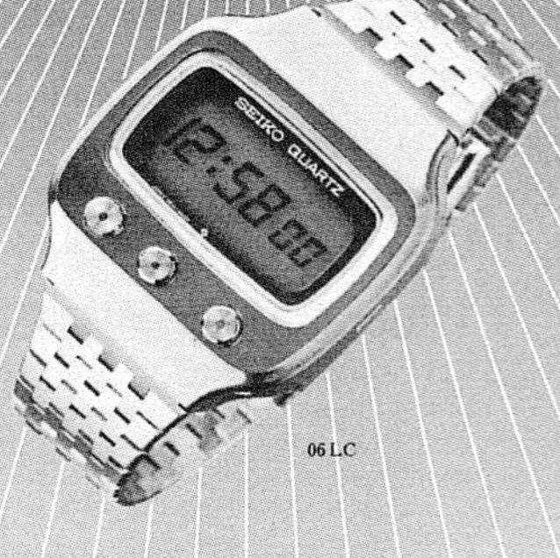

06LC

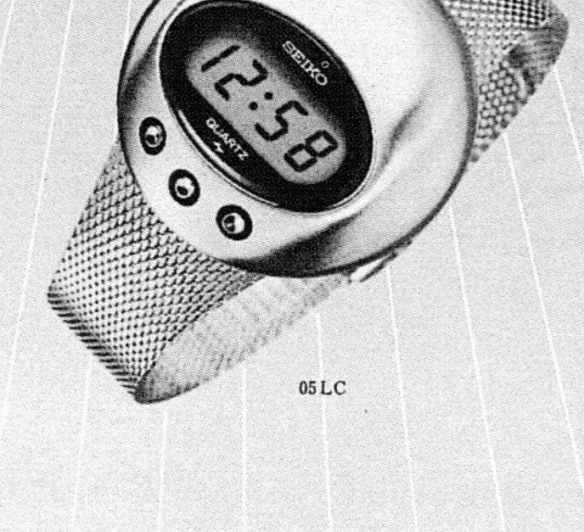

05LC

いままでの腕時計のイメージをまったく変えた液晶表示式の水晶発振式デジタル腕時計セイコークオーツLCV・F・A（06LC、05LC）が、いよいよ発売されます。

液晶表示式腕時計は、これまでの腕時計と異なり機械的に動く部分がまったくなく、時計機能のすべてが電子回路によってコントロールされ、時刻はデジタル表示されます。デザイン、機能の両面で腕時計のイメージを一新する「セイコークオーツLC」の登場により、世界の腕時計の歴史に新しいページが開かれました。

〈液晶とは〉

液晶は固体と液体の中間的な性質をもつ有機化合物で、電気や温度変化、圧力などの刺激を受けるとその部分だけ色がついて見えたり、透明度が異なったりする性質をもっています。液晶表示時計では、このうちの電気的刺激に感応する性質のものを利用して、時刻を表示しています。

「セイコークオーツLC」に使われている液晶表示体はFE型ネマチック液晶と呼ばれる高品質のもので、5万時間以上という画期的な長寿命をもっています。また、現在発表されている液晶表示は白ヌキがほとんどですが、「セイコークオーツLC」の表示は黒で書いたようにあざやかなコントラストをもった黒で、世界にもほとんど例がありません。1971年にプロトタイプを発表して以来、セイコー技術陣の努力の成果がここに製品となって登場したわけです。

〈時計技術の集大成〉

「セイコークオーツLC」は時間標準に水晶振動子を用いた水晶発振式腕時計で、セイコークオーツ発売以来の経験によって開発されたLSIなどをはじめとする数々の技術と液晶表示体の研究成果とが、集大成されています。

06LCは時・分・秒の6桁表示、05LCは時・分の4桁で秒は時と分の間のコロン（：）の点滅によって表示します。いずれも時刻合わせはワンタッチのプッシュボタン式。暗い所でも内部照明装置によって時刻を読み取れます。

〈製品仕様〉

表示：FE型ネマチック液晶（シングルクリスタル・ディスプレイ）
表示方式：時・分・秒の12時間制デジタル表示
水晶振動数：32，768Hz
携帯精度：平均月差±10秒以内（常温）
使用電池：小型銀電池1個
電池寿命：2年以上（内部照明ランプを平均1日10回、1回当たり約1秒点灯した場合）
電子回路：C MOS－LSI

〈作動原理〉

セイコークオーツLCは、5つのブロックで構成されています。発振部①の水晶振動子の発する信号は、分周部②、分配・駆動部③のC MOS－LSIによって瞬時に時、分、秒の電気信号に変えられ、液晶パネル④に表示されます。

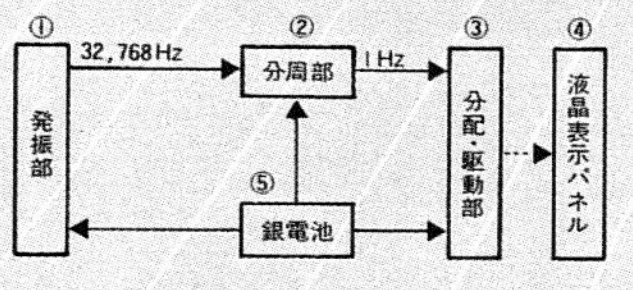

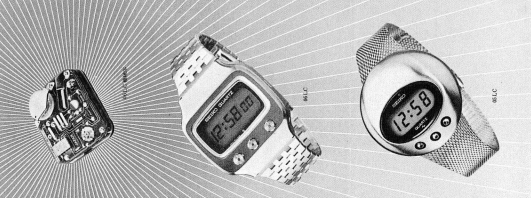

In the early 1970s digital technology was understood to be the wave of the future for timepieces. In 1972, Hamilton Watch Company and Electro Data introduced Pulsar, the first retail version of a digital wristwatch with an LED (light emitting diode) display. This watch presented one a challenge that was hard to overcome for an LED. It required two hands to operate, since the energy needed to illuminate the display had to be engaged by pressing a button. That same year, the Twisted Nematic Liquid Crystal Display (TNLCD) was invented at Hull University in England, after years of research, and made it possible to reflect light onto a screen at a lower power level than the LED. Within a year the LCD (liquid-crystal display) had evolved and was enough that it could be employed in small small-scale devices, and in October 1973, the Japanese watch company Seiko introduced the Quartz LC VFA 06LC, using the first six-digit, liquid crystal field-effect display indicating hours, minutes and seconds, which had been developed by Suwa Seikosha, (later known as Epson). Adopting styling that set it apart from standard watches, 06LC had a titanium casing, a stainless-steel link band and a rectangular screen that remained lit in a black, slightly curved frame and could be read in the dark. In addition to providing sharp contrasts, the internal photochemical and chemical interactions of the LCD had a lifespan of 50,000 hours. The fact that LCDs consumed so little power that constant illumination was now possible, which allowed Seiko's engineers to include seconds in the time display. The result was a changing read out that underscored the user perception of the accuracy of the watch. With the addition of pushbuttons that allowed the user to set time down to the second and change minutes and hours independently, 06LC was not simply a new watch, it was a new machine. With the introduction of the 06LC, the digital watch and the Japanese watch business was set on an ascendant trajectory that would last for much of the next decade.

A large body of opinion in the motor-cycle world insists that the SS 750 Desmo is the most beautiful bike ever designed. Everything about it catches the eye. It has Fabio Taglioni's signature 90° V-twin desmodromic engine, originally designed in 1970 for the Ducati 750GT. Beautiful in form, and pleasing in its original round crankcase with the Ducati name cast in Art Deco style lettering and made to last, Taglioni's engine has been the basis of all Ducati V-twins since. The story of the bike is a good one. The original 750GT turned out to be much more than just a serviceable road bike and it was immediately pressed into race service. For the Imola 200 race in April 1972 Taglioni and his team prepared 750 V-twins for British ace Paul Smart and Italian racer Bruno Spaggiari. No one thought they would win, least of all the rival MV Agusta team, with world-champion Giacomo Agostini in pole position, or the Japanese teams, then at the height of their power. In a sensational upset the two Ducatis outperformed the big factory teams and dominated the race, running virtually in a one-two formation, with Paul Smart edging Bruno Spaggiari for first place. The legend was born, and as a mark of celebration, Ducati quickly put into production the SS 750, essentially a replica of the victorious Imola machines. The styling of the new SS 750 was a *tour de force* and flew in the face of Italian racing tradition, where everything was painted red. The duck-egg green and silver colour scheme was like nothing else on the road. The bikini fairing was sleek and elegant, and the side covers were beautifully scalloped and slotted, as if jet-propulsion was somehow hidden under the seat. And, with its forward-leaning V-twin engine, the bike not only looked fast, it had the race pedigree to prove it. The original SS 750 was produced only in 1974 in a limited edition of 400 bikes. It was subsequently put into production for another two years but with a different carter engine.

The 240-year-old Riedel brand has been a family glass-making business for eleven generations, creating hand-blown and now machine-made products. Professor Claus Josef Riedel, the ninth generation of glass makers, was the first to realize that the shape of the glass influences the flavours and features of different wines. By replacing traditional coloured and cut glass with a thinly blown, long-stemmed, simple shape, he transformed stemware into the first functional wine glass, reducing the glass to its essential form: bowl, stem and base. This crucial change began with the Sommeliers range, introduced in 1973, in Orvieto, Italy. Claus Riedel created the world's first gourmet glass series, developed with the help of the Association of Italian Sommeliers (ASI). The series consisted of ten different shapes and included the Bourgogne Grand Cru and Bordeaux glasses, which were designed in 1958 and 1959 respectively. At that time wine glasses tended to be of a moderate size, and at 27 cm (10.75 in) high the Bourgogne Grand Cru was gigantic. The bowl was proportionately larger than normal and had a globular drop shape flaring to the rim. Riedel found that the size of the rim influenced the bouquet, taste, appearance and texture of the wine. At the same time, the wine was directed on to the taste zones of the palate in various ways, according to how the drinker tipped his or her head while taking a sip. After wine is poured, it begins to evaporate immediately, with aromas filling the glass in layers, which are further exaggerated by swirling the wine. The larger the size of the glass, the more aromas are revealed and the more enjoyment gained from the experience. Georg Riedel, Claus's son, developed the Sommeliers series further. Almost yearly new glasses were added, not only for wine but also for champagne, fortified wines and spirits. The most recent introduction is the mysterious black tasting glass, which came on the market in 2003. This glass was specially designed for blind tasting. Without being able to see what is in the glass, one can fully concentrate on smell and taste. Today the Sommeliers collection consists of no less than forty different glasses. When the series started, the glasses stood out for their unusual dimensions and perfect balance. Nowadays the Sommeliers range produces the standard glass for wine tasting. Its flawless crystal, its high-quality, handmade execution and its special design make it stand out against all competitors. Even machine-produced glasses imitate the size and shapes of this range, but the refinement of a Riedel Sommeliers glass can never be matched.

Bordeux Grand Cru
design 1961

Tinto Reserva
design 1987

Hermitage
design 1995

Zinfandel/Chianti Classico
design 1991

Mature Bordeux
design 1973

Loire
design 1997

Rheingru
design 1973

Montrachet
design 1973

Sauternes
design 1989

Alsace
design 1973

Michel Ducaroy

With the cultural

turmoil of the 1960s giving way to economic and social uncertainty in the 1970s, it was for designer Michel Ducaroy a 'time of restlessness'. It was also a time of possibility for furniture designers, with new materials regularly coming on-stream and opening up fresh creative possibilities. Ducaroy, exactly half-way through a twenty-six-year stint as head of design with French company Ligne Roset, responded with what today is still seen as a breathtakingly bold, if somewhat 'period', departure: the world's first all-foam sofa. The Togo three-seater sofa is made entirely of Dacron, a polyester fibre, and has no frame of any kind. Covered in loose upholstery, the foam is quilted into a form that suggests all manner of associations, from a bent stovepipe to a tube of toothpaste or a large caterpillar. Ducaroy

played to the material's squishy qualities by creating an almost shell-like mass that positively sucked the leg-weary owner into its welcoming folds. Togo proved so popular at the Paris Furniture Fair of 1973 that Ducaroy and Ligne Roset were soon working on creating a range of comple-mentary pieces, including 'fireside' chairs and a corner seat, which allowed two sofas to be put together for a particularly extravagant effect. Although its rather hedonistic style and not inconsiderable cost were seemingly at odds with the oncoming economic crises of the 1970s, Togo was popular from the outset and remains so today, to the extent that Ligne Roset continues to produce it. Ducaroy remained fascinated by the possibilities of all-foam furniture. He had already designed an earlier foam chair in 1968, which was effectively a smaller version

of the Togo without the pleats. A flexible, mattress-style sofa bed followed in 1976 and an attempt, in 1981, to marry all-foam construction to a less unified form than the Togo, but it is the Togo which is considered contemporary today.

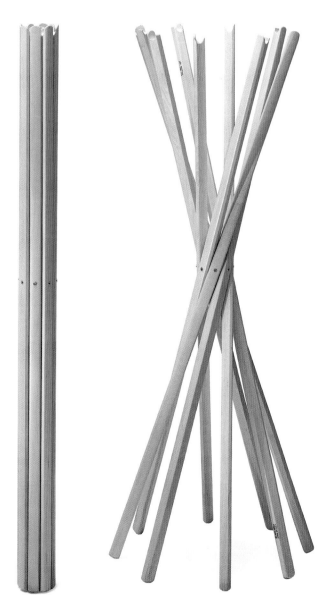

The Sciangai folding clothes-stand consists of eight beechwood rods screwed together into a cluster at the centre. In fact, despite its elegant finish, the Sciangai is little more than a compact bundle of sticks. Yet, when released, these sticks fold out in a spiral, like the struts of a double-sided parasol or a Native American tepee, spinning out from the centre to create one of the most striking clothes-stands around. In choosing to call their stand 'Sciangai', the designers have created a visual pun: Sciangai is the Italian name for the game of 'Pick up Sticks', where one stick is removed from a pile without disturbing the others. This sense of fun is carried through in the design, which combines elements of playfulness and modernity. The clothes-stand is disguised when folded, but unfolded it quickly expands into a spiral shape, changing from a diameter of 41 cm (16.5 in) to one of 65 cm (26 in). It is available varnished, in black, or in bleached or wengé-stained oak. Created by the architects Gionatan De Pas, Donato D'Urbino and Paolo Lomazzi, the Sciangai is portable furniture reduced to its most primitive form. In some respects its collapsible nature follows on from the design group's pioneering development of temporary architecture and inflatable furniture during the 1960s, most famously the Blow Chair of 1967, as well as a more general interest in flexible, adaptable mobile living. In 1979, at the Milan Triennale, the Sciangai won a prestigious Compasso d'Oro award. De Pas died in 1991, but D'Urbino and Lomazzi continue to be one of the most prolific design partnerships around today.

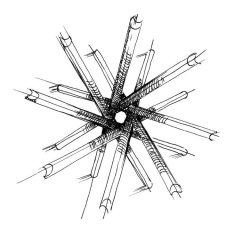

76-4

Sciangai (1973)
Gionatan De Pas (1932–91)
Donato D'Urbino (1935–)
Paolo Lomazzi (1936–)
Zanotta 1973 to present

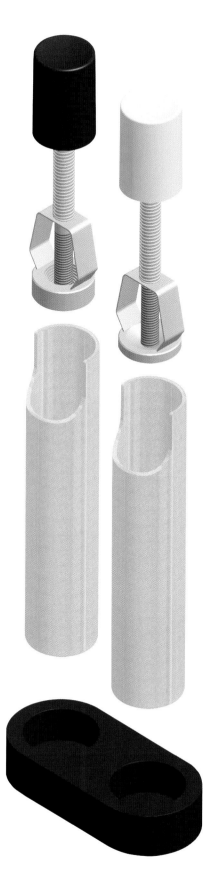

Rud Thygesen and Johnny Sørensen are known for their furniture design using laminated wood that is the embodiment of the high-quality Danish design tradition. Both designers attended the School of Arts, Crafts and Design, School of Furniture Design in Copenhagen, graduating in 1966, and in doing so became members of the last generation of furniture designers to experience the golden age of Danish furniture. The work produced by their company since 1966 fully employs the Danish design sensibility developed at the school. The pair's design output reflects a dedication to craftsmanship and quality of materials, while also displaying ingenuity and invention. All their projects are designed as industrial products. The pair consider use of materials and the potential of technology as key parameters in the design process. The Salt and Pepper Rasps illustrate the sophistication and inventiveness that is characteristic of the duo's approach to design. The rasps are made from aluminium and are easier to use than the traditional form of the wooden mills as they are operated with one hand only. The clever design has a patented rasp mechanism that enables the user to hold the mill in one hand, and use the thumb press to activate the grinding mechanism that releases freshly ground seasoning. The two slender cylindrical rasps sit in a purpose-designed holder. The success of the design is in its beauty and innovation, in keeping with the Danish design tradition. The work of Rud Thygesen and Johnny Sørensen enjoys an international reputation, and many of their designs can be found in collections throughout the world, including The Museum of Modern Art.

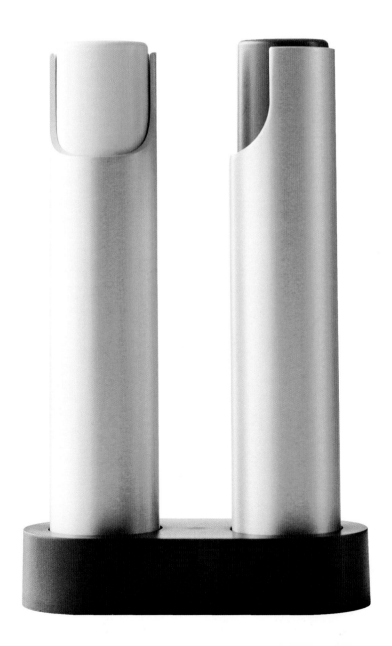

LIGHTER

With Fixed Flame

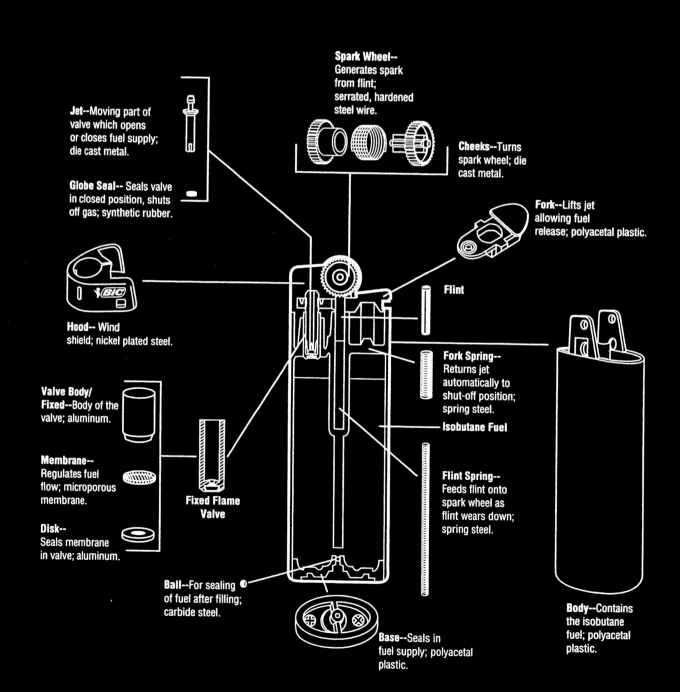

Spark Wheel-- Generates spark from flint; serrated, hardened steel wire.

Jet--Moving part of valve which opens or closes fuel supply; die cast metal.

Cheeks--Turns spark wheel; die cast metal.

Globe Seal-- Seals valve in closed position, shuts off gas; synthetic rubber.

Fork--Lifts jet allowing fuel release; polyacetal plastic.

Flint

Hood-- Wind shield; nickel plated steel.

Fork Spring-- Returns jet automatically to shut-off position; spring steel.

Valve Body/ Fixed--Body of the valve; aluminum.

Isobutane Fuel

Membrane-- Regulates fuel flow; microporous membrane.

Fixed Flame Valve

Flint Spring-- Feeds flint onto spark wheel as flint wears down; spring steel.

Disk-- Seals membrane in valve; aluminum.

Ball--For sealing of fuel after filling; carbide steel.

Base--Seals in fuel supply; polyacetal plastic.

Body--Contains the isobutane fuel; polyacetal plastic.

There is nothing original about the basics of the Bic lighter's design. Cigarette lighters powered by gas and petrol had existed for decades before its arrival, and despite the extraordinary success of the Bic, other models based on older designs, such as the Zippo (1933), continue to thrive. The mechanism the Bic uses to ignite its gas, as with most lighters, is among the very oldest of human inventions: a flint, struck to make a spark. Indeed, the only thing that made the Bic lighter new or different in what was already a crowded marketplace was its disposability. Unlike its competitors, the Bic was designed to be cheap to buy, and to have an extremely limited lifespan. After 3,000 flames, its fuel would run out and it could not be refilled. In manufacturing the Bic lighter, a company that had already achieved market dominance for its disposable pens, was entering a very different field. However, the idea was not as strange as it first seems. Both lighters and pens are pocket- or handbag-sized and highly portable. This portability means they can easily be lost, and it is far less galling to lose a cheap disposable lighter or pen that can be purchased almost anywhere than a more expensive item. Secondly, smoking utensils actually had a long history of disposability. For example, clay pipes, the first vessels that brought smoking to something approaching a mass market broke easily and were designed with disposability in mind in much the same way as cigarette lighters. When designing its lighters Bic had to bear in mind certain considerations that had not been an issue with pens. Primary among them was safety, which is why, having decided that its next product would be a lighter, the company bought established French lighter manufacturer Flaminaire in 1972. Bic drew on the company's considerable legacy to aid a team led by Leandre Poisson, bringing out the first Bic disposable lighter in 1973. It is almost superfluous to detail the lighter's breathtaking market success since then: 4 million are sold every day.

766

Bic ® lighter (1973)
Flaminaire Design Team
© Societe Bic 1973 to present

3000 flames

The smart choice.

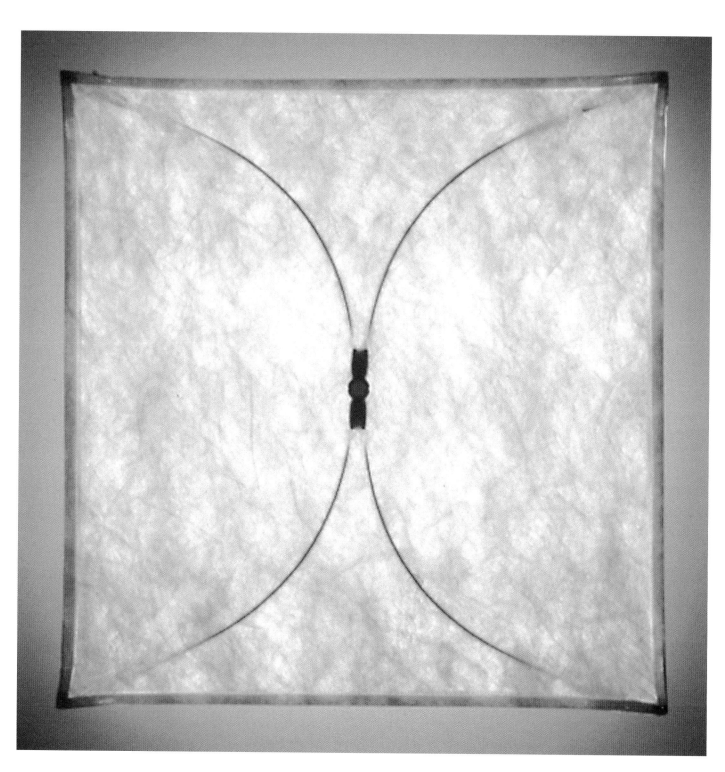

The Ariette 1/2/3 lamp, which can function either as a wall or ceiling fixture, approaches illumination in a novel way. The transparency of the synthetic fabric diffuser, comprised of a material called Tyvex, combined with the unusual texture and reflected colour from the supporting structure, make Ariette more of a sculptural light installation than a common or garden lamp fitting. The solution adopted for the 'square canvas' supporting structure is fresh and inventive. It effectively acts as a casing with reinforced borders. Inserted into an opening on the side towards the wall are the light element and the hooks to fit the lamp on to the wall. In the opposite side, four coloured fibreglass elastic rods are slotted in. These rods, which are fixed on to the internal corners, effectively stretch the square canvas, and this subsequently enables the lamp to stand independently, without any other supports. The lamp has also been designed to take into account ease of assembly/disassembly, therefore the packing volume is considerably reduced. Ariette is a key model in the range of innovative diffuser lamps created by Afra and Tobia Scarpa for the Italian lighting company Flos. At the heart of this range is a commitment to exploring the possibilities of new materials, not only in terms of structure but also in the interplay between material and lighting effect. Yet in terms of its truly original and quite beautiful synthesis of material and light, combined with the practicality of its design, the Ariette is probably one of the finest achievements of the relationship between the Scarpas and Flos.

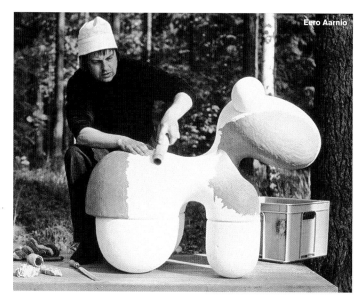

Eero Aarnio

These small, colourful, abstract ponies look as if they had been intended for small children, but Aarnio conceived them as playful seating for adults. The user could either 'ride' the horse by facing the front, or sit sideways on it. The padded, fabric-covered stools with tubular frames make clear reference to the contemporary Pop sensibility in which the designer takes an object that is commonly thought of in one manner and twists it into something else. Aarnio is playing with our established expectations of what adult furniture should be and how we should decorate our homes. In doing so he transforms the much beloved children's hobbyhorse into something for adults. During the late 1960s many Scandinavian designers started to experiment with plastic, fibreglass and other synthetic materials. These new materials allowed for new forms and new solutions to the traditional ideas of what seating could look like. Led by Aarnio and fellow Scandinavian Verner Panton, these designers investigated the boundaries of what furniture could be and what different forms it could take. Aarnio even designed a chair named the Pastille that could function as a sledge in wintertime and a small raft in the summer, in addition to it usual role. Both Panton and Aarnio placed an emphasis on geometric shapes that were then transformed into usable pieces of furniture. Not since the experiments of Gerrit Rietveld and Marcel Breuer in the 1920s had there been such an interest in testing the boundaries of what constituted a chair. As Aarnio himself said, borrowing from Gertrude Stein, 'A chair is a chair, is a chair, is a chair, but a seat does not necessarily have to be a chair. It can be anything as long as it is ergonomically correct.' The Pony is simply a child's chair all grown up, in terms of scale at least. It attempts to translate that child-like sense of joy and playfulness to the adult arena. The Pony chair is currently available by special order from Adelta, and the upholstered stretch fabric of white, black, orange and green still provides adults with an object of imagination and joy.

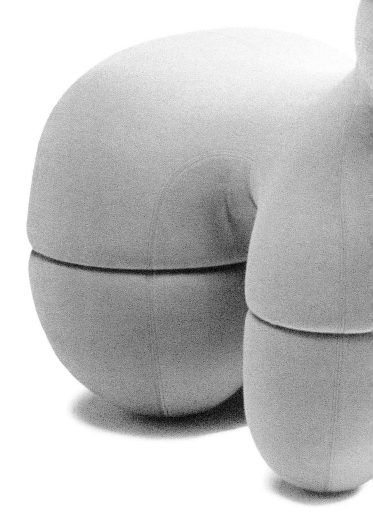

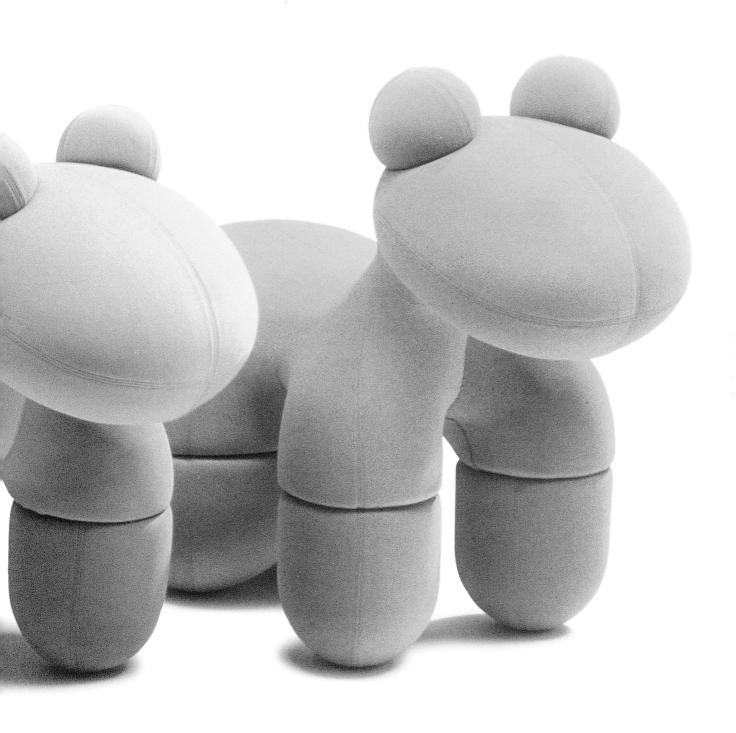

Hans Beck

Hans Beck designed this system of children's figures in 1974 at the request of his employer, Horst Brandstätter, owner of geobra Brandstätter, a German company who started making plastic toys in the 1950s. After the company's early success manufacturing hula hoops had died away, Horst Brandstätter started to think about a new system-based toy that would be less susceptible to the of whims of fashion. Over a period of a few years Beck spent many hours observing children playing, and developed a design that promoted creative play while encouraging imagination and motor control. The result was these 7.5 cm (3 in) high figures, whose scale was determined by the size and dexterity of the small hands of children. They feature a spherical, rotating head, with changeable hair or headgear, articulated limbs and gripping hands. These design features allowed for the basic figure to be finished and clothed in a variety of outfits and hand-held accessories. Over the thirty years since its introduction, the range has grown to over 2,000 products, comprising complete worlds that include not just figures, but animals and vehicles. Part of its continuing popularity may be due to the apparent simplicity of these geometric yet characterful figures. Hans Beck has consistently resisted requests to produce war-based or horror characters as well as inevitably short-lived, trend-based characters. The initially small family of little people was launched in the midst of the mid-1970s oil crisis and has grown to become the core of the company, which now has subsidiaries in ten other countries. In total the company has produced more than 1.7 billion figures, and not just for children. Although most are probably sitting in children's toy boxes and playrooms throughout the world, there are plenty of adults as keen on collecting the little figures, prompting collectors' websites offering potentially high prices for original boxed sets.

playmobil ⓑ SYSTEM

Die natürliche Umwelt der Erwachsenen in die verkleinerte Kinderzimmerwelt übertragen können, dem Kind Gelegenheit geben, im aktiven Spiel die Wirklichkeit nachzuempfinden – das ist die in ihrer Art einzigartig realisierte Idee von b-playmobil.
Das bewußt einfache kindgerechte Design von Figur und Umweltzubehör läßt der Phantasie des Kindes weitgehenden Entfaltungsspielraum. Fordert schöpferische Aktivitäten geradezu heraus. b-playmobil ist dadurch ein pädagogisch wert-

volles Spiel. Das System eignet sich auch ausgezeichnet als Rollenspiel für mehrere Kinder.
Die Figur ist 7,5cm groß (Maßstab 1:24) und rundum einfach sympatisch. Sie wiegt 11g und ist entsprechend standfest, besteht aus hochwertigem Kunststoff (ABS) und ist dadurch äußerst robust – das Kind kann auch ruhig einmal darauf treten – präsentiert sich in freundlichen, charakteristischen Farben und entspricht den DIN-Sicherheitsanforderungen für Spielzeug. Und was sie alles kann:

stehen,   beugen,   bücken,   sitzen,   aufstützen,   Kopf drehen (180°),   Arme drehen (360°),   reiten . . . . .

 Darin liegt der Schlüssel des Spiels. Alle Utensilien (gleicher Maßstab) sind darauf ausgerichtet:

. . . und greifen.   Schaufel,   Besen,   Hammer,   Schubkarren,   Straßenwalze,   Bierkasten und, und . . .

Seiner jeweiligen Umwelt paßt sich die Figur durch einfache aber sehr charakteristische Utensilien an –

Warnweste beim Straßenbau.
Arm- und Beinschmuck beim Indianer,
Mantel oder Königsschleppe beim Ritter –

Die Utensilien werden einfach aufgeschnappt und lassen sich auswechseln.

Durch die vielfältigen Möglichkeiten schöpferischen Spielens konnte der Altersbereich mit 4-10 Jahren ziemlich weit gesteckt werden.

b-playmobil ist ein System ohne Vorbild.
Und: Untersuchungen haben ergeben, daß b-playmobil bei Kindern und Eltern ausgezeichnet ankommt. Das ist die beste Empfehlung für Ihren Erfolg.

Serien und Inhalt der Sets umseitig.

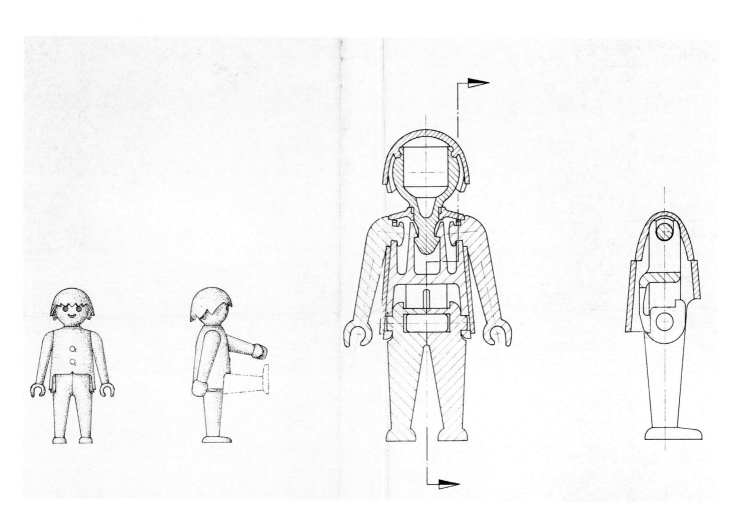

The Italian word 'servomuto' translates into English as 'dumb waiter', a most suitable name for Achille Castiglioni's table design from 1974. Made from a base of polypropylene, a steel rod and a table top in layered plastic laminate or hard polyurethane, this lightweight side table facilitates absolute utility while remaining elegant in its visual simplicity. The use of few component parts in manufacture makes this an affordable proposition for many commercial and domestic environments. The extending steel rod acts as the supporting stem of the table and the waist-height knob on the top invites the user to effortlessly move the table around at a whim. This makes it ideal for use in cafés or bars, where ever-changing numbers of customers may call for changes in the furniture layout, too. The size of the tabletop is ideal for drinks, snacks, an ashtray or a cup of coffee. The protruding rod running through the centre of this round surface announces its purpose for, indeed, it prohibits the positioning of such objects as a lamp, large books or dining plates. This table has been designed for quick uses. The Servomuto was the third design by Castiglioni in his I Servi series of accessory products using the same base and rod components. The first two items were the Servofumo ashtray and the Servopluvio umbrella stand, which were both designed with Achille's brother Pier Giacomo and created for the Splügen Bräu beerhouse in Milan in 1961. They were originally produced by the Italian lighting company Flos, but in 1970 the furniture manufacturer Zanotta took on the designs and invited Castiglioni to continue adding more to the series. This particular design, available in black, white or aluminium finishes, has subsequently been joined by another twelve items, including the Servomostre poster stand (1984), the Servolibro book stand (1985), the Servomanto coat rack (1985), the Servonotte clothes stand (1986), the Servobandiera flagstaff (1986) and the Servino bottle cooler (1987). The series is still produced today by Zanotta.

770
Servomuto (1974)
Achille Castiglioni (1918–2002)
Zanotta 1975 to present

The Input Ice Bucket, which formed part of the twenty-one-piece Input range of containers for Crayonne, was instrumental in affording plastic accessories the kind of quality image in the UK that continental manufacturers such as Kartell had already achieved with its products. In 1973 Airfix Plastics was keen to produce more distinctive, good-quality household products than its usual buckets and bowls, and subsequently approached design consultants Conran Associates to work with it on product development. The first result was the Input range of containers, marketed under the Crayonne brand. The range of twenty-one 'containers' comprised bowls, dishes, trays, vases, pots and an ice bucket. Some had lids and some were open and certain models were fitted with different ceramic, melamine or, in the case of the ice bucket, insulating inserts. Colours were vibrant red, yellow, green or white. The units were not named at all. They were simply given a number, which meant that since their use was never prescribed they could be used for any purpose, in either the home or office. The Input range was built up logically. All units were based on the same diameter and height ratios, and this afforded it an integrated quality. In terms of materials and technology, each piece was produced using heavy-duty ABS plastic, chosen for its strong, solid finish which was scratch-proof and shatter-resistant. A particularly low-rate injection-moulding cycle enabled the units to be made nearly twice as thick as other ABS products, adding to the impression of solidity, which was similar to that of Bakelite. When it was introduced in 1974 the Input range became a best seller in Habitat, the British retailer, and was chosen by The Museum of Modern Art in New York as an exemplary product, illustrating how attitudes to a material could be changed through design. In 1974 the range also received a Design Council Award for Consumer Goods, commending the joint attempt by Airfix Plastics and Conran Associates to upgrade the image of plastics in the UK. Unfortunately, the oil crisis in the mid-1970s meant that the plastics boom collapsed, and products such as the Input Ice Bucket were no longer economically viable.

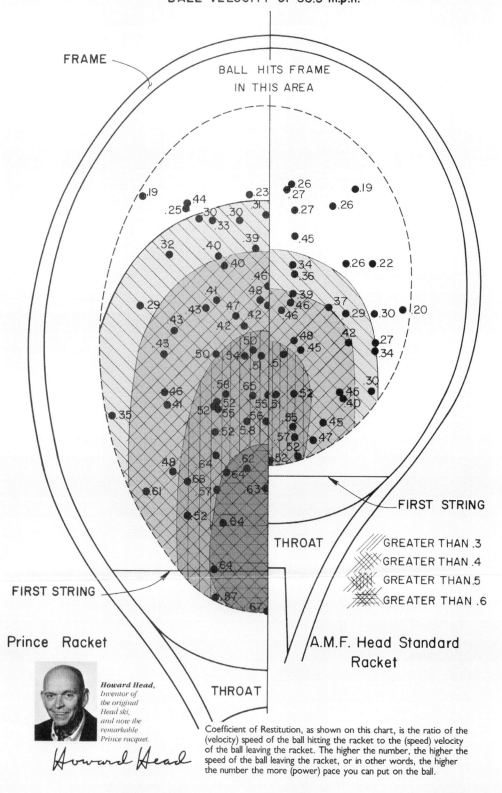

COEFFICIENT OF RESTITUTION
RACKETS HELD BY VISE
BALL VELOCITY OF 38.5 m.p.h.

FRAME

BALL HITS FRAME
IN THIS AREA

FIRST STRING

THROAT

/// GREATER THAN .3
X GREATER THAN .4
XX GREATER THAN .5
XXX GREATER THAN .6

FIRST STRING

Prince Racket

A.M.F. Head Standard
Racket

THROAT

Howard Head,
*Inventor of
the original
Head ski,
and now the
remarkable
Prince racquet.*

Howard Head

Coefficient of Restitution, as shown on this chart, is the ratio of the
(velocity) speed of the ball hitting the racket to the (speed) velocity
of the ball leaving the racket. The higher the number, the higher the
speed of the ball leaving the racket, or in other words, the higher
the number the more (power) pace you can put on the ball.

The design of the tennis racket, essentially a wooden stick with a handle and a small, teardrop-shaped head, remained very little changed for about 300 years. The designer, Howard Head, began experimenting in the late 1960s, using technology that his company had already applied to pioneer new designs in ski manufacture. This involved the use of metal and plastic honeycomb, and resulted in the first composite racket in 1969, although it was not until 1974 that the design was perfected by Head. US tennis player Jimmy Connors was one the highest-profile exponents of a new metal alloy technology. However, it was Arthur Ashe, tennis's ultimate gentleman, who used this stiff, lightweight frame to beat Connors in the 1975 Wimbledon final. The new racket allowed him greater control and power, and his win immediately brought the design to public attention. Further innovations introduced glass fibre and the newly developed carbon fibre, many times stronger than steel. The use of carbon composites allowed for a larger racket head, a bigger 'sweet-spot' – the contact area where higher velocity of the ball is developed – and better control of off-centre ball contact. With an overall length of 69 cm (27 in), the head of the racquet is 31 cm (12.2 in) long and 23 cm (9 in) across. Howard Head was also responsible for the first oversized racket, the 110 sq in racket for the manufacturer, Prince, in 1976. Much of the power of today's game is attributed to the composite racket technology pioneered by Head, and subsequent developments in composite technology have resulted in the Head Titanium Tennis, which became the world's first 'Intelligent' racket with a micro chip in the handle, introduced in 2000. World tennis champion André Agassi is currently one of Head's highest-profile racket users.

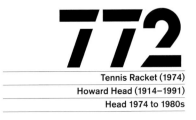

Arthur Ashe

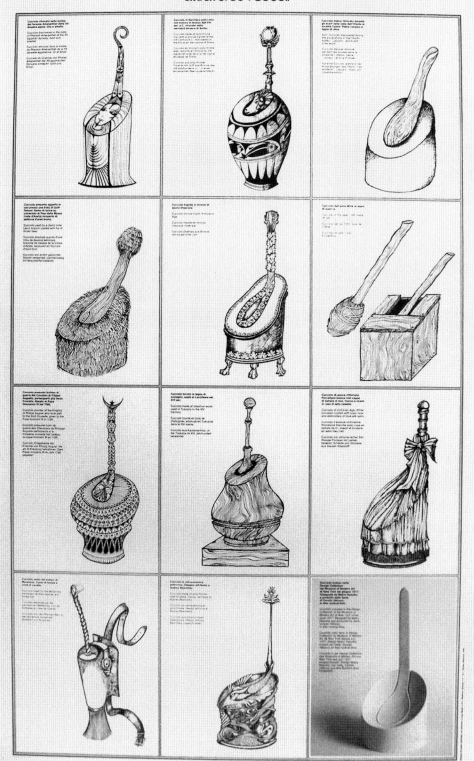

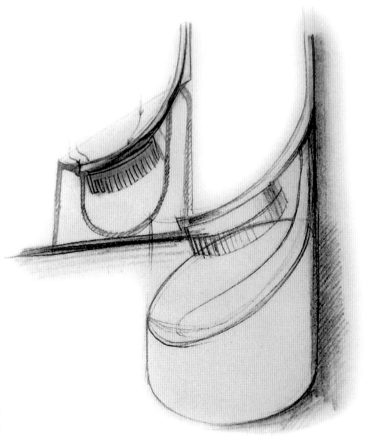

The sculptural form of the Cucciolo Toilet Brush belies its purpose as a simple tool designed to perform one of the most unpleasant of household tasks. Awarded the Compasso d'Oro prize in 1979 and put on display in the Design Collection of the Museum of Modern Art in New York, the humble toilet brush, usually something to be hidden away in the corner of the bathroom, invisible and unremarkable, has been transformed by Makio Hasuike into an object of beauty. When Hasuike was approached by Gedy, he had already turned his hand to the design of toilet brushes. He started by considering aspects of hygiene. The most hygienic object he could think of was a plate or dish, so he began to think of a brush-holder with no hidden areas. Hasuike was also aware that the bathroom had evolved from being a place that only household members would use to a room that was on show to guests, so he wanted to allow the owner a sense of pride in the object. Not only should it be functional, economical and durable, it should also be a joy to use and something to be looked at and admired. The resulting design was a simple form with a shallow cavity to collect the drops of water from the brush. The cavity was easy to clean and was covered by the brush itself. Born in Tokyo, Hasuike moved to Italy in 1963, founding his own studio in Milan in 1968. During his forty-year career he has designed a wide range of products, from furniture to domestic appliances, household products to luggage. In 1982 he added the role of entrepreneur to his extensive repertoire by creating the highly successful and innovative company MH Way, specializing in the design and manufacture of bags and accessories. The Cucciolo was such a success that for years it was the signature design of Gedy, spawning many copies and launching a very different idea of what bathroom products could look like. Today, it continues to be the company's best seller and is available in eleven different colours.

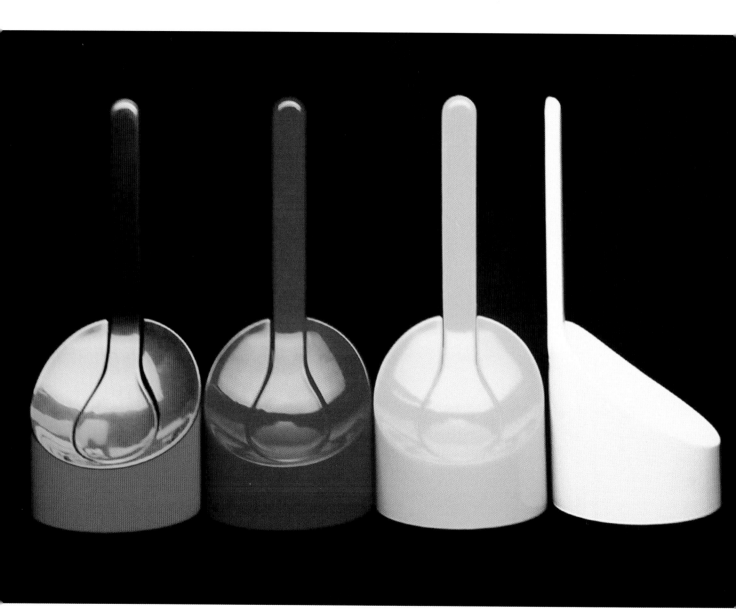

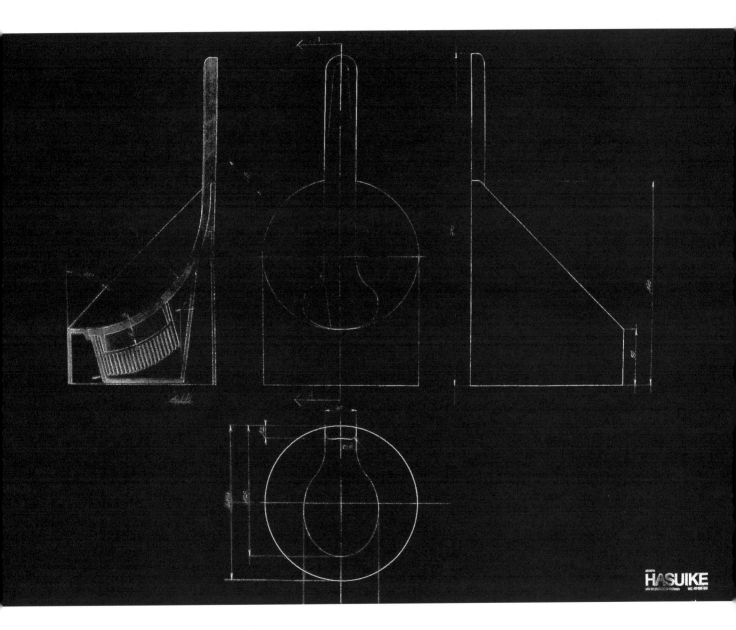

Peter Holmblad was not a trained designer. He was originally employed as a salesman by Stelton, then just a small company making stainless-steel items for domestic use. However, he clearly had an understanding of the significance of design and had one major advantage in this respect: he was Arne Jacobsen's foster son. It was through this family connection that he began to reform Stelton's product range, successfully transforming the company's fortunes in the process. By the late 1970s he had become the owner of the firm and achieved fame in a small way, not as the designer of a corkscrew, but as the person who had badgered the initially unenthusiastic Arne Jacobsen into designing his well-known Cylinda-Line series. Jacobsen's set of tea and coffee pots, plus an immaculate cylindrical ice-bucket, were produced in brushed stainless-steel and won for the company a good degree of international recognition and, in the process, the prestigious ID prize in 1967. Although Holmblad wanted Arne Jacobsen to extend the range of products (he was hoping for a cocktail shaker), Jacobsen was not interested in alcohol and could not be persuaded. After his death, Holmblad developed the range by introducing small kitchen tools. He had been originally responsible for the idea of basing Jacobsen's product line on a series of cylinders, and he had also prepared some of the initial sketches, so he had the experience to design the new additions himself. His straightforward modernization of the corkscrew was originally made in nickel-plated steel. The screw is now produced in steel, but is teflon-plated and meshes seamlessly with the rest of the company's products, becoming something of a star in its own right. Along with the corkscrew, the series consists of a bottle opener, cheese/bar knife, butter knife, cheese slicer and cheese plane.

Peter Holmblad

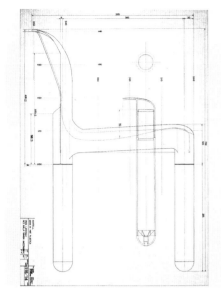

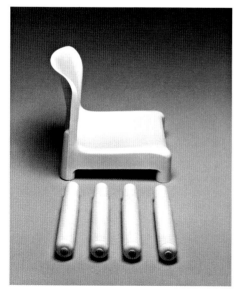

The cartoon-like quality, soft curves and compact proportions of Carlo Bartoli's 4875 Chair owe much to its two famous predecessors at Kartell: Marco Zanuso and Richard Sapper's Stacking Child's Chair of 1960 and Joe Colombo's Model 4867 Chair of 1965. However, unlike both earlier chairs, which were originally moulded in ABS, the 4875 was made from polypropylene, a newly discovered plastic. While ABS gave the earlier chairs the same high-gloss finish imparted from the mould, polypropylene was a more versatile, harder-wearing plastic, had better engineering qualities and was much less expensive. When the 4875 was put into production in 1974, it was one of the most inexpensive chairs of its kind on the market. During a chance meeting with the founder of Kartell, Giulio Castelli, he expressed his desire to work and experiment with plastics. Castelli invited him to pursue his new-found interest at Kartell. Bartoli began by carefully examining the structure of both Colombo's and Zanuso and Sapper's chairs. He used the same single-body structure incorporating the seat and backrest, together with four pivots for the legs, in one moulding. Four cylindrical legs were then moulded separately. Propitiously, during the two years that it took to develop the design, polypropylene was invented. Kartell took advantage of this momentous advance in plastics technology and decided to manufacture the 4875 in the new material, with the addition of small ribbings under the seat to reinforce the leg joints because of the less rigid qualities of polypropylene. By the 1970s plastics had fallen out of fashion, so the 4875 Chair never achieved the same status of its predecessors at Kartell. While Kartell's earlier successes reflected the economic boom of the 1960s when optimism and experimentation were lauded and synthetic materials and bright colours embraced, by contrast the oil crisis of 1973 and the subsequent shortage of petrochemicals led to a more circumspect outlook with environmental concerns placed high on the design agenda. Nevertheless, the chair became an immediate best seller and in 1979 the 4875 was selected for the Compasso d'Oro award.

The Rubik's Cube took the toy industry by storm in the early 1980s and became one of the most recognized and beloved puzzles of the twentieth century. The 'Magic Cube' as it was originally named, was the invention of Ernö Rubik, a Hungarian architect and professor of design who had been toying with the idea since the mid-1970s. The colourful cube was small enough to be taken to school and perplexing enough to seem educational. Superficially, the Cube appeared as fifty-four coloured squares comprising six colour groups, each representing one of the six sides. The idea was to jumble the colours by randomly twisting the Cube, then to attempt to  rearrange them into their original configuration, which was much easier said than done. In 1980 the Cube was exported by Ideal Toys under the name 'Rubik's Cube' and soon became the new must-have item on every child's wish list. Part of its success may have depended on linking the inventor's name with the product. The idea of the reclusive Eastern bloc professor appealed to something in the Western psyche, and solving the Cube was a sure sign of a similar genius to come. Soon, it was no longer a question of completing the Cube, but how fast you could do it. Essential to its beauty was the apparent simplicity of Rubik's design: twenty-six small cubes ('Cubees'), held together by one central mechanism, to form a large cube that could be twisted horizontally and vertically through 360 degrees. It was this central piece, invented by Rubik, that marked him as an innovator; he had previously attempted to hold and rotate the cubes using elastic bands, without success. The Cube inspired countless mathematical debates, competitions and even a Saturday morning cartoon called 'Rubik: The Amazing Cube'. It had sold more than 100 million units by 1983, and it could be argued that the Rubik's Cube played a part in transforming the Hungarian economy in the early 1980s. The original Rubik's Cube continues to be produced today, along with various other Rubik's puzzles. With its bold colours and simple shape the Rubik's Cube will always be remembered as one of the most successful toys of the twentieth century.

776

Rubik's Cube® (1974)
Ernö Rubik (1937–)
Ideal Toy Company/CBS 1980 to 1985
Seven Towns 1985 to present

In the Banco Catalano designers Óscar Tusquets Blanca and Lluís Clotet successfully fused a number of design dilemmas into a beautiful, coherent and functional object. During the early to mid-1970s Tusquets Blanca and Clotet were part of a small group of Spanish designers that became known for their iconoclastic approach to design. Angered by the fact that they were unable to find manufacturers willing to take risks and put their ideas and designs into production, in 1964 they formed their own company: Studio PER. More like-minded designers and creatives, including Bocaccio Design, joined them and in 1974 BD Ediciones de Diseño was born. Inspired by Antoni Gaudí's public seating for the Park Güell, the Banco Catalano has an elegant outline and is based on ergonomic principles, making it sleek and comfortable. Its production uses minimal materials. The bench is constructed in sheet metal, using a technique known as 'déployé' where the metal is stretched and stamped to produce a concertina effect. The result is a bench that is strong, but which has an illusion of transparency, so creating continuity with its surrounding space. The design is modular and consists of a one-metre seat that can be joined side-by-side or back-to-back to accommodate any spatial requirement. This sophisticated and stylish example of street furniture is used to this day. By use of its materials and stunning form, combined with the adaptable nature of the design, Banco Catalano epitomizes BD Ediciones de Diseño's position as a leader of Spanish design.

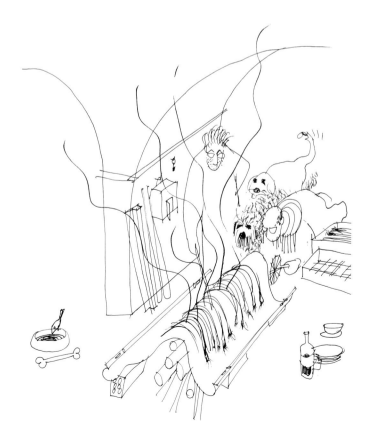

Óscar Tusquets Blanca and Lluís Clotet

777

Banco Catalano (1974)
Óscar Tusquets Blanca (1941–)
Lluís Clotet (1941–)
BD Ediciones de Diseño 1974 to present

Launched in 1974,

Volkswagen's Golf represented a milestone in car design on a number of levels: firstly, it was created at a time when the influence of the immediate postwar generation of Italian car stylists was waning and the design of the mass-produced car had become a priority. Secondly, it marked a new direction in car design in which the 1930s approach to stream-lining, characterized by organic curves, was replaced by new aerodynamic ideas which favoured straight lines and a wedge front. In turn Volkswagen was looking for a radically different car with which to replace its long-serving Beetle and turned to Giugiaro's Turin-based company, Italdesign, to provide them with one. Having worked with Dante Giacosa at Fiat, Giugiaro understood that car design was at its best when engineering ideas were fused with artistic ones. The result was a small car, with significant internal space and an elegant, faceted body-shell. A minimal radiator grille was placed in the sharply raked bonnet and just enough of a rear end was left to give the car a sporty feel. The

HAUPTABMESSUNGEN

1 —— GOLF CABRIO

(2) —— KÄFER CABRIO

result was a highly balanced design in which each line played a key part and was carefully selected. The straight horizontal line across the car's midriff provided a central focus and everything else related to it. The car had an immediate appeal and sold in huge numbers. Various other models were introduced at a later date, including the Cabriolet. Giugiaro had succeeded in creating a car-styling revolution which was to influence many other models developed through the 1970s and early 1980s, among them his own little Panda for Fiat of 1981. The introduction of straight lines and particularly of the wedge front in the VW Golf heralded a new era in which comfort and practicality were paramount.

778

VW Golf A1 (1974)
Giorgetto Giugiaro (1938–)
Volkswagen 1974 to 1983

Working on the principles of the 'French' press, the Chambord Coffee Press made it possible for anyone to make a good cup of real coffee in the home. Its ease of use has made it instantly and enduringly popular. The shape and construction of this coffee maker allows for the most simple method of brewing real coffee. The ground coffee is placed in the conical glass beaker, the hot water is added, and the lid is put in position, with the in-built filter above the water level. Then after a few minutes, or when the brew is to the desired strength, the plunger is depressed and the filter forced through the coffee. The result is a granule-free brew made with an ease, which appeals to a wide range of people. The Chambord emphasizes the company's core philosophy that good design should not be more expensive; this ethos brought not only good design but also good coffee to the masses. The 'French' press was actually invented by the Italian Calimani in 1933. However, since then Bodum has become synonymous with the brewing process, and variations on the Chambord are found in most European homes. This coffee plunger is the original cafetière designed by Carsten Jørgensen for Bodum in 1982. The combination of the heat-resistant Pyrex glass beaker, chrome frame and black, durable bakelite plastic knob and handle have made it renowned worldwide for its timeless design. It is as popular today as when it was first launched and is, in essence, a functional work of art. The uncomplicated and modest design is accompanied by practicality: the Chambord can be completely dismantled, allowing ease of cleaning and replacement of any parts that may break or get damaged, such as the beaker or filter. With the Chambord, Bodum aimed to develop a new design language for coffee makers, incorporating beauty, simplicity and excellent materials into everyday life. Using the Chambord offers a cosmopolitan twist to coffee drinking and freedom from instant coffee. The design is internationally successful and is used in the home from kitchen to table, and in cafés and restaurants alike.

ORTHOPEDICALLY CONTOURED, MOULDED
THERMOPLASTIC BACKREST AND SEAT

BACK-TILT MECHANISM
CAP
COIL SPRING
PIVOT VALVE
UPPER CASING
LOWER CASING
CONNECTING SUPPORT TUBE

SEAT SLIDING MECHANISM
SEAT & BACK TILT MECHANISM
SPRING
STOP WASHER
RETAINER PIN

SEAT HEIGHT
ADJUSTMENT MECHANISM
THREADED POST
UPPER CAM
LOWER CAM & ADJUSTING NUT
SUPPORT COLUMN
SUPPORT SPRING

HIGH STRENGTH
RUBBER/VINYL BELLOWS

780

Vertebra Chair (1974–5)
Emilio Ambasz (1943–)
Giancarlo Piretti (1940–)
KI 1976 to present
Castelli/Haworth 1976 to present
ItokiCrebio 1976 to present

The Vertebra Chair was the first office chair to respond automatically to the user's movement, using a system of springs and counterbalances to support everyday work. The name Vertebra was chosen to express the intimate relationship between the user's back and the movement of the chair. It is considered one of the first office chairs to embody the idea of ergonomics, the study of how people work and how designers can support that work. The Vertebra Chair created a standard by which all subsequent office chairs would be judged by introducing, to both the design community and consumers, new design features and terminology. These included features such as automatic seat and back movements that responded to the user's motions and thus eliminated the need for manual adjustment. The term 'lumbar support' was established with the introduction of the Vertebra, as chairs previously prescribed the user's position but did not necessarily support them. After the Vertebra, chairs were expected to perform by following and responding to the user's movements. With the Vertebra, for example, the user would only flex the lower back when leaning forward because of the placement of the hinge between the seat and back. More importantly, the chair would only ever tilt forward with the sitter, to a maximum of six degrees, bringing the backrest forward as the sitter's legs pressed down with a forward motion. The mechanisms were mostly under the seat-pan, or the two tubes, of 4 cm (1.6 in) thick, supporting the chair's back, which carry the key mechanisms that allow the chair to be adjusted. Vertebra also introduced a new visual vocabulary to furniture design, with its cast-aluminium base and flexible tubular-steel frame. Chairs that perform are now commonplace, but the Vertebra Chair still stands as the benchmark. It won several design awards and has had only very slight alterations over the years. The work of Ambasz and Piretti introduced a new dialogue about furniture that continues, just as their Vertebra Chair does, thirty years later.

Stools and steps are of course indispensable for reaching high shelves, but traditional designs have a considerable drawback. They must do two contradictory things: first, they must provide a secure base to stand on and second, they should be mobile. In the past the second element was sensibly neglected to prioritize the first. This meant, however, that if one wanted to move, say, a pile of books from one shelf to another nearby, one would have to climb on a stool, get the books, set them on the floor, reposition the stool and then place the books in their new home. While the traditional stool thus allows the job to get done, it can be laborious. Wedo (Werner Dorsch) solved this problem so neatly that the Kickstool has become an extremely common sight in libraries, universities, schools, warehouses and other places that use lots of shelving. It has three castors mounted on its base, allowing it to roll freely. This means that, as the name suggests, it can be pushed across the floor by foot, leaving the arms free for carrying books or files. These castors would make the stool dangerously unstable to stand on, however, if it were not for the really innovative part of the design. Once weight is placed on top of the stool – for instance, by standing on it – the entire stool sinks a centimetre, locking the castors and bringing the broad circular rim of the base into contact with the floor. This makes it extremely stable, with a broad footprint and a low centre of gravity. This stability is assisted further by the stool's circular plan, meaning that the stool has a step on all 'sides', so it does not have to be aligned after being repositioned, a further boon if your hands are full. The design is really extraordinarily simple, but its sheer superiority to other, more traditional solutions has made the Kickstool an emblem of the librarian's and archivist's trades.

Folding bicycles have become very common on urban streets around the world. The Brompton has a devoted following, prompting users' web-sites for swapping stories and singing its praises. The development of this bike, like several other significant small-wheeled folding bicycles, has occurred mostly in the UK, and mostly carried out by men usually quite unconnected with the world of bicycles, working out ideas on kitchen tables or in garden sheds in the tradition of quirky British inventors. The Brompton, a fantastic parcel of small wheels and hinged steel tubes, was designed by Andrew Ritchie, who had previously been involved in landscape gardening. The Brompton's success has grown out of several factors: frustratingly slow urban traffic conditions, high instances of bicycle theft and a general interest in cycling as a healthy, clean and convenient means of transport. This level of interest has prevented the Brompton from being just a specialist product and it has become an increasingly common sight among suited commuters as well as a cult item among young men more often seen on BMXs. Amazingly, at a time when the majority of bicycles are manufactured in Taiwan, even if they are assembled in the UK or USA, the Brompton is manufactured not just in the UK, but in London, which is some feat in itself. Andrew Ritchie, on finding no willing manufacturer to take on his invention, started manufacturing the Brompton himself and has committed his factory to constantly refining the manufacturing process, as well as the design and engineering, so that the Brompton just keeps getting better. To fold and unfold the bike requires a couple of big wing-nut type fixings to secure the two hinges, while the rear triangle and wheel simply swing underneath the frame through 180 degrees. Once mastered, the operation is very easy and can be completed in approximately 20 seconds. It is also lightweight – approximately 12 kg (26.5 lb) – and a very reasonable ride. The Brompton may not be the bike to go round the world on, but is definitely the one to choose for getting around almost any city, with wonderful convenience, speed and freedom.

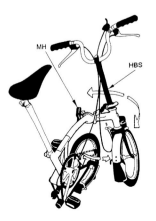

MH

HBS

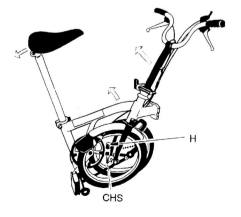

H

CHS

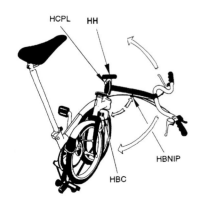

HCPL HH

HBNIP

HBC

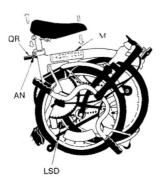

QR

M

AN

LSD

The Papillona Lamp is not only one of the most elegant models to have emerged from the consistently innovative relationship between the designers Tobia and Afra Scarpa and the Italian lighting company Flos, but it also reinvents both formally and technologically the freestanding electric Luminator lighting system, which had revolutionized modern lighting technology in the 1930s since it was easy to carry. The formal analogy that most readily comes to mind with the Papillona is that of a long-stemmed flower. The graceful stem is constructed via the conjunction of two sheets of extruded aluminium that open out into a crystal flower-head of metallic prismatic glass. The Scarpa approach to design embraces a commitment to the Italian craft tradition as well as a particular commitment to experimenting with new materials and their applications, and in this respect the Papillona is no exception. The attention to technical detail, as evinced in the Papillona, is precise and prescient. Every angle and junction is beautifully articulated and the indirect light cast by the prismatic glass reflector-diffusers has a strong geometric presence. The stem is hollow inside in order to conceal the wiring, and the bases and diffuser support are meticulously finished in painted and die-cast aluminium. The lamp is also revolutionary in that it is one of the first models to incorporate halogen lighting technology, meaning that the Papillona was endowed with a longer lamp life and higher lumen output per watt as well as improved beam control. Afra and Tobia, the latter the son of the influential architect Carlo Scarpa, also worked in commercial architecture and interior design, with perhaps their best-known work being for the Benetton clothing company. The Papillona, because of its elegant, organic ration-alized form and energy-efficient halogen technology, was used to striking effect in many of the Benetton company offices, including Benetton offices in Paris, designed in 1980. The lamp has been a permanent fixture in Flos's production catalogue since it was introduced in 1975.

Tratto Clip.
Più bello da usare o da guardare?
O da vendere?

Tratto Clip è piú bello da usare o da guardare? Difficile rispondere. Una cosa è certa: in pochi mesi ha invaso l'Italia, è diventato quasi un fatto di moda. Si fa vedere - e si fa vendere! - dappertutto.
In altre parole, oltre che un bello strumento per scrivere, Tratto Clip è anche un grosso successo commerciale.

E vuole continuare ad esserlo, e ad esserlo sempre di piú. Per questo è pronta a scattare, in autunno, una delle piú importanti campagne pubblicitarie del settore.

Pubblicità sui quotidiani,
sui periodici,
sui mezzi di trasporto.

Mezzi pubblicitari	
14 quotidiani: i piú importanti in ciascuna regione.	56 annunci di grande formato
11 settimanali e mensili: i piú diffusi e i piú letti in Italia.	34 annunci a pagina intera.
Tram e autobus in 5 grandi città.	1775 cartelli e tabelloni giganti.
Conclusione: milioni di persone vedranno piú e piú volte la pubblicità Tratto Clip.	

Tratto Clip.
Più bello da usare o da guardare?
O da premiare?

Tratto Clip è piú bello da usare o da guardare? Difficile rispondere. Una cosa è certa: la Giuria del "Compasso d'Oro" - un premio famoso per i suoi rigorosissimi criteri selettivi - lo ha scelto fra 1167 partecipanti, quale uno dei piú significativi esempi, nell'ultimo decennio, del design italiano.

È una conferma, una prestigiosa conferma, della validità di un prodotto che sin dal suo primo apparire ha superato ogni piú rosea previsione in fatto di vendite.

Ma la conferma forse e senza forse piú importante - quella,comunque, cui la Fila tiene di piú - è la fiducia di chi, come Voi, ha il compito piú delicato: mettere Tratto Clip nel taschino dei consumatori. Una fiducia che Tratto Clip farà di tutto per continuare a meritarsi.

Since its creation the Tratto Pen has helped form the curves, corners and scribbles of countless writings and drawings. It is no wonder that this elegant pen is a feature on many designers' desks. Manufactured by Fila, the Tratto Pen was designed by the Milan-based product design company, Design Group Italia. Established in 1968, Design Group Italia has since dedicated itself to creating innovative industrial designs in myriad sectors. With the introduction of the original Tratto Pen, the company started a line of writing instruments that would reshape the traditional pen into a modern, innovative and sleek design object, giving all users the pleasure of rendering a piece of work with an inspiring writing instrument. Design Group Italia launched the Tratto Pen fineliner, 1975–6, whose lithe form and exquisite mark-making ability assured it an instant triumph, and in 1978, with the addition of a clip to the original 1976 classic, the Tratto Clip fineliner was introduced. Both the original fineliner and the clip fineliner were highly praised, winning the Compasso d'Oro in 1979. The Tratto's success continued throughout the 1980s and, with the introduction of a synthetic point in 1990, the Tratto Symbol synthetic point pen was born. In that same decade the Fila Tratto Matic ballpoint pen (1994) and Tratto Laser needlepoint pen (1993) became available to the public. These pens continued the legacy of their predecessors with an organic and pure form, and the introduction of new nibs ensured Tratto's popularity in the writing world. The Tratto Pen has proven itself instrumental in creative expression; the pen's success lies in the hands of countless thoughts yet to be transcribed.

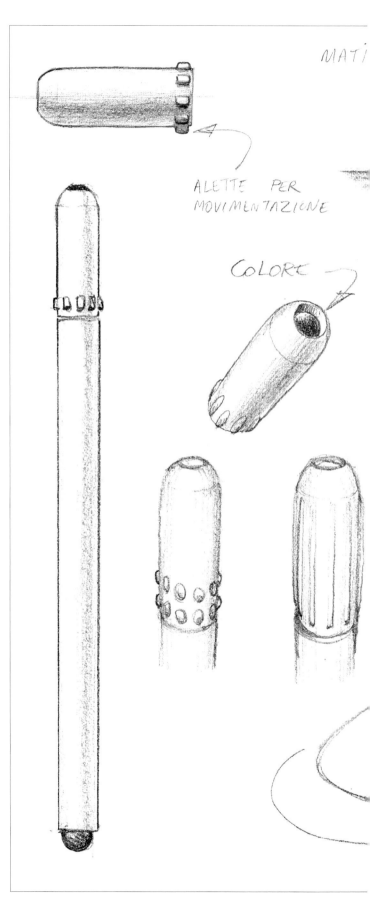

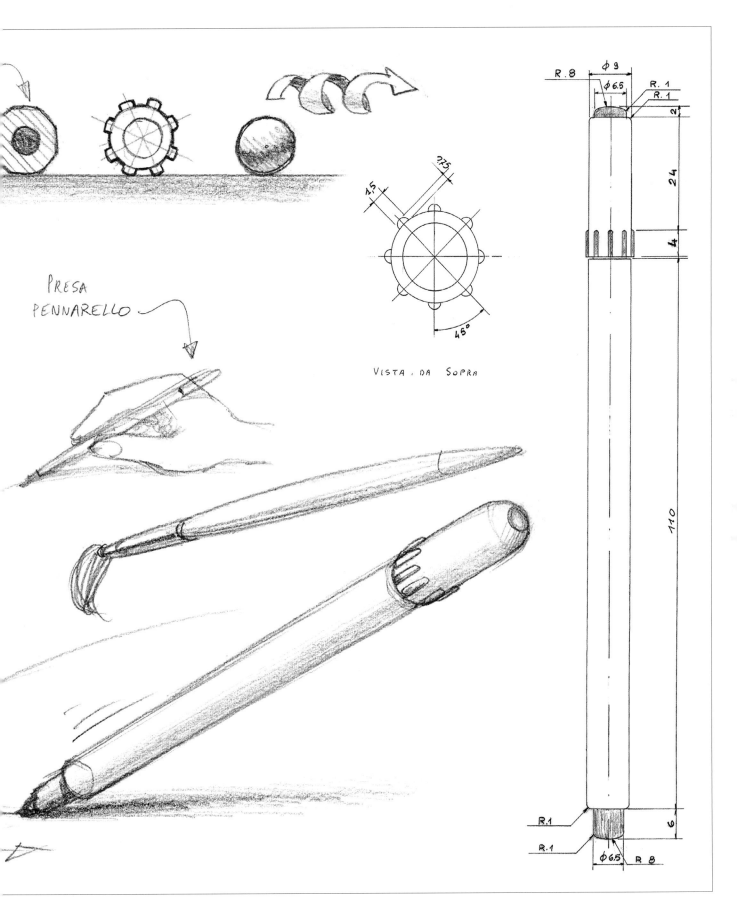

PRESA
PENNARELLO

VISTA DA SOPRA

φ9
φ6.5
R.8
R.1
R.1
2
24
4
110
6
R.1
R.1
φ6.5
R.8

1.5
0.75
45°

Riki Watanabe, an industrial designer, was one of the first to establish an independent design firm, Q Designers, in Japan in the late 1940s. This simple stainless-steel tray, designed by Watanabe, is one of the most copied products of this kind and its simple, almost anonymous appearance belies its rich and complex history. The tray can be used for many purposes, and looks equally good in offices or at bedsides, but was commonly used by the cashier of shops and restaurants in Japan. It was intended to be the first stainless-steel pen tray. It was so successful that it spawned many imitations, despite Watanabe's complaints. When the original manufacturer, Daiichi, went bankrupt in the late 1990s, 'bootleg' versions were produced using original moulds, but without the designer's permission. This increased Watanabe's determination to put the trays back in production. Through his long-term friend Sori Yanagi, he was introduced to the Sato-Shoji Company, and in 1999 the trays were on the market again, this time in an improved version. The form was slightly rounder than the original, as were the edges, which adds a touch of softness to a product that could otherwise be seen as slightly medical. The original trays were available only in a mirror finish, but now they are available in three different surface finishes: mirror, brushed and blasted, in three different sizes. At the time of the relaunch the tray was renamed the Uni-Tray after 'unique' and 'universal'. In 2001 the tray was awarded a G-Mark, the Japanese Good Design Award, nearly thirty years after it was originally designed. Today, the 'Martian' hallmark and 'Riki' engraved on the back of the tray are two signs which are proof of its authenticity.

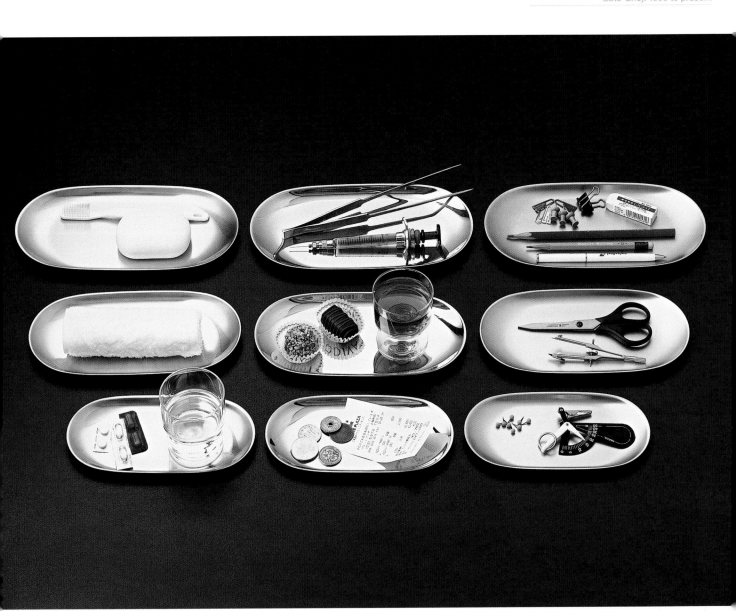

The development of Rosenthal's Studio Line range is largely due to Philip Rosenthal. In the mid-1950s he began commissioning well-known designers to produce ranges of high-quality modern domestic porcelain for the American market. This proved successful and in 1961 the modernized range was named the Studio Line. The strategy for the Studio Line has been developed and expanded over the years, but central to the concept is a range of high-quality, well-marketed domestic ware, designed by some of the best-known industrial designers and artists of the day and sold through a restricted set of upmarket department stores and special shops, where it can be shown to best advantage. The award-winning Suomi range, designed by Timo Sarpaneva, is one of Rosenthal's more popular lines and has remained in production since its introduction in 1976. Sarpaneva was by training a sculptor and, although he is best known for his work in glass, the Suomi range has a quality reminiscent of his passion for creating beautiful shapes. Originally produced in an undecorated white porcelain, the service, has a rounded-square form echoing the shape of a water-smoothed pebble. 'Suomi' (Finnish for Finland) is also produced with a range of more or less discreet surface decoration of faint indentations. The patterned variants have titles like 'Rangoon', 'Anthrazit', 'Pure Nature' and 'Visuelle Poésie', but it is not clear whether Sarpaneva, whose own sculptural work is abstract and often monumental, was consulted over the decoration. The Pompidou Centre permanent collection of contemporary design in Paris accepted the Suomi range in 1992, simply reiterating the success of this project.

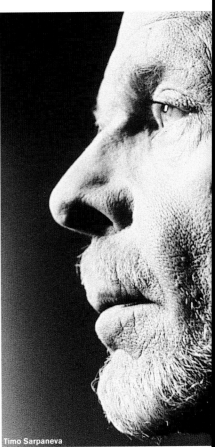

Timo Sarpaneva

Bikes often have to be kept outside, and can be very expensive pieces of equipment. If that was not enough to tempt thieves, they also double as a getaway vehicle. Before the Kryptonite K4 lock, the most common way of thwarting the light-fingered was to chain the bike to a rack or railing and secure the chain with a padlock. There was a flaw with this design. The basic padlock was simply an appropriation of existing materials to solve a problem, rather than a specific design solution. Even the best padlocks could be foiled by a vulnerable chain, and a pair of bolt-cutters could render pretty much any chain and lock useless within seconds, turning the bike into a statistic. The separate padlock and chain were fiddly, unwieldy and ugly.

Michael Zane's solution to this problem was the essence of simplicity. He did away with the chain altogether, and designed a lock that was basically a glorified padlock. He achieved a purity of design almost immediately by focusing on the strongest element of the existing arrangement. Thus the Kryptonite K4 was born, the first lock built with the bike in mind. The Kryptonite consists of a U-shaped rod of vinyl-coated zinc and nickel-plated steel, secured by a drum-shaped barrel lock that is thick enough to thwart all casual attempts at theft, a claim the company is happy to regularly test. Famously, Zane stress-tested a prototype of the lock in 1972 by leaving it locked to a signpost in Greenwich Village, New York, for thirty

days. The lock held. But the highest endorsement comes from the customers: the Kryptonite was a word-of-mouth success for what started as a one-man operation. And it is a product that has endured. Updated versions of the U-lock are still manufactured, which all originated from this design, and now sell in fifty countries. However, in what amounts to an 'arms race' against thieves, ingenuity is also applied by the other side, and in 2004 it was discovered that some models of the lock could be picked with a ballpoint pen. The design has since been updated to defeat this flaw, and the vulnerable locks have been exchanged by the company.

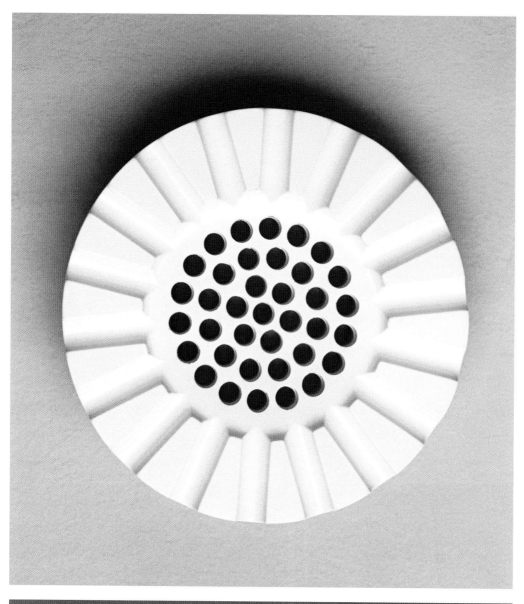

Architecturally trained

Anna Castelli Ferrieri is one of only a few women to have succeeded in the male-dominated Italian design world of the twentieth century. Starting her career in the office of Franco Albini in 1941, Castelli Ferrieri assisted the minimalist architect in his quest to rebuild depressed postwar Italy. She eventually set up her own practice in 1959 in collaboration with Ignazio Gardella, when they worked together on the design of various architectural projects, including Alfa Romeo's technical offices in Arese and the Kartell Building in Binasco. The latter was built in 1966, the year Castelli Ferrieri started as a design consultant for Kartell, the influential manufacturer of plastic domestic objects founded by her husband Giulio Castelli in 1949. Ferrieri started working with plastics at a time when the durable and versatile material was proving popular with consumers. As new plastic composites were invented, Ferrieri was one of the first to identify the new material properties and transform them into suitable products, such as with her first success, a stacking unit system made from ABS plastic in 1967. Almost ten years later, this ashtray was designed using injection-moulded melamine, a heavy, rigid, nonporous and unbreakable plastic that was perfectly suited to ashtrays due to its heat-resistant qualities. The material was a more durable competitor to ceramic and its quality and colour range more consistent and diverse. Of course, the design of the ashtray is highly practical: the concentric rings undulating on the base surface prevent propped cigarettes from sliding into the discarded ash. It is also stackable and easy to wash, making it suitable for use in bars and restaurants. Castelli Ferrieri has been Kartell's art director since 1976, and her repertoire of plastic designs has helped shape the company's history. Most of her pieces are still in production, sustaining her vision of affordable and mass-produced products.

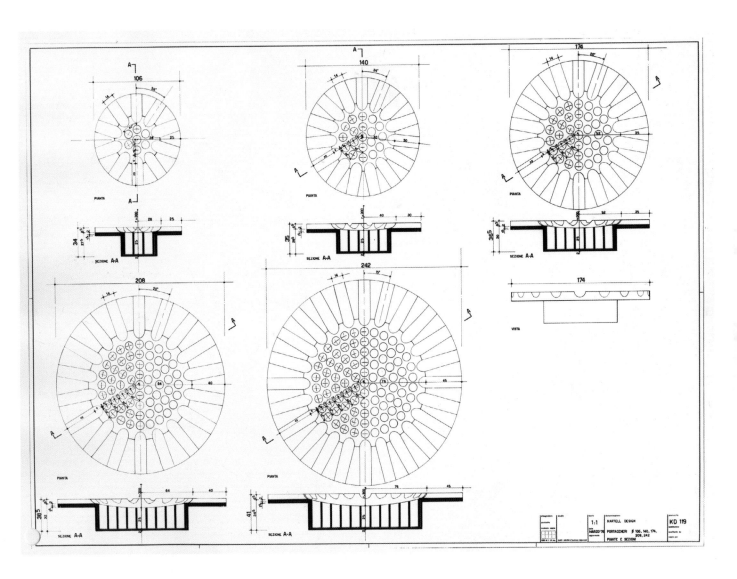

Of the 120 objects designed by Vico Magistretti, 80 per cent are still in production. This is a remarkable feat for any designer, let alone one who has been working since the 1940s, and which can only prove that his work has been consistently ahead of its time. Although his training was in architecture, he turned to furniture design in 1960 and began designing pieces in plastic that would be part of larger production series. His interest in 'anonymous' objects, or those that 'can go on repeating themselves in time with slight differences,' dominates many aspects of his work, especially those which do not appear to be overly designed. Sonora, which in Italian means something that has a resonant sound, is a large dome-shaped pendant lamp, bringing with it much presence and an element of the understated. The thin cable, barely seen, gives the impression that the lamp is gently floating in the air. Magistretti's desire to create simplified objects, without any excess, can be seen in this beautiful lamp, originally created in metal. It was in production throughout the 1970s and 1980s in two sizes – 50 cm (20 in) and 80 cm (32 in) – and was replaced by Murano glass in 1990. O luce recently reintroduced the lamp in blown metacrylite as Sonora 490, with clear, opaline or coloured versions and in a slightly larger size of 90 cm (36 in). The elegance is still there, and the lamp continues to be a source of aesthetic pleasure. The Sonora Lamp was followed by the Atollo Lamp in 1977, for which the dome lamp was given a base to create a table lamp. Magistretti, the honorary designer for the Royal Society of Arts and the winner of two Compasso d'Oro awards, with twelve pieces part of the permanent collection of The Museum of Modern Art in New York, can perhaps credit his success to his lack of interest in issues of 'style', and his ability to take traditional pieces and imbue them with a sense of modernity.

In the Glass Chair of 1976, Shiro Kuramata presented a new take on the traditional armchair, a standard in furniture design in the West. The chair is reduced to its essential elements, resulting in a stripped-down but complex form that spans art and design, both concepts that Kuramata successfully challenges. The use of glass for every element of the chair turns our expectations upside down and inside out, and results in a substantial and solid chair being rendered almost invisible. Yet, despite its radicalism, Kuramata's design is still functional: the chair still serves as a chair, and its material makes it sturdy despite its ethereal appearance. In much of his design work, including the Glass Chair, Kuramata challenges the limits of the material world. In his skilful and daring use of materials he tried to make things disappear, and repeatedly created 'borderline objects' at the critical point of transformation where, as Ettore Sottsass once commented, 'material becomes light, weight becomes air'. The Glass Chair illustrates Kuramata's characteristically deft handling of materials. Here he employs glass in plate form, minimizing any visual impurities such as joints and seams. The result is a piece that is a pure minimal design, one that truly spans disciplines with an intellectual and practical rigour without compromise.

In 1946, for one his earliest pieces of furniture, Vico Magistretti designed a bookcase that resembled a step-ladder propped against a wall. Nearly thirty years later Magistretti again borrowed typology and inspiration in part from ladders in his Nuvola Rossa bookcase, with its collapsible frame and six removable shelves. Drawing on a history and tradition of anonymous design, he created a new, now reworked object which was both immediately useful and of continuing relevance. The Nuvola Rossa is clever but not a statement. It is liveable, warm and vaguely familiar, but not dated. It is casually elegant, but not stylized. The shelves, with their equated distances, function as a wall or a room divider, creating a new environment on each side. Magistretti's remarkably persistent, unwavering approach stands in sharp contrast to that of many of his contemporaries. When Cassina launched Nuvola Rossa in 1977, a new, highly stylized, self-expressionism had begun to take hold in Italian design, casting aside mass production as a tool. In the midst of wave upon wave of ideology and style, Magistretti designed a simple but elegant, modest but clever, highly saleable, mass-produced bookcase, working in close partnership with the manufacturer. Cassina continues to produce Nuvola Rossa in natural, black, or white lacquered beechwood, just as it has each year since its launch. This enduring legacy sets the Nuvola Rossa bookcase apart and, although it does not yet qualify under Magistretti's own rule that a good design lasts perhaps fifty or even a hundred years, it is surely close enough.

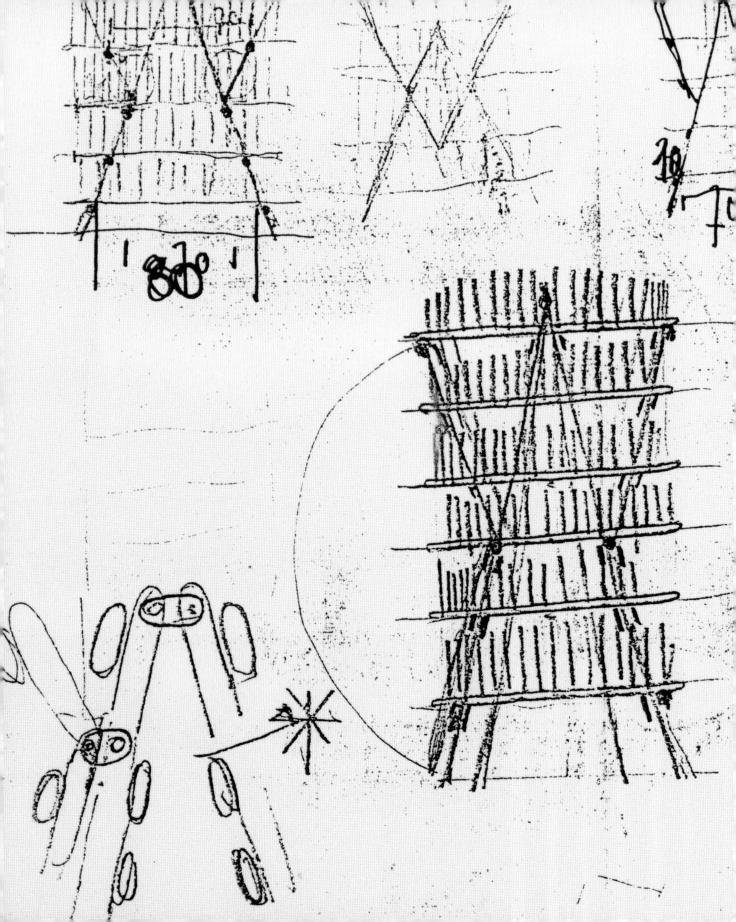

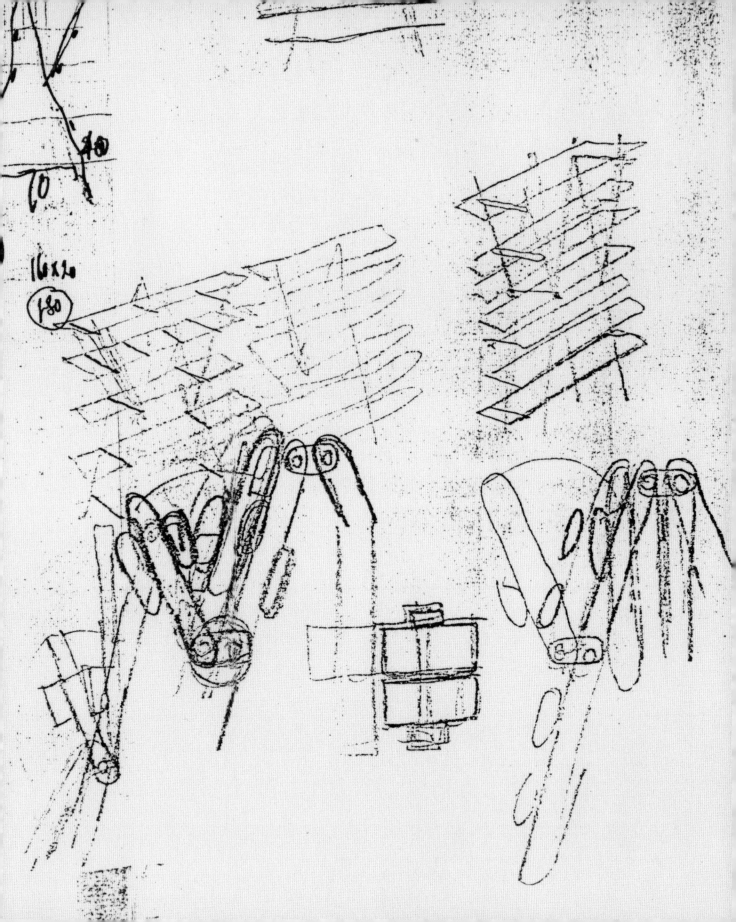

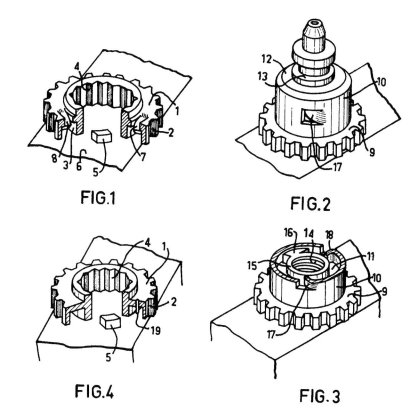

FIG.1

FIG.2

FIG.4

FIG.3

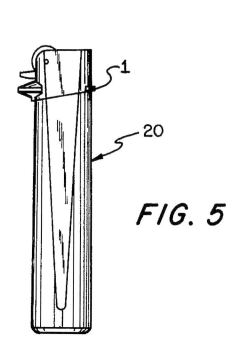

FIG. 5

In 1963 the US tobacco industry had reached its per capita peak of 4,345 cigarettes per individual per annum. Clearly, products that facilitated the habits of tobacco consumers would mean big business. Introduced in 1961 by the French firm Dupont, the Cricket lighter was the first disposable lighter. It had a round column, with a plastic body containing its butane fuel and a metal housing for its wick. On its heels, however, came the Bic lighter, which became the best-selling lighter worldwide. Consensus was that the oval-shaped, slightly less expensive competitor, the Bic, was easier

to hold than Dupont's product. Consequently, Dupont added planes to their lighter's surface, indicating the orientation of the flame. Dupont was located in Faverges, a few miles away from Annecy, where the American razor company, Gillette, had a factory. Gillette's CEO Vincent Ziegler, would take the company through its peak performance years, and Gillette was engaged in a process of diversification. Intent upon entering the then booming smoking accessories business, Gillette acquired 80 per cent of Dupont in 1972 and established an independent Cricket Company in Balme-de-

Sillingy. In 1977 Cricket issued its newly redesigned lighter, the Cricket Maxi, in the now classic bar-shaped body with fixed flame technology that ensured a safe, predictable flame every time. Since then the Cricket Maxi has held its position as one of the world's largest-selling disposable lighters. In 1981 Americans smoked 684 billion cigarettes, an all-time high in national consumption. In 1985 Gillette sold Cricket to the Swedish Match Company, a firm dedicated to the sale of tobacco products, matches and lighters. Beyond the dependability of its construction, the lighter continues to be known for

safety, as well as a style-conscious marketing strategy. It is now available in nineteen variations that address the various ways in which a lighter might be used, and its surface decoration is constantly changing. With new variations available every three months, the Cricket has become eminently collectible.

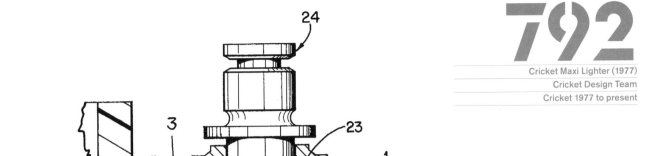

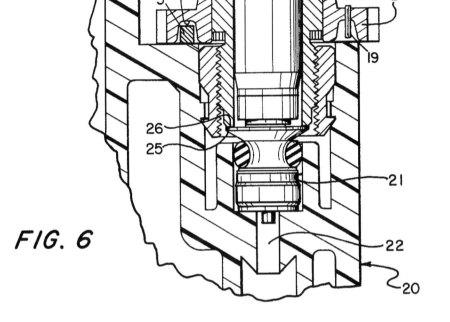

FIG. 6

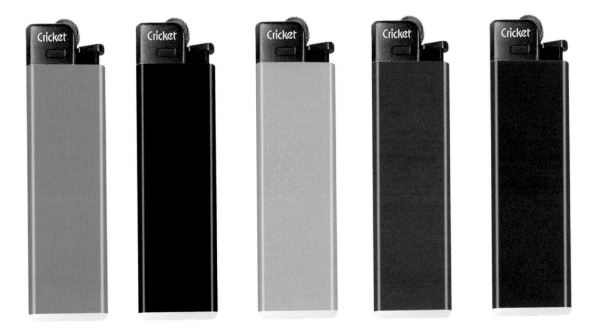

Erik Magnussen's insulated Vacuum Jug for
Stelton reflects perfectly its designer's instinctive feeling
for form coupled with his strict, almost austere approach
to function. The flask is an essay in simplicity in design: its
method of production, the materials it is made from and
the way it works are each an object lesson in economy
and fitness for purpose. The jug was the first product
Magnussen designed for Stelton after he succeeded Arne
Jacobsen as the company's chief designer. The jug was
intended to complement Jacobsen's famous Cylinda-Line
of 1967, a seventeen-piece stainless-steel range of
tableware that included a cocktail shaker and an ice
bucket, but that lacked a vacuum jug. Magnussen
developed a design that utilized an existing glass bottle
liner (thus immediately reducing production costs) and
introduced a unique, T-shaped lid with a rocking stopper
mechanism that opened and closed automatically when
the jug was tilted, allowing it to be operated easily and
with one hand. Originally the jug was made in stainless
steel to match the other products in the Cylinda-Line,
with the lid made from POM plastic, a material that hardly
absorbs the taste or smell from tea or coffee. From 1979
the body of the jug was also produced in shiny, scratch-
resistant ABS plastic and available in several different
colours. The use of plastics turned an otherwise expensive
item into an affordable one. The low cost of materials and
the simple production method reduced production costs
by as much as 50 per cent. The bright, shiny colours also
suited the jug's sleek lines and simple economic form,
thus adding considerably to its desirability. The jug became
an instant success and continues to be one of the company's
best-selling products. The jug was awarded the Danish
Design Centre's ID Prize in 1977, the same year as
its introduction. Today the jug is available in sixteen
different colours.

The Atollo lamp is perhaps one of Vico Magistretti's most famous lamps and was winner of the Compasso d'Oro award in 1979. It is a table lamp made of painted aluminium; its simple geometrical composition transforms an accessible domestic object into an abstract sculpture. The lamp is composed of two distinct elements: a cylindrical support and a spherical top. The top is connected to the lamp's base by an element so slim that, when the lamp is turned on, the unit appears to be suspended in mid-air. The diffuser projects the light into the upper conic segment of the base. The outer surfaces of the lamp are completely smooth, which both invests the object with an elegance of material shape and allows a play of light on the surface that enlivens the geometrical composition. The many lamps that Magistretti has designed throughout his career are a combination of abstract geometries and light effects. Details such as joints, wires and plugs are always concealed; what prevails in these objects is a great formal simplicity and balanced composition. Magistretti displays a unique ability to obtain an essential and balanced composition through the assembly of different geometrical shapes. As he once said, 'I love geometrical shapes. I love creating essential shapes that seem mere wisps.' The Atollo is a perfect example of Magistretti's overall approach to design and represents the results of a successful collaboration between the industrial designer and the manufacturer that helped to underpin the success of Italy's postwar furniture industry. The lamp's concept was realized by Magistretti in a series of sketches, but it took time for the manufacturer to put such a technically complex idea into production. O luce is the oldest Italian lighting design company still active today. The early 1970s were a new and important era for O luce, coinciding with a transfer of ownership from the Ostuni family to the Verderi family. For many years Magistretti was an art director and chief designer for the company, where he conferred his unmistakable stamp and where the Atollo was one of its most successful products.

Mål

bredde 22½ cm,
dybde 15 cm,
højde med telefonrøret
pålagt 8½ cm.

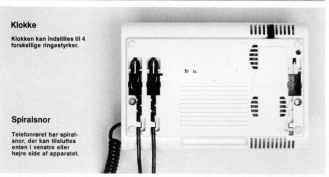

Klokke

Klokken kan indstilles til 4
forskellige ringestyrker.

Spiralsnor

Telefonrøret har spiral-
snor, der kan tilsluttes
enten i venstre eller
højre side af apparatet.

F78

F78 telefonapparatet er et
lavt bordapparat, der er
nemt og hurtigt at bruge.

Tastatur

Apparatet har tastatur –
ved opkald indtaster De
det ønskede telefon-
nummer ved at trykke
let med fingerspidsen
på de pågældende tal.

Tasterne ✳ og ⊞ er
reserveret til fremtidige
specielle formål.

Post- og Telegrafvæsenet   Henvendelse

i Sønderjylland:

Telegrafkontoret
Sønderport 47
6200 Åbenrå
Telefon 04-00 19

på Møn:

Telekontoret
Østervangsvej 2
4780 Stege
Telefon 03-81 46 45

Grå

Grøn

Umbra

Farver

F78 fås i fem forskellige
farver: grå, gul, grøn, rød
og umbra. De skal først
meddele, hvilken farve De
har valgt, når apparatet
leveres.

Rød

Gul

P&T-reklame 1979. Tryk Johnsen+Johnsen A/S, København

F78

telefon i ny
design med
tastatur

This telephone heralded the start of the 1980s revolution in telecommunications technology. The unassuming telephone, by Danish product designer Henning Andreasen, quietly became the standard-issue product for consumers in a number of countries and sold extremely well in the United States. Its presence spread out of offices and homes and on to the streets in the late 1980s when Andreasen levered the same design cues into a best-selling phone box for the Swiss telecom company, ASCOM. The phone consists of a red, beige or white gently curving body with simple black push-buttons set in a grid at the centre. The black handset rests along the back of the body. The success of the phone lies in its pioneering use of technology that would become standard in later years. The phone was one of the first to replace the ring dial with push-button technology and also one of the first to replace the old-fashioned bell ringer with an electronic tone ringer. Its popularity is partly due to the growing desire for cutting-edge electronic consumer goods during the 1980s. Andreasen is perhaps better known for his simple, stainless-steel Folle Stapler of 1979 for Folle of Denmark, but the popularity of the F78 means that it is certainly his most used product. Its simplicity and popularity were recognized when it won the Dansk Design Centre's ID Prize in 1978 and also when it was exhibited at The Museum of Modern Art in New York. The phone is now out of production, but the recent surge of nostalgia for the 1980s has lead to a thriving second-hand market for the product.

Mario Bellini – architect, industrial designer, furniture designer, journalist and lecturer – is one of the most notable figures in today's international design community. His Cab chair, produced in Milan by Cassina since 1977, endures as a symbol of late twentieth-century Italian innovation and craftsmanship. An enamelled tubular steel frame is completely encased by a form-fitting leather cover, closed by four zips that run along the inside legs and under the seat. Reinforced only by a plastic plate within the seat, the effect is taut, luxurious and uniform. In the uncertain economic climate of the 1970s, Bellini's Cab chair stood as an expression of two important Italian manufacturing ideals. On the one hand, its steel frame construction, appropriate to mass production, adhered to the rationalist (and often highly restrictive) directive from manufacturers to keep costs low. On the other hand, its use of fine, smooth leather and saddle-stitch detailing at the seams underlined Italy's desire to promote its important craft heritage in the international marketplace. Although committed to design innovation that reflected a global move towards light, flexible and affordable furniture, Italian manufacturers were also aware that high-quality craftsmanship, incorporated into avant-garde design, could boost export levels. Whereas tubular steel furniture up to that point relied on contrasting materials for visual impact, Bellini here combines the two elements, metal and covering, to create an enveloped, elegant structure. By 1982 the chair had become synonymous with high-quality Italian design; two companion pieces joined it in production – an armchair and a sofa – all available in tan, white and black. Bellini has held several distinguished posts, as editor of *Domus* magazine (1986–91), as professor of industrial design at the Domus Academy in Milan (1986–1991) and as a member of the Scientific Council for the Milan Triennale's Design Division (since 1979). In his early career he acted as chief design consultant for Olivetti (from 1963) and it has been suggested that the leather skin of the Cab chair is a reference to traditional typewriter casings. The series is still in production.

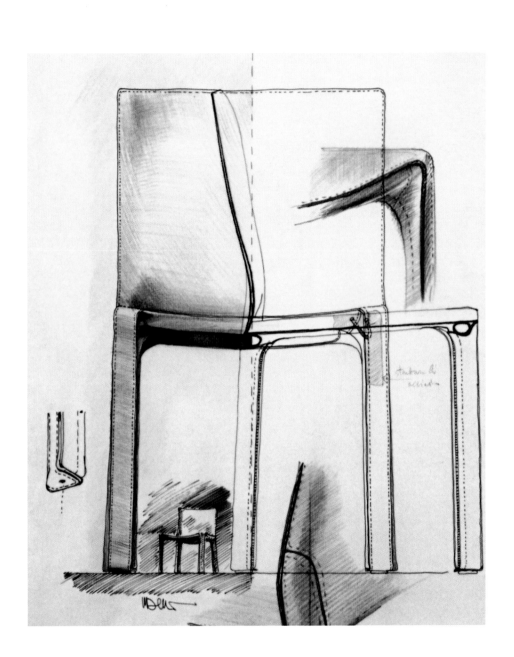

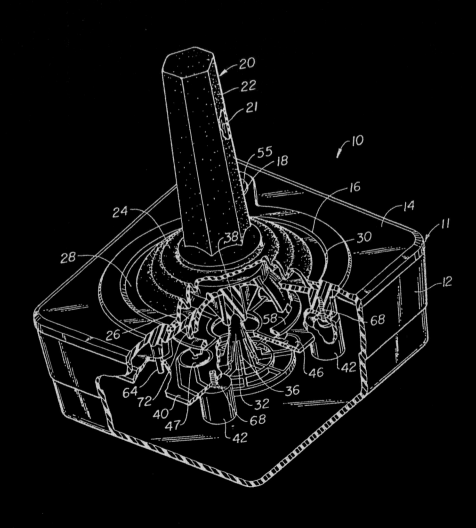

The Atari Joystick CX40 standard controller was and still is an object that has garnered much love over the years from its faithful fans, even though Atari made several controllers between 1977 and 1996. It originally came with the CX2600 Video Computer System, a rectangle with a black corrugated plastic top with six silver switches and a fake wood-grain front piece. This system came with two CX40 Joysticks, one paddle controller, an adapter, a TV/game switch and a cartridge for the game Combat. It was the most successful video game console ever launched, and sold over 30 million units. Since it was the first machine without fixed games, the latest games on the market could be bought as separate cartridges. Atari, owned by Nolan Bushnell, sold the company to Warner Communications in 1978. The designers of the video computer system, Steve Mayer, Joe Decuir and Harold Lee, were working on an earlier version at the time, and the CX2600 was developed after the handover. The CX40 Joystick, with the single red button in the top corner, was revolutionary in its flexibility, and allowed users to physically interact with the game they were playing. Kevin McInsey and John Hyashi, the key designers, placed a black plastic plate over the board which had four heavy Phillips screws, while the inside had a printed circuit board, a spring for the red fire button, a white handle within the rubber joystick and a plastic ring. With one button and a stick that could move in eight directions, the innovation lay in the fact that it was the first controller that could be disconnected from the main console. There were two key problems with the design, however: the ring inside the case would wear down quickly, and the red fire button would eventually stop working. But both issues were solved due to readily available replacement parts. The first 400,000 Atari 2600s were packaged with an earlier CX40 design that had one notable external cosmetic difference from the other joysticks, which is the lack of the word 'TOP' for the forward/ up position of the Joystick. Internally, the Joystick had a completely different inner mechanism which was intended for an earlier product that Atari was in the midst of developing. The CX40 worked with much-loved games such as Asteroids, Missile Command and Adventure, as well as with all other Atari systems, and has been an influence for the future generations of home video games.

Designed by Richard Sapper, a pioneer of postmodern industrial product design ideology, the 9090 Espresso Coffee Maker was awarded the Compasso d'Oro at the 1979 Milan Triennale. The stainless-steel columnar coffee pot was praised not only for its sleek lines and 'exceptional' success in reinventing the espresso coffee maker, but also for its innovative design. Although a high-profile postmodernist, Sapper's 9090 design illustrates clearly a basic modernist idiom, namely that form follows function. The wide base gives the coffee maker both sturdiness and stability, but also the ability to boil the water evenly and quickly to avoid scorching the coffee. Sapper's design included a non-drip spout and a widely heralded innovative click system that opened and closed the pot to allow water and coffee to be added. In previous pots of this type the norm was for the pot to be opened using a screw system. Designed between 1977 and 1979, the 9090 exemplified Alessi's intuition that the kitchen would be a good arena for new strategic initiatives. The idea was based on the belief that there was a market for a new and different cafetière that could be both more expensive and more technically complex than other available models. With the Bialetti Moka cafetière dominating the market in Italy, the Alessi strategy was to commission a state-of-the-art design that would retail for a much higher price than any in their existing range. Sapper's solution, still in production today, was a revolutionary coffee maker with no traditional neck or spout, futuristic in shape and with pared-down decoration.

The Proust Chair

takes its form from a typical eighteenth-century Baroque armchair, but it is decorated with dazzling bursts of colour in imitation of pointillism, the painting technique that came out of the French Post-Impressionist movement at the turn of the century. The juxtaposition of a traditional chair shape with a more modern and seemingly

inappropriate type of decoration was meant as a comment on the state of contemporary design. Mendini wanted to show that design had reached an impasse, that new forms were not possible and that decoration had supplanted design itself. The pointillist pattern is also a metaphor for the writer Marcel Proust, after whom the chair is named, and who lived and worked at the

same time as the Post-Impressionists. He was allegedly an admirer of the painter Paul Signac, from whose paintings the surface pattern of the chair was taken. Proust presented the theory that time is in constant flux, the past being as relevant as the present, and the only way to understand time was through intuitive memory. Mendini's quotations from mass culture

and historical styles have an echo of Proust's beliefs, and his work can be seen to be the major precursor of Postmodernism. Alessandro Mendini, one of the most important and influential Italian designers of the late twentieth century, was one of the founding members of the design group Alchimia in Milan in 1976. Alchimia was the natural successor to the Italian

Anti-Design movements of Superstudio and Archizoom. Mendini declared, 'There is no more originality' and proposed a new code of the banal. The Proust Chair was one explanation of this code; a redesign of an existing object as a means of emphasizing the banality of the alteration. The chair, originally made by Studio Alchimia, now exists as two versions, the first of which was

not intended for commercial production. This version is still made by Atelier Mendini, with each one hand-painted, and includes Mendini's signature. The second version was put into mass production by Cappellini in 1994, and differs in that the pointillist-patterned textile is printed. The Proust Chair is one of a series of redesigns by Mendini. He also produced a sideboard painted in imitation of Wassily Kandinsky's style. Another tactic was to redesign a series of famous chairs by Gerrit Rietveld, Marcel Breuer, Gio Ponti, Joe Colombo, Michael Thonet and Charles Rennie Mackintosh, adding decoration to their classic forms.

Proust Chair (1978)
Alessandro Mendini (1931–)
Studio Alchimia/Atelier Mendini
1978 to present
Cappellini 1994 to present

BILLY

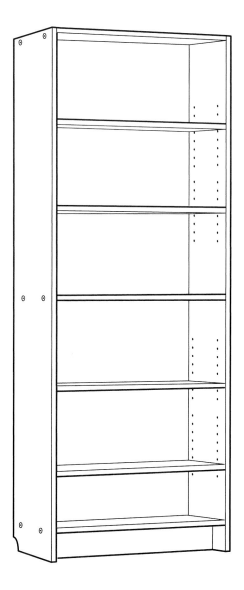

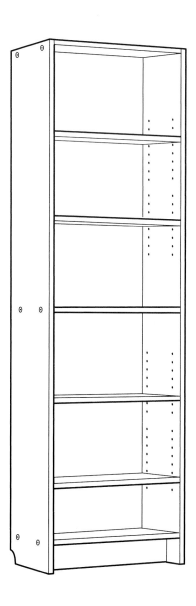

Billy Shelf (1978)
IKEA of Sweden
IKEA 1978 to present

The Billy Shelf is a design phenomenon. This simple, flexible, self-assembly storage system is one of the most popular design products in the world. Since it was launched by IKEA in 1978 it has sold around 28 million pieces. Of course, IKEA is also a phenomenon in its own right. Founded in 1943 by seventeen-year-old Ingvar Kamprad as a mail-order company specializing in affordable, functional and well-designed furniture, the company currently represents the leading home furnishings brand in the world, with more than 200 stores in more than thirty countries, boasting in 2004 over 400 million visitors and a turnover of 13,570 million euros. The IKEA concept has remained true to the spirit of Scandinavian Modernism and its democratic principles of good, affordable design for all. The company's spectacular success can be attributed to a great extent to its pioneering approach to the concept of self-assembly, and it was one of the first companies to introduce the concept of flat packs. IKEA established the idea of fully integrating home furnishing by developing modular, interlinking systems as opposed to individual, one-off products. The Billy system is the key exemplar of IKEA's *raison d'être*. Essentially Billy is a storage system that has evolved from simple, adjustable shelving units to a whole series of bookcase and storage combinations featuring corner units, glass doors, CD towers and TV benches, to name just a few of its components. Billy is essentially particle board, which is cheap to mass-produce and easy to assemble. These components are veneered in a selection of materials ranging from birch and beech, to white, dark and grey metallic finishes. IKEA has always sold bookcases, but Billy is optimized in terms of flexibility and material consumption, which are two of the all-important cornerstones of sustainable design. The IKEA mantra of functional, low-cost design has seduced a global audience and the clean lines, high versatility and low cost of its best-selling Billy system have greatly contributed to this Scandinavian seduction.

1

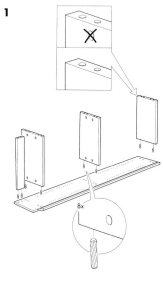

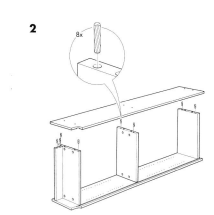

2

8x

3

6x

4

6x

5

4x

6

4x

7

4x

8

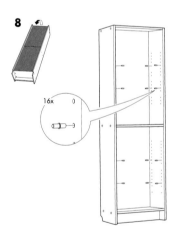

16x

9

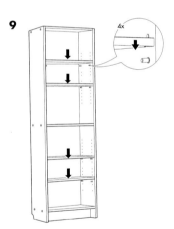

4x

10

The ET 44 calculator, created by Dieter Rams for Braun, came on the scene soon after the price plummet of the early electronic calculators. Initially, the earliest inventions cost the same price as a car. The introduction of the first integrated circuits and LEDs to replace gas-filled display tubes had an immediate effect on the overall unit price. Not only were prices tumbling, but all the calculating components for a four-function calculator could be packed on a single IC, which was the real key towards true pocket-sized dimensions. Rams was born in 1932 and still lives in a house he designed near Frankfurt close to the Braun factory complex where he worked for nearly forty years. He studied architecture and interior design at the Werkkunstschule Wiesbaden, graduated in 1953 and briefly worked in an architects' office before joining Braun in 1955. He soon expanded his remit to design products, packaging and advertising alongside his original position in buildings and interiors. Everything was designed in-house, with Rams overseeing all aspects of the team. During his career with Braun, Rams's black, minimalist designs were punctuated with beads of colour to create more intuitive designs. Said Rams, 'Braun products… must stay in the background, must harmonize with any environment. Strong colours could upset and confuse.' This design ethos is manifested in his definitive ET 44 Pocket Calculator, whose matt black finish is punctuated with glossy convex buttons. Building on the progressive designs and reputation he consolidated in the 1960s, while his peers designed veneered domestic products to look more like furniture, Rams broke away from the pack to create products with their own aesthetic of black minimalism. At the onset of Ram's relationship with Braun in the 1950s, his creations were considered avant-garde, so it was hoped his designs for complementary domestic items would encourage tastes to catch up and co-exist with Braun's products.

8O1

ET 44 Pocket Calculator (1978)
Dieter Rams (1932–)
Dietrich Lubs (1938–)
Braun 1978 to 1981

Aldo van den Nieuwelaar

The A'dammer, which is essentially a cupboard system with vertical roll-down shutter cabinets in lacquered ABS plastic, is a perfect embodiment of the perennial Pastoe philosophy of sober minimalism, and is as vital now as ever in the current 'New Functionalism' cultural landscape. Using a minimum of resources and materials, the A'dammer was an attempt by architect Aldo van den Nieuwelaar to make a user-friendly form that would not dominate any given space. The basic modular shape of the design, which is defined via its clever, highly practical shutter mechanism, allows the cupboard to either occupy space as a freestanding object or form part of a whole system of A'dammers. The model comes in various permutations to avoid monotony. The legacy of the Dutch De Stijl movement, and in particular the work of Gerrit Rietveld, can clearly be seen in the formal rationale of the A'dammer. In the same way that Rietveld reduced forms to an abstract composition of line and surface, so van den Nieuwelaar has reduced the A'dammer to an abstracted, refined and formally minimalist piece of furniture: cool, calm, collected, and free of artifice and excess. Moreover, the A'dammer was explicitly designed to embrace the industrial manufacturing process. The A'dammer was created at a time when elsewhere in Europe, particularly in Italy, design tendencies were veering towards the celebration of decoration and eclectic excess that would eventually lead headlong into Postmodernism. Works conceived by Memphis and Alchimia, produced during the same period, embodied this new direction, but were at the opposite end of the design scale to the A'dammer in terms of design approach. The quiet Dutch composure of the cupboard would prove to be perennially popular, its success a sign that the dignified utilitarianism embodied in its design can endure the unpredictable whims of the market.

8O2

A'dammer (1978)
Aldo van den Nieuwelaar (1944–)
Pastoe 1978 to present

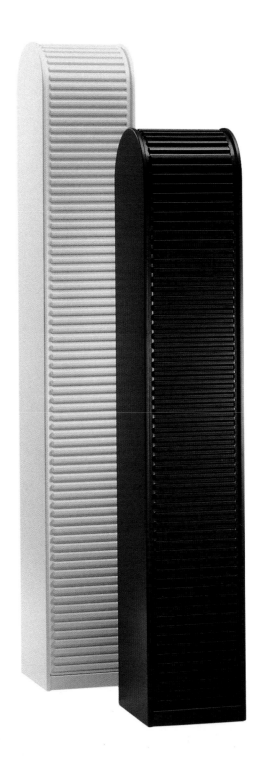

Mattia Esse (1978)
Enrico Contreas (1942–)
Mattia & Cecco 1978 to 2003

In 1978 sailing-boat

designer Enrico Contreas embarked on
what was to become his most famous
project, the multi-hull Mattia Esse.
Contreas began his career at Pirelli where
he designed an inflatable boat, the PV4.
His passion for the sailing-boat, however,
inspired him to start his first multi-hull
project in 1971, leading to the Mattia Esse,
which first set sail on Lake Como, Italy, in
1978. The catamaran, built of fibreglass
with a mainsail of 12.42 mq a jib and and a
large asymmetrical spinnaker of 15.5 mq,
is intended for two people to sail. The sail
area and special design of the hulls, with
their lean bow and unique stern that looks
as though it has been cut with a knife,
make the Mattia Esse one of the fastest
catamarans ever built. The line of the keel
allows the bow to stay a little above the
waterline, making the boat more agile and
providing overall stability to the hull.
Simultaneously, the level of the bow keeps
the catamaran from capsizing. For this
project Contreas was awarded the
prestigious Compasso d'Oro in 1981.
He went on to set up his own shipyard,
Mattia & Cecco, building more sports
boats, including the famous Mattia 18
and the comfortable Mattia 56 for cruising.
Enthusiasm for this boat ensured that
many Mattia class races were held around
the world in order to gain attention for this
particular design. There were over 600 of
the Mattia Esse produced at the height of
its popularity, before it was replaced by the
Mattia Esse Sport, which is the same size,
but faster and with a slightly longer beam.
The original Mattia is no longer in production, but remains one of the most
beautiful sailing catamarans ever built.

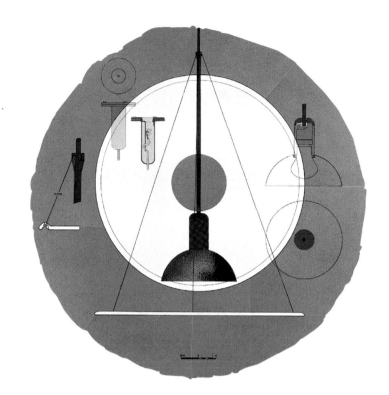

Achille Castiglioni is quite rightly considered one of the greatest designers of the last century. He was the winner of the prestigious Compasso d'Oro prize no less than eight times and his long and prolific output can be mapped out via the light fittings he designed for Flos, one of Italy's most respected lighting companies. An obvious enthusiast and acknowledged master of the subject, Castiglioni designed more than twenty-five lamps for Flos during his career. Many of these lamps represent Castiglioni's trademark wit and lightness of touch, but are also recognized as icons of twentieth-century design. Several of them are included in museum collections around the world. The Frisbi is one of these, and its popularity and apparent simplicity have caused it to appear regularly enough for it to seem commonplace. This is despite its unusual solution to the everyday problem of deflecting glare from a hanging light. Castiglioni's approach to lighting design often started with an in-depth appraisal of a particular bulb. The results of this research would generate the eventual form of the light, while maximizing the inherent qualities of its light source. This lamp followed on from earlier research completed with his brother, Pier Giacomo, and was designed to provide both soft, reflected light and direct light all from the same fitting. This was achieved by means of a suspended white translucent metacrylate disc with a large central hole. This hole directs light down on to a tabletop, while the opal plastic disc holds, diffuses and reflects the remainder of the light. The remaining components consist of a small spun and polished metal bowl, which houses the incandescent bulb. This bowl is fixed to the stem, from which three tiny steel wires are suspended. These in turn support the opal plastic disc, which appears to float magically in space when seen from a distance.

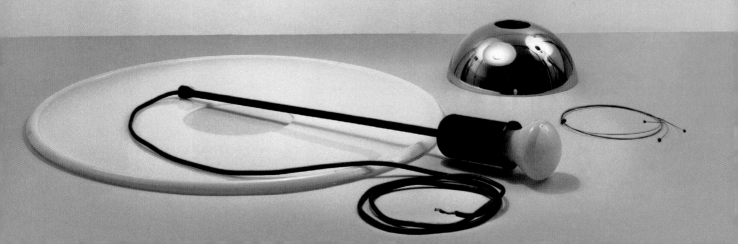

805

5070 Condiment Set (1978)
Ettore Sottsass (1917–)
Alessi 1978 to present

The 5070 Condiment Set designed by Ettore Sottsass for Alessi is characteristic of the company's ethos that the essence of modern design is to create objects which make the commonplace special. Synonymous with postmodernist design practice and theory of the 1980s, Sottsass is one of Italy's most expressive and successful designers. He began his design association with Alessi in 1972 and the 5070 Condiment Set marks one of his early works for the company. The beauty of the design lies in its simplicity and it has been widely copied. Sottsass's design defined what was expected of a successful condiment set. The containers are sophisticated crystal glass cylinders, each topped with a polished stainless-steel dome, and stand neatly on their holder. The high quality of the materials evokes a sense of style while being practical (the glass reveals the contents and how much remains), and the holder serves both to carry the set and to keep the separate jars together. The essence of the piece, in many ways, lies in the design of the holder: the convenient handle allows it to be handed around easily, thus promoting the ideal of social and communal eating. This subtle design feature directly references Italian cuisine and eating traditions, while the set as a whole remains truly utilitarian, essential as a table centrepiece and an item of daily use. Designed in late 1970s Sottsass's 5070 Condiment Set was ahead of its time and gave an insight into the future, providing an early indication of the design style that would become dominant through the 1980s, with Italian design leading the scene and clearly enjoying its position at the forefront of consumer popularity. The proof of the enduring success of the set is in its ubiquity in its country of origin. Found widely in Italian restaurants, bars and homes, the classic 5070 Condiment Set created an industrial and domestic standard for the table since its launch.

R=18

R=5

R=22.5

R=14.5

R=4

R=2

R=2

35

184.5

133

38

16.5

15

1.5

1.5 14 53 1 8 29 8 1 53 14 1.5

181

184

SEZIONE

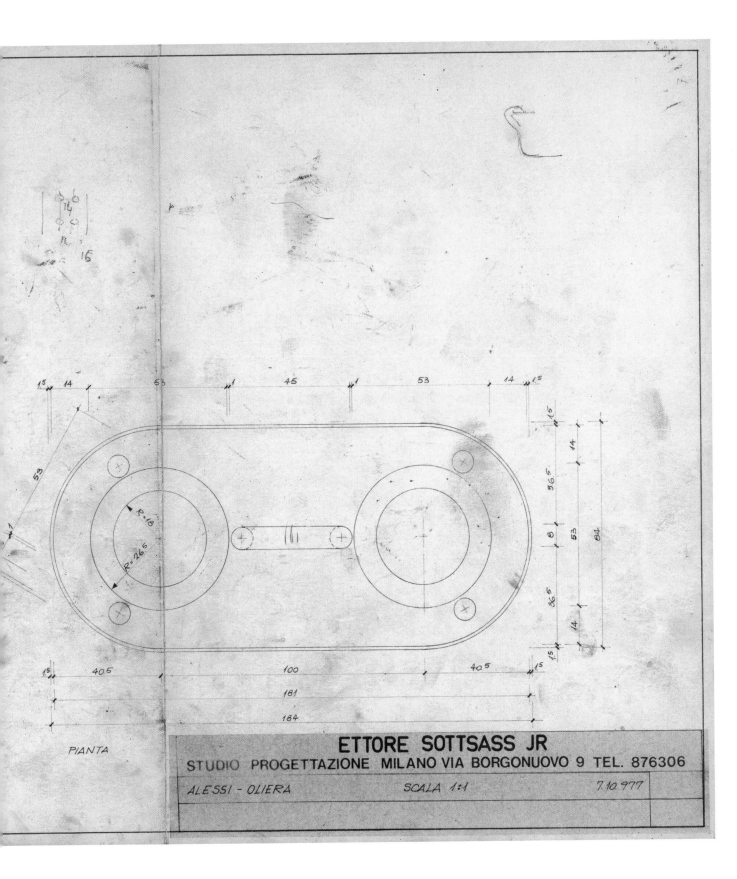

PIANTA

ETTORE SOTTSASS JR
STUDIO PROGETTAZIONE MILANO VIA BORGONUOVO 9 TEL. 876306

ALESSI - OLIERA   SCALA 1:1   7.10.977

No chair is more representative of modern café culture than the Gacela Chair, designed by Joan Casas y Ortínez. It is perhaps not coincidental that it was designed in the late 1970s, historically a moment of cultural regeneration for Spain, both in social terms and in design. Constructed out of an anodized aluminium tube, the Gacela's simple, clean lines make it a versatile design fit for indoor or outdoor spaces. A graphic designer, industrial designer and lecturer, Casas y Ortínez started working with Spanish manufacturer Indecasa in 1964. His Clásica collection of stacking chairs, of which Gacela is part, is today hailed as a classic of European café furniture. The Clásica collection is the result of more than twenty-five years of Indecasa history. The products in the collection have a series of common elements in their construction and use of anodized aluminium tubing, and are constantly being updated with different finishes to reflect changing fashions. Gacela was designed with either aluminium or wooden slats and cast aluminium joints for additional strength. The aluminium slats are also available painted in powdered polyester or can be given a personal touch with adhesive labels suitable for external use. Gacela's lightness, durability and stackability have over the years made it a best seller. The chair is the perfect example of Casas y Ortínez's statement that: 'Design for me means creating products for industry, for sale, that are functional and please thousands of people and that over the years will acquire classic status, becoming part of our surroundings.'

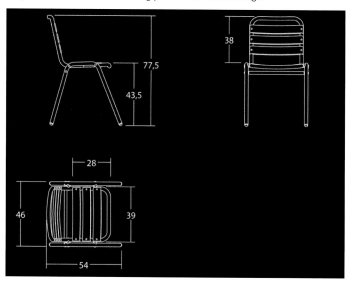

806
Gacela (part of Clásica collection) (1978)
Joan Casas y Ortínez (1942–)
Indecasa 1978 to present

The design of the Maglite suggests

a strong consideration of its purpose, being free of superfluous decoration – practically a tool for lighting. The casing, precisely made by machine, employs high-quality rubber seals and high-resolution optics and there is even a spare bulb housed within the body of the torch. The Maglite was introduced in the USA in 1979 and aimed at the public safety sector. It was intended to be an improvement on existing torches available to the police, fire-fighters and engineers: a portable lighting source in lightweight, anodized aluminium that would be reliable and robust. Its inventor, Anthony Maglica, a Croatian emigrant, came from a working-class background with experience as a machinist. He set up his own company to supply precision parts for the aerospace and military industries. Maglica recognized that the two key ingredients in the growth of his business were a superior product and a high level of customer care, and his company enjoyed further growth with progressive innovation set against competitive production costs. The reliable and durable Maglite was positively received by its target market and, with a commitment to product innovation and refinement, Maglica quickly developed a family of torches based on the key features of the original design. The differing sizes and weights exploited new markets and found a receptive consumer within the domestic market. Anthony Maglica demonstrated further skills as a business leader with an acute understanding of market demands. By 1982 his company, Mag Instrument, employed 850 people and his Maglite range was distributed worldwide. The original form and ideals of the Maglite remain unchanged, whether the torch is miniaturized to be carried on a key-ring or uses the trademarked Rechargeable Flashlight System.

807

Maglite (1979)
Anthony Maglica (1930–)
Mag Instrument 1979 to present

MAGLITE®
FLASHLIGHTS

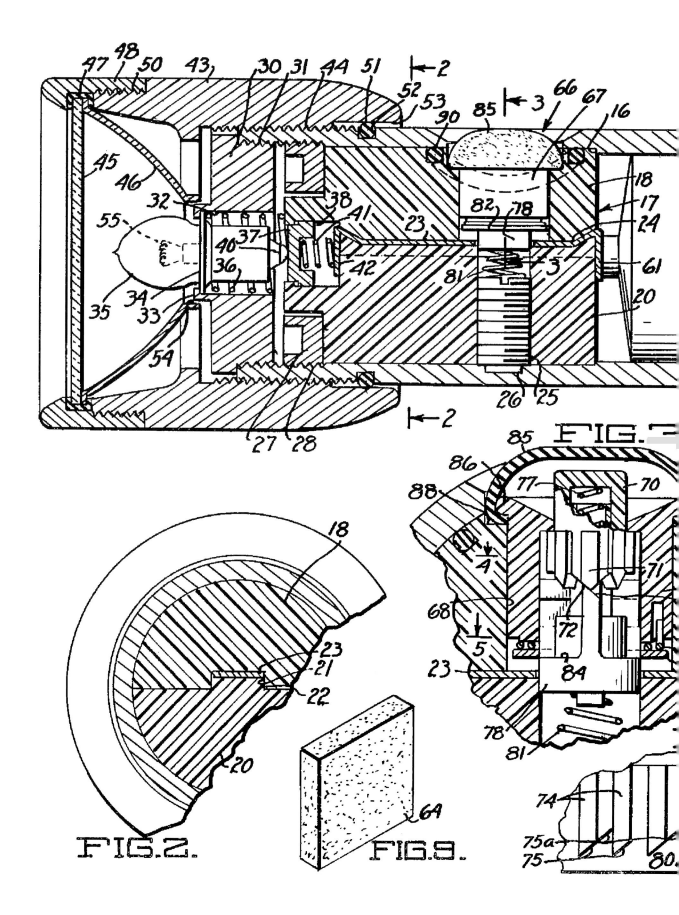

FIG.3.

FIG.2.

FIG.9.

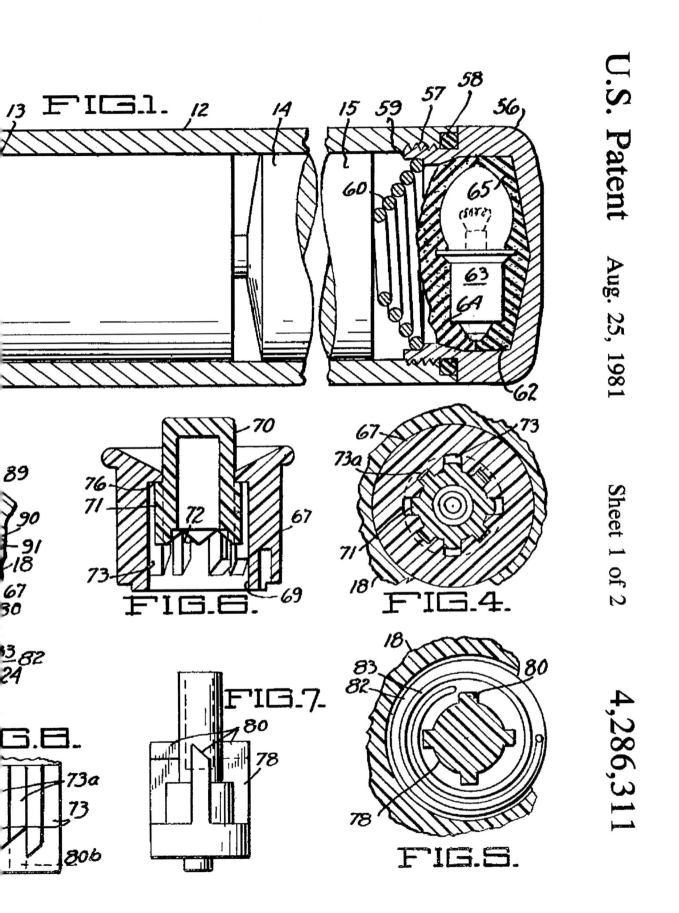

FIG.1.

FIG.6.

FIG.4.

FIG.7.

FIG.8.

FIG.5.

Boston Shaker (1979)
Ettore Sottsass (1917–)
Alessi 1979 to present

The Boston Shaker, part of the Boston Cocktail Set, represents Ettore Sottsass's deeply rooted belief that his products should be instruments to enhance the experience of the user, rather than being purely functional. The set, which takes its name from a traditional American Boston cocktail shaker, comprises a wine cooler, stand, ice bucket, ice tongs, shaker, strainer and stirrer. The design comes from an in-depth investigation into professional tools for bars and for wines, which was carried out in the late 1970s by Sottsass along with Alberto Gozzi of the Scuola Alberghiera, Italy's famous training school for the hotel trade. The Shaker itself is composed of polished stainless steel and thick glass, adding a sense of decadence to the business of shaking, stirring, muddling and mixing, and takes its cue from the perfect cocktails prepared with such expertise by debonair actors such as David Niven in movies of the 1950s. Sottsass, born in 1917, studied at the Turin Politecnico before setting up his studio in 1960 in Milan. He held the position of design consultant with Olivetti from 1958 to 1980. There he revolutionized the company's design approach, adding a subversive edge to the modern typewriter that delighted Olivetti and the public alike. His work there also attracted the attentions of the Alessi family, who invited him to their Crusinallo base, and in 1972 he began designing for the quirky accessories giant. Sottsass continued to produce simple yet sophisticated products for Alessi over a number of years, designing the classic crystal glass condiment set and the best-selling Nuovo Milano cutlery range, as well as overhauling Alessi's corporate identity. Sottsass's philosophy was influenced by his travels in 1961 to India, where he discovered existentialism, as well as time spent in California mixing with the Beat generation. He had a strong desire to get away from the perfect form, to rediscover fun and create surprise and improvisation between the user and the environment, whether in large-scale architectural schemes or small-scale tableware and cutlery.

Balans Variable Stool (1979)
Peter Opsvik (1939–)
Stokke 1979 to present

The Balans range was a new type of office seating, designed following revolutionary ergonomic principles. First developed in Norway in the 1970s by the Balans group, which included Hans Christian Mengshoel, Oddvin Rykkens, Peter Opsvik and Svein Gusrud, and introduced at the Copenhagen Furniture Fair of 1979, the Balans line now encompasses twenty-five different models covering a wide range of seating types, from office chairs to upholstered living-room chairs, rocking chairs to folding stools. The Balans Variable Stool is perhaps the best known and certainly most recognizable of the Balans range. It was one of the first models, designed by Peter Opsvik, and demonstrates clearly how the Balans range overturned accepted principles about how a chair is used and what it should look like. It is perhaps the only valid redesign of the archetypal chair, a fact that fits neatly with Opsvik's own principles of sustainable design: 'When a planet is overwhelmed by products and users for an endless number of articles, it can appear a paradox to develop new products. Nevertheless, I am convinced that products will enjoy a longer existence where devotion, far-sightedness and thoughtfulness contribute to their development, than those governed by fashion and trends.' It is only in the last thirty years or so that people have been required to sit at an office desk for hours on end, often with detrimental effects on the lower back and spine. Designers responded by struggling to find a perfect sitting position. However, they soon found that any position became uncomfortable after a certain period of time. Balans solved the problem by not searching for one position, but by allowing the sitter to assume as many positions as possible. It was this idea of introducing movement that was key to the Balans series. The Balans Variable Stool encourages movement by a shift in the angle of the seat and the introduction of knee supports and rockers. These improve the posture of the back by shifting the user's weight forwards and changing the angle between the hips and legs, allowing the knees to support the body and the back muscles to soften and relieve tension, as well as allowing the sitter to adopt a number of different positions.

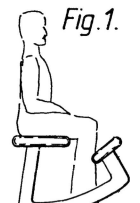

Fig.1.

Fig.2.

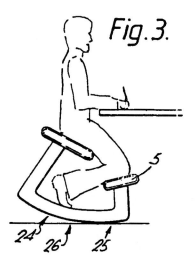

Fig.3.

Fig.4.

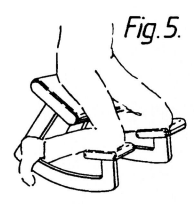

Fig.5.

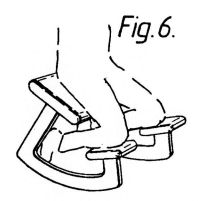

Fig.6.

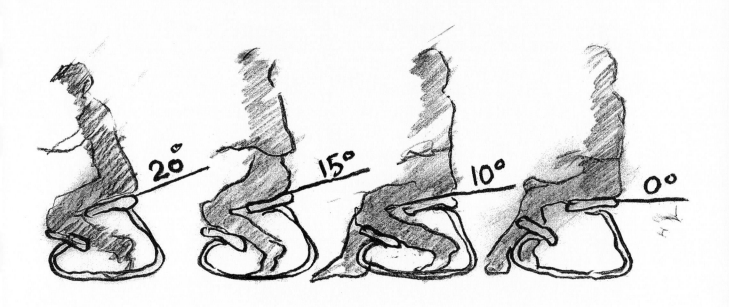

ABSOLUT HELSINKI.

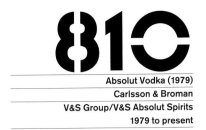

Absolut Vodka (1979)
Carlsson & Broman
V&S Group/V&S Absolut Spirits
1979 to present

Following a brilliant approach in the design and marketing campaign, the launch of Absolut Vodka in America in 1979 was a huge success and that year alone 100,000 bottles were sold. Within a few years Absolut had already become a modern icon, perhaps benefiting from the political climate at the time and the fact that the vodka had no Russian connections. Lars Olsson Smith produced 'Absolut Rent Bränvin' ('Absolutely Pure Vodka') by means of a new distilling process he had invented in 1879, called continuous distillation. A century later Absolut was reintroduced and labelled as a product coming from one factory, well and wheat field. The bottle was designed by a Swedish team led by Gunnar Broman and Lars Börje Carlsson, who found inspiration in a traditional medicine bottle they had discovered in an antique store in Stockholm. Carlsson & Broman agency came up with a simple bottle which did not look like a spirit bottle because of its rather short neck and minimalist metal screwtop. Originally vodka was sold as a medicine against colic and the plague and, therefore, the notion of a medicine bottle was not inappropriate, persuading the company to use a glassworks which had produced medicine bottles since the 1730s. Instead of using a paper label, the design team decided to abandon the idea of a label entirely, saying it would only distract from the purity of the product. They announced Absolut's purity by writing the name directly on the bottle, and thus the bottle itself became the advertisement. The print advertisements have now become famous in themselves, and all use the bottle as their point of focus. In the first advertisement the bottle appeared as a haloed saint, creating a visual pun or interplay between the bottle and the purity of the drink, and the idea of the pun or referencing famous signage in popular culture has been the model for the company's endorsements ever since. More than 1,000 advertisements have since been published, and have included collaborations with such celebrity artists and designers as Keith Haring, Jean-Paul Gaultier, Julian Schnabel and Andy Warhol. In 2002 *Forbes Magazine* ranked Absolut the world's number one luxury brand, and in 2004 the company celebrated the manufacture of its one-billionth bottle.

Lars Olsson Smith

The Walkman, launched in 1979, was readily accepted and – with nearly 50 million sales worldwide – it transcended markets and cultural influences because of its portability. Its case, just slightly larger than a cassette, has undergone several superficial changes, though as a cultural and design icon, the concept of the Walkman marks a turning-point in postwar industrial design. Akio Morita, the Sony chairman, understood the need for the consumer to enjoy music in any situation or environment, whether travelling or during activity. It was to be a personalized accessory that remained true to Sony's quest for small-size, functional designs. The Walkman did not deny the overview of design and the Walkman uses a style between the influence of the German design studio, Braun, and Japanese minimalism. Technically the Walkman was the world's smallest cassette player and provided a high quality of sound. The design offered the user a new level of freedom and soon became a highly successful fashion accessory, as worn by Kevin Bacon in the eighties hit movie, *Footloose* (1984). It was originally aimed at the youth market, with a 'blue jean' metallic colour, and the dual headphone jacks were named 'guys' and 'dolls', which were soon changed to port 'A' and 'B'. The

Walkman followed in the footsteps of the earlier Pressman recorder, now transformed into an audio player by removing the recording circuit, speaker and microphone, which were replaced by stereo amplifier and miniature headphones. Sony was formed in 1946 and quickly established market stature through the combination of advanced technology, marketing and an astute understanding of consumer needs. Their success highlighted the consumer demand for a personalized and flexible supply of music and voice and led the way for further developments, including the Walkman and the Watchman. Originally inspired by American ideas, the company matured to create a Product Planning Centre that adopted an understanding for lifestyle marketing and an approach that blended technology of product with rationality and modernity. The Walkman marks an important moment in the cross-fertilization of a successful industrial design product with the demands of popular culture. The design of the Walkman led to over forty-three designs and variations, each becoming smaller, slimmer – attempting to acquire the same dimensions as the audio cassette held inside.

Kevin Bacon in *Footloose* (1984), directed by Herbert Ross

811
Headphone Stereo Walkman, TPS-L2 (1979)
Sony Design Team
Sony, production years vary by country

The music
is on his side.

'Buy Post-it Notes' is most likely to be scribbled on a piece of paper that has a strip of low-tack glue on the back and is stuck somewhere that was not designed to be used as a notice-board in the first place. Originally thought of as a hymn bookmark, the Post-it has acquired mythical status in innovation history. This is echoed by the numerous creation stories attributed to its moment of eureka. It is, however, a story of two scientist-inventors, their persistence and the innovation culture of the company they worked for. It took some five years of internal company use for the versatile 3M company to release the now unmistakable, unavoidable, unbelievably useful, not-so-sticky, canary-yellow notes in 1980. In 1968 Dr Spencer Silver was working on improving tape adhesives. He formulated an adhesive that was strong enough to stick on to surfaces, but left no residue after removal. The first attempts at finding the right application included notice-board surfaces and spray-on cans. The fitting application, 'the product niche', was discovered by Art Fry, then a new-product development researcher. He had the idea of using scrap-paper bookmarks for what was to become the world-recognized Post-it Notes. However, the note was in direct competition with cost-free scrap paper, which made for difficult arguments about investment in the project. In 1977 test markets failed to show consumer interest. Fry and the supportive products development manager, Geoff Nicholson, didn't give up. Through intensive internal company promotion and a massive consumer sampling strategy in 1980 the Post-it took off and made its way, in viral-like acceptance, into offices and homes alike. The presence of the yellow Post-it Note has since migrated to the screen-based digital world, not just as a dedicated notes programme but even as far as the language used for attaching notes. The wide range of applications and the cultural significance the Post-it has propagated since its introduction is a testament not only to the clarity and brilliance of the invention and its design but also to the power of simple tools which respond to human behaviour.

812

Post-it ® Notes (1980)
Spencer Silver (1941–)
Art Fry (1931–)
3M 1980 to present

With its black outlines, garish primary colours, wobbly leg and slipping ring, the Dúplex stool looks as if it belongs in a cartoon rather than a designer drinking establishment. So perhaps it is not surprising that during the 1970s its creator, Barcelona-based Javier Mariscal, was best known as a graphic designer and underground comic-strip illustrator. In its combination of standard and stable with sketchy and unconventional, Mariscal's design, which is one of his first attempts at creating furniture, is reminiscent of an archetypal cartoon drunk, as though trying to pull on a dignified mask over a colourful, intoxicated interior. Part of a design project for the Dúplex Bar in Valencia, in collaboration with the interior designer and bullfighter Fernando Salas, the stool charts the beginnings of a switch from function to expression as the guiding principle of design. Indeed, Mariscal's palette of black, white and primary colours, combined with the Dúplex's linear geometry, makes the stool seem like a three-dimensional descendant of Piet Mondrian's De Stijl paintings, fused with various aspects of Pop and Op Art. It mixes styles and disciplines, and design with art, and can be brought under the general umbrella of Postmodernism, but more importantly it stands as an 'anti-design' object, a counterpoint to De Stijl-style purity of design. Consequently, the Dúplex stool announced a new style that would characterize Barcelona's renaissance as a centre for design during the 1980s, which culminated in Mariscal's creation of Cobi, the mascot for the 1992 Barcelona Olympics.

813

Dúplex (1980)

Javier Mariscal (1950–)

BD Ediciones de Diseño 1980 to 2003

81-4

Praxis 35 (1980)
Mario Bellini (1935–)
Olivetti 1981 to 1988

Building on its well-earned reputation in the development of portable typewriters, electric portables and communication technology, Olivetti launched the first portable electronic typewriter in 1981. In common with all Olivetti's products, the Praxis 35 was not only technologically advanced, it also bore the trademark looks and elegance of an holistically designed object. By 1981 Bellini had already worked on countless projects with Olivetti (he first collaborated with the company in 1963), including the iconic rubber-membrane-interfaced Divisumma18 and the wedge-shaped Logos 68 printing calculators in1973. The Praxis 35 (along with the 30, 40 and 45) incorporated a 'daisy-wheel' print head, which was not only very light, but also meant that users had an extensive range of typefaces from which to choose. Its clean and sober lines reflected an era in Olivetti's history when corporate design was increasingly recognized as a desirable feature. Indeed, the aesthetic language was easily identifiable in contemporary products by designers such as Ettore Sottsass and George Sowden. This contributed to a recognizable Olivetti 'shape' that was widely imitated by competing typewriter manufacturers. Ergonomic factors also played a big part in the design process at Olivetti during this time. A great deal was invested in research in this area, with studies being published that treated the many elements of office equipment as a system that could be developed for optimum comfort and efficiency. This is reflected in the Praxis 35 in the 13-degree-inclined keyboard surface and wrist support, as well as in the clear graphics and flaps to protect particular switches. Known for its innovative graphics and advertising campaigns, Olivetti employed some of the most celebrated designers of the era in order to show its products in the best light. The Praxis 35 was no exception, featuring in advertising posters by Milton Glaser, and even forming the basis of a fourteen-page article in Vogue that sang the machine's praises from a design point of view, declaring 'Praxis makes Perfect.'

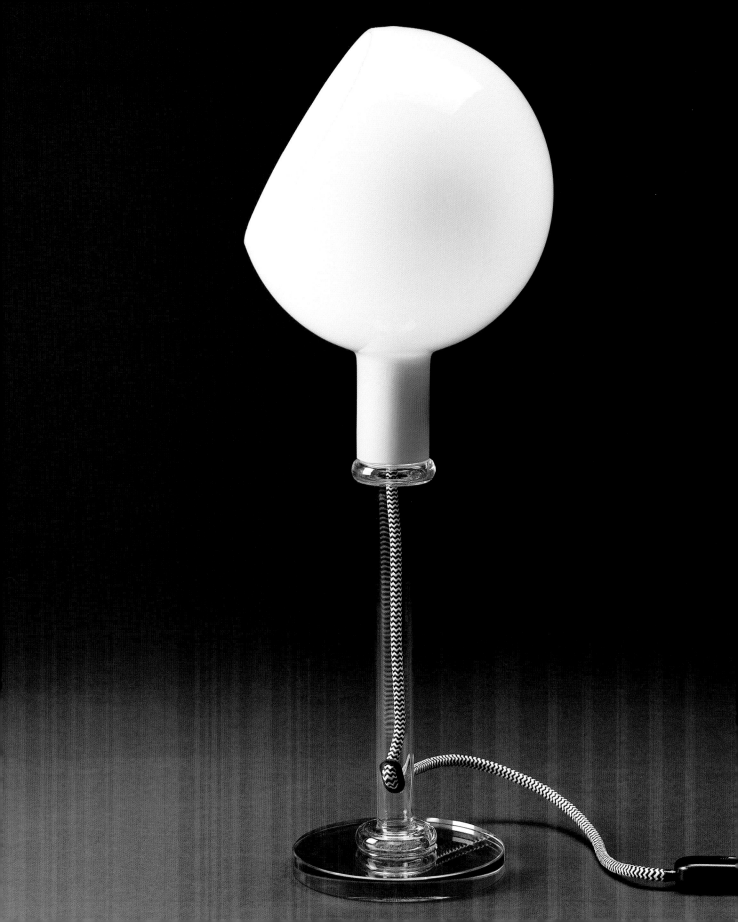

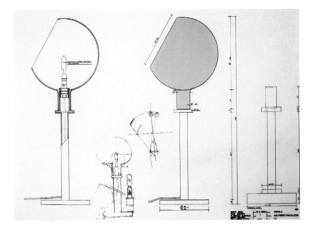

The Parola lamp is a halogen standard lamp, comprising an opaline glass shade on a glass stem and base. It is also available in wall-mounted and table versions. It was designed by Gae Aulenti in conjunction with Piero Castiglioni for the Milanese glass manufacturer FontanaArte. Aulenti is an architect best known for her museum buildings, exhibition installations and interiors. In 1979 Aulenti was appointed artistic director for FontanaArte, a post she held until 1996. She appointed a team of designers to run the main areas of design activity, including Piero Castiglioni (son of Livio), in charge of lighting. Aulenti's aim was to build upon the tradition, continuity and identity of the company, revisiting its roots as a producer of high-quality glass furnishings since the 1930s, when it was founded as a branch of the Fontana company by Gio Ponti. She also aimed to develop products that made full use of all the glass processes at the company's disposal, including blown, cast and industrially produced plate glass, and to demonstrate craftsmanship combined with the latest manufacturing processes. The Parola lamp, one of the first products produced under her directorship, exemplifies this approach. It is made from three elements, each demonstrating a different glass process. The shade is a glass sphere with a slice removed, imitating a partial eclipse, made from blown opaline glass. The stem, through which the electrical cable is visible, is of clear glass, and the bevelled base is made from ground natural crystal. The 'eyeball' shade harks back to a form popular in the 1960s, and Aulenti herself had used a similar form for an earlier design. The Parola lamp is a good example of the classical yet modern approach for which Aulenti is renowned. Rendered in palely coloured glass, the lamp becomes a luxury rather than a utilitarian object, at home in both traditional and modern interiors. Aulenti described her attitude to lighting design as follows: 'I never thought of lamps in terms of technical lighting or like a machine for making light, but like forms in a harmonious relationship with the context for which they are created.'

Japanese designer Toshiyuki Kita designed the Wink chair to be lower than the average lounge chair and to accommodate a more reclined sitting posture, and was the first item that brought Kita international recognition. At the time, Wink aimed to reflect both the more relaxed attitude of a younger generation as well as traditional Japanese sitting habits. Design-wise it is an achievement in comfortable, flexible and adaptable seating thanks to side knobs at the base, which allow the chair to be transformed from an upright to a lounger. The two-part headrest can also move backwards or forwards into a 'winking' position for more support. Aesthetically,

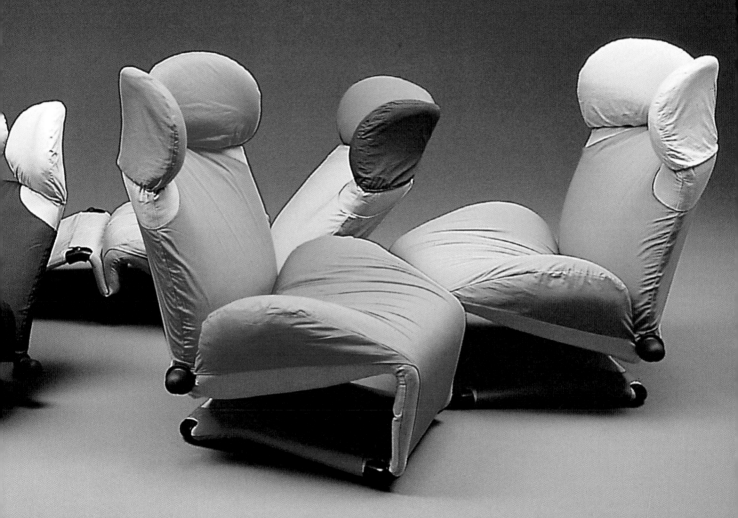

the Wink chair has a humorous, cartoonish appearance, typical of many 1980s furniture pieces. Its panda-like, folding 'ears' and the pop colours of its zips led to its nickname 'Mickey Mouse', yet these features are not solely stylistic: the zips were added so the upholstery could be removed and washed. A designer with roots in both European and Japanese culture, Toshiyuki Kita always straddled two worlds. After studying architecture at the University of Osaka, Toshiyuki Kita went to Milan to work in the offices of Mario Bellini and Silvio Coppola, opening his own studio in 1971. Since then Kita has designed for manufacturers such as De Padova,

Moroso, Tecnolumen, Cassina and Sharp. In keeping with his interest in cartoon-like images, he has also designed for Kreon, creating light fixtures with the New York graffiti artist Keith Haring. Toshiyuki Kita has never associated himself with a particular school or movement, and instead chooses to develop a wholly individual style full of wit and technological competence, which is well summarized in his Wink chair. In 1981 the Wink chair was selected for the permanent collection in The Museum of Modern Art in New York.

The Fiat Panda, produced until 2003, was launched as a utility vehicle, but also as an everyday car, and its legacy has outlasted its style. Giorgetto Giugiaro, the designer, initially studied art, and decided instead to go into technical design. At a mere seventeen years of age he was offered a job at the Fiat styling centre in 1959. Giugiaro began creating cars with sharp edges and straight lines, known as the 'folded paper school of design', and was behind the design of a number of Lamborghinis and Ferraris. The Panda is a testament to this particular style, with its box-like shape and large, square-shaped headlights, finished with five chromed lines diagonally gracing the front of the grille. The Panda came out of the generation of cars created by the 'Robogate' system, which was a robotized production line that assembled the bodywork. The engine and transmission of the Fiat 127 were the source of inspiration for the Panda and, while the design of the Panda may have been revolutionary, its mechanics were not, although its silent suspension made for a smoother ride. Many features contributed to the Panda's utility-car role: the rear seat could be folded flat to make a bed, folded up to act as a bottle carrier, or removed altogether to increase the load space. The front seats had removable, washable covers. The fabric-covered dashboard could also be removed, and the Panda could be specified with a full-length, roll-back canvas roof. A victim of tightening safety legislation, the Panda started to be phased out across Europe from 1996, and production halted seven years later. The Panda was recently revisited by Stefano Giovannoni, known for his work with the Italian manufacturer Alessi. By joining forces, Alessi and Fiat decided to bring back the Panda spirit, and created a two-tone car, with a polypropylene white band running around the lower section, while the upper part is black, recalling the actual animal. But gone is the old feel for utility, replaced with new facia, door mouldings, front radiator grille and upholstery. Although the concept of the car has been recreated, the original Fiat Panda established the trend for a car that was affordable, reliable and could move easily between smooth city roads and rough country lanes.

Panda

Nuovo restyling del frontale con barrette cromate inclinate e proiettori rettangolari di grande formato.

Sedili con nuove imbottiture e rivestimento in morbido tessuto.

Marsupio portaoggetti sottoplancia rivestito con il nuovo tessuto dei sedili.

Pannelli porte rivestiti di tessuto e dotati di tasca rigida.

Padiglione rivestito con un pannello preformato.

Posacenere incassati nei fianchetti laterali posteriori.

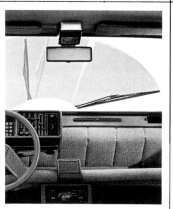

Tergicristallo a due velocità: la prima è ad intermittenza (su Panda 45 Super).

Elettroventilatore a due velocità e ideogrammi dei comandi illumina (su Panda 45 Super).

Nuova coppa coprimozzo a profilo aerodinamico (su Panda 45 Super).

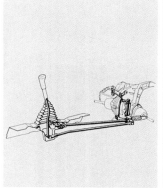

Nuovo comando del cambio con sistema a doppio leveraggio (su Panda 45 Super).

Sospensione posteriore con nuove balestre monolama: più confort e silenziosità di marcia.

Tetto apribile di tipo sdoppiato (optional).

Nuove Panda Super

L'auto in libertà

Funzionalità senza rinunce

nchetti posteriori rivestiti.	Cristalli posteriori laterali con apertura a compasso.	Bagagliaio con rivestimento isolante.	Aletta parasole destra con specchietto di cortesia.
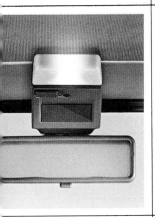			
cchio retrovisore interno con zione anabbagliante e sede per logio digitale (optional su Panda Super).	Specchio retrovisore esterno regolabile dall'interno (su Panda 45 Super).	Accendisigari (su Panda 45 Super).	Lunotto termico con lavatergilunotto. Di serie su Panda 45 Super, optional su Panda 30 Super.

nture di sicurezza con arrotolatore ptional).	Orologio digitale sopra lo specchio retrovisore interno (optional su Panda 45 Super).	Cambio a 5 marce (optional su Panda 45 Super).	Ruote in lega con pneumatici maggiorati (optional su Panda 45 Super).

a ricchezza dell'allestimento

i optional qualificanti

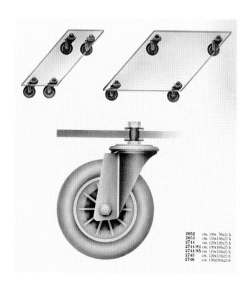

2652   cm. 140x.70x25 h
2653   cm. 150x150x25 h
2744   cm. 120x120x25 h
2744/S4 cm. 100x100x25 h
2744/S5 cm. 110x110x25 h
2745   cm. 130x110x25 h
2746   cm. 150x100x25 h

There are virtually no design elements to this table, yet it speaks eloquently of advanced design sensibilities in the late 1970s and early 1980s. Gae Aulenti's table comprises four outsize rubber-tyred wheels that raise a sheet of glass only a few centimetres above the floor. It is minimal yet expresses durability: the wheels would normally be found on industrial machinery rather than in the living-room. There is also a degree of humour in the juxtaposition of these heavy-duty components with a mere sheet of glass, and the inappropriateness of their appearance in the home. With this light touch Aulenti succeeded in humanizing the sterility of Modernism. Yet she has not turned to craft traditions and the marks of hand production to achieve this, as other designers might. Her humanity derives from a thorough and disciplined control of the language of engineered components at her disposal. The enduring success of this design derives from its simplicity. It is a visual embodiment of Mies van der Rohe's dictum that 'less is more' and is a perfect expression of the Modernist belief in industrial materials, honestly employed. The absence of elements that could be said to add style contributes to the timelessness of the design. More specifically, the design should be regarded in the context of the High-Tech movement in architecture that celebrated industrial materials and components and found perfect expression in the Pompidou Centre in Paris by Rogers and Piano, completed in 1977. In 1980, the year she designed this table, Aulenti was also working on projects at the Pompidou Centre and, more famously, on the interiors of another Parisian gallery, the Musée d'Orsay, for which she is perhaps best known. The table is manufactured by the Italian firm FontanaArte. Among Aulenti's other clients are Olivetti and Knoll, for whom she has designed furniture, lighting and interiors. In the late 1990s, with Piero Castiglioni, Aulenti designed lighting for iGuzzini. She is one of very few female Italian designers of her generation to have enjoyed international recognition.

818

Tavolo con ruote (1980)
Gae Aulenti (1927–)
FontanaArte 1980 to present

Best known for their wry re-appropriation of industrial components to create such instantly recognizable products as the Mezzadro stool, the Castiglioni brothers were also masters of observing and solving the minute, mundane problems presented by everyday objects. And so it was that when Achille was asked by manufacturer Cleto Munari to contribute a design for a collection of silverware for everyday use, he began by undertaking rigorous analysis of his chosen subject, the oil and vinegar cruet. The result, christened 'Acetoliere' and produced initially in limited numbers by Rossi & Arcanti (in silver plate and crystal) and today by Alessi, is unmatched in its functionality, its 'Tin Man' features displaying the delightful character with which Castiglioni regularly imbued his work. Acetoliere's improvements upon a standard oil and vinegar cruet are manifold. The oil dispenser is larger than the vinegar because it is usual for more oil to be used. The hinged lids, their flat surface broken up with a shape reminiscent of a cat's head, are counterbalanced with weights that allude to saxophone keys and rock gently open as pouring begins. The handles are clasped at the top, and each vessel is balanced like a pendulum and will not tip without positive movement. There is no protruding spout; instead, a lip that is bent inwards catches the drips. Castiglioni added a tray and salt cellar to the silver-plated stainless steel and glass set for Alessi's production of the set. A beautiful piece in its own right, the salt cellar dispenses with the common but awkward bung in the base in favour of a pressed-steel stopper in the top containing the shaking holes and a central pin allowing it to be pulled out. The sheer number of highly detailed components means the set is expensive to produce, but the attention paid to each and every element has ensured that its use is a continual pleasure.

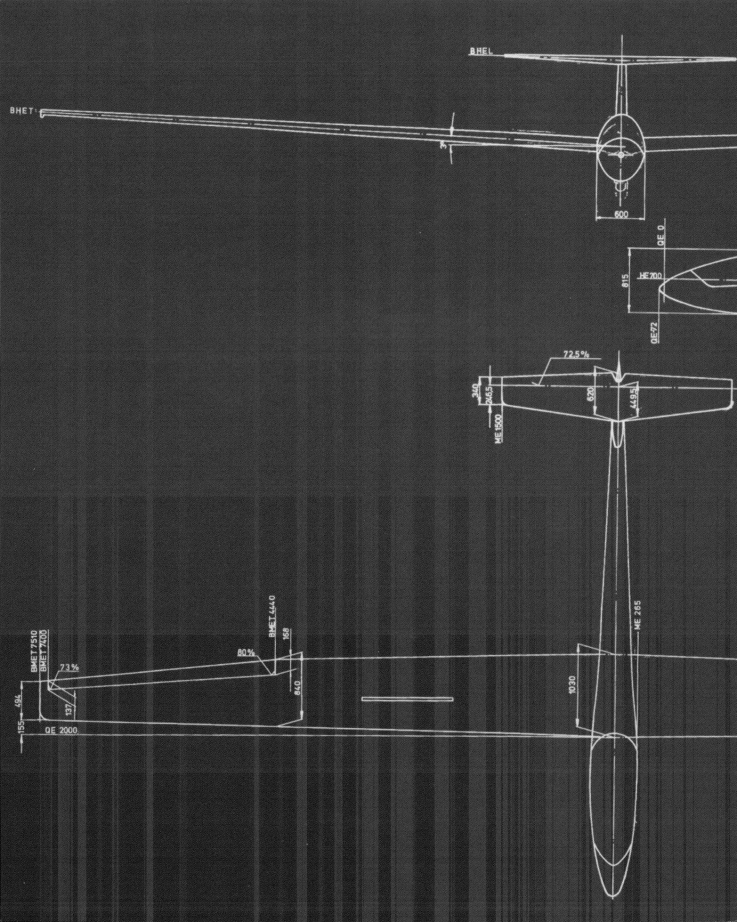

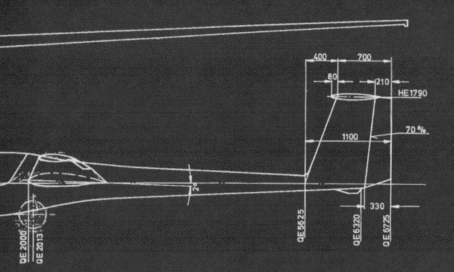

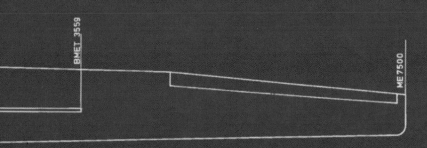

Flying in a glider is considered to be the closest we can come to flight at its most natural and exhilarating. With a light fibreglass body, weighing in at only 255 kg (102 lb), and a comparatively enormous 15 m (49 ft 2 in) wingspan, the Grob 102 Standard Astir III was designed to become, and to stay, airborne as easily as possible. Like most sailplanes, the Grob 102 has no engine and needs motor-powered assistance before it can fly. One method is simply to use another plane to transport the glider into the skies and then release it at high altitude. Another is to attach a drum cable to the undercarriage of the glider, securing the other end of the cable to a stationary vehicle. When the cable is reeled in, the glider moves forwards and once it has reached above its stalling speed it lifts up into the air. Still attached, it climbs to a high enough altitude for flight before it is finally released. German company Grob-Werke opened its aerospace division in 1971 and from 1974 the company used purpose-built airfields for its research and development. The Grob 102 Standard Astir III was one of the results of its labours. This glider was specifically designed to be easy to handle in the air and, being relatively inexpensive, it was soon popular with glider and flying clubs. The generous size and good visibility of the single seat cockpit and its maximum speed of 250 kph (155 mph) also made it a favourite. This delicate-looking craft, with its capsule-like cockpit and elegant wings, was also used in a daring feat to break the world record for sailplane altitude. Robert Harris first flew a glider in 1978 and this one experience was enough to make him determined to break the existing altitude record of 14,236 m (46,267 ft) attained by Paul Bickle on 21 February 1961. Conditions had to be perfect and after years of preparation, in 1986, Harris was towed into the air in a Grob 102. With favourable lifts and great skill, he managed to reach 15,077 m (49,000 ft) above the Sierra Nevada Mountains before being forced to return to earth, thus setting a record that is still unbroken.

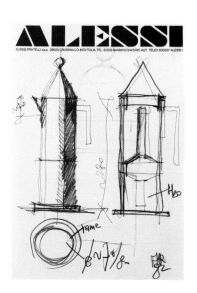

La Conica was the result of La Taviola di Babele (Tea and Coffee Piazza), a project formed between Alessi and Alessandro Mendini in 1983. Mendini and ten other architects, Aldo Rossi amongst them, were invited to reinterpret domestic objects that were emblematic of the home, and this collection was documented, providing valuable research for Alessi. Rossi approached the design of household products as architecture in miniature, which is clearly reflected in his design for the La Conica coffee maker. He was fascinated by the geometric simplification of basic architectural forms, with the cone being a recurrent theme in Rossi's work. In response to the brief, Rossi embarked on a programme of rigorous research into the making and serving of coffee, a subject that was to become something of an obsession for him, and one which he saw as perfectly symbolizing the dialectic relationship between architectural townscapes and the 'household landscape' into which his miniature monument would fit. The coffee maker was to become something of a motif in Rossi's architectural drawings, appearing as buildings in the urban panorama. The set was Rossi's first mass-produced design, and came under the 'Officina Alessi' trademark, a range of innovative and experimental products designed by selected architects and designers as a counterpart to Alessi's range of stainless-steel products. The Officina Alessi products catapulted Alessi to the centre of a fierce debate on Postmodernism, although Rossi himself refused to accept the Postmodernist label. The timeless quality of La Conica is a testament to his stance. In all his work Rossi eschewed fashionable and popular styles in favour of a more universal style, encompassing historical and cultural influences without labouring the point. The designs resulting from the Babele project were produced in silver, with only ninety-nine copies manufactured for each design. But La Conica, the first product of the Officina Alessi brand, has now become symbolic of 1980s design, with far more than ninety-nine copies being produced and sold.

821

La Conica Coffee Maker (1980–3)
Aldo Rossi (1931–97)
Alessi 1984 to present

Ettore Sottsass was by the 1970s a leading figure among Italy's design vanguard, successfully establishing a new design language for, most notably, Olivetti. In 1980 Sottsass founded Sottsass Associati with Marco Zanini, Matteo Thun and Aldo Cibic. In 1981 he joined forces with Cibic and Zanini, along with Michele de Lucchi, George Sowden and Nathalie du Pasquier, to form the Memphis Group, exhibiting at that year's Salone del Mobile in Milan. The response to their first collection of furniture was outstanding. Among the works in that collection were pieces that came to exemplify the postmodern spirit. Some were more enduring than others. Among the most articulate of these pieces was the Sottsass-designed Callimaco lamp, ostensibly a 500-watt halogen floor lamp with an integral dimmer. The intense white light, which emanated from the small cone at the top of the 1.8 m (6 ft) brightly coloured lacquered aluminium base, enlivened the object, which otherwise was mute about its purpose. With a wide green cone at its base, attached to a yellow tubular stem and a significantly smaller red cone at its top, Callimaco defies the convention of standing a lamp next to a sofa or a chair to illuminate reading. At 500 watts, the light it produces is too bright to be observed directly and the use of halogen lights in a domestic setting and the opaque torchère were relatively new phenomena. Consequently, with a handle attached to the central tube, a signature Sottsass detail, it enters into the postmodern dialogue between past and present. And although it makes visual references to megaphones, Callimaco confounds expectations by the fact that it conveys not sound, but light, intensely radiating from its mouthpiece-like canopy. In the context of a myriad postmodern flights of fantasy, Callimaco is a provocation and an authoritative standard bearer of Memphis.

The Commodore C64 is widely credited with having taken the computer out of the world of gadget-lovers and into the public domain. It is still the best-selling computer in history, with approximately 30 million having been sold between its launch in 1982 and 1992, when the last Commodore 64 was pushed off the assembly line, shortly followed by Commodore's bankruptcy in 1994. Without the advent of the Commodore Design Team (including Al Charpentier, Robert Yannes, Charles Winterable, David Ziembeicki and Bruce Crockette), today's games consoles, such as the X-Box or the Nintendo Game Cube, might not exist. Based on Commodore's existing VIC-20, the C64 was an easy-to-use, programmable computer contained within a lap-sized grey plastic slab that plugged into a television and brought the world of video arcades into the home. Needless to say, its success was more to do with what was inside the casing than the casing itself. In part this is due to the fact that the C64 was designed with low cost as the primary concern. 'For $595, you get what nobody else can give you for twice the price', ran one Commodore marketing slogan. It was packaged and sold (by retailers like Toys 'R' Us and K-Mart) like toasters or any other domestic appliance. Indeed, in Germany, the C64 was often referred to as 'the breadbox' as a result of its utilitarian design and the fact that jamming a cartridge into the back of it was like stuffing sliced bread into a toaster. Despite the emergence of the faster Commodore 128 in 1985 (and the company's attempts to shut down production of the C64 in order to promote the newer computer), the C64 remained most people's computer of choice. Commodore produced many variations on the original C64, including a Golden Jubilee version issued to commemorate one million sales that was provided with a gold casing. Such was the ubiquity of the C64 that there are many who believe that it is partly responsible for the development, during the 1980s, of free- and shareware.

When the Sinclair ZX81, one of the first 'plug and play' computers, was launched in the UK in 1981, it caused a revolution in the home computer market, largely because it was both affordable and accessible. Sir Clive Sinclair, the designer of the ZX81, had founded his ground-breaking electronics company Sinclair Radionics in 1961 and had already brought the world its first pocket calculator, digital wristwatch and pocket TV, and had gained a considerable reputation for innovation. The ZX81 was launched as the first mass-market computer; it was aimed directly at the home user rather than the professional or computer specialist. It had a wedge-shaped casing measuring 167 x 175 x 40 cm (65 x 69 x 16 in), a touch-sensitive keyboard, used the Sinclair BASIC program and came in two versions: either as a self-assembly kit or as a ready-assembled machine, needing only connection to a television set and power supply to be fully functional. The ZX81's streamlined profile in black ABS plastic was light-years ahead of other home computer models and it was also unexpectedly cheaper, retailing at an exceptional £50 in kit form and £70 for a ready-built model. The ZX81 was the first affordable home computer model to make an impact on the high street. In 1981 few shops in the UK sold computer equipment but, in a bid to reinvigorate its image, the British newsagent chain W H Smith agreed to stock the ZX81 in its stores. The response was extraordinary, and by February 1982 Sinclair Research was making over 40,000 ZX81 models a month to keep up with demand. Within only two years of release the ZX81 had sold over a million units. Although primitive by today's standards - with only 1K memory, no colour and no sound - the ZX81 had tapped into the previously unexplored home computing market, and kick-started a trend that continues its phenomenal growth today.

82-4

Sinclair ZX81 (1981)
Sir Clive Sinclair (1940–)
Sinclair Radionics 1981 to 1986
Sinclair Radionics/Amstrad 1986 to c.1993

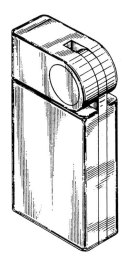

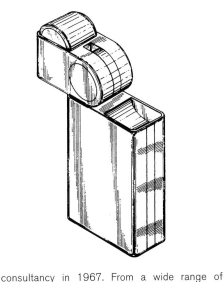

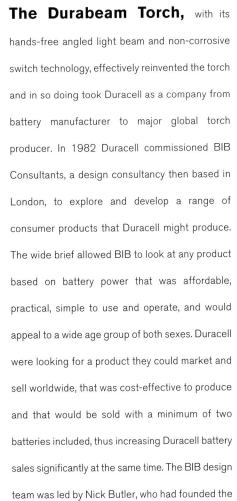

The Durabeam Torch, with its hands-free angled light beam and non-corrosive switch technology, effectively reinvented the torch and in so doing took Duracell as a company from battery manufacturer to major global torch producer. In 1982 Duracell commissioned BIB Consultants, a design consultancy then based in London, to explore and develop a range of consumer products that Duracell might produce. The wide brief allowed BIB to look at any product based on battery power that was affordable, practical, simple to use and operate, and would appeal to a wide age group of both sexes. Duracell were looking for a product they could market and sell worldwide, that was cost-effective to produce and that would be sold with a minimum of two batteries included, thus increasing Duracell battery sales significantly at the same time. The BIB design team was led by Nick Butler, who had founded the consultancy in 1967. From a wide range of suggestions put forward at the concept stage, the idea of a range of functionally unique and attractive torches rapidly gained favour, particularly when the existing problems associated with using torches were explored. Research showed that torches were used infrequently and because they were left unused for long periods of time the switch contacts corroded. The BIB solution here was to switch the torch on by opening the beam head module through the arc of its available travel, thus cleaning and wiping the switch contacts each time the torch was turned on. BIB also solved the question of how to deal with a problem while holding a torch in one hand to illuminate it. The Durabeam light beam was angled so that the torch could be put down and its light projected on to the problem, leaving both hands free to sort out the problem. There are five torches in the range – the Pocket, Standard and Lantern, with the additional Tough and Cycle torches. The uniqueness and simplicity of the Durabeam Torch both in terms of practicality and appearance ensured the continued sales and popularity of the range for the twelve years of its production. Together with the practical aspects of the design, the yellow moulded chassis and black ABS battery covers and head cap have been widely imitated by other torch manufacturers in Europe and the Far East.

#1250　ステンレスカトラリー

テーブルナイフ	¥893	230mm
テーブルフォーク	¥578	183mm
テーブルスプーン	¥578	183mm
フィッシュナイフ	¥735	207mm
フィッシュフォーク	¥525	170mm
スープスプーン	¥578	170mm
デザートナイフ	¥735	210mm
デザートフォーク	¥473	170mm
デザートスプーン	¥473	170mm
ティースプーン	¥368	140mm
ケーキフォーク	¥368	150mm
コーヒースプーン	¥315	118mm
ヒメフォーク	¥315	140mm
フルーツナイフ	¥630	170mm
シュガーレードル	¥420	130mm
バターナイフ	¥525	170mm
サービススプーン	¥1,050	220mm
サービスフォーク	¥1,050	220mm
ソースレードル	¥1,365	165mm
アイスクリームスプーン	¥368	150mm
グレープフルーツスプーン	¥399	160mm
カニフォーク	¥420	183mm
マドラー	¥525	220mm
パスタフォーク	¥714	198mm

#2250　黒柄カトラリー

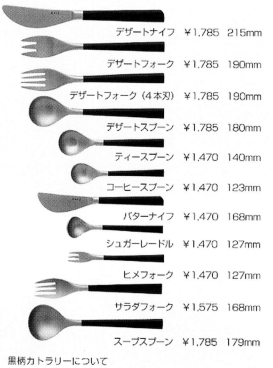

デザートナイフ	¥1,785	215mm
デザートフォーク	¥1,785	190mm
デザートフォーク（4本刃）	¥1,785	190mm
デザートスプーン	¥1,785	180mm
ティースプーン	¥1,470	140mm
コーヒースプーン	¥1,470	123mm
バターナイフ	¥1,470	168mm
シュガーレードル	¥1,470	127mm
ヒメフォーク	¥1,470	127mm
サラダフォーク	¥1,575	168mm
スープスプーン	¥1,785	179mm

黒柄カトラリーについて

　ハンドル部はカバ材積層強化木を使用し柔らかい持ち心地で飽きがきません。若干吸水性があるため水に浸けて放置するとハンドルが緩む原因になります。食器洗浄機では使用しないで下さい。

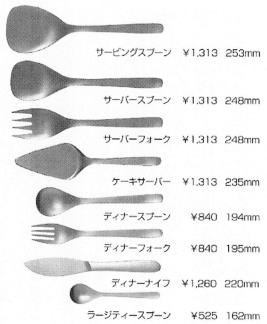

サービングスプーン	¥1,313	253mm
サーバースプーン	¥1,313	248mm
サーバーフォーク	¥1,313	248mm
ケーキサーバー	¥1,313	235mm
ディナースプーン	¥840	194mm
ディナーフォーク	¥840	195mm
ディナーナイフ	¥1,260	220mm
ラージティースプーン	¥525	162mm

The work of Sori Yanagi, pioneering industrial designer, represents a perfect marriage of form, function and aesthetic. Inspired by natural forms, his 18-8 range of stainless steel flatware is produced by Japanese steel distributor Sato-Shoji and seeks to bring practicality, style and a pleasing tactile quality to any dining table. Each setting consists of five elegant and durable pieces of flatware plus four serving utensils. The characteristic organic shapes reflect the designer's preference for 'gentle and rounded forms that radiate human warmth'. Yanagi believes the designer's role is not to repackage old ideas but to take them forward, and to counteract the throw-away habits of thoughtless consumerism. When purity of design is achieved through conscious decisions that flow with the grain of nature, an object as basic as a pitcher becomes almost noble. In his work, Yanagi has always sought to blend functionalist philosophies with traditional Japanese design. Hands-on and workshop-based, Yanagi creates hundreds of prototypes for each design in order to attain a flawless model, before handing over to a team of craftsmen with a natural rapport for materials and their practical application. Yanagi began his career in the architectural office of Junzo Sakakura, where he first met Charlotte Perriand, and became her assistant from 1940 to 1942. In 1952 he opened his own office in Tokyo and soon after became a founding member of the Japan Industrial Designers' Association. As modernization and Westernization overwhelmed post-war Japan, Yanagi promoted design that did not compromise the traditional Japanese environment. As a prime example of this, the 18-8 flatware set has been in continuous production since its first manufacture.

Donald Judd

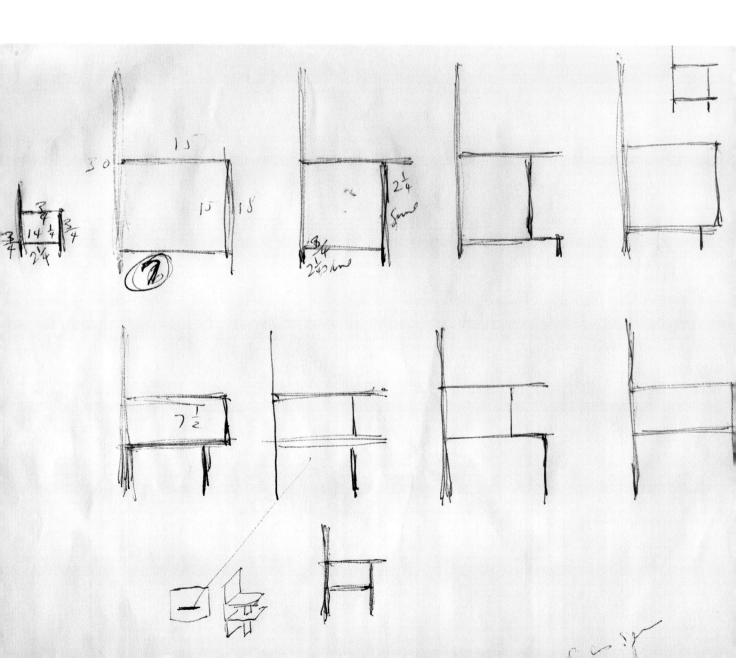

827

Chair (1982)
Donald Judd (1928–1994)
Jim Cooper and Ichiro Kato 1982 to 1990
Celedonio Mediano 1982
Jeff Jamieson and Rupert Deese
1990 to 1994
Jeff Jamieson 1994 to present

In 1993 Donald Judd contributed an essay entitled 'It's hard to find a good light' to the exhibition catalogue accompanying a retrospective of his furniture in Rotterdam in the Netherlands, in which he held steadfast to his lifelong belief that a chair is simply a chair, as art is simply art. Judd insisted that his furniture remain separate from his art, that they never be shown together and that his furniture never be distributed through galleries. Any perception of similarity between his art and his furniture, he declared, should never be understood as intention. This characteristically rigid dogma propelled Judd to the centre of the debate on the nature of art, architecture and design throughout his life. Judd's works of art, his 'specific objects', explored volumes, spaces, materials, colours and forms, and banished narrative absolutely. All meaning existed solely within the physicality and manufacture of each piece. Removing context also meant removing any reliance on the illusion of space. Rather than representing space, his works occupied space, and thus entered actively into a dialogue with the viewer. Moving from his art to his furniture, and to his chairs in particular, we find the same approach. These works of furniture explore the same themes of volume, space and colour, and exist as nothing more than what they are, whether a functioning chair or table. Judd designed his earliest chairs for his own use following a move to Marfa, Texas, in 1977. These were made out of pine and built by both Judd and Celedonio Mediano, the construction foreman on his ranch. Inspiration for these early designs most certainly came from Judd's own collection of works by Gustave Stickley, Gerrit Rietveld, Mies van der Rohe, and Alvar Aalto, and from his library of both popular and obscure texts about design from 1880. His best-known chairs, however, date from a later period, when he first began creating chairs for sale. Made of solid woods, including mahogany, cherry and Douglas fir, and more finely finished, these chairs were produced in editions between 1982 and 1990 by the New York-based fabricators Jim Cooper and Ichiro Kato. Experiments with chairs and other furniture in enamelled aluminium followed. Judd went on to introduce more open geometry, lightweight construction and use of colour into his designs. These uneditioned designs were produced in a number of locations, including workshops in Yorkshire in England and Galway in Ireland.

German electronics powerhouse Braun is a celebrated creator of everyday domestic products that excel in design and practicality, from the first radio sets in the 1920s to Dieter Rams' music systems in the 1950s and the world's first electronic toothbrush in the 1990s. Ludwig Littmann's MR30 Stabmixer marked another first for the company: the first hand-held blender made entirely from one piece of plastic. Produced in 1982, the Stabmixer embodies the ergonomic design and cutting edge technology valued by Braun. The mechanics are concealed within a slender 'wand', mixing foodstuffs at high speed, mimicking the action of a manual implement but using the power of the latest electronic technology. The rotating electric blade is protected and cloaked within the plastic body. The device, due to its handheld nature and minimal form mimicked the action of traditional, manual kitchen implements but used the latest electronic means. This slimline alternative to the cumbersome tabletop blender was a direct response to changing urban lifestyles, where less space and time demanded new design solutions. Not only did the MR30 require less storage and cleaning and provide more versatility than traditional alternatives, it also appealed to a new generation of consumers who wanted kitchen appliances to replicate the streamlined designs coming into other areas of the home. As with many Braun products, the MR30 has since been refined and redefined. While the design of the wand unit has remained largely unchanged, the basic chopping motion of the MR30 has been superseded in later models. Littmann studied at the Folkwang School of Design in Essen in Germany before joining the Braun in-house design team in 1973. He has been responsible for many design innovations and remains the designer behind the development of the 'wand' mixer and its numerous contemporary forms.

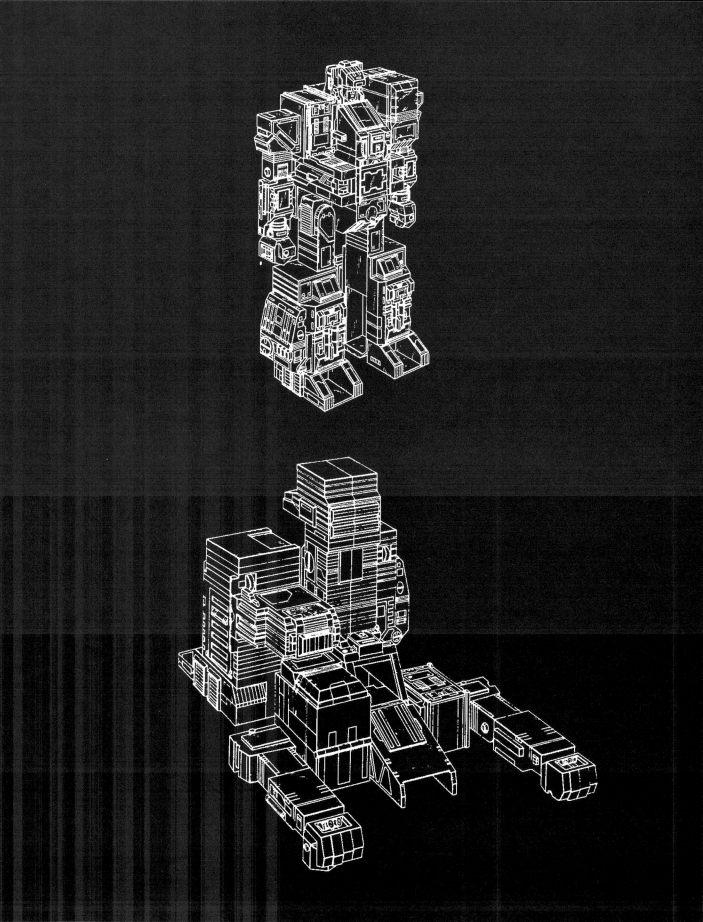

The Transformers were initially created in the early 1980s by Takara, Japan's second largest toy company. Takara's series of toys then caught the attention of the American toy manufacturer, Hasbro. Takara had been producing a series of toys called Microman, from which the Transformers concept and mould was taken, but the Transformers' unique aspect was the fictional history that was developed for them: the toys, a collection of robots, inhabit the planet Cyberton, and the good guys, the Autobots are in the midst of a million-year war with the Decepticons. This story led to the creation of Generation 1, the first of a series of robot-to-vehicle figures produced from 1984 to 1990, as well as an animated TV series, a Marvel comic collection and a movie. The Transformer is a humanoid robot, with a series of segments and hinges that swivel, and can reconfigure into a plane, car or animal. This was the first toy that could change its shape, and immediately became popular in Japan, the United States and Europe. Hasbro brought the toys to the United States in 1984, while Japan continued to produce its own versions, which had different names and packaging from the models sold in the United States. When Hasbro brought the toys to the United States, the company hired John Romita, a comic book artist for Marvel, to redesign the figures to a more humanoid appearance in order to make them more marketable. The initial Autobots and Decepticons inspired several series: Generation 2, Beast Wars, Machine Wars, Robot Masters and many more. Their popularity has continued since the 1980s, and today they have a number of loyal adult fans as well as a new, dedicated audience, especially with the recently revived Robots in Disguise series. With the unique combination of legendary story and the innovative idea of creating toys that can be both a car and, with a couple of twists and turns, an upright robot, the Transformers created a new relationship between toy and fiction.

829

Voltes V Transformer (1982)
Kouzin Ohno (1959–)
Takara 1982 to 1983
Hasbro 1984 to present

The quirky yet sleekly sophisticated appearance of the Costes Chair epitomizes the 1980s 'neomodern' aesthetic. Veneered in a rather austere mahogany, with an upholstered leather seat, its design pays homage to Art Deco as well as to traditional gentlemen's clubs and shows how Philippe Starck was unafraid of borrowing from a diverse range of styles and sources to guide the user or viewer into understanding the cultural signifiers of his designs. The chair was originally designed as part of the interior scheme for the Café Costes in Paris, but is now mass-produced by the Italian manufacturer Driade. Starck first came to prominence in 1981, when he was one of eight designers selected to refurbish and design furniture for President Mitterand's private apartments in the Elysée Palace. On the strength of this he was commissioned to design the interiors for the Café Costes. Starck produced a luxuriously avant-garde interior that was dominated by an axial, theatrical staircase, at the top of which was a large clock, perhaps a reference to the historical legacy of Paris cafés as places that sell time as much as food and drink. The three-legged chair was designed, apparently, so that the waiters wouldn't trip over the legs, and the three-legged motif would soon become something of a Starck signature. The Café Costes rapidly became a popular haunt for a young design-conscious crowd, a growing breed in the 1980s. It represented the epitome of chic and the place to see and be seen. Starck went on to become one of the most famous designers of the late twentieth century, and in the process, and no doubt due to his showmanship and ability to command the attention of the world's press, helped to establish the cult of the celebrity designer.

830

Costes Chair (1982)
Philippe Starck (1949–)
Driade 1985 to present

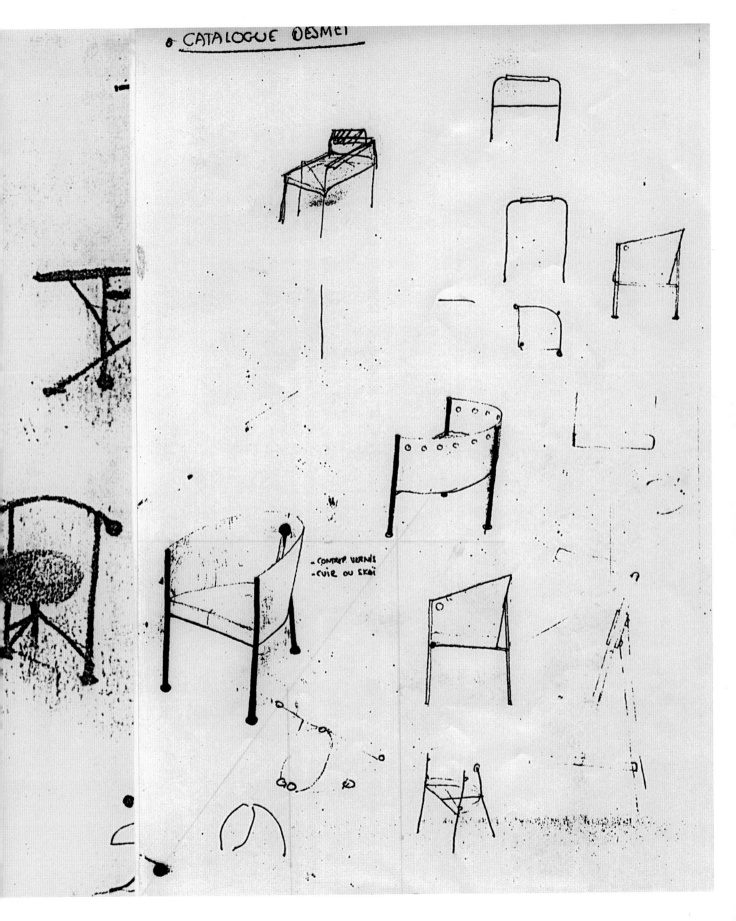

CATALOGUE DESMET

- CONTRP. VERNIS
- CUIR OU SKAÏ

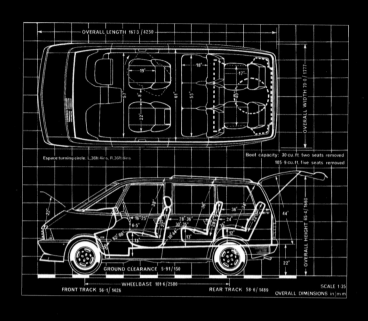

OVERALL LENGTH 167·3 / 4250

OVERALL WIDTH 70·0 / 1777

Espace turning circle. L.36ft 4ins, R.36ft 8ins

Boot capacity: 30 cu.ft two seats removed
105·9 cu.ft. five seats removed

OVERALL HEIGHT 65·4 / 1660

GROUND CLEARANCE 5·91 / 150

WHEELBASE 101·6 / 2580

FRONT TRACK 56·1 / 1426

REAR TRACK 58·6 / 1489

SCALE 1·35

OVERALL DIMENSIONS in / mm

The arrival of the Espace, the first mono-volume 'people carrier' or MPV (multi-purpose vehicle) ushered in an age of family-orientated car design focused on lifestyle, rather than performance or prestige. The car has a complex genesis. The original concept for a 'minivan' for Matra was the work of Geoff Matthews and Fergus Pollock at Chrysler Europe. When Chrysler's European facilities were sold to Peugeot, the concept was transferred to Matra who set about forging a relationship with Peugeot's primary rival, Renault. Under the creative leadership of Matra designer Antoine Volanis, the design was refined in response to Renault's brief for a radical new product. The design needed to feature an uncluttered flat floor for front-to-back mobility, five or seven independent seats (with two front swivelling seats), and bodywork made from composite material attached to a galvanized chassis to keep the vehicle's weight down. Renault took responsibility for the final design, marketing and sales, while Matra handled vehicle development and production. The first Espace appeared in 1982 and was initially greeted by the press and consumers alike with a degree of scepticism, since the vehicle confronted their prejudices by rejecting the traditional executive automotive archetype. However, the concept rapidly gained acceptance, and over four successive vehicle generations the Espace has commercially and aesthetically led the European large MPV market. With each successive version, Renault has innovated, in terms of safety, driving pleasure and travelling comfort, to the point where today's model is a match for any 'conventional' executive car. Consequently the German prestige brands have been forced to ape Renault's formula and create their very own MPVs. The striking 'one box' form, with its evocative tapered front end, draws inspiration from that other iconic French design of the 1970s, the TGV train, thus creating a conceptual template for Renault design. Renault continues to take risks under the inspired creative leadership of Patrick Le Quement, most notably with the (sadly short-lived) radical two-door Avantime, an Espace coupé promoting space as the new luxury. It was the last MPV to be manufactured for Renault by the Matra factory.

ЛОМО®

The legendary LOMO-Compact-Automate is a modest-looking camera manufactured by the LOMO Russian Arms and Optical factory in St Petersburg. The Compact is an improved interpretation of a Japanese camera. Acknowledging its sophisticated glass lens and extremely high light sensitivity, the factory set out to produce an improved, robust version. Though its brief was to develop a small, reliable camera to serve the masses, the design team, which was led by Mikhail Holomyansky, exceeded all expectations. The LC-A's Minitar 1, a wide-angle lens that functions in dim conditions, allows the Compact to deliver colour-saturated images. The camera, which was available in Vietnam, Cuba and East Germany, with its manual film advance, and 1/500-second to two-minute exposures, allowed for low light exposures that did not require a flash, and was therefore suitable for street photography. The exposure system of the LOMO LC-A does not have a photometer measuring the light, and instead has a photoresistor that loads a capacitor or an integrating device. As more light enters the photoresistor, the faster the capacitor will load which, on a specific voltage, triggers the shutter. The original Compacts have Russian lettering, with some models having framelines and icons to measure distance in the viewfinder and, while there are models which lack these features, every Compact has LEDs in the viewfinder. Today's global homage to the LOMO was spearheaded by a group of Austrian students holidaying in Prague. Entranced by the camera's exceptionally vivid prints, they founded the Lomography Association in 1992, and cultivated and endorsed a number of 'Lomo Embassies' across the world. When production of the camera ceased due to competition from cheaper models, particularly from China, Lomo enthusiasts campaigned to recommence production, drafting in the support of the then mayor of St Petersburg, one Vladimir Putin. To compound the pressure, LOMO enthusiasts set about curating high-profile exhibitions in New York and St Petersburg to convince the powers that be of the Compact's renewed popularity. Such perseverance paid off, and the dynamic Lomography Association became the exclusive worldwide distributor of the LOMO-Compact-Automate. However, in 2004 the camera was definitively discontinued due to high costs of production, to the great disappointment of its enthusiasts.

832

LOMO-Compact-Automate (1982)
Mikhail Holomyansky (1941–)
LOMO 1983 to 2004

Winner of the 2002 Japan Good Design Award, Global Knives created a sensation when launched onto the world's culinary stage as an alternative to traditional European-style cutlery. Japanese industrial designer Komin Yamada was commissioned to develop a superior, radical knife made with the best materials and employing the most modern design concepts. The result was the avant-garde Global Knife, which was first designed in 1982. Yamada had access to a large budget for his exploratory and innovative design, allowing him to create a chef's knife that was of such a standard in both appearance and performance that it appealed equally to the professional and domestic market. Made from an extremely high-grade stainless steel (molybdenum/vanadium), Global Knives all have remarkably sharp blades owing to being ice-tempered and hardened. This process results in a blade that holds its sharp edge longer than other steel counterparts and is resistant to rust, stains and corrosion. Yamada's design concept embraced three essential influences: Italian design, German durability and Japanese precision and was conceived as 'a knife one feels like touching'. With close reference to tradition, as with the Samurai sword, the Global Knife is carefully weighted to ensure perfect balance in use. Smooth contours and seamless construction prevent any food and dirt particles from collecting on the knife, making it the ultimate in hygienic kitchenware. As a functional object the Global Knife is explicit of the Arts and Crafts dogma: design through beauty of materials. Yamada's knife has a beauty of form that is matched by the beauty of its metallic colour. The design indicates a shape that the material would naturally assume and the resulting design of Yamada's research is a simple elegant solution. There is no unnecessary material included and with the handle being given a thick, round form, it is inviting to handle. Further evidence of Yamada's genius, with the two-millimetre diameter 'black dot 'design on the handle, the 'too smooth' or 'too cold' impression is avoided, resulting in the decorative signature design that doubles with the practical effect of securing a firm, warm grip.

Global Knife (1982)
Komin Yamada (1947–)
Yoshikin 1983 to present

Japanese Slim vs. the Germans

Continued From First Dining Page

high-carbon stainless steel and need to be sharpened or at least honed very often, Global knives are made from a new alloy of stainless steel called molybdenum/vanadium, which is harder than other stainless steels. According to the maker, it does not stain or corrode, and the blade is extraordinarily sharp because it is evenly tapered lengthwise and crosswise rather than only at the edge, as European knives are.

European knives are meant for heavy-duty chores, like cutting meats, boning poultry, chopping vegetables and dicing. Global knives are designed for more precise work; they would fit in at a sushi bar.

In my testing, I concentrated on the two most important knives in the cook's arsenal, the chef's knife and the paring knife. The eight-inch chef's knife, the only truly neces-

GLOBAL, Wüstof-Trident and F. Dick knives are sold at most good cookware shops, like Bridge Kitchenware in Manhattan, as well as by mail and on the Internet.

Eurokitchen and Bath (877-436-2842, www.eurokitchens.com) carries the full line of Global knives. The Master Grinding Service (800-282-4622, www.PlanetDelicious.com) has all three brands, as well as others.

sary knife, is the one with the slightly rounded blade. It is used for chopping, slicing and even pounding and crushing (when you slam an ingredient with the side of the thick part of the blade). The paring knife, at the other end of the spectrum, has a four-inch blade and is used for delicate tasks.

I put the three chef's knives through their paces, by slicing, chopping, dicing and mincing: raw beef, whole uncooked chicken and vegetables like onions, carrots, potatoes and bell peppers. I tested the parers by coring and slicing tomatoes, hulling strawberries, peeling zest from lemons and slicing shallots.

The first thing in a knife you react to is the handle. The F. Dick has a traditional riveted and molded handle, and the Wüsthof-Trident Grand Prix's is molded high-impact polypropylene. That type of handle is becoming increasingly popular because it is pleasing to look at and to hold. The material is nonabsorbent, durable and easy to keep clean. The lightly textured surface feels good in the hand, and rounded edges allow for a more comfortable grip.

The Global handle is flatter and can be turned easily to shift the blade from one cutting angle to another. The advantage of this became evident as soon as I began slicing meat. I started with a straight up-and-down cut, then experimented with angled cuts. The blade performed like a fish knife, with just the slightest flex, yielding thinner slices. I was also able to cut angled, paper-thin slices of beef.

Both the Wüsthof-Trident and F. Dick

knives were sharp, but their bulk was no[t] maneuverable as the Global's, and the h[an]dles seem made for one grip only — balance of the knives is designed for up-a[nd] down motions. Their weight pulled th[em] straight down as if to a magnet, so [the] angled cuts were far more difficult th[an] vertical cuts.

The slim Global knife sliced vegetab[les] with precision. Its light weight made comfortable for julienne or small dice. [The] thin blade moved easily through solid c[ar]rots and potatoes, and minced cucumber[s so] finely they were almost puréed. The G[er] man knives sliced well because they wer[e] sharp, but the thickness of the blades did [not] allow for the same delicacy; the slices w[ere] more smashed.

However, when it came to chopping, [the] heavier European knives had a distinct [ad]vantage. Because they are well balanc[ed,] chopping is done with an easy rocking [mo]tion. With both I chopped vegetables [and] meats quickly and cleanly. The kniv[es'] weight was a particular advantage whe[n it] came to chopping dried fruit, cutt[ing] through poultry, or using the flat side of [the] blade for crushing garlic; chopping [was] simply easier.

The Global knife required some ex[tra] muscle to accomplish the same tasks.

The Global parer's shape is disti[nctly] different from the familiar Western par[ing] knife, with an unusually broad base an[d a] straight edge along the length of one sid[e. I] assumed it was designed for looks rat[her] than practicality. But as soon as I picke[d]

Tony Cenicola for The New York Times

had a revelation. When I gripped the
handle, my forefinger fitted neatly into the
notch below the blade, keeping my hand
away from the work surface while I cored
and sliced small fruits and vegetables. I
enjoyed holding the knife this way, and
found that it fitted my hand well.

I liked the slightly flexible blade for peeling and the straight edge for slicing against
a cutting board. But I preferred the European knives over the Global knife for many
tasks usually done with a paring knife:
delicate work preparing garnishes and decorative carving in fruits and vegetables.
And I preferred the slightly larger, molded
handle of the Wüsthof.

Taste in knives is, of course, personal.
And cutting is not the only issue. Any good
knife will require care to remain sharp and
durable. German knives can be sharpened
with an electric grinder or honed with a
diamond steel. Global's manufacturer rec-
ommends sharpening the blades with ceramic steels or a whetstone, requiring more
of a commitment than most home cooks are
used to.

In the end, as much as I wanted to think of
the Global knives as the Excaliburs of the
kitchen, I realized that no one knife fits all.
This new blade works best for slicing, but
for chopping, I'm keeping my trusty
Wüsthof.

Philips Compact Disc (1982)
Philips/Sony Design Team
Philips/Sony 1982 to present

Requests

from the sports broadcasting industry for
instant replays in the early 1960s set manufacturers on the
road to today's DVD technology. Philips intervened in this market with
its LaserVision video disc in the early 1970s. Despite years of development,
however, the LaserVision did not offer any significant advantages over the recently
introduced video cassette, and had no recording capability. In 1978 Sony teamed up with
Philips to develop a standard, universal compact disc to hold audio and finally, in 1982, a
prototype compact disc (CD) emerged, heralding the birth of the digital revolution. Unlike the audio
cassette and vinyl record, the CD was not subject to mechanical wear, and it produced a distinctly richer
sound than the average record, especially for dynamic music styles such as jazz and classical. With a
diameter of just 11.5 cm (4.5 in), each CD comprises a thin, highly reflective metallic layer pierced by a series
of pits of varying lengths on the readable side of the disc. A thin layer of acrylic and a thicker layer of durable
polycarbonate protect these pits. Each pit appears to the laser that reads the disc as a slightly raised bump of a
certain length, corresponding to a predefined value linked to a rapidly changing series of digital signals which are
translated into images, sounds or data. The prototype was adjusted in size to accommodate the whole of
Beethoven's Ninth Symphony, with the final commercial version offering 77 minutes of music, significantly longer
than a double-sided LP. First vinyl and then compact audio cassettes were gradually supplanted by CDs. Further
technological advance has produced a CD that can store increasingly large amounts of data that are easily
recordable, error-free and reproducible. This transformation of the analogue world into a digital one has
produced a revolution in visual culture and our ability to manipulate what before could not be changed or even
seen, from special effects on the cinema screen to the inner workings of the human body via non-intrusive
medical equipment. The characteristics of the CD have allowed electronics and consumer goods to
flourish beyond the original vision of the early 1970s: the ability to store large amounts of digital data
in a reasonably indestructible but common format has inspired new product design. Individual
segments of content can be located without laboriously sifting through mountains of
information and new forms of interactivity and education have been shaped. The easy
retrieval of data makes possible risk-free archiving and sharing of information.
While common terminology may differentiate between a music CD, a
DVD and a CD-ROM, all three are conceptually identical and
remain largely unchanged from the very first
compact disc.

A range of functional office products, storage bags and folders made of translucent, corrugated plastic sheet was an innovation in the complete office accessories market when it first appeared in 1982. The system was quite simple but stood in marked contrast to existing ranges, which were mainly standard paper and cardboard products. Makio Hasuike used prefabricated, extruded plastic sheets and 'tailored' the folders, bags and storage boxes. Only by folding and bending did the product reach its final three-dimensional shape. The hardware-like handles and clips are carefully designed and mass-produced in different colours by injection-moulding. This a very basic product range based on intelligent research into using new and long-lasting materials, which are industrially manufactured and sold for low prices, and fulfil all necessary functions with high design values. The product line is constantly added to, offering valuable space for additional design ideas and variables for the future. After more than twenty years in production this accessory line is as popular today as it was at its launch. The range has been kept fresh with new surfaces and hardware design. But the basic concept of a clear container, folder and storage line has remained fundamentally unchanged during this time, and the product's success can be seen in its many imitations all over the world.

When, on a Friday night in 1981 design company Memphis opened its controversial show in Milan, its new visual style and philosophy of furniture, accessories and fashion was met with enthusiasm. The event was seen as an innovative confrontation with the design concept of the Bauhaus, classical modernism and the dreary engineering product design prevalent at the time. In this postmodern context Michele De Lucchi created his First Chair, a symbolic furniture design that appealed because of its shape and figurative details. It was rather uncomfortable to sit in, and seemed more to resemble a skinny sculpture than a practical chair. Its attraction could be found in the different design elements and materials used. The shape's resemblance to a sitting figure is obvious, but does not help to make the product work as an everyday chair. Its sense of lightness, mobility and fun appealed to the viewer, provoking an emotional response. The chair was originally made in small series in metal and lacquered wood, looked handmade or crafted – a typical prototyping production method that reduced risks but created high costs. As with many of the products created by the Memphis group, the First Chair represents a brief period in design trends, but Memphis decided to keep this chair in production to the present day. The First Chair, along with a number of De Lucchi's works, were acquired by the prestigious collection at the Centre Georges Pompidou, Paris, in 2003. A graduate of architecture, De Lucchi moved into radical architecture with Memphis, then began designing products for Artemide and Kartell, and was the Director of Design at Olivetti from 1992 to 2002. Today, his firm, aMDL, is a gathering of architects and designers, working within ideas of architectural thinking, industrial design and global communication, with offices based in Milan and Rome.

Michele De Lucchi on the *Domus* magazine cover, May 1981

Small, portable knives have existed in some form or another since the days of ancient Rome, with folding knives unearthed during excavations in Pompeii and Herculaneum. The modern descendants of those blades have taken the forms of various pocketknives, jackknives, switch-blades and folding utility knives. Of these, utility knives embody the most articulated statements about the technological experience of average individuals. Tools that can be used on bicycles, computer hardware, electrical appliances and personal hygiene are all among the multi-part devices we can buy. One of the most remarkable of these tools was the Leatherman PST (Pocket Survival Tool). In 1975, frustrated by faulty hotel plumbing and a cranky car as he travelled across Europe, Tim Leatherman returned to the United States determined to use his engineering background to create a tool that included the full-size pliers he had needed and the other tools travellers like himself would have wanted. After years in development he arrived at the Pocket Survival Tool that Leatherman and his business partner, Steve Berliner, would bring to the market in 1983. For Leatherman devotees the PST was the ultimate all-in-one tool. Too large for a pocket knife, it came with its own belt-attachable sheath and included more devices than any item the company has produced since that time. This 224 g (8 oz) tool included needle-nose and regular pliers; wire cutters; a clip point knife; a serrated knife; a diamond-coated file; a wood saw; scissors; extra small, medium, large and Phillips-head screwdrivers; a tin/bottle opener; heavy-duty wire strippers and a lanyard attachment. Manufactured in the United States, the PST was made of a highly corrosive-resistant stainless steel. And, although far from being its most effective appliance, the pliers become the PST's primary tool. When taken from the sheath, the pincers are the only tool visible while all others are comfortably concealed in the handles. Four of the PST's blades are locking and accessible from the exterior; two of those blades can be accessed with one hand. Guaranteed for twenty-five years, the Leatherman Pocket Survival Tool's quality is unimpeachable. In addition, balancing finely sculpted tools in small, similarly sized parallel groupings in each handle, the PST possesses the internal logic that creates great beauty in the natural order. For all of these reasons the original Pocket Survival Tool, which is no longer in production, has become a collectors' item.

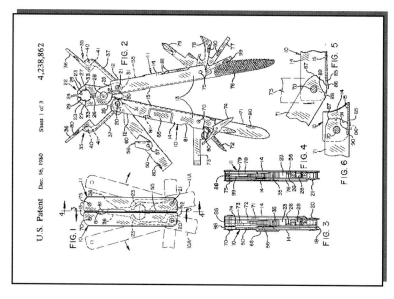

FIG. 1
FIG. 2
FIG. 3
FIG. 4
FIG. 5
FIG. 6

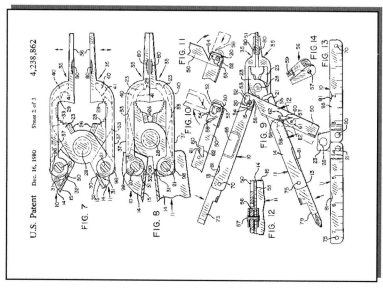

FIG. 7
FIG. 8
FIG. 9
FIG. 10
FIG. 11
FIG. 12
FIG. 13
FIG. 14

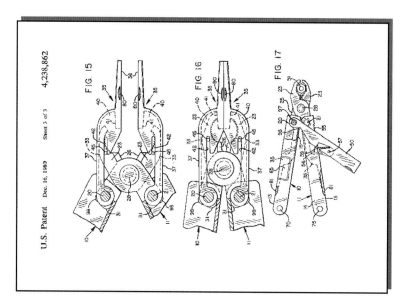

FIG. 15
FIG. 16
FIG. 17

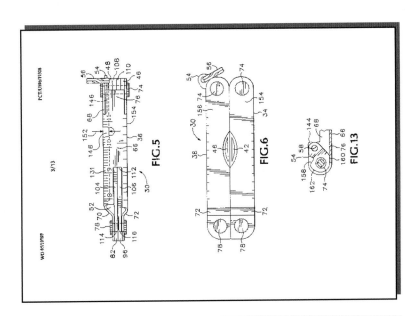

FIG.5

FIG.6

FIG.13

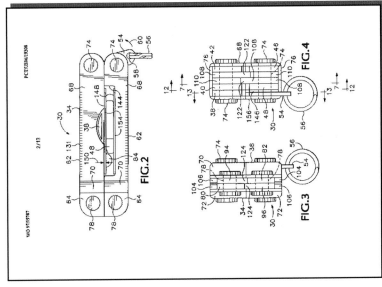

FIG.2

FIG.4

FIG.3

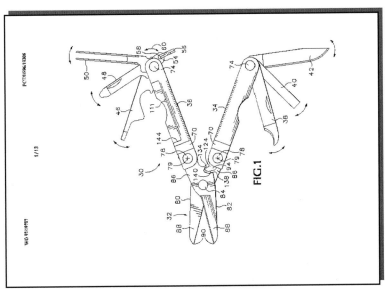

FIG.1

Ulf Hanses

The Streamliner functions both as a colourful, tactile and robust plaything for children and a visually striking aesthetic object for adults. Its simple, solid wooden form and smooth, sensual high-lustre paint finish also embody the Swedish design philosophy of beautiful, functional design on a human scale. The aim of the Kalmar-based company Playsam, which was founded by Carl Zedig in 1984, was to produce well designed, functional and aesthetically pleasing toys.

Ulf Hanses, a Swedish industrial designer, was the first to attract Playsam's attention. Hanses had previously created a range of toys for disabled children during the early 1980s, and these subsequently caught the eye of Zedig. Hanses's existing designs went on to form the basis for the Streamliner, a simple wooden car model, stripped down to its formal essence, with an emphasis on its smooth tactile and colourful visual properties. The toy made its first appearance at the Nuremberg Toy Fair

838

Streamliner (1983)
Ulf Hanses (1949–)
Samhall 1984 to 1989
Playsam 1989 to 1999
PlayMe Toys 2000 to present

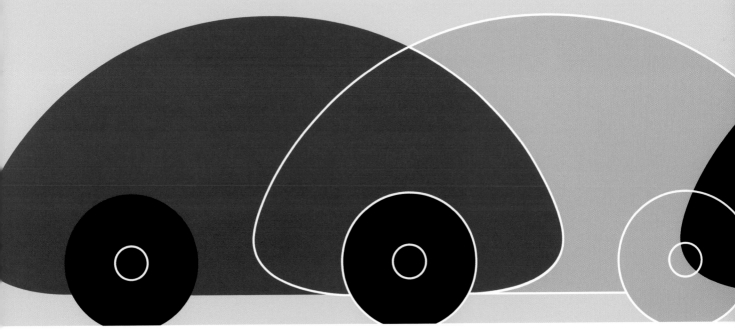

SVERIGE BREV

in 1985, and would provide the fledgling Playsam with its first major success. Hanses's Streamliner can be viewed very much within the Swedish tradition of making wooden toys. Appropriately enough, Hanses hails from the Dalarna region, an area known for its indigenous craft tradition, and particularly renowned for producing the colourful Dala (or Mora) wooden toy horses, currently recognized as a national folk-art symbol of Sweden. The enduring and universal appeal of the Streamliner is a testament to its simple, honest and egalitarian design credentials, which seem to chime more than ever with the prevailing eco-sensitive cultural climate. In 1998 Streamliner was selected as Swedish Design Classic by a jury from Svensk Form Council and the National Museum of Fine Arts, Sweden, and in 2004 was selected to be a Swedish stamp showing the best of Swedish design over the past sixty years.

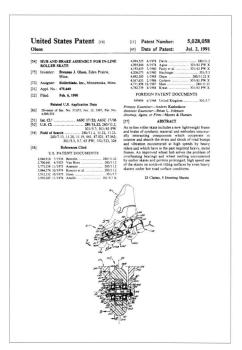

United States Patent [19]

Olson

[11] Patent Number: 5,028,058
[45] Date of Patent: Jul. 2, 1991

[54] HUB AND BRAKE ASSEMBLY FOR IN-LINE ROLLER SKATE

[75] Inventor: Brennan J. Olson, Eden Prairie, Minn.

[73] Assignee: Rollerblade, Inc., Minnetonka, Minn.

[21] Appl. No.: 475,449

[22] Filed: Feb. 6, 1990

Related U.S. Application Data

[62] Division of Ser. No. 57,055, Jun. 12, 1987, Pat. No. 4,909,523.

[51] Int. Cl.5 .... A63C 17/22; A63C 17/06
[52] U.S. Cl. .... 280/11.22; 280/11.2; 301/5.7; 301/63 PW
[58] Field of Search .... 280/11.2, 11.22, 11.23, 280/7.13, 11.28, 11.19, 941, 87.021, 87.042; 301/5.3, 5.7, 63 PW; 152/322, 326

[56] References Cited

U.S. PATENT DOCUMENTS

2,048,916 7/1936 Benzlin 280/11.22
2,706,641 4/1955 Van Horn 280/11.2
3,773,339 11/1973 Aranson 280/11.2
3,844,574 10/1974 Konono et al. 280/11.2
3,912,332 10/1975 Jones 301/5.7
3,992,025 11/1976 Amelio .... 301/5.7 X

4,094,525 6/1978 Davis 280/11.2
4,095,846 6/1978 Agins .... 301/63 PW X
4,193,679 3/1980 Pauly et al. .... 301/63 PW X
4,208,073 6/1980 Hechinger 301/5.3
4,492,385 1/1985 Olson .... 280/11.22 X
4,567,633 2/1986 Corkery .... 301/63 PW X
4,711,458 12/1987 Shim 280/11.22
4,762,739 8/1988 Kraus .... 301/63 PW X

FOREIGN PATENT DOCUMENTS

959494 6/1964 United Kingdom ... 301/5.7

Primary Examiner—Andres Kashnikow
Assistant Examiner—Brian L. Johnson
Attorney, Agent, or Firm—Moore & Hansen

[57] ABSTRACT

An in-line roller skate includes a new lightweight frame and brake of synthetic material and embodies structurally interacting components which cooperate to counter and absorb the strain and shock of road bumps and vibration encountered at high speeds by heavy riders and which have in the past required heavy, metal frames. An improved wheel hub solves the problem of overheating bearings and wheel melting encountered by earlier skates and permits prolonged, high speed use of the skates on nonlevel riding surfaces by even heavy skaters under hot road surface conditions.

23 Claims, 5 Drawing Sheets

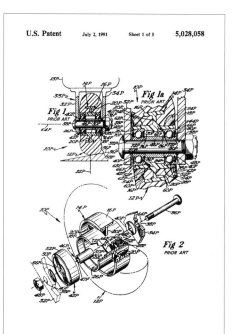

Fig 1 PRIOR ART
Fig 1a PRIOR ART
Fig 2 PRIOR ART

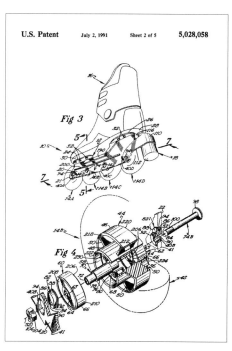

Fig 3
Fig 4

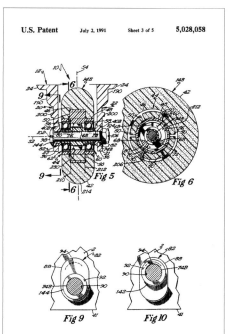

Fig 5
Fig 6
Fig 9
Fig 10

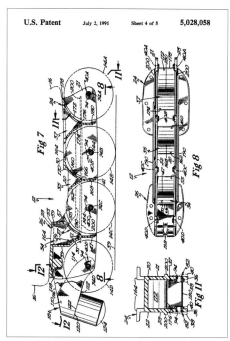

Fig 7
Fig 8
Fig 11

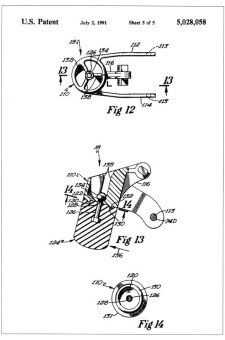

Fig 12
Fig 13
Fig 14

Lightning TRS (1983)
Rollerblade Design Team
Rollerblade 1989 to 1991

The Lightning TRS introduced the concept of the in-line skate to a mainstream audience, creating not only a skate but a worldwide exercise phenomenon. The inspiration for the skate was the discovery of an old in-line skate by two ice hockey-playing brothers keen to find something suitable for off-season training. Brennan and Scott Olson developed the design through over 200 prototypes, arriving at the first modern in-line skate, initially manufactured in the basement of their parents' Minneapolis home. The brothers continued to refine the concept, but it was only when they sold the company that sufficient research

and development funds permitted the launch of the Lightning TRS in 1989. Previous in-line skates had suffered from significant design flaws. They were prone to collect dirt and moisture in the ball-bearings of the wheel, the solid wheels were easily damaged and the unintuitive brakes were front-mounted and adapted from traditional roller skates. The Lightning remedied these problems through a series of innovations. The skates featured revolutionary fibreglass frames, providing the required stiffness for a chassis featuring polyurethane wheels. Ergonomically resolved, the skate was far easier to put on, take off and

adjust than its predecessors. The design also made novel use of a rear-mounted brake, producing a product that behaved like an ice-skate, enabling users to skate more naturally. Nordic and Alpine skiers rapidly adopted the Lightning as a key training aid, but Rollerblades' strategic marketing efforts in the mid-1980s successfully positioned in-line skating as a new sport, leading to its widespread recreational use. Their success is such that 'Rollerblading' has become the generic descriptor for the industry, leaving competitors in their wake. Rollerblade continues to lead the in-line skate industry, with over 250 patented innovations.

Swatch 1st Collection (1983)
Swatch Lab
ETA 1983

With the introduction of a wide range of new timepiece technologies in the 1970s, analogue mechanical watches suddenly appeared obsolete, with previously revered Swiss products among the worst hit. On 1 March 1983 The Swatch Group (originally founded by the Swiss watch industry as the Corporation for Microelectronics and Watchmaking Industries, SMH) introduced Swatch, in a collection of twelve models. The new Swatch watch was the result of a bold and somewhat desperate move on the part of the failing Swiss watch industry to arrive at new technologies and strategies for achieving a radically different but high-quality product. Designed by Ernst Thonke, Jacques Müller and Elmar Mock, the first Swatch boasted an accurate quartz analogue product with only fifty-one parts, instead of up to 150 parts that are found in conventional watches, allowing automated assembly and an original price of $39.90 CHF. Conceived as a fashion watch in a period of unusually high consumption, it was assumed that an average Swatch owner would buy more than one. Swatch's manufacturers recognized that the watch was an emotional purchase and for both men and women it represented statements about how they wanted to be perceived. Drawing upon the psychological potential of an accessory to express multiple facets of personality, the Swatch market strategy has created character by employing high-profile talents to design subsequent collections. GB001, the first Swatch, had a black plastic wrist band and housing for its glow-in-the-dark, white face and strikingly legible, sansserif numbers in an analogue configuration with an optional day/date window. These features have undergone constant change with subsequent designs. The first Swatch set standards such as silent movement, ultrasonic welding, injection moulding and waterproof, damage-resistant housings. Those standards have since been applied to 140 different styles annually by the likes of Matteo Thun, Alessandro Mendini, Keith Haring, Yoko Ono, Vivienne Westwood and Annie Liebowitz. Initial sales targets for this collection were set at 1 million timepieces in 1983 and 2.5 million in 1984. To date, more than 250 million have been sold, transcending the typical 'peak and decline' market patterns of fad and fashion accessories.

This two-litre stainless steel 9091 Kettle from 1983 – gleaming, elegant and substantial – can be considered the first true designer kettle. It was created by Richard Sapper, who was inspired by the barges and steamships blowing their foghorns as they sailed up and down the Rhine. Sapper and the kettle's Italian manufacturer, Alessi, hit the market at just the right time. The 1980s were a decade predicated on style over substance and the kettle's large dimensions 19 cm (7.5 in) tall by 16.5 cm (6.5 in) wide, its sleek, shiny dome and its high price tag put it right at the centre of the ideal home. In design terms, there is a certain hauteur to the upright dome, a geometric purity that distinguished it from the cosy, homely traditional shapes of earlier kitchenware. The kettle is easy to fill and pour, and its sandwiched copper base ensures good heat transmission for use on any stove, including glass or Agas. A polyamide handle is set back on the kettle to avoid steam hitting the hand, and a sprung mechanism operated by a finger on the handle opens the spout for pouring or filling. Whether it is entirely effective in its aim is a point of debate. But what really sets the kettle apart is its whistle. Sapper always said it was important to 'bring a bit of pleasure and fun to people.' Its pipes, pitched in E and B, are specially made by craftsmen in the Black Forest. Some describe the whistle as sounding like a locomotive, others liken it to a harmonica. Unusually for a designer, Richard Sapper never attended a school of design or architecture, which perhaps explains his free-thinking approach. Instead, he took in a wide gamut of subjects including philosophy, anatomy, graphic design, engineering and economics. After completing his studies he worked at Daimler-Benz before leaving Germany for Milan in 1957, where he worked with a number of big name designers including Gio Ponti and set up a partnership with Marco Zanuso.

The Can Family is one of the best examples of simple, pared-down elegance in design and combines quality with its use of inexpensive plastic and multi-purpose application for the kitchen, bathroom and all living areas. Such simplicity was new and almost shocking, but by the end of the century the style was to become almost ubiquitous. Copies became commonplace and Authentics, the German company behind the Can and the revolution in plastic households goods, found itself facing liquidation in 2000. The Can is one of the signature products in the Authentics Basics range. Available in six sizes, it was designed by Hansjerg Maier-Aichen, who had worked with Authentics since 1968 and who took over the reins of the company in 1975. Maier-Aichen redirected the company's position in 1996, concentrating its efforts in the design and manufacture of plastics to produce inexpensive but high-quality household products for everyday use. A key step in this new direction was the introduction of internationally acclaimed designers such as Konstantin Grcic, Matthew Hilton and Sebastian Bergne to the company's stable of designers. Making the most of the inherent qualities and production techniques of plastics, the new Authentics range introduced designs that could not be achieved in other materials and, thanks to a subtle colour language of translucent hues, set a much copied trend in motion. The high production values, simplicity and reduction of form were consciously meant as an antidote to fashionable products with gimmicky variations and correspondingly short life spans, lending a sense of worth and emotional resonance to what was usually regarded as a 'cheap' material, especially where household goods were concerned. A restructuring of the company in 2001 has seen Authentics restored to financial health and the Can Family continues to be one of its best sellers.

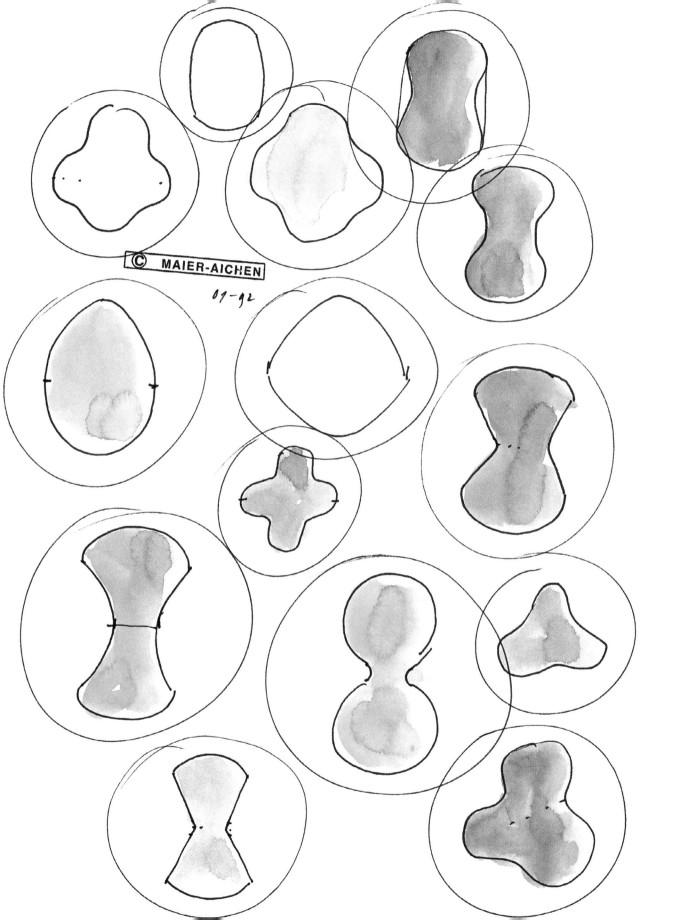

© MAIER-AICHEN

01-92

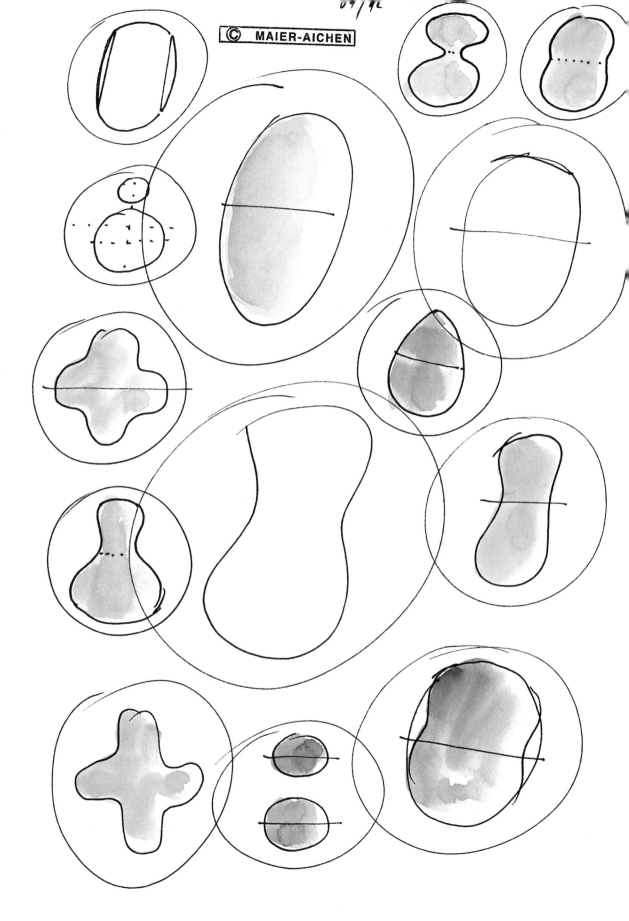

Right from the beginning Apple has set high standards in terms of both computer hardware and interface design, which other manufacturers have aspired to but never achieved. The Macintosh was born out of a shared humanist approach to design by Steve Jobs (joint founder of Apple Computer) and Hartmut Esslinger (founder of frogdesign), beginning in 1982. Set up in 1976, only five years after Intel had marketed its first 4004 CPU microchip, Apple was looking to demystify the computer and market its potential further. In 1981 fewer than 3 per cent of the US population owned a computer in the home, and so a great new opportunity had been identified. Apple therefore deliberately turned its attention away from the business market – which was dominated by IBM – and towards the personal market. Jobs would say, 'IBM has it all wrong; they sell personal computers as data-processing machines, not as tools for the individual'. The Macintosh, with its all-in-one beige box, minimal (but stylish) detailing and 9-inch screen, was therefore conceived as a product that would be easy to use and small enough to suit the home environment. Released on January 24, 1984, the Macintosh only had 128k of memory, no numeric keypad or function keys, which were sacrificed because of their high cost. But frogdesign shared a humanistic ethos, subverting Sullivan's dictum that 'form follows emotion'. It was previous work for Wega and Sony that brought Esslinger to Jobs' attention and together they developed a sophisticated, holistic and enduring design language that successfully encompassed product, brand, and company, and set a precedent for the brand-centred 1990s. Effectively introducing the brand to a wider international public, the Macintosh computer was honed like a mini shrine for the user to worship at (values that have been successfully built upon to this day). Indeed, the Macintosh was often photographed in pseudo 'Zen' gardens, with the gravel carefully raked around the monitor's base and keyboard, suggesting quiet contemplation and spiritual well-being. Essentially, the design of the Macintosh, with its user-friendly interface, played a key role in breaking down the fear that potential users felt about computers. Help was at hand with this strange new phenomenon called 'home computing', from a product aspiring to be more like a friend than a foe.

8-4-4

Sheraton Chair 664 (1984)
Robert Venturi (1925–)
Knoll 1984 to 1988

This chair breaks all the rules of modern design. Most chairs designed within a modernist idiom focus on the integration of material, form, surface and structure. Here these elements contrast rather than integrate. The chair rejects modernist ideology and instead focuses on image, sign content and psychological value. The chair's structural material is laminated plywood, as found in modern chairs of the 1940s and 50s. However, plywood is used here less as expressed structure and more as a surface in space, like a billboard, on to which other messages can be projected. The shape of the chair seen from the front suggests, in a kind of cartoon cut-out version, the silhouette of a Sheraton chair from the late eighteenth century. The surfaces are decorated with a coloured floral pattern suggesting upholstery of a later period, overlaid with a black, geometric motif reminiscent of 1960s Pop graphics. None of the above elements fits logically or consistently together. All are in contradiction and yet all are about chair culture. The design is one of a collection of nine chairs all similarly configured, with furniture references ranging from eighteenth-century Queen Anne to Art Deco. They were designed by Robert Venturi, an architect who is widely acknowledged as one of the fathers of postmodern design. Venturi's influence stems from his book *Complexity and Contradiction in Architecture* (1966), a critique of the limitations of Modernism and a call for a more inclusive approach to design. Venturi articulated the psychological and narrative value to be learned from historical, vernacular and commercial culture. Venturi called for 'both and' rather than 'either or' as a means of providing richness of meaning. In typical rhetorical fashion he famously subverted Mies van der Rohe's even more famous dictum 'less is more' with 'less is a bore'. In these chairs Venturi incorporated many of the ideas explored in his architectural work and writing. The collection's importance is in its challenge to the increasingly dogmatic and semantically limited palette of Modernism.

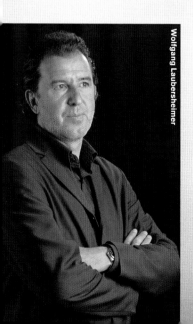

Wolfgang Laubersheimer

The Gespanntes

Regal (Taut Shelf) belongs to the 1980s 'new design' wave. The ironic and idiosyncratic form of the shelf, with its quirky tilting action in springy sheet steel, not only discards the traditional predilection for right-angled geometries but also eschews the modernist mantra of designing with mass production in mind. Wolfgang Laubersheimer, co-founder of Pentagon, a group of five experimental designers who set up in Cologne in 1985, has admitted that the Gespanntes Regal emerged as a result of a commission from a client to build a one-off book shelf. While studying sculpture in Cologne, the designer had experimented with hot-rolled steel and steel sheet, observing the changes in the material's properties under certain conditions of tension and pressure. Initially, Laubersheimer attempted to build a small book shelf solely of 4 mm (0.16 in) steel sheets, but found that the result was unstable. Subsequently, the designer fixed a steel rope at one side of the longitudinal axis. At first this appears to be purely a decorative motif, but it serves a crucial function: this simple yet extremely effective device provides the springy steel shelf with tension and, ultimately, stability, as well as imbuing the piece with an endearingly off-beat personality. The final bookcase model was made of waxed and welded hot-rolled 3 mm (0.12 in) steel sheet, which was left raw and untreated. Paradoxically, although the Gespanntes Regal was clearly created as an individual statement, a sculptural piece that seems to fly in the face of the homogenized design approach of the mass market, it is also currently one of the most successful production pieces of Nils Holger Moormann. As one of the main champions of new German design, the Bavarian company has pioneered many experimental works by young, often unknown designers, and Wolfgang Laubersheimer's Gespanntes Regal has become one of its defining, not to mention perennially popular, designs.

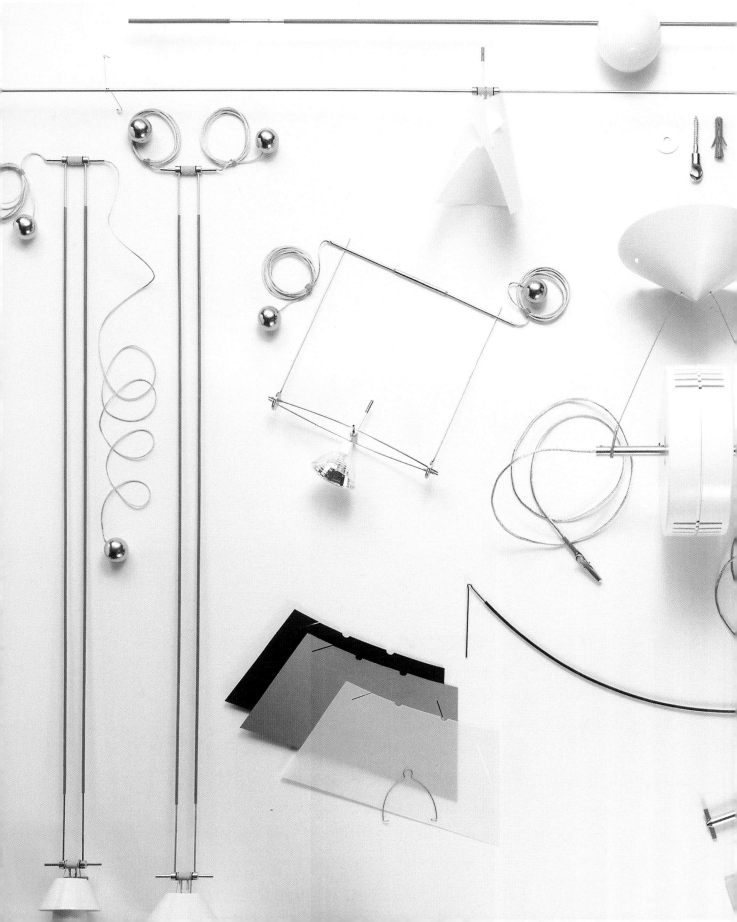

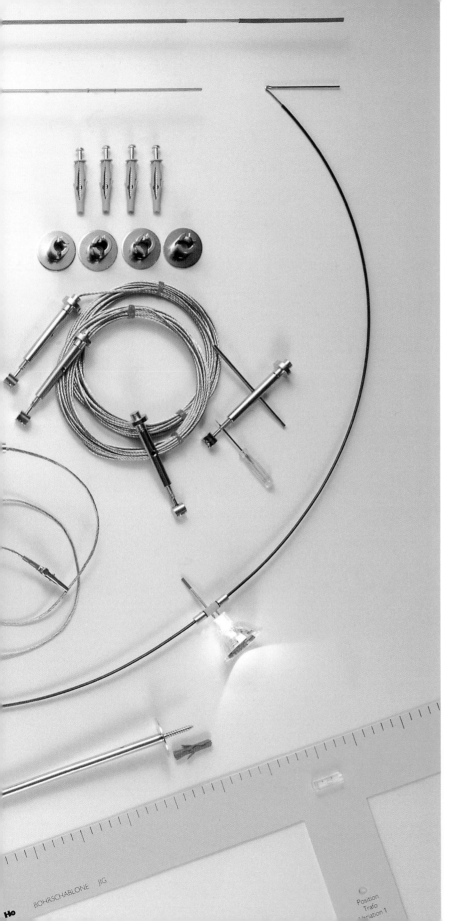

Ingo Maurer trained as a graphic designer, but started working with lighting in the 1960s. Yet it was not until 1984 with Ya Ya Ho that his work came to the attention of a wider audience. Despite its eccentric personality, which tends to draw much media attention, the lighting system immediately became a good seller after its launch and helped to establish Ingo Maurer and his company as a quirky and capable lighting design and production team. Ya Ya Ho was the world's first mass-produced lighting system using live 12-volt cables. Different lighting devices with halogen lamps are hung from bare wires, which are suspended between walls. With the structure provided by the walls, the system can be assembled in a number of configurations, and functions more like a deconstructed track lighting system. The system includes a transformer to adjust the incoming voltage down to 12 volts, which is then transmitted through the live cables. The lights can be placed anywhere along the wires, each allowing differing light qualities or uses. This playfulness is typical of Maurer's approach to design. He explores a lighting technology and then assembles an idea out of finely detailed components to make highly individual, sometimes whimsical, yet fully functioning lighting objects. The inherent flexibility of this system means that Ingo Maurer and his team are often invited to make dramatic installations in galleries and showrooms around the world. These are usually built using components from Ya Ya Ho, as well as its more recent sister product, Ba Ka Ru, another flexible lighting system using bare 12-volt wires. Its success can be seen in the thousands of copies, echoing this same system.

Défilé Issey Miyake, La Villette/Paris, 1999

Massimo Morozzi launched his career as one of the founding members of the radical design group Archizoom in Florence in 1966, along with Andrea Branzi, Paolo Deganello and Gilberto Coretti. Developing their manifesto during a time of political upheaval, the group challenged the undisputed functionalist formula of design and its compliance with the growing industry base. Most of Archizoom's ideas were voiced as concepts, with only a handful of designs actually realized. When the group dissolved, Morozzi continued with his design research before turning his attention once again to furniture and objects in the 1980s. In 1985

he presented the Pasta Set project to Alberto Alessi, owner of the renowned Italian housewares brand Alessi. At first Alberto was attracted to the shape of the object, yet mystified by its function. He was not alone: a survey revealed that approximately half of those interviewed did not recognize the design as a saucepan for boiling water. Nonetheless, the manufacturer had the confidence to put it into production. The decision paid off. In actual fact, Morozzi had introduced a clever functional innovation into the over-crowded market of kitchen utensils, which rapidly inspired endless imitations around the world. Morozzi had the idea of incorporating a metal

colander with plastic handles inside the pan, so that the user could simply lift the pasta out of the boiling water without the need to drain it in a separate colander in the sink. As the water heats the metal colander during the cooking process, the pasta also remains hot when removed from the water. The lid has a hollow plastic knob for the steam to escape. This remarkably obvious yet meticulously considered design has been described by Alberto Alessi as 'simply a homage to pasta.' The Pasta Set won the Gold Medal at the Ljubljana Bio 11 in 1986 and was later joined by Morozzi's Vapour Set in 1990, a similar design for steam cooking.

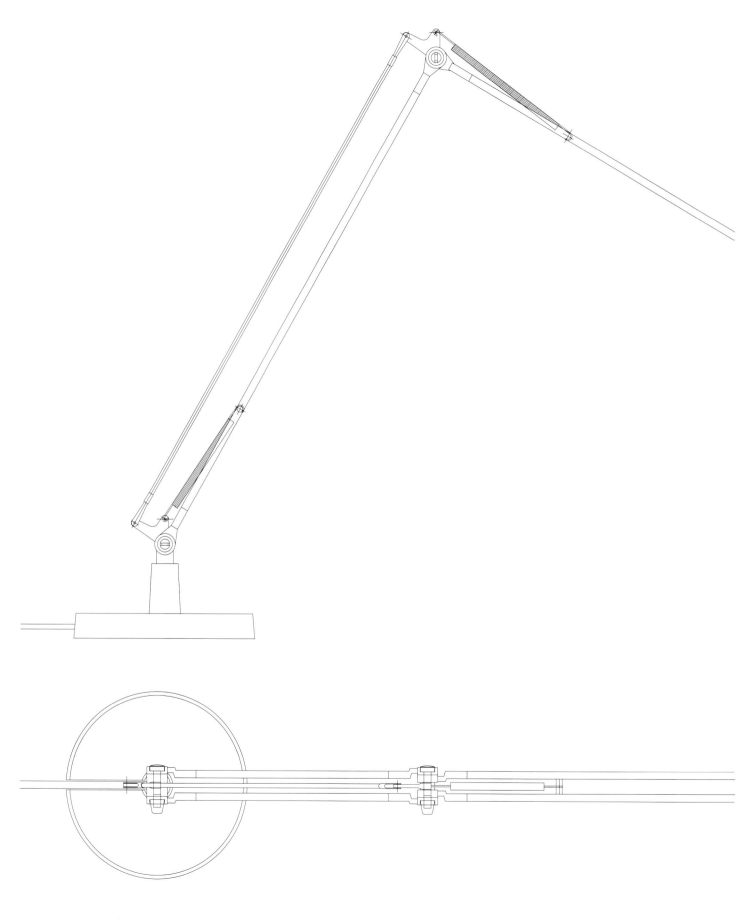

Berenice (1985)
Alberto Meda (1945–)
Paolo Rizzatto (1941–)
LucePlan 1985 to present

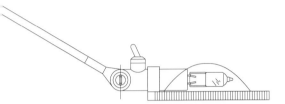

The Berenice table lamp is one of the signature hi-tech products of Milan-based lighting company LucePlan, founded by Riccardo Sarfatti, Paolo Rizzatto and Sandra Severi Cristalli in 1978. Alberto Meda joined them in 1984 and, together with Rizzatto, began designing the innovative range of LucePlan lights. The Berenice table lamp, which uses low-voltage halogen, has a slim and elegant form and a fluid, rather than mechanical, action to it when repositioned. The use of a transformer enables the electricity to be conducted through the structure without the need for additional wires on the armature itself. The lamp has a highly complex structural and material specification. It is assembled from forty-two components using thirteen different materials, including metals, glass and plastics. The metal armature is made from stainless steel and die-cast aluminium elements, with reinforced nylon joints that can stand up to friction when the position of the lamp is adjusted. The head of the lamp is made from Rynite™, an injection-moulded thermoplastic polyester resin, often used for the manufacture of tough miniature components, such as those used in rifles. The coloured glass reflector (in blue, green or red) is made from borosilicate glass, again chosen for its heat resistance, durability and also because it can be manufactured using strong colours. The lamp is a subtle, pared-down version of the industrially styled task lamp popularized by Italian designers in the 1970s and 1980s. Like Richard Sapper's Tizio lamp, the Berenice is based on the close analysis of structure, technology and compositional elements. Alberto Meda's approach to design stems from his training in mechanical engineering. He combines technological innovation with a sparse, light and elegant style. Often pushing materials to their limits in terms of their structural and ergonomic possibilities, he creates objects that are both functional and sculptural and therefore at home in different environments, from the office to the living room. In 1987 the Berenice table lamp received a special mention at the Compasso d'Oro awards, and in 1994 Meda and Rizzatto were awarded the European Design Prize for their work.

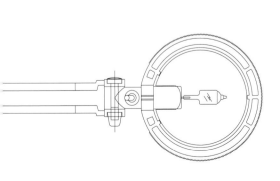

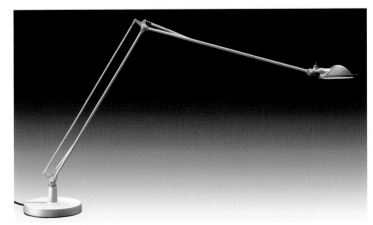

American designer and bicycle racer Jim Gentes founded Giro in 1985 with, as its launch product, his ground-breaking triathlon helmet, which exploited the potential of lightweight materials and aero-styling. The design was in response to the US Cycling Federation who made helmets mandatory in their races, which alienated many existing racers. The helmets available were heavy, awkward to wear and lacking aerodynamics. However, it was the Aerohead helmet that made a name for Gentes and Giro and changed forever the manufacture and appearance of cycling helmets. The helmet's design was based on wind-tunnel research and employed the latest developments in aerodynamic form. Its shell was made of expanded polystyrene, resulting in a helmet that was extremely light and strong. The lycra cover provided a friction-reducing protective skin, and meant the helmet could be personalized. The

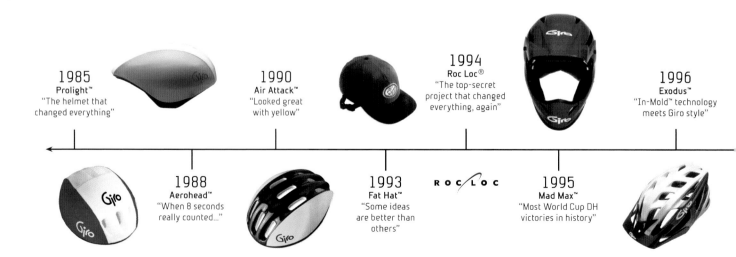

1985
Prolight™
"The helmet that
changed everything"

1990
Air Attack™
"Looked great
with yellow"

1994
Roc Loc®
"The top-secret
project that changed
everything, again"

1996
Exodus™
"In-Mold™ technology
meets Giro style"

1988
Aerohead™
"When 8 seconds
really counted…"

1993
Fat Hat™
"Some ideas
are better than
others"

1995
Mad Max™
"Most World Cup DH
victories in history"

Giro Aerohead revolutionized the international arena of sports cycling when American cyclist Greg LeMond first wore one in the final time trial of the 1989 Tour de France. LeMond's striking appearance was in stark contrast to his competitors, including the then yellow jersey holder, Laurent Fignon, who wore the traditional helmet. The Aerohead proved its worth as LeMond flew round the course and took the yellow jersey from Fignon by just eight seconds: the smallest margin in the history of the Tour de France. From that point onwards the look and construction of competitive cycling helmets was inspired by the Giro Aerohead. This, unsurprisingly, also filtered through to non-professional safety headwear. Today Gentes and his Giro brand continue to develop the performance potential in sports design using the latest technological advancements.

1998
Ravine™
"Giro wrote it's name
in the snow"

2000
Nine™
"For riders who
don't like helmets"

2002
Universal Fit™
"Right on target"

1997
Boreas™
"Cooler than no
helmet at all"

Switchblade™
"For the new school
sessions"

1999
E2™
"Looks like a truck,
feels like a convertible"

P.O.V.™
"A better view"

2001
Pneumo™
"Can you see through
your helmet?"

Semi™
"Like your favorite hat"

The 9093 Whistling Kettle

designed by American Michael Graves is one of the most commercially successful mass-produced products to come out of the postmodern design movement of the 1980s. Commissioned by Alessi as a hob kettle specifically aimed at the American mass market, Graves's design followed Richard Sapper's earlier 9091 Kettle (1983), also produced by Alessi. The success of the design is in the simplicity of the concept. The red moulded plastic bird whimsically suggests a source for the kettle's whistle. This visual and physical pun is reminiscent of ceramic bird whistles and decoration found on nineteenth-century American Federal tea and coffee services. The broad appeal of this kettle lies in its overt humour and wit and in its muted but effective use of pattern and colour. With the simple clean form, minimal decoration and restrained use of materials, the kettle is fundamentally an example of straightforward modernist design. However, it is the twist of the addition of the bird and the use of bold colour in the handle that breaches the bounds of Modernism. When launched in 1985, the kettle became an instant success, appealing to the top end of the consumer market with its combination of mischievous and radical design, and with high sales figures it earned its label as a Postmodern design classic. The kettle is still in production and is now available with a matt finish as well as the original polished surface and differing colours in the handle and bird. Further, Alessi has produced a cordless electric Whistling Kettle. As the water in the kettle boils it automatically switches off before enough steam is produced to blow the whistle, rendering the iconic bird silent and purely ornamental.

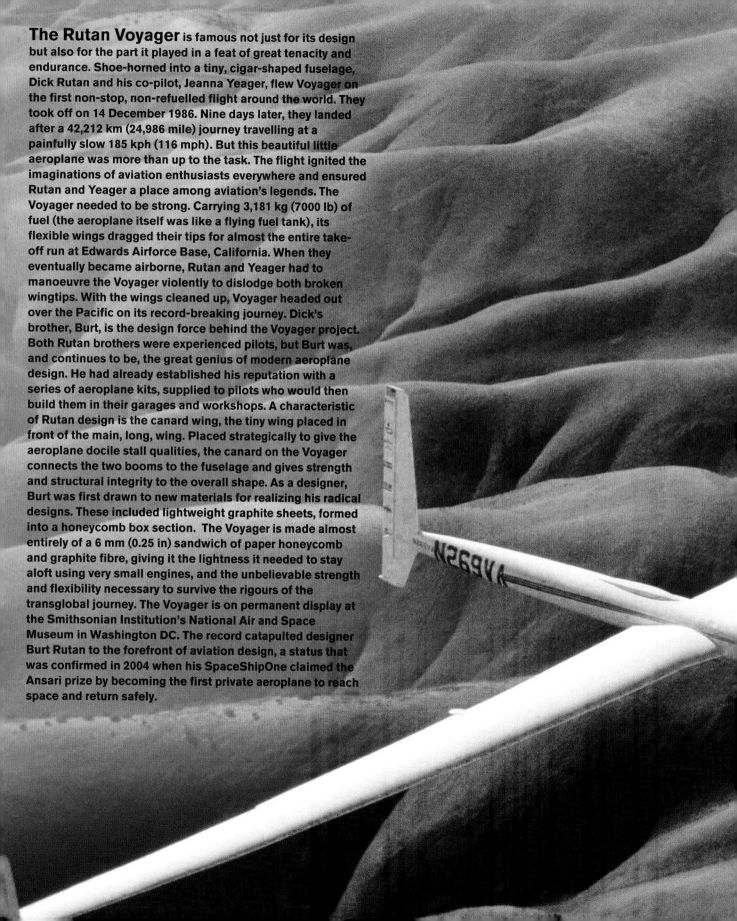

The Rutan Voyager is famous not just for its design but also for the part it played in a feat of great tenacity and endurance. Shoe-horned into a tiny, cigar-shaped fuselage, Dick Rutan and his co-pilot, Jeanna Yeager, flew Voyager on the first non-stop, non-refuelled flight around the world. They took off on 14 December 1986. Nine days later, they landed after a 42,212 km (24,986 mile) journey travelling at a painfully slow 185 kph (116 mph). But this beautiful little aeroplane was more than up to the task. The flight ignited the imaginations of aviation enthusiasts everywhere and ensured Rutan and Yeager a place among aviation's legends. The Voyager needed to be strong. Carrying 3,181 kg (7000 lb) of fuel (the aeroplane itself was like a flying fuel tank), its flexible wings dragged their tips for almost the entire take-off run at Edwards Airforce Base, California. When they eventually became airborne, Rutan and Yeager had to manoeuvre the Voyager violently to dislodge both broken wingtips. With the wings cleaned up, Voyager headed out over the Pacific on its record-breaking journey. Dick's brother, Burt, is the design force behind the Voyager project. Both Rutan brothers were experienced pilots, but Burt was, and continues to be, the great genius of modern aeroplane design. He had already established his reputation with a series of aeroplane kits, supplied to pilots who would then build them in their garages and workshops. A characteristic of Rutan design is the canard wing, the tiny wing placed in front of the main, long, wing. Placed strategically to give the aeroplane docile stall qualities, the canard on the Voyager connects the two booms to the fuselage and gives strength and structural integrity to the overall shape. As a designer, Burt was first drawn to new materials for realizing his radical designs. These included lightweight graphite sheets, formed into a honeycomb box section. The Voyager is made almost entirely of a 6 mm (0.25 in) sandwich of paper honeycomb and graphite fibre, giving it the lightness it needed to stay aloft using very small engines, and the unbelievable strength and flexibility necessary to survive the rigours of the transglobal journey. The Voyager is on permanent display at the Smithsonian Institution's National Air and Space Museum in Washington DC. The record catapulted designer Burt Rutan to the forefront of aviation design, a status that was confirmed in 2004 when his SpaceShipOne claimed the Ansari prize by becoming the first private aeroplane to reach space and return safely.

Initially designed as a floor lamp in 1986 and then subsequently released in table and hanging versions (both 1986), the Costanza lamp is, at first glance, the minimum distillation of what such an object should be: base, shaft and shade. And, of course, it is in this elegant simplicity and lack of superfluous ornament that much of this lamp's 'timeless appeal' lies. Yet perhaps a better reason for the Costanza's classic status lies in the way in which Rizzatto's design incorporates qualities of both flexibility and modernity within its apparently timeless and strictly traditional appearance. The Costanza, in the floor and table versions, is supported on a telescopic aluminium shaft, which allows the user to adjust the height of the lamp to suit its particular setting. While it adopts the most traditional of conical forms, the lamp's shade exploits modern materials to make the product better suited to the demands of contemporary living. Made of silk-screened polycarbonate, it is light, rigid, easily washable and just as easily replaceable. Still, one of Rizzatto's greatest achievements in the design of the Costanza is the way in which he demonstrates how a minimal or essentialist approach to design does not completely preclude ornament. This is most particularly demonstrated in the Costanza's distinctive rod-like switch. While the switch exists for practical reasons (it means that you do not have to fumble under the shade or rummage for the cord in order to operate the light), it also serves an aesthetic purpose. The switch is rather longer than is strictly necessary, designed to attract attention and as a counterpoint to the lamp's slender stand. In short, the Costanza seems to have been designed to make its owner aware of the fact that an object that lacks ornament is often the most ornamental object of all.

Spain did not figure largely in the development of twentieth-century design history. However, following the death of Franco, in the 1970s the country bounced back with a renewed optimism. One such example was the emergence of a group of like-minded industrial designers and theorists who came together in Barcelona in 1977 to form the research group 'Grupo Berenguer'. Comprising Jorge Pensi, Alberto Liévore, Noberto Chaves and Oriol Piebernat, the design team set about defining a more modern, refined and functional style, away from the extravagance of the city's architectural heritage of Antonio Gaudí. Working within the realm of furniture, lighting, product design and architecture, Pensi eventually chose to branch out independently with the founding of his own design studio in 1984. Pensi's research steered his interests towards the use of aluminium in furniture. His design for the Toledo Chair was originally intended for outdoor use at Spanish street cafés, but its subsequent popularity brought sales success across the world. The designer opted for a slender-lined, polished and anodized cast aluminium structure, lending the chair a slick and refined appearance coupled with comfort. The slits in the seat and backrest, which are apparently inspired by Japanese Samurai armour, allow rain to drain through the corrosion-resistant chair. The Toledo Chair is light and stackable, essential criteria for outdoor café culture. As a logical accompaniment, Pensi also designed a café table and introduced fabric, leather or polyurethane seat and back upholstery options for the chair. The phenomenal success of the award-winning Toledo Chair, produced by Amat, marked the start of a prosperous career for Jorge Pensi, who has become one of Spain's leading design consultants. His skills have been called upon to design furniture for international manufacturers including Thonet, Cassina and Knoll.

The Swiss have turned time-keeping into an art form, celebrated the world over by those willing to pay a premium for a Swiss-branded timepiece, of which the Official Swiss Railway Watch is one of the most recognizable. Its uncomplicated watch face is designed specifically for checking the time quickly. The circular face provides a clean backdrop to the simple block-shaped hour markers and the handsomely proportioned minute and hour hands. In contrast to the monochrome background, the bright red second hand, which replicates the station master's hand-held red departure signal, offers a constant reminder of the passing seconds. The stainless-steel case and black leather strap add to the authoritative styling. Lettering on the face includes the Mondaine company name above the small red and white company logo, the letters SBB CFF FFS which stand for 'Swiss Federal Railways', and the words 'Swiss Made' just below the 6, as confirmation of the watch's provenance. The Official Swiss Railway Watch was introduced in 1986 by Mondaine, the Swiss luxury goods group, as an inspired replica of the classic Swiss Railway Station Clock designed in the 1940s by Swiss industrial designer Hans Hilfiker. The clock originally found fame with the addition of a red hand that was employed as a beacon, visible from great distances on the station platform. Robust, understated and with unfailing technical accuracy, the clock came to epitomize Swiss efficiency, and the travelling public were quick to take it to their hearts. Shrewdly capitalizing on the clock's status, Mondaine produced their successful wristwatch version, which continues to be sold in twenty countries, and has been adapted to form new shapes and sizes. Although available in different shapes and sizes, it is the original circular-faced version that is most revered. Undoubtedly, it is likely to remain as one of the most successful monikers of Swiss branding for decades to come, as ubiquitous perhaps as the original railway clock, which still appears on each and every platform throughout Switzerland.

The Ko-Ko chair, constructed from black-stained ash and chromed metal, reflects its designer's fascination with contemporary Western culture. Shiro Kuramata's furniture designs reflect the confidence and creativity of postwar Japan. During this period of economic prosperity Kuramata was one of a number of artists who sought to synthesize Japanese tradition with ground-breaking new technologies and Western influence. He used modern industrial materials such as acrylic, glass, aluminium and steel mesh to create functional yet often poetic and humorous pieces. His desire to eliminate gravity in his constructions, to create lightweight pieces appearing to float in space, is a consistent theme. Kuramata's designs are dependent on a minimalist aesthetic and concept of proportion that derive from traditional Japanese architecture and methods of storage. He received a traditional training in woodcraft before pursuing his studies in design at the Kuwasawa Design Institute in Tokyo, where he was taught

Western concepts of design. He worked for a major fashion company, San-ai Company, designing their floor and window displays, as well as their graphic designs, before going on to work in the interior design section of Matsuya department store in 1964, the same year he opened his own design office in Tokyo. He gained prominence in the 1970s and 1980s for his many furniture designs and commercial interiors such as the series of international boutiques for the fashion designer Issey Miyake. In the early 1980s Kuramata became involved with the Milan-based group, Memphis, headed by Ettore Sottsass. The Ko-Ko chair falls into the lines of Postmodernism, as encouraged by Memphis, in terms of its abstracted form, which refers to an object to be sat upon, with the slight gesture of a backrest hinted at by the steel band. The object becomes a chair by the delicate intonation of its purpose.

855

Ko-Ko (1986)
Shiro Kuramata (1934–91)
Ishimaru 1985
IDÉE 1987 to 1995
Cappellini 1986 to present

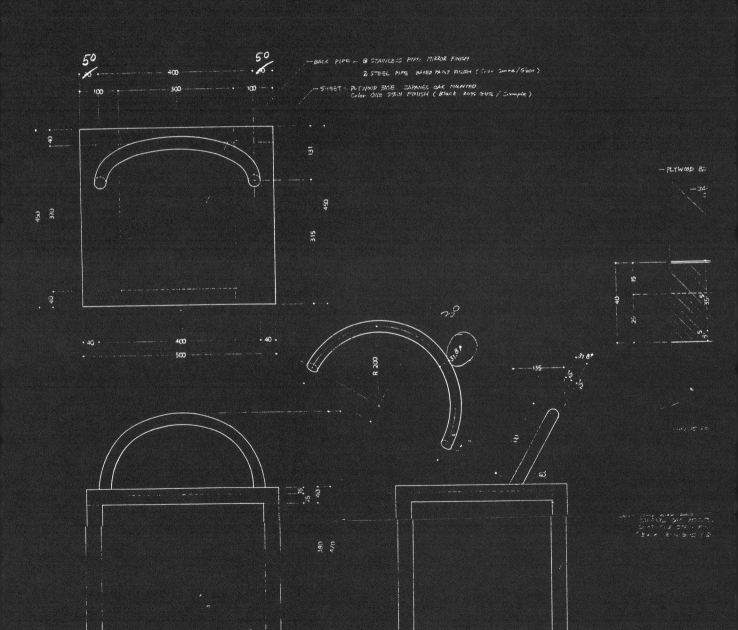

Toshiyuki Kita has made a career out of introducing contemporary design into traditional Japanese crafts. Over the past three decades, Kita has taken his designs to craftspeople in isolated villages in Japan, employing their nearly obsolete skills in the manufacture of commercially viable products for an international audience. Threatened with extinction because of competition from mechanized mass production and the emergence of wholesalers, the ancient crafts of *washi* (paper) and *urushi* (lacquer) are of particular interest to Kita. Reinterpreting the graphic forms of traditional tableware, the innovative 1986 Wajima ceremony series includes a fruit bowl, soup dishes and rice boxes. It was designed for traditional lacquer manufacturer Ohmukai-Kosyudo and employs an ancient lacquer technique in the traditional colour palette of red and black. Moving between both Milan and Osaka since 1969, Kita has commented that the Japanese are persuaded to appreciate their own heritage and culture only by design products that are successful in the West. While the forms of the Wajima pieces may look thoroughly Japanese to a Western eye, Kita has in fact pushed the boundaries of Japanese design to create something quite startling to the native viewer. The modernity of these pieces lies in their extended scale, while traditional Japanese lacquerware is quite diminutive, and their graphic, functional form. Kita makes a virtue of the strong colour combinations and sculptural forms of traditional lacquerware by exaggerating them, bringing them to a size of decorative objects to be admired.

The Thinking Man's Chair was one of Jasper Morrison's first industrially produced designs after leaving the Royal College of Art, London, in 1985. Morrison has explained his inspiration for the design as being 'a chance encounter with a quite elaborate wooden armchair with a missing seat cushion.' The structure of the armchair seemed to him to be very modern and became the starting point of the design. The finished chair's skeletal form of varnished metal tubes, with a seat and back composed of flat bars, and the elegant use of line refer to simple garden furniture as well as to traditional chair craftsmanship. The addition of subtle witty details, such as the small discs on the end of each arm on which people can rest their glasses and bottles, reveals a charm that fits nicely with the chair's slightly idiosyncratic appearance. Zeev Aram, an entrepreneur and champion of modern design, had gambled on Morrison after seeing his degree show and asked him to design a chair for an exhibition he was holding in his London shop, Aram Designs, in 1987. Amongst twenty-three pieces by distinguished artists and designers such as Eduardo Paolozzi and Norman Foster was the then unknown Morrison and his clever Thinking Man's Chair. By chance Giulio Cappellini visited the exhibition and was so impressed by Morrison's design that he stopped by his studio on his way to the airport the next day and invited him to come to Italy. He sent Morrison a ticket the following day, and thus began a long and mutually inspiring relationship between manufacturer and designer that continues to this day. Although the chair's reductive skeletal appearance reveals an early preference for the pared down, the design as a whole seems almost fussy when compared to Morrison's later designs, almost as if it has too much personality. Morrison said, 'I must have sketched the idea a thousand times before I honed it to something worthy of a prototype. It was a painful process and in many ways a formative project.' The evidence of his endless sketches can be seen in the terracotta painted version, which has white chalk-like notes with the dimensions and the radii scribbled down on the legs and arms, literally describing the shape of the chair. The other versions, all which are intended for both indoor and outdoor use, are less of a chair-in-progress and are produced in gypsum white, dark grey, and green.

857

Thinking Man's Chair (1986)
Jasper Morrison (1959–)
Cappellini 1988 to present

The generous size and classical outline of the How High the Moon armchair seems to contradict its use of the

unaccommodating industrial material steel mesh. Yet the chair offers great comfort far beyond immediate expectations

and the design remains important as an example of provocative and intellectual thinking. The design is exquisitely detailed

and its large volume reduced by the transparency of the material. The skeletal structure of fine steel mesh is a legacy of

Shiro Kuramata's strong modernistic background. Mesh has appeared in Kuramata's work before, but in a more planar,

two-dimensional way. With the design of How High the Moon, Kuramata has defined the key structural elements of seat,

back, arms and base. The simple delineation of these volumes reads as a whole through the singular use of material. The

sculptural qualities of Kuramata's design bring the chair into the realm of art. The curved planes balance harmoniously

with the flat, and play against the inherent rigidity of the material. In some ways, too, the production methods reinforce the

notion of artwork. Although the raw material is low-cost, the design requires fine, labour-intensive welding of pattern-cut

and pressed sheet metal, plated with copper or nickel, that create an expensive seating design. Kuramata would not

substitute the production technique of hundreds of individual welds for any other solution that would compromise the

transparency and fine lines of planes meeting each other. Kuramata brought carefully considered detail and harmony to

his design approach, although these elements were combined with an extraordinary understanding for materials and form,

rarely seen in furniture design. His approach to acrylic, glass and steel was highly influential for a generation of designers

following in his path.

858

How High the Moon (1986)
Shiro Kuramata (1934–91)
Terada Tekkojo 1986
IDÉE 1987 to 1995
Vitra 1987 to present

859

Sity Sofa (1986)
Antonio Citterio (1950–)
B&B Italia 1986 to present

At first glance there does not appear to be anything too extraordinary about the Sity sofa system. However, historical context is vital in understanding this product. Sity, which was designed by Antonio Citterio for the Italian furniture manufacturer B&B Italia, was a model of restraint and good manners in comparison with design during the 1980s. The Sity has set the template for what is still considered tasteful contemporary furniture design today. B&B openly discuss the importance of this sofa in the company's monograph stating it 'is a courageous step forward in the search for a system of seating conceived as a flexible and separable structure capable of reorganizing the now complex living scene'. This modular system came with certain core elements – including a straight sofa, a curved version or one with a chaise – while over twenty other pieces, including a bed, could be added to the core or scattered around the room. Indeed the bulbous, circular chaise that can form one end of the sofa arrangement is still being widely copied by furniture makers and designers across the globe. Unifying elements of the various pieces included their black plastic feet and tubular armrests. Several items also came with the option of a roller headrest. It was certainly appreciated at the time – Citterio was awarded the Compasso d'Oro for the system in 1987. However, possibly because of the era it was created in, the importance of Sity tends to be overlooked. The critics and historians are naturally drawn to the wild colours, shapes and rhetoric of the Memphis movement that appeared to encapsulate an entire decade's decadence. Yet, this is one of the most influential pieces of furniture to come out of the 1980s.

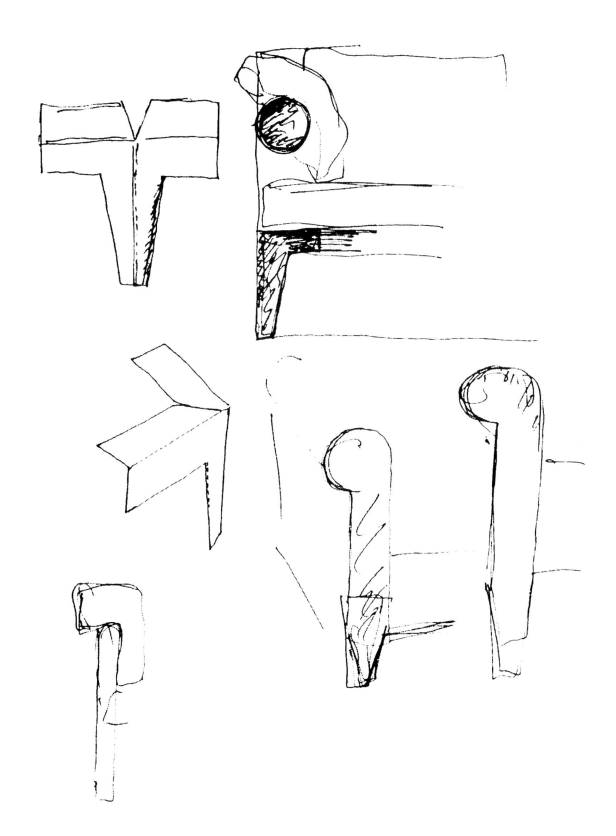

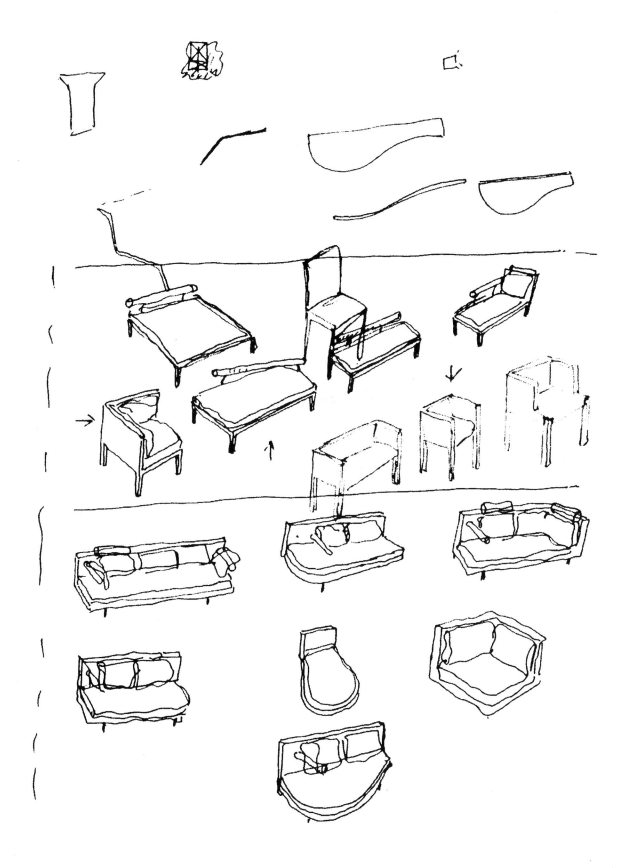

The Lockheed Lounge

was conceived by Marc Newson as 'a fluid metallic form, like a blob of mercury' based 'loosely, very loosely' on the chaise longue in Jacques-Louis David's 1800 portrait of Madame Recamier. The neoclassical reference, however, is tempered by the use of aluminium and rivets, hard industrial materials and the exuberantly languid curves influenced by Newson's love of surf culture. The Lockheed Lounge was Newson's break-through piece, forming the centrepiece of an exhibition of furniture designs at the Roslyn Oxley Gallery in Sydney, Newson's hometown. Having studied jewellery and sculpture as a student, Newson had not really thought of becoming a designer as such, but an interest in materials and industrial processes, together with an instinctive approach to design instilled by a childhood upbringing surrounded by 1960s Italian design classics, naturally led him to start designing furniture. Newson created the Lockheed's fluid form out of foam, having seen the technique used to create surfboards, and made a fibreglass mould from this. He tried to laminate it, but nothing would stick to the façade. He then spent 'a couple of miserable months' hammering hundreds of aluminium panels into shape with a wooden mallet and attaching them with rivets. The result reminded Newson of an airplane, so he named the piece after the American aircraft manufacturer. The exhibition won Newson a certain amount of acclaim. The National Gallery of Southern Australia bought the Lockheed Lounge for £3,000, and it featured in various design magazines. Having seen photographs of the Lockheed Lounge, the Japanese entrepreneur Tetuo

Madonna in the music video, *Rain* (1993)

Kurosaki, owner of the Tokyo furniture company Idée, purchased one model and then offered to put Newson's designs into production. Newson moved to Tokyo, and when Kurosaki began exhibiting Newson's work in Tokyo and Europe, most notably at the Milan Furniture Fair, Newson's reputation was sealed. In 1993 the Lockheed Lounge appeared in Madonna's video for 'Rain', bringing him immediately into the international spotlight.

860

Lockheed Lounge (1986)
Marc Newson (1962–)
Pod 1986

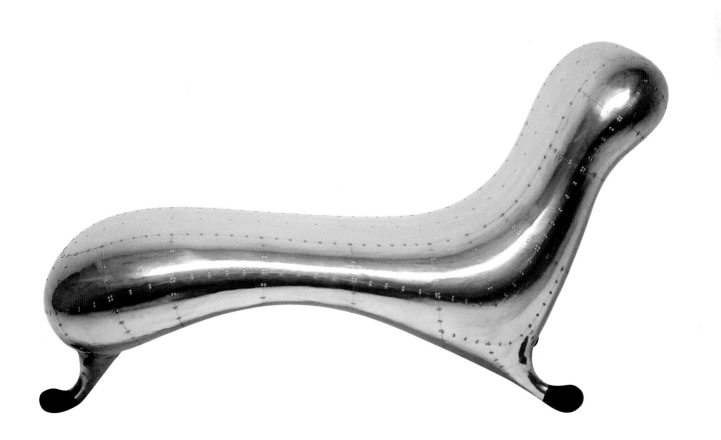

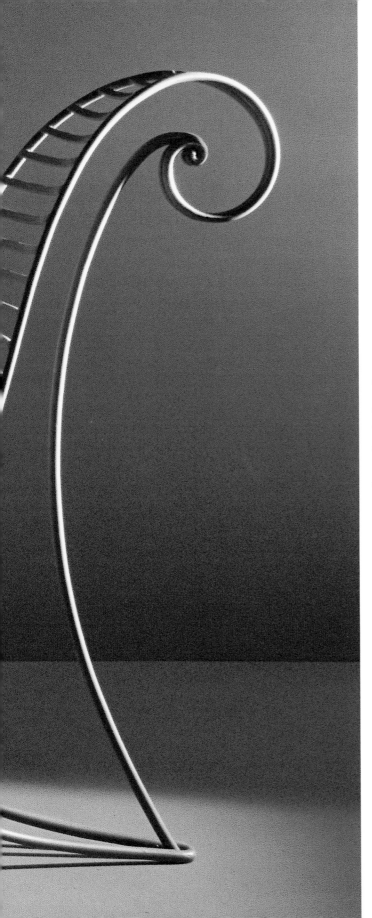

861

Spine Chair (c.1986)
André Dubreuil (1951–)
Ceccotti Collezioni 1988 to present

This is a design that breaks with twentieth-century conventions of metal furniture. Unlike bent tubular-steel chairs of the 1930s, its form does not derive purely from functional requirements. And unlike chromed metal chairs, the surface openly bears the marks of its manufacture. It is evidently a handmade piece of furniture that lacks the mechanical aesthetic employed for metal chairs before the 1980s. Postmodernism of the 1980s permitted designers to appropriate elements of historical styles, an approach to design that had been denounced by the Modernist movement earlier in the century. The form of the Spine Chair refers to the baroque style in, for example, the scrolls under the seat and the suggestion of cabriole legs, without slavishly reproducing them. Its curves are luxurious and decadent, as is the excessive use of steel in its manufacture, far more than is structurally necessary. The name of the chair draws our attention to its anthropo-morphism; it is almost like a ribcage hanging in front of a spine. Animal and human references in design were also common Postmodern traits. The Spine Chair was made in London by a French designer-maker, André Dubreuil, who collaborated with Tom Dixon, Mark Brazier-Jones and Nick Jones in Creative Salvage, a group of makers specializing in objects and furniture usually made from scrap metal during the early 1980s. Dubreuil's aesthetic was most similar to Brazier-Jones's. By the end of the decade, both were making highly individual furniture with historicist overtones in limited editions for the luxury market. In the 1990s Dubreuil returned to France and manufacture of the Spine Chair was licensed to Ceccotti Collezioni in Italy. Different versions of the chair have been manufactured; some are painted black while others are simply made of waxed steel.

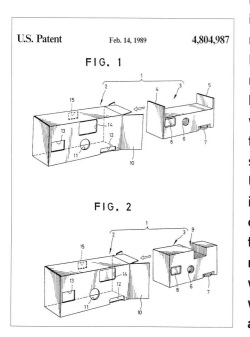

U.S. Patent   Feb. 14, 1989   4,804,987

FIG. 1

FIG. 2

Fuji introduced the world's first 'single-use' or disposable camera in 1986. The Quicksnap Camera was designed to appeal to first-time users and those wanting a quick and inexpensive way of picture taking, which unexpectedly opened up new areas of photography. The disposable camera was not a new idea: a little-known French model, the Fex Photo-Pack-Matic of 1966, was claimed as the first and the American Lure (sold as 'Rank' in Britain and 'Blick' in Italy) was marketed around 1975. A plastic recyclable camera, the Imp, was available in 1951 and was subsequently sold under the name Pro (1953) and Mini-Mate (1971). The camera was returned to the manufacturer for film processing, to be reloaded with film and sold again. None of these earlier cameras saw much commercial success. Kodak reacted to Fuji's move with the single-use Fling 110 cartridge camera in 1987. It had developed a similar product years earlier, but had never marketed it because of fears that traditional film sales might be harmed. Fuji quickly returned with the 35 mm Quicksnap, which offered a larger negative, producing better-quality pictures. New models which were brightly packaged, and ergonomically designed, now using 35 mm film, were increasingly compact and lightweight, some featuring built-in flash, panoramic formats, waterproofing and multiple lenses. With no sales prior to 1986, 22 million single-use cameras were sold in the United States and 62 million in Japan by 1993. The single-use market increased rapidly and, in 2000, sales represented 20 per cent of the total camera market. After the Quicksnap's launch, Fuji established a system to collect cameras after processing and return them to factories for recycling. By 1998 a reverse manufacturing process was put into place whereby reuse and recycling were built into the product design stage, with related parts being grouped into units for more efficient disassembly, and plastics being directly moulded into new components. In 1992 a full-scale recycling programme was introduced, so that the company was able to claim that its cameras were 100 per cent recyclable. Kodak claimed to get back 70 per cent of the cameras it produced and to reuse 86 per cent of the material from those cameras. By 1990 it had recycled over 400 million cameras. Although the majority of single-use cameras continue to use film, as digital technology has fallen in price the single-use sector has felt the impact. In 2003 Pure Digital Technologies of San Francisco launched its Dakota 2 megapixel single-use digital camera. The camera takes 25 digital pictures and the whole camera is returned to the retailer where the images are printed and put on to a photo CD before being returned to the photographer. The company retains the camera. An even bigger threat is the rise of the camera phone, which will leave little room in the market for single-use cameras, film or digital.

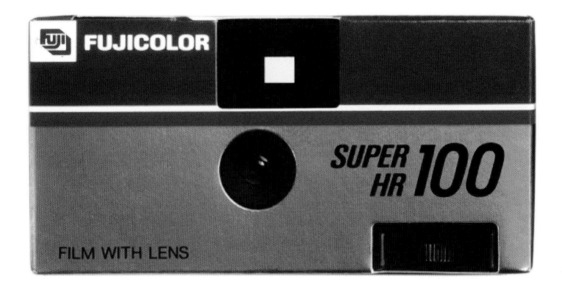

Michele De Lucchi and Giancarlo Fassina presented a prototype of the Tolomeo lamp to Artemide's product developers. The garish and provocative style associated with the Memphis Group (established by Ettore Sottsass, with De Lucchi and Andrea Branzi in 1981) had been stripped away in favour of an approach that explored notions of tension and movement. Stylistic features were being replaced with a more considered approach to structure and the production processes were being made available with technological advances. Tapping into Artemide's inherent desire to drive innovation, De Lucchi had proposed a light that could adjust and hold still at any angle, using a cantilevered structure and a system of spring balancing. The diffuser, which could be fully rotated, was matt anodized aluminium, while the joints were polished aluminium. The lamp is available in three versions, with interchangeable supports for the table and the floor and with a clamp for a desk. The Tolomeo lamp displayed more flexibility than its predecessor, Tizio, designed by Richard Sapper for Artemide, but also demonstrates an example of reworking earlier designs such as the Luxo L-1 by Jacob Jacobsen. This new addition to the vast Artemide collection was quickly proclaimed a perfect union of form with function. The Tolomeo won a Compasso d'Oro award in 1989 and has gone on to attain significant sales for the company. The original version has now been developed to suit every imaginable lighting situation as a table, floor, wall or ceiling lamp. Available in polished and anodized aluminium, the light is still selling strongly across the world today.

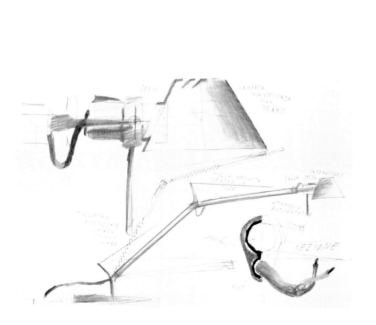

863

Tolomeo (1986)
Michele De Lucchi (1951–)
Giancarlo Fassina (1935–)
Artemide 1987 to present

Advertisement by Guido Buratto and illustration by Andrea Baruffi for Artemide USA: *Where is Tolomeo?*, 2004,

Michele De Lucchi

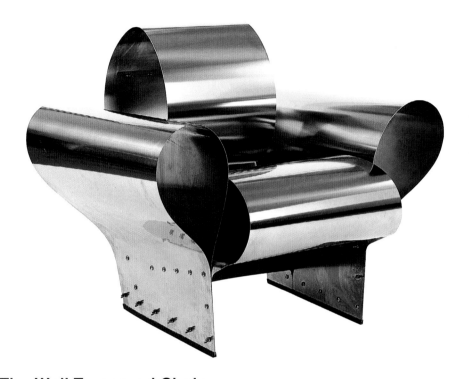

The Well Tempered Chair,

well named to reflect the tamed behaviour of the die-cut stainless-steel sheets, from which it is made, originated from a playful design workshop led by Ron Arad at Vitra's museum in Weil am Rein. Designer Arad had requested sheets of sprung steel for experiments. Luck had it that the particular material that was available was both flexible and resistant in the right measures to support, on its rolling shapes, the weight of a sitting person. It took Vitra over a year to source the right material again when Rolf Fehlbaum decided to put this piece into production as part of the 1986 Vitra edition. The production ended in 1993 when the steel used was no longer manufactured. The chair is made of four volumes: back, seat, and left and right sides, that act as legs and arm rests. Each is made of a single leaf of steel gently bent over itself so that its ends are clasped together into a plane. The back and seat connect on their flat sides to form a petal-like sitting area and the sides are bolted to a metal connector beam at the base to create the sumptuous flexible arm rests. The innovative contribution being the substitution of upholstery and mechanism by the actual construction. The simplicity of the structure echoes the formal idiom of a classic armchair. The unconventional sitting feeling, similar to that of sitting on a water bed, made this chair into a surprising design in the middle of the postmodern eighties, in spite of its modernist truth to the material's values. Arad, both a designer and a trained architect from the Architectural Association in London, and designer, talked of this cut-and-bolt piece as one of the last he designed with the idea of being able to make it in his own studio. This was the first project for a company other than his own One Off Ltd. In 2002 Arad designed the successor, Bad Tempered Chair, made in a sandwich of carbon fibre and Kevlar held together by polyester.

paper model
cut & glue

There is something non-specifically anthropomorphic about the S

Chair. Perhaps it is the cinched waist, curvaceous hips and suggestion of a spine and ribs.

Or perhaps the chair is zoomorphic and more resonant of a serpent than of a human form. Either way, the S

Chair's appeal is fundamentally organic, arising from its sinuous, ribbon-like form and the use of natural rush upholstery. The outline

is created from a welded bent-metal rod, around which the rush is woven. The S Chair bears comparison with two older classic

designs. The Zig–Zag Chair (1932–33) by Gerrit Rietveld featured a continuous folded plane to create the back, seat and

support. Rietveld's chair was necessarily made of wood, whereas Verner Panton's eponymous Panton Chair (1959–60)

translated the idea of a single rippled skin into moulded plastic. The undulations of the S Chair seem more freehand

than either of these designs, but the ribbon-like form and cantilevered seat suggest comparisons. Rietveld was

searching for unornamented purity, Panton yearned for industrial simplicity and Dixon sought sensuousness by

similar means. The chair marks a transition in Tom Dixon's career. His earlier works, both as part of the group

Creative Salvage and alone, were generally one-offs or limited-edition metal objects,

often created from recycled metal. He initially made S Chairs in his own London

workshop but quickly licensed the design to Cappellini, which continues to produce it in Italy. Dixon has gone on to design a number of

successful products, as well as heading the design department of the furniture store Habitat since 1998. Today he is one of the most

influential British designers, and the S Chair is one of his most significant designs. Cappellini has experimented with velvet, leather and

other finishes, as well as rush upholstery, and the S Chair features in every Cappellini collection, often signalling the keynote of the

season. The rush original, however, remains the most sensual S of all.

865

S Chair (1987)

Tom Dixon (1959–)

Cappellini 1991 to present

_ FARE PROVA SFODERABILE (escetto pelle)
— APPOGGIO SU 2 FASCETTE NYLON
— SOVRAFFODERA NELLO STESSO TESSUTO.

● SEDIA "S" CHAIR — TD1

_ BENE LE FINITURE
_ INCLINARE SEDILE DI 15 mm.
_ PIEDE IN GOMMA TONDO.

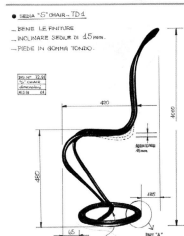

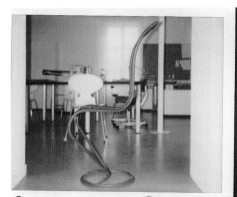

Sedia "S" CHAIR — Tom Dixon — 4·91

Sedia "S" CHAIR — Tom Dixon — 4·91

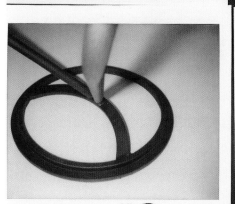

Sedia "S" CHAIR — Tom Dixon — 4·91

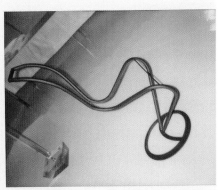

Sedia "S" CHAIR — Tom Dixon — 4·91

The I Feltri chair, made of thick wool felt, resembles a modern-day shaman's throne. While the base is soaked in polyester resin, making it strong enough to hold its shape and take the weight of a person, the top, by contrast, is soft and malleable, enfolding the sitter like a regal cloak. The idea of enveloping and enfolding is a theme that recurs in Pesce's work. Sometimes it is used as a comforting, maternal metaphor, and at other times it is intended to be more threatening and claustrophobic. Although Pesce is labelled an artist, architect and designer, he is also renowned for being a renegade and revolutionary. Above all, Pesce's work is characterized by his innovative use of materials, his obsession with exploring and developing new production techniques, and his insistence on producing objects that provoke controversy and challenge complacency. I Feltri was first premiered at the 1987 Salone del Mobile as part of Pesce's 'Unequal Suite' presented by Cassina. The pieces of this suite, a wardrobe, table, modular sofa and armchair, were entirely different from each other in style and aesthetic. What they did share, however, was an unskilled, 'disobedient', handmade appearance, intended as an antithesis to the high style, high production values predominant at the time. Pesce felt passionately that objects should have their own personality and true individuality. His aim was to mass-produce originals to produce a diversified series of objects that would reconnect craft with industry. Pesce had intended that by using low-tech, inexpensive manufacturing processes, the chair could be mass-produced in Third World countries from discarded rugs, and then distributed widely. Cassina, however, was not interested in such high ideals. 'I remember them telling me that they were obliged to take care of their own workers,' Pesce recalls. Today, the chairs are exquisitely crafted out of thick felt and priced accordingly.

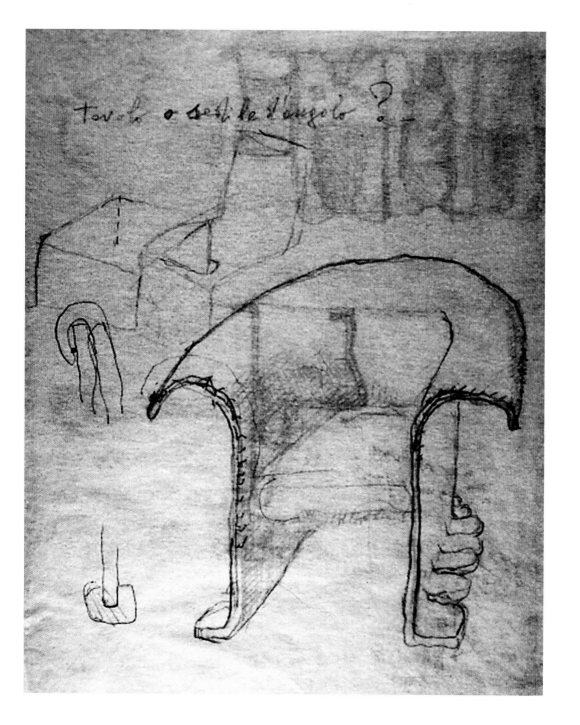

The Braun AB 314 Alarm Clock has become a benchmark in alarm clock technology and a torch-bearer for the Braun philosophy of quality and innovation combined with the modernist mantra of form following function. The AB 314 is a continuation of a travel alarm clock tradition pioneered in the early 1980s by Braun and Dietrich Lubs, the company's head of design, with the AB 310/312/313 series. These models were characterized by their small size and square, flat shape, which made them ideal travelling companions. The AB 314 quartz model moves forward by embracing a small, super-flat travelling clock complete with flip-down protective lid featuring a world time-zone map, as well as an alarm guard, snooze function, built-in flashlight and clock face illumination. The flat, square shape lends itself to portability in even the smallest pieces of luggage, and the lightweight, high-quality plastics provide an optimum surface quality and high durability. In graphic design terms the face is basic yet stylistically eloquent. Lubs was responsible for Braun's product graphics from 1971 and this shows in the graphic schema, particularly in the ordered and balanced articulation of the black plastic face, punctuated by clear and legible white numbers and hands. The simple monochrome tableau has a few colourful interlopers such as the yellow second hand, and green snooze and red light buttons, but these interventions actually serve to heighten the graphic appeal of the model rather than to create any unnecessary distraction. Subsequent permutations of the AB 314 have included models with voice- and reflex-control technology, whereby the alarm can be switched off using voice or actions respectively, rather than by manual means. The AB 314 has recently been superseded by the ABR 314 model, but for reliability, legibility, portability and style the original AB 314 is often cited as the definitive alarm clock.

868

Milano (1987

Aldo Rossi (1931–97

Molteni & C 1987 to presen

The Milano chair is an example of the happy coexistence of tradition and innovation. It was conceived to be made of hard wood, with versions in cherry wood or walnut, and its slatted backrest and seat are surprisingly comfortable, making the most of the flexibility of the slatted wood.

Aldo Rossi was primarily concerned with architecture and urban living. He had always considered design to be more of a hobby, and his collaboration with Alessi in the early 1980s was initially met with dissatisfaction, as the concept drawings that he presented for the Conica and the Cupola Coffee Makers were imprecise and lacked any measurements. Yet, Rossi's designs naturally convey his theories and the Milano chair, with its references to traditional design, reflects his belief that architecture cannot dissociate itself from its city's heritage. However, Rossi was a critic of Modernism, and was convinced that the solution for contemporary urban living could not be resolved by the modernist ethos of form following function.

The Milano chair, with the sweeping lines of the backrest, is a concession to this predicament, and with its ergonomic shape it looks somehow at odds with the principles embodied in Rossi's imposing structures and innumerable drawings. Rossi probably felt more freedom designing industrially designed objects, as these imply a use that needs to adapt to different settings and are not rigidly inserted into an urban environment. A series of beautiful drawings illustrate how the Milano chair might be used in different situations: in an informal meeting around a table, with a dog on the floor or in a studio setting.

The Milano chair is part of the important body of work cut short by Rossi's premature death, but continues to stand as a strong emblem of both his architectural and design work.

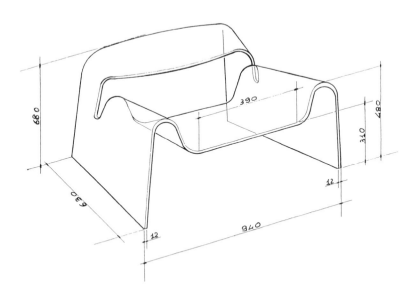

Although a seriously weighty piece of furniture, Cini Boeri and Tomu Katayanagi's Ghost Chair looks as light as air. Made from one slab of solid glass, this is a daring piece of design produced by one of the furniture industry's few truly innovative companies, Fiam Italia. Vittorio Livi founded Fiam in 1973, although it was not until a decade later that he made his most significant technological breakthrough. With a table called Ragno he produced what is thought to be the first item of furniture ever made from one single sheet of bent glass. In the following years he refined the technique until, in 1987, Boeri and Katayanagi gave Livi's technological innovation the poetic expression it deserved. Cini Boeri, a Milanese architect and designer, had been developing a number of ideas for Fiam when one of the senior designers, Tomu Katayanagi, suggested a glass armchair. 'All my principles were against it,' she recently recalled. 'Glass is cold and gives a sensation of fragility.

It doesn't offer comfort and an armchair must, on the contrary, offer warmth, relaxation and safety.' It was not until she saw the 'magical paper maquettes' proposed by Katayanagi that she became open to the idea and discovered 'the desire to take up the challenge and see if such a thing was possible to produce.' With Livi's assistance, the technical problems were resolved and the chair has since become a firm icon of avant-garde furniture design. Amazingly, the chair is capable of bearing a load of up to 150 kg (330 lb), even though the curved floating crystal glass is a mere 12 mm (0.5 in) thick. Fiam still produces Ghost Chairs today, warming large sheets of glass in tunnel furnaces before bending them into shape. Numerous designers, including Philippe Starck, Vico Magistretti and Ron Arad, have designed for Fiam since, but few have ever matched the startling, almost surreal, impact achieved by Boeri and Katayanagi with their fantastic Ghost Chair.

Although the design bears the same name as a previous 1960 light, Taraxacum '88 is a completely different design. Achille Castiglioni designed it for the Milan lighting fair, Euroluce, and it was immediately adopted by the Triennale Museum to illuminate some of its galleries. Taraxacum '88 (its name is Latin for 'dandelion') is made of twenty die-cast polished-aluminium equilateral triangles, each accommodating three, six or ten bulbs. A number of these triangles are hinged together to form an icosahedron, a twenty-sided form, the Platonic shape closest to a sphere. It is produced in three sizes, with a total of 60, 120 or 200 Globolux light bulbs. Castiglioni famously said of Taraxacum '88: 'It is a bit of a

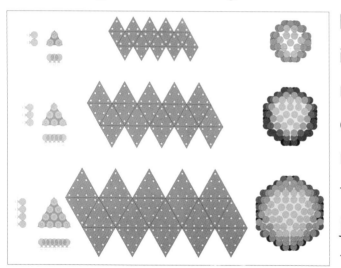

blow to energy-saving, but a big chandelier is meant for community areas, lobbies and rooms that need a lot of light for special occasions, so it also needs to be decorative.' The design also reflects his belief that designers should not push innovation just for the sake of it, but pursue it when there is a valid reason. Castiglioni conceived Taraxacum '88 as a light that could replace the classic multi-flame chandelier, with its emphasis on decoration. Taraxacum manages both to be a modern chandelier with a simple, coherent design, and to provide the same lighting scope provided by many flames. Its clustered shape was born out of Castiglioni's idea of taking individual light bulbs and grouping them together like a bouquet. Following Castiglioni's own classification of his work, Taraxacum '88 could be seen to belong to the 'redesigned objects' category, meaning traditional objects that the designer had perfected or updated according to current needs and technological developments.

870

Taraxacum '88 (1988)
Achille Castiglioni (1918–2002)
Flos 1988 to present

Achille Castiglioni

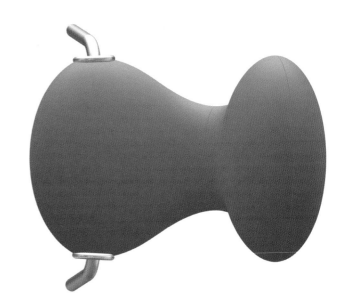

871

Embryo Chair (1988)
Marc Newson (1962–)
Idée 1988 to present
Cappellini 1988 to present

Marc Newson

A period spent living in a seafront beach hotel steeped in surfer culture plays a large part in Marc Newson's 1988 Embryo Chair. Aged just twenty-five and with no formal design training when he created it (he had chosen instead to study jewellery and sculpture at Sydney College of the Arts), Newson took a material related to the sea – the neoprene used to make wetsuits – to fashion a bright pink, distinctive design whose organic form recalls that of an embryo, giving the chair its name. It is a perfect example of Newson's signature style: fluid, swelling shapes reminiscent of 1960s science fiction married with the appropriation of industrial materials to create wildly imaginative futuristic forms. The original chair has changed little since its debut at the Powerhouse Museum exhibition, 'Take a Seat', in Sydney in 1988. It still features a one-piece body made in polyurethane foam, whose back tapers to a waist before widening out into a seat supported on three tubular metal legs. Newson's gift here and through much of his work is to take a material not intended for use in furniture production and make that material integral to his design, creating a statement that is witty and innovative but also sophisticated and gorgeous. Nearly two decades since its creation the Embryo is still in production, in Japan by Idée and in Europe by Cappellini, and it still looks fresh and exciting, characteristics obviously associated with Newson's own strong influences. Growing up with contemporary futuristic designs such as Joe Colombo's Boby Trolley in the beachfront hotel his mother managed, admiring modern classic cars like the Aston Martin DB5 and the 1960s Lamborghini, and drinking in the fantastic film sets of production designers like Ken Adam (the man responsible for the futuristic look of *Dr Strangelove* and James Bond's *Dr No*) obviously played their part in shaping Newson's imagination. He has since designed everything from a bottle opener and toilet-roll holder to a recording studio and the interior of a Falcon 900B long-range jet.

Shiro Kuramata's poetically minimalist creations were instrumental in raising the profile of, and setting the benchmark for, Japanese design during the second half of the twentieth century. One of the Tokyo-based designer's finest and final legacies is the Kiyotomo Sushi Bar in Tokyo, in which you find this delicate yet functional chair, a masterwork in transfiguring form and material into extraordinary lyricism. The chair started life as an exhibition piece, and was created for a furniture event held at the Axis Gallery in Tokyo and Isetan Department Store in Shizuoka in 1988. The exhibition was organized to promote the image of Shizuoka and in particular to celebrate its strong cabinet-making tradition. Leading designers were invited to create furniture showing the possibilities of wood, thus providing a boost to the local timber production and manufacturing industries. Prior to designing the Chair for Kiyotomo, Kuramata had established his reputation with materially and formally innovative and unorthodox furniture pieces, such as the Glass Chair of 1976 and the steel-mesh How High the Moon armchair of 1986. Early in his career Kuramata had studied in the Woodcraft Department of the Tokyo High School of Industrial Art. Therefore, the design for the Chair for Kiyotomo represented an ideological homecoming of sorts. The lacquered wood of the chair has been crafted with a precision and minimalist meticulousness that is very much in the Japanese aesthetic tradition, yet the wood base is combined with a steel pipe and chrome back, providing a contemporary twist. Although the Chair for Kiyotomo began as a conceptual piece, it gradually evolved, with the technical assistance of Japanese furniture manufacturers Furnicon, into a fully functional product. The Kiyotomo Sushi Bar is soon to re-open under the name of 'Shiro', in hommage to the designer. At the time of Kuramata's death in 1991, the chair was still displayed in the Sushi Bar, and today is available upon request.

Designed by Antonio Citterio and introduced in 1990, Vitra's Chair AC1 is notable for its lack of levers. At the time of its launch, the office industry had become obsessed with height adjustability, producing chairs that were full of gadgets but tended to look rather cumbersome. In this environment the Swiss manufacturer's pared-down product came as a refreshingly elegant change. The adaptable material, Delrin, is used for the backrest shell, with CFC-free foam polyurethane upholstery. The revolutionary aspect of the chair was that it had no concealed mechanism, making it look very clean and light. Instead, the flexible back connected, via the armrests, to two points on the seat. This allowed the position of the seat's surface to change with the angle of the back, meaning the two elements were completely synchronized. The chair responded to the positions of the user's body and moved with them – all without having to twist a lever. As Vitra's sales pitch for the product pointed out: 'Because the materials used are flexible and because the shape of the chair fits the body so well, you automatically sit more dynamically and thus better in ergonomic terms.' The length and height of the seat, lumbar support and the counter-pressure of the back-rest could all be adjusted depending on the height and weight of the user. The chair worked well while, importantly, looking very attractive. Like many of its rivals, it came in an array of different fabric finishes and the five-legged, star-shaped base could be bought in plastic as well as polished or chrome-plated aluminium. In its most photographed form it often used a geometric checked backrest fabric created by Alexandre Girard. Citterio also designed a sister model, the bulkier AC2, for the more executive end of the market.

Chair AC1 (1988)
Antonio Citterio (1950–)
Vitra 1990 to present

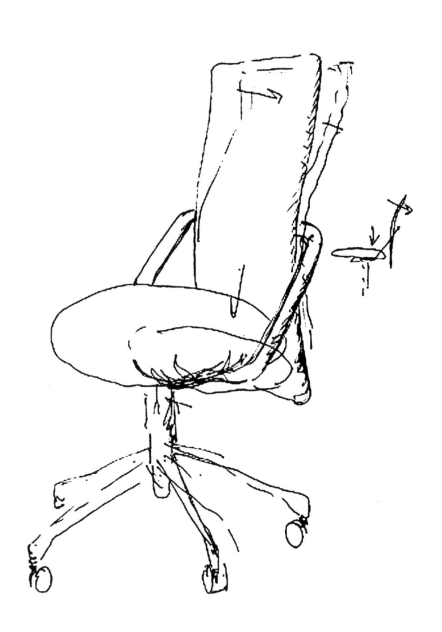

The Ará is one of many lighting designs by the irrepressible designer, Philippe Starck. Although the design maintains the characteristics of many lamps, with a circular foot/base, an upright, tapering stem and an adjustable hood to protect and direct the light source, the light is switched on and off by adjusting the head up and down. It is a design that displays a language and uses forms that are characteristic of Starck's enormous portfolio of work. The Ará is an illustration of powerful design and marketing sensibilities at a point when Starck was emerging as an international household name associated with high-quality brand-associated products. The lamp uses highly reflective chrome steel that evokes glamour, wealth and an intelligent understanding of contemporary design. The organic, flame-shaped shade is a form Starck has used throughout his work, from small-scale door handles and toothbrushes, to furniture, through to the massive sculptural 'flame' on top of the 1990 Asahi Building in Tokyo. It is this distinctive vocabulary that assists the Ará towards the achievement of classic status, while at the same time calling attention to itself as a Starck-designed object. The balance between the three components of base, column and shade is weighted towards the symbolic value of the shade. The personality of the design is represented through the evocative shape of this component and marks the Ará as quite different from other table lights. The shade articulates, like many other lamps, to fulfil functional requirements, but the balance between shade, column and base creates a cohesive whole that represents Starck's successful and individual juxtaposition of shapes. Starck was appointed artistic director at Pierre Cardin in 1969 but it was his commission in 1984 for the interior and furnishings of Café Costes in Paris that drew him into the more commercial public eye. With a skill for self publicity and eloquent charm, Starck welcomed the many opportunities that came his way. He approaches and understands new technologies both as a designer requiring their application, and as a consumer wishing to embrace them. Philippe Starck displays the characteristics of one of a handful of 'super-designers' who have managed to influence a generation of designers and manufacturers and who have had a powerful impact on domestic and interior landscapes.

The Kivi Votive is an object so simple it barely seems to have been designed at all. It is made from surprisingly chunky, lead-free crystal and comes in eight colours: clear, cobalt, lavender, yellow, red, green, light green and light blue. These colours may have been inspired by the colour cubes by Leo Moser and Moser Glassworks, the famous Bohemian glassmakers established in 1857, who have been using nine shimmering colours in some of their stemware. While the colours may have been influenced by the Czech manufacturer, glassmaking is very much part of the Finnish tradition and has been ongoing for the last 300 years. In this design the glass enriches and enhances the light produced by the candle, adding to the ambience of the room. The votive can be used on its own or in a cluster as a centrepiece of a table and, importantly for a product like this, is competitively priced. There is no doubt that since its launch Kivi has managed to transcend fashion and has established itself as a quiet, contemporary classic by adhering to iittala's values of durability, quality, modernity and a feeling of joy. Orvola went on to win Finland's most important design award when he picked up the Kaj Franck prize in 1998, and works in a range of materials including ceramics, cast iron and textiles, as well as making avant-garde sculptures, tableware and dinnerware.

Jasper Morrison's

Ply-Chair Open Back not only fulfils the criteria of a classic design but also offers an insight into Morrison's thoughtful approach to the design process. The overtly spare outline indicates a utilitarian outlook towards seating design. The strict formulation of front legs and seat suggests pure functionalism, balanced against the gentle curve of the back legs and back rail to support the sitter. A further concession to comfort is subtly disguised beneath the thin plywood skin of the seat, where concave cross bars provide a cushioning effect. The construction and fixing devices are exposed, revealing the composition and simplicity of the design. The Ply-Chair was conceived for an exhibition, 'Design Werkstadt', in Berlin during the city's 1988 Year of Culture. Morrison described his inspiration: 'At the time I was obsessed by the kind of wooden chair you find in old bars and restaurants all over Europe, straight-forward, no-nonsense chairs.' He designed and constructed the chair with limited equipment, in a material he considered relevant to his exhibition and as a reaction to the stylistic exuberance of the period. With sparse facilities to hand (sheet plywood, a jigsaw and some 'ship's curves'), the design evolved from two-dimensional cut shapes to a three-dimensional seating design. 'It was an experiment to try to assess the "invisible" qualities of an object and the impact the contents of a room may have on the atmosphere of a space and further, how these objects may interrelate,' Morrison explained. Rolf Fehlbaum of Vitra recognized the enduring qualities of the design and went on to produce the Ply-Chair with an open back and a second version with the back filled in, 'which is more comfortable, but less exciting'. The Ply-Chair is representative of Morrison's attitude to the design process and as such it is a benchmark for a renewed wave of 'thoughtful' design that he is responsible for and that has strongly influenced the last fifteen years of design practice and consumer taste. The shared use of plywood provides a reference to early masterpieces by Marcel Breuer and Alvar Aalto, as the material provides a common ground, and the spare, elegant functional profile brings the Ply-Chair to the comparable value of these predecessors. Morrison's sensitive approach to design involves finding usefulness and longevity in his projects. This utilitarianism belies extravagance and short-term fashions and proves Morrison's designs to be of lasting quality.

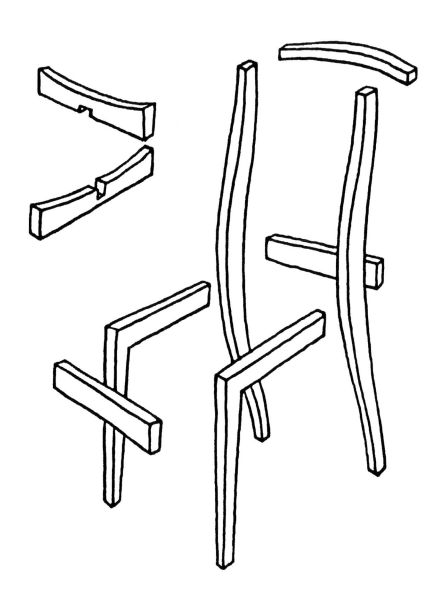

The Wood Chair was originally designed by the Australian designer Marc Newson for an exhibition in Sydney of chairs made from Australian wood. In choosing to take part in the exhibition, he was faced with the challenge of adapting his own design style to accommodate the inherent qualities of wood, an unusual choice of material for him then and since. Intent on stretching a wooden structure into a sequence of curves in order to emphasize the natural beauty of the material, Newson set about finding a manufacturer capable of producing the chair to his specifications. Every company he approached told him that his design was impossible to make until, eventually, he tracked down a manufacturer in Tasmania who agreed to produce the chair in a supple local pine. In the early 1990s Newson began working with Italian furniture manufacturer Cappellini, who offered to make reproductions of some of his early designs, including the Wood Chair. Central to Newson's work is the discipline underlying his instinctive sense of form: 'I have always tried to create beautiful objects with challenging technologies.' He once said that this discipline stemmed from a lifelong love of making things, from constructing toy cars and boats in his grandfather's garage as a boy and later, as a young designer, hand-sculpting the Lockheed Lounge in a Sydney backyard. Newson has always striven to express order, and most importantly, simplicity, in revealing the essence of a product and its materials. The Wood Chair is an early example of this design philosophy, taking the inherent qualities of the material, in this case Tasmanian pine, and literally stretching it to expose its natural beauty and design possibilities. Newson studied jewellery and sculpture at the Sydney College of the Arts. After graduating in 1984 he designed and made limited editions of sculptural furniture, first in Sydney, then in London and Tokyo. As his international reputation rose throughout the 1990s Newson opened larger studios in Paris and London to execute more ambitious industrial projects. His approach to design is not simply to tinker with existing typologies, but to take a long, lateral look at them and imagine how the perfect version might be.

Miss Blanche is believed to be inspired by a dress with red roses worn by Vivien Leigh in the film *A Streetcar Named Desire*, by Tennessee Williams. The cheap artificial red roses floating in acrylic are meant to represent the frailty and vanity of Blanche DuBois. The roses also make ironic reference to the faded charms of chintz upholstery, and the arms and back of the chair are gently curved, suggesting a feminine elegance. However, the angularity of the piece as a whole and the manner in which the aluminium legs are inserted into slots carved out of the underside of the seat, making them clearly visible, introduce an uncomfortable tension that acts as a counterpoint to any notions of feminine sweetness. One of Japan's most important designers, Shiro Kuramata loved the idea of contrast and extremes, combining seemingly non-negotiable concepts such as transparency and solidity. Miss Blanche represents the culmination of a period in Kuramata's career that explored the notion of transparency. Kuramata felt attracted by transparent materials, because he claimed that transparency belongs to no one place in particular, but simply exists. He particularly loved working with acrylic, which he saw as an ambiguous material, cold as glass, yet warm as wood. Throughout his work he strove to go beyond the limits of the material world, often trying to make things 'disappear', and repeatedly created objects at a borderline or at the critical point of transformation where material becomes light and weight transforms to air. Miss Blanche was created for KAGU Tokyo Designer's Week '88. Samples of artificial flowers were collected from all over Japan, and numerous models of the chair were constructed in order to achieve the perfect illusion of floating flowers. During the final stages of production the acrylic was laid in its mould and the roses were held in place with tweezers. Kuramata reportedly telephoned the factory every thirty minutes to make sure the floating effect was achieved.

When Ross Lovegrove designed the Basic Thermos Flask in collaboration with Julian Brown, the aim was to combine structural and technical innovation. In the finished design the improvements in production and materials used are visualized in the thermos flask itself. The transparent plastic does not in any way conceal the construction, purpose or material. The thermos flask explores the relationship of the inside and the outside by using transparent polycarbonate plastic and the material is redefined as a durable material in this flask. The Basic Thermos Flask consists of only three transparent parts, which are assembled by threads: a round bottom, ribbed on the inside for strength; a funnel-shaped cover; and a spout with integrated handle. These parts can be assembled with great ease, integrating the silvered glass vacuum flask like a treasure. In recent years, Lovegrove has become an advocate for organic design. For him, the use of computers to create these designs is as important as studying nature, resulting in often wonderful solutions that cannot be emulated by any artist or designer. Combining modern technology with general knowledge and inspiration from nature has made Lovegrove a very influential designer. The Basic Thermos Flask is one of the first products to illustrate this new attitude. Ross Lovegrove studied industrial design at Manchester Polytechnic and then completed his studies with a master's degree at the Royal College of Art, London, in 1983. Upon graduation he worked for prestigious continental companies like Frog Design and Atelier de Nîmes, returning to Great Britain in 1986 to found a London-based studio with Julian Brown. In 1990 the collaboration ended and Lovegrove started his own Studio X.

Basic Thermos Flask (1988–90)
Ross Lovegrove (1958–)
Julian Brown (1955–)
Alfi 1990 to present

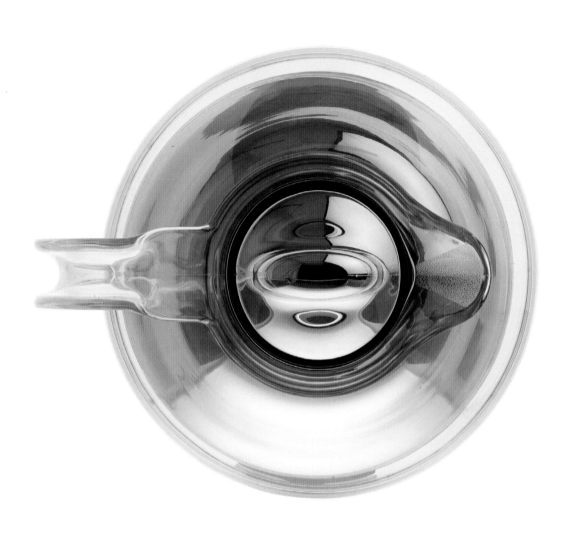

New Zealander John Britten was the maverick genius of late twentieth-century motorcycle design. From the late 1980s until his death in 1995 this engineer and designer dominated the world of racing motorcycle design with his radical and successful racing motorcycle, the Britten V-1000. Britten's machine was hand-built and assembled around his own 1,000-cc 60-degree V-twin engine. The beautifully designed engine is light, immensely strong, impressively smooth for a V-twin and powerful, capable of achieving an incredible160 brake horsepower at 11,500 rpm. Not simply an eccentric and beautiful object, the V-1000 was very fast and very successful. Right from the start it beat production race bikes from established factory teams, and not just on local New Zealand tracks but also on the international stage. Most sensationally, in 1997 it won at Daytona, the cradle of American super-bike racing. Britten's most radical design decision was to abandon the conventional frame. He came up with the idea of clustering as much of the weight as possible around the engine, creating a short-coupled and quick-handling machine. The engine is the heart and soul of the Britten and all the external design decisions flow from it. Using Kevlar and carbon fibre, everything from seat to wheels to suspension was bolted to the engine, which became the central stressed unit. The seat is simply a carbon-fibre beam extending rearward from the cylinder head. The rear suspension is actually mounted in front of the engine, and connects to the rear swinging arm via a long rod. With its powder blue and lipstick pink colour scheme, it turned heads from the moment it was unveiled. Britten realized his dream of combining beauty, speed and function in one racing machine.

With numerous awards and titles, Vico Magistretti has been recognized as one of the pioneers of the postwar Italian design phenomenon. After thirty years of designing furniture and with scores of successful products credited to him, Magistretti designed the Silver Chair in 1989 for De Padova, where it continues to be produced. The Silver Chair illustrates one of the most consistent and significant themes of Magistretti's work in that it manages a captivating balance of idiosyncratic originality and reference to the traditional. This is made possible by his preference for conceptual simplicity, which manifests itself here as a reinterpretation of an earlier design using new materials. According to Vanni Pasca in his 1991 book about him, Magistretti is fascinated by

'anonymous traditional objects' in part because he sees them as able to 'go on repeating themselves in time with slight differences, because they're basically resistant to conceptual wear.' The Silver Chair is a reinterpretation of what he considered to be an archetypal bentwood chair, similar to Chair 811 attributed to either Marcel Breuer, Josef Hoffmann or Josef Frank, and featured in a Thonet catalogue from 1925. The original would have been made of solid steam-bent beech with rattan, cane or perforated plywood like standard Thonet products made since the nineteenth century. Silver Chair is made of polished welded aluminium tube and sheet material, with a polypropylene seat and back giving a fresh interpretation to an old form, comfortably familiar and yet new. It is available with or

without arms, castors and a pedestal base and, just as Thonet chairs were suitable for a variety of environments, the Silver Chair was intended to address the needs of a changing contemporary dynamic between home and office. In an interview published by De Padova in 2003, the Silver Chair is best explained by Magistretti himself as 'a homage to Thonet, who had produced a similar chair. I thought it would be a good idea to use and reinvent it, also because I've always loved Thonet chairs, even if these are no longer made of wood and straw…. At the same time they are a homage to other objects usually seen around us: they remind me of the baskets used for eggs in the Japanese market in Tokyo, with their square holes which I loved so much and from which I took inspiration for this chair's seat and back.'

When the Braun AW 20 wristwatch appeared on the market in 1990 it represented a logical development for Braun, arriving as it did after the success of the company's alarm and wall clock ranges. Its beautifully minimalist form and precision detail also captured the *zeitgeist* of the early 1990s with its back-to-basics retreat from the ostentation of the 1980s. In doing so the AW 20 restated the Braun philosophy of innovation combined with a pure and simple design vision. The AW 20 was designed by Dietrich Lubs, deputy head of Braun Design from 1995 to 2002. Lubs joined the Braun Design Department in 1962 and subsequently designed some of the company's most successful and iconic products, including the precedent-setting Control LCD ET 44 Calculator in 1978, and, more presciently, the AW 20's horological predecessors, the ABW 30 Wall Clock and the AB 314 travelling alarm clock series, both from 1982. In common with its

predecessors the AW 20 precision quartz movement watch is beautifully proportioned, quietly detailed and functionally and ergonomically precise. All extraneous fuss has been removed, resulting in a face that is a triumph of Minimalist graphic design; Lubs himself was responsible for Braun's product graphics from 1971. The AW was produced in black or chrome and originally featured numerals, but after 1994 the design displayed the minute scale only and articulated a monochromatic sensibility. However, a measured splash of colour appears on the minute hand and date detail, thereby lifting the watch's design dynamics. Luxury as well as durability is also implied in the stainless-steel casement and flawless leather strap. Dietrich Lubs's AW 20 wristwatch ceased production in 1998, but in design terms it has influenced all subsequent Braun watches, as well as many other current mainstream market models.

The beauty of Titania is that it appears almost transparent when looked at from the front but solid if seen sideways on and, by the merest touch of the hand, the light moves, giving a new experience each time. A lead counterweight allows the height to be adjusted with the minimum amount of fuss. The lightness of the outer shell allows it to be hung from virtually any part of the ceiling. Designed by Paolo Rizzatto and Alberto Meda, from a distance the lamp appears rather complex and fragile, yet in fact it is elegant and easy to use. The striking, elliptical outer casing, made from lamellar aluminium, holds a number of 'blades' made of silk-screened polycarbonate, which come in five different colours. By simply slotting a different shade, either green, yellow, blue, red or violet, into the outer shell and over the white light source, the colour of the light changes. The interchangeable blades simultaneously act as a reflector of the central light source, and as a dissipater of heat from the bulb. While it was obviously a contemporary reinterpretation of the classic reading lamp, Titania's design seemed to come out of the ether. It managed to be both contemporary and decorative, while at the same time being highly engineered and vaguely organic; perhaps not completely surprising as Meda's background was in engineering. The elliptical shape, while somewhat unusual for a hanging lamp, was the result of the requirements of the way in which the illumination functioned, and therefore defined the contour. A floor model with an aluminium stand was introduced in 1995, but it is this suspension lamp which attracted much attention. Discussing his philosophy on design Meda once said: 'A subtle object eludes the logic of imagination and simple visibility; it isn't flashy, it doesn't shout out at you, but instead takes the path of non-invasiveness, of de-materialization, of miniaturization.' It is a sentiment that sums Titania up nicely.

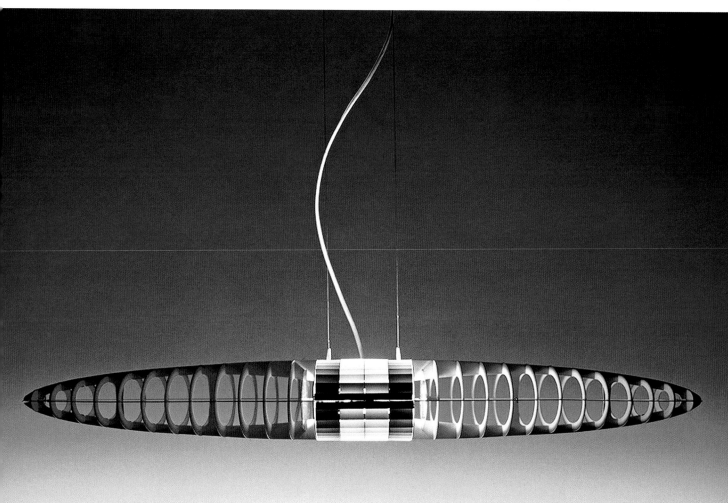

883

Titania (1989)
Alberto Meda (1945–)
Paolo Rizzatto (1941–)
LucePlan 1989 to present

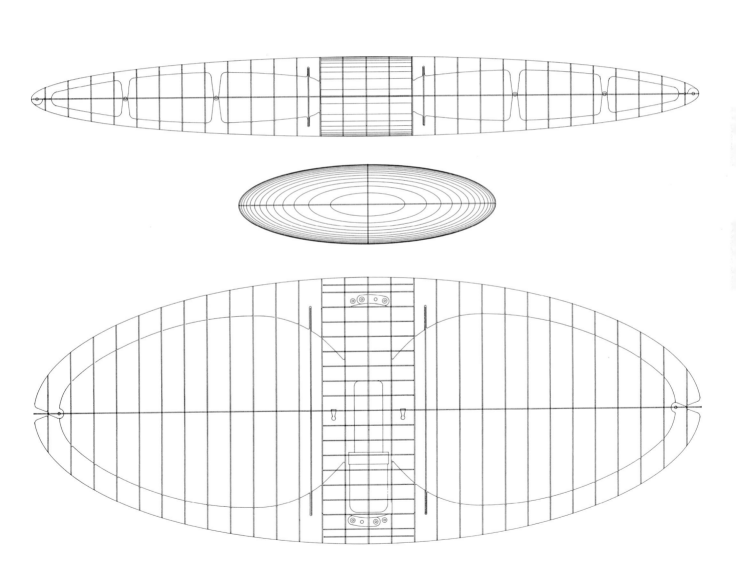

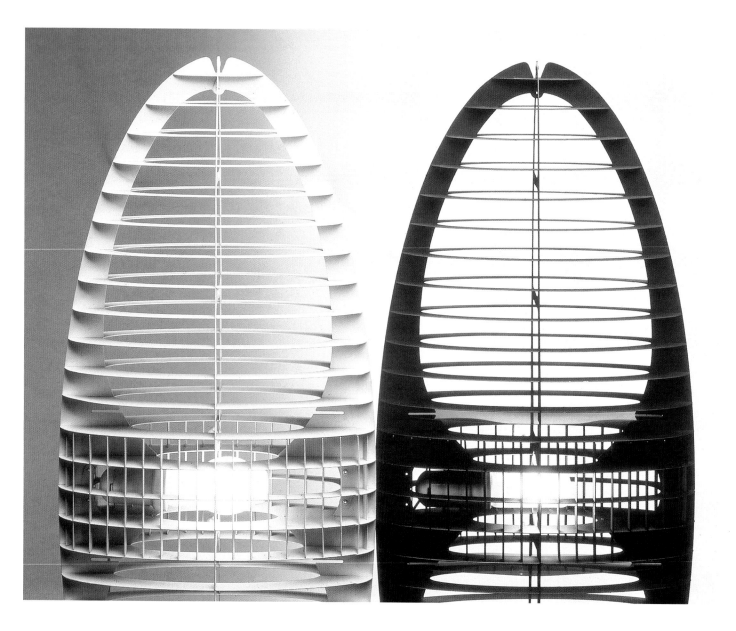

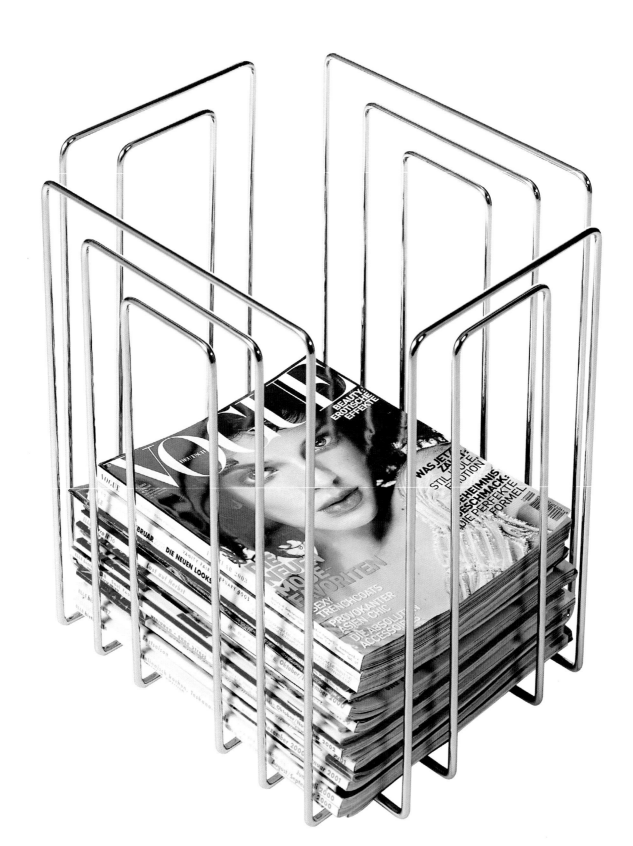

The magazine or newspaper rack is a design object that is found as often in the home as in the office. Launched in 1989, Willi Glaeser's version gives a contemporary twist to this ubiquitous design object. Swiss designer Glaeser is known for his pared-down work using chrome-plated steel wire to create objects with a high level of practicality, solid in form yet elusive. Glaeser had the ingenious idea of rethinking the use of the rack and combining it with a waste bin, turning it into something more than just a holder for ephemeral printed material. Engaging with modern concerns for sustainability and recycling, Glaeser's rack holds newspapers, magazines and waste paper neatly and in an ordered manner, allowing them to be easily collected and recycled. The Wire Newspaper Rack is available in two sizes, one to hold standard broadsheet publications folded in half, and the smaller size to cater for folded tabloid newspapers, magazines and waste paper. The clean and straightforward form of this modern, functionalist design has no added decoration or features. A thoughtful example of precision-crafted design, the rack secured its position as a prime example of high design and eco-awareness that developed in the late 1980s.

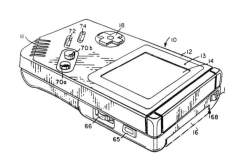

It would not be an

exaggeration to suggest that the Nintendo Gameboy, the compact video game system, created a tidal wave in design, fashion and economy for the portable game console. Nintendo, a company whose beginnings as a card manufacturer date back to 1889, began making video games in the 1960s with a number of early failures and difficulties. But when Gunpei Yokoi, a graduate in electronics, joined in 1965, he rose from the initial post of maintaining the assembly-line machines to an electronic game designer, later becoming the head of the Research and Development team. It was at his suggestion that his team, in the mid-1980s, created a hybrid of the NES and Game & Watch hand-held consoles, which led to the Gameboy. When it was

originally launched it was received with some scepticism, because it had a small screen of less than two square inches, which was monochromatic even though the technology to create colour consoles had existed for some time. But these factors worked in the Gameboy's favour: the size of the screen allowed the whole gadget to be portable, with a weight of only 300 g (10.6 oz), and the lack of colour permitted lengthy battery economy. It was a self-contained system, with the patented Nintendo cross-key joystick. The console offered Game Link, with a connecting cable, allowing two players to compete against each other at the same game. Furthermore, it was the first to provide a jack for headphones so that the high-pitched digital sounds could be heard in stereo solely by the player. The Gameboy's ultimate success lies, perhaps, in its brilliant marketing idea of packaging the system with the ideal game. This game was Tetris, created by the Russian

mathematician Alexey Pajitnov and spotted in 1988 by Nintendo's American CEO at a trade show. Similarly to Super Mario Brothers and the NES, Nintendo launched its portable console with Tetris, selling one million Gameboys in 1989 in the United States alone. The craze became an international sensation, with over 60 million sold, establishing 'Gameboy' as part of every child's vocabulary during the 1990s. The Gameboy has evolved through several versions since the launch of the much-loved original, including the Gameboy Advance SP, which was released in 2004.

The Orgone chaise longue has come to be a signature design of the Australian, Marc Newson. Its organic shape, hence the name, and bright, exotic colours have appeared regularly in his work across genres from household objects to concept cars and interiors since he came to prominence in the 1990s. The piece found an audience after it caught the eye of the renowned Italian manufacturer, Giulio Cappellini. At the time Newson was working with Japanese entrepreneur Teruo Kurosaki, whose Idée business manufactured several Newson designs from the late 1980s, prompting the designer's four-year stay in Japan, his first venture beyond his homeland. Newson's upbringing in Australia meant that while he could and did absorb the influence of European Modernism by choice he was not bound to it as part of a rigorous design education. This left him free to explore his wide-ranging fascination with contemporary visual culture and the act and technology of making things. The Orgone clearly borrows from Newson's Australian roots, as its fibreglass form with gentle curve resembles a surfboard with the waist nipped in. The hourglass Orgone shape would reappear in a celebrated later project when Newson designed the 021C Concept Car for Ford in 1999, incorporating the Orgone pattern into the interior carpet and even the tyre tread. Cappellini still produces the Orgone, as well as a variation in the shape of the Orgone Table, which is essentially the same design but with an additional leg.

Orgone (1989)
Marc Newson (1962–)
Cappellini 1989 to present

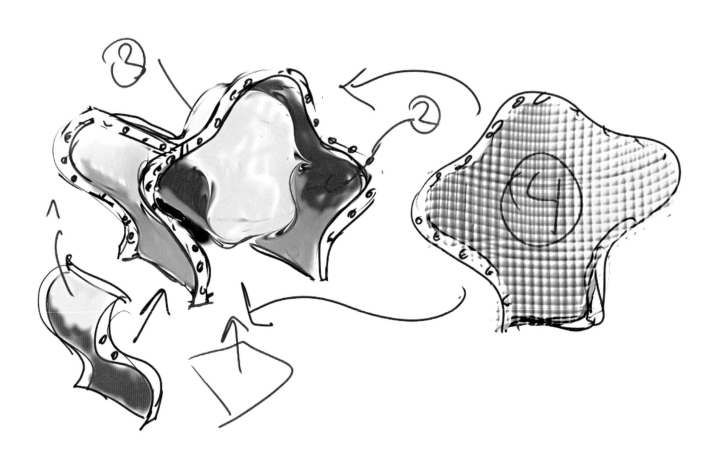

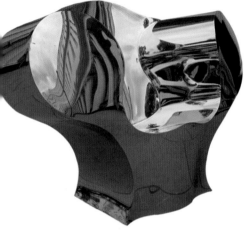

The initial Volume 1 series of the Soft Big Easy evolved from Ron Arad's desire to retain the clarity and immediacy of his sketches once they were translated into form. He 'sketched' directly on to steel with spray paint, cut each element out with electric shears, assembled the rough form by spot welding, and bent and beat final touches before completing the final welding of seams. After the rough, almost primitive, impact of these one-off designs, the Big Easy gradually evolved into the more commonly seen Volume 2 series. With the advent of the Volume 2 series, these overstuffed armchairs were no longer a passing experiment, they were now being collected and priced accordingly. This second series was produced in two editions of twenty with mild steel replaced in one by stainless steel and in the other by patinated black steel. They were followed in 1999, by the New Orleans series made out of pigmented polyester and reinforced with fibreglass. Gone was the idea of a bold sketch merely imposed upon volume and in its stead stood chairs formed from glistening, undulating curves of steel without the faintest trace of seam or line. Arad was a trained artist-turned-architect from a family of artists, and his references to, inspiration from, and respect for, art are not without thought or import. He avoids existing categorizations and orthodoxy in favour of innovation, and one can draw parallels between the importance of the seminal Big Easy series and his unconventional path to success. The Big Easy is a modern restatement of art within design, and the series marked a transition in 1989 both for Arad and for design generally. Since 1990 Arad began mass producing the Big Easy with the Italian manufacturer, Moroso. The new series included an upholstered as well as a plastic version, rotationally moulded from recycled pigmented polyethelane. Arad's production of his first edition works were always chairs for sitting, but each prompted a frenzy of buyers pursuing the chairs as visual pieces. This cult of collecting had little precedent in modern design in 1989. By his refusal to adhere to the norm, he became the precedent. He had designed a series of chairs and had built a business by ignoring orthodoxy.

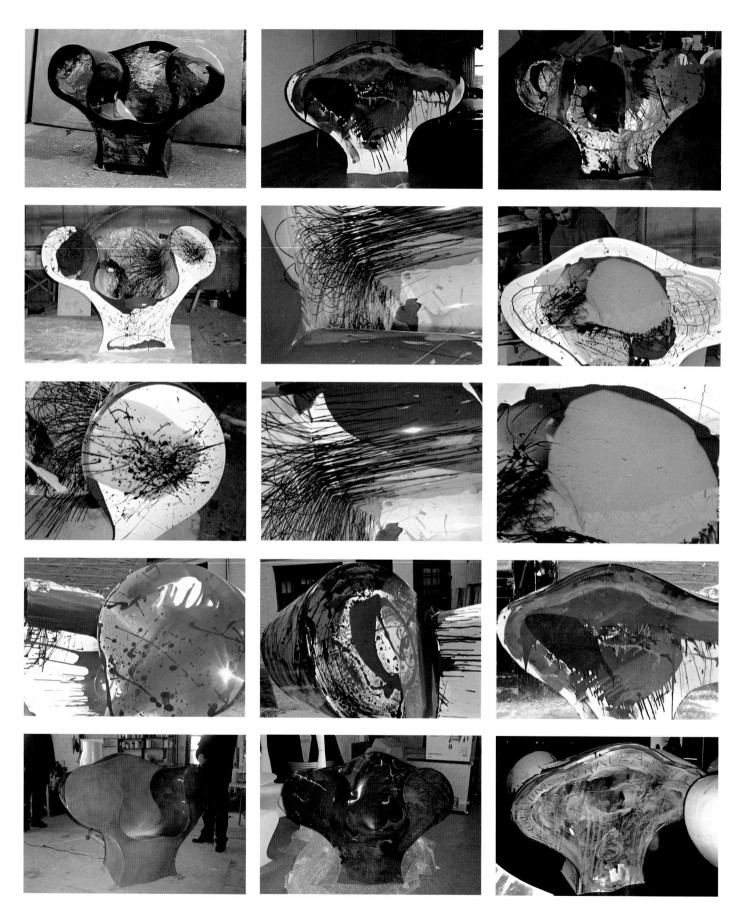

Flemming Bo Hansen's WATCH

was designed at a time when digital timepieces were considered to have had their day and were deemed to be totally out of fashion. However, Hansen's design challenged this assumption with staggering success, both in terms of sales and acclaim. The slim, square-faced digital watch was soon elevated to iconic status and received many international design awards. The design pioneered the aesthetics and design of personal wrist-watches, an achievement confirmed by its inclusion in leading design museum collections, including the permanent collection of The Museum of Modern Art in New York. Flemming Bo Hansen was an apprentice at Georg Jensen and worked with the company in Copenhagen, New York and Tokyo. Combining design and craft sensibilities, he developed a personal design philosophy of 'simplicity by elimination', with his work focusing strictly on functionality, yet not at the expense of style or beauty. His WATCH is elegant and simple in form, style and features. With no light, alarm, stopwatch or additional features, this honed-down wristwatch has a purity that focuses on time and a design that eliminates all distractions. The large proportions of both the rectangular face and the easy-to-read numbers serve to make the design a rare object of late 1980s modernist ideals. With its ground-breaking simplicity, Flemming Bo Hansen's watch design used efficiency and focus to full effect. Bo Hansen formed a partnership with manufacturer Ventura that became synonymous with distinctive design, success-fully challenging and influencing contemporary notions about watch design. With a clarity of approach Bo Hansen embraced and accepted the restrictions of designing an instrument to be worn on the wrist, resulting in a design that cast off previous traditions.

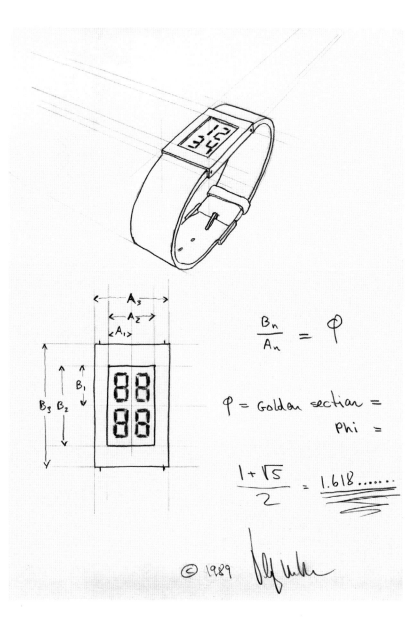

$$\frac{B_n}{A_n} = \varphi$$

$$\varphi = \text{Golden section} =$$
$$\text{phi} =$$

$$\frac{1 + \sqrt{5}}{2} = \underline{1.618\ldots\ldots}$$

© 1989

WATCH (1989)
Flemming Bo Hansen (1955–)
Ventura Design On Time 1989 to 1999

889

Flower Vase Ephemera (1989)
Shiro Kuramata (1934–1991)
Ishimaru 1989
Spiral 1989 to present

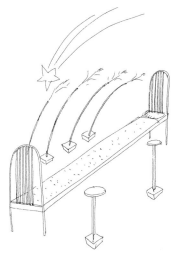

In Japan flowers and flower arranging form an important component of traditional interior decoration. The flower arrangement reveals the artistic and material tastes, education and cultural practices of the householder. The flowers used, and the receptacle in which they are placed, are chosen to create a specific theme. Taking this Japanese tradition and fusing it with Western modes of design and culture, Shiro Kuramata developed a fresh way of looking at the flower and its vase, which incorporated the functionalist approach important to Japanese design. Kuramata first produced the Ephemera Vase for a solo exhibition at the Yves Gastou Gallery in Paris in 1989. Each long-necked vase resembles a wilting flower, or a human head bent in prayer, referencing themes of solitude and the transient nature of organic and human life, which is reinforced by the vase's name. Several of the vases were placed alongside a bed for the exhibition 'Il Dolce Stilnovo della Casa' at the Palazzo Strozzi in Florence, where they could be said to resemble flowers placed for the dead. Constructed from acrylic, aluminium and stained alumite finish and holding a single flower each, Kuramata's stem-like vases receive and transform natural and artificial light, making them appear transparent and less dense. Kuramata's fascination with acrylic was based upon its ability to capture, enclose and permeate light within an object. He effectively used this property to destabilize and reinvent the apparent form and structure of objects, while retaining their literal form and function. By inventing a new design language concerning the ephemeral, and playing with gravity, Kuramata questioned the relationship between form and function, imposing surreal and minimalist ideals on familiar objects. In Europe, Kuramata's work has had a profound effect on the progress of design to the extent that, at the time of his solo show in Paris, the French Ministry of Culture awarded him the title of 'Chevalier de l' Ordre des Arts et des Lettres'.

How to twist
the rules
of the game.

© 1992 The Knoll Group

KnollStudio

Introducing Cross Check. One of seven new designs by Frank Gehry for Knoll. 105 Wooster Street, New York City.

For other locations or more information call 800 445-5045.

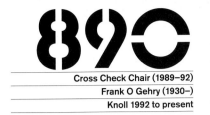

The best designs are sometimes those that arise from the simplest ideas. In this instance the aim was to exploit the structural and flexible properties of laminated maple strips to make every part of the chair. The strips are woven together, giving the characteristic check pattern that is reminiscent of rattan or basketwork furniture but on a vastly larger scale. The undulations of the interconnecting, laminated strips give the chair structural stability that is both flexible and durable. It is not incidental that the chair also has a strong visual presence and is instantly recognizable. Its conception dates from a period when chairs began to be treated almost as works of sculpture, and their designers fêted like artists. While remaining totally practical, the Cross Check Chair is traded in limited, signed editions like an artwork, and collected as much for its experimental formal qualities as for its usability. The Cross Check Chair was designed by the Canadian-born architect Frank Gehry, best known for radical organic buildings such as the Disney Concert Hall in Los Angeles and the Guggenheim Museum in Bilbao. It was not his first foray into furniture design, nor his first experiment with materials. The inspiration for the Cross Check Chair was, claimed Gehry, the woven structure of apple crates that he remembered from childhood. In 1989 furniture manufacturer Knoll established a workshop in Santa Monica, California, close to Gehry's own studio, and for the next three years the architect experimented with laminated wooden structures. The frame is constructed of 5 cm (2 in) wide hard white maple veneers and extremely thin strips, which are laminated to 15.24 to 23 cm (6 to 9 inch) ply thickness with high-bonding urea glue. Thermoset assembly glue provides structural rigidity, minimizing the need for metal connecters, while allowing movement and flexibility in the backs of the chairs, for added comfort. The collection of chairs and tables was previewed at New York's Museum of Modern Art in 1992 and has won Gehry and Knoll numerous design awards.

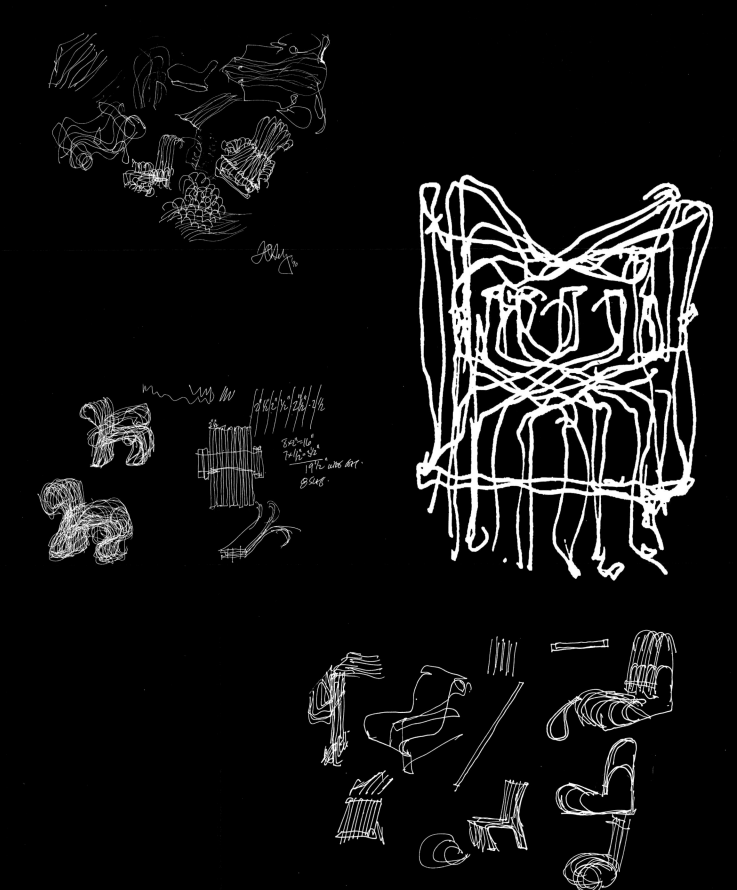

Cross Check Collection, 1992. Left to right: Power Play Club Chair and Off Side Ottoman, High Stacking High Back Chair, Hat Trick Arm Chair, Face Off Cafe Table, and Cross Check Chair

Nach Allerorten Sommer

ist uns das Reisen zumute. So lange, bis wir die Landkarte nicht mehr in ihre Falten

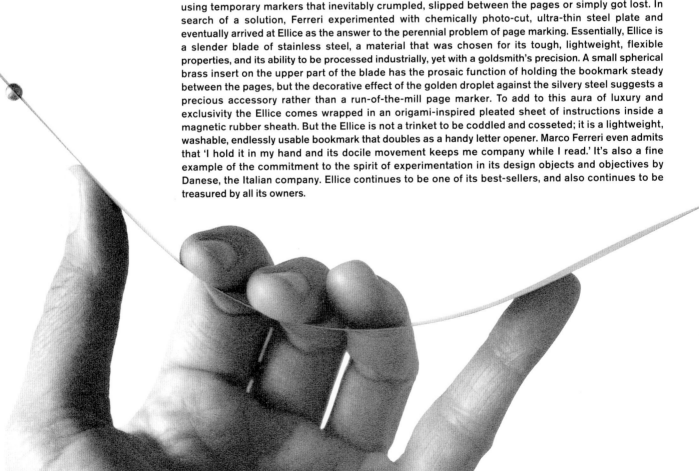

Marco Ferreri's Ellice takes as its starting point the humble bookmark, but completely reimagines it into a jewel-like yet fundamentally functional work of art. Architect and designer Ferreri was inspired to create a bookmark when he continually experienced the pitfalls and annoyances of using temporary markers that inevitably crumpled, slipped between the pages or simply got lost. In search of a solution, Ferreri experimented with chemically photo-cut, ultra-thin steel plate and eventually arrived at Ellice as the answer to the perennial problem of page marking. Essentially, Ellice is a slender blade of stainless steel, a material that was chosen for its tough, lightweight, flexible properties, and its ability to be processed industrially, yet with a goldsmith's precision. A small spherical brass insert on the upper part of the blade has the prosaic function of holding the bookmark steady between the pages, but the decorative effect of the golden droplet against the silvery steel suggests a precious accessory rather than a run-of-the-mill page marker. To add to this aura of luxury and exclusivity the Ellice comes wrapped in an origami-inspired pleated sheet of instructions inside a magnetic rubber sheath. But the Ellice is not a trinket to be coddled and cosseted; it is a lightweight, washable, endlessly usable bookmark that doubles as a handy letter opener. Marco Ferreri even admits that 'I hold it in my hand and its docile movement keeps me company while I read.' It's also a fine example of the commitment to the spirit of experimentation in its design objects and objectives by Danese, the Italian company. Ellice continues to be one of its best-sellers, and also continues to be treasured by all its owners.

Conceived by the French designer Philippe Starck this cast aluminium lemon juicer was created for the Italian manufacturer Alessi. The Juicy Salif has become synonymous with the design culture that first appeared in the 1980s, and has achieved the seemingly impossible task of making a juice squeezer controversial. Often the focus of heated debate and criticism, the Juicy Salif polarizes opinion. Widely derided as being hopelessly non-functional, impractical and difficult to both use and store, it has also become a piece that is a mainstay for any museum collection or book of modern design. For those who consider design from a principally aesthetic viewpoint, the Juicy Salif is a jewel-like and much-loved reference point within the world of practical, utilitarian and often visually monotonous kitchen utensils. It can be viewed as a stroke of genius from a designer who constantly evades popular assumptions. Its simplicity of form can be seen as an inspired reinterpretation of an everyday object. Starck challenges the norm that a squeezer must comprise three elements: the squeezer, sieve and container. The Juicy Salif hones down the form to a single, elegant shape that can be placed over a glass so that, following the laws of physics, the juice flows directly into the glass. It is this simplification that also fuels the opinions of his critics and makes the juice squeezer the ultimate symbol of extravagant hedonistic consumerism. The lack of the fundamental sieve and container parts results in the pulp and pips ending up in the glass and the sharp spindly legs are liable to dent all but the toughest of work surfaces. But love it or hate it, the Juicy Salif undoubtedly exemplifies a shift in late twentieth-century product design. It is this product, more than any other freely available and affordable item, that defines the move from the consumer's priority being one of *need* to one of *want*.

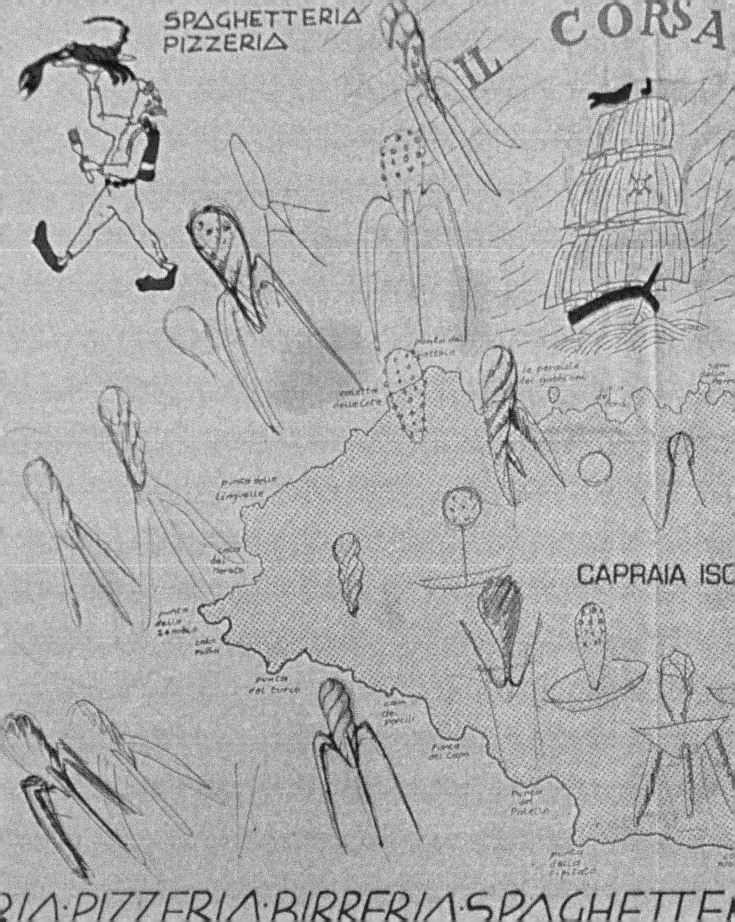

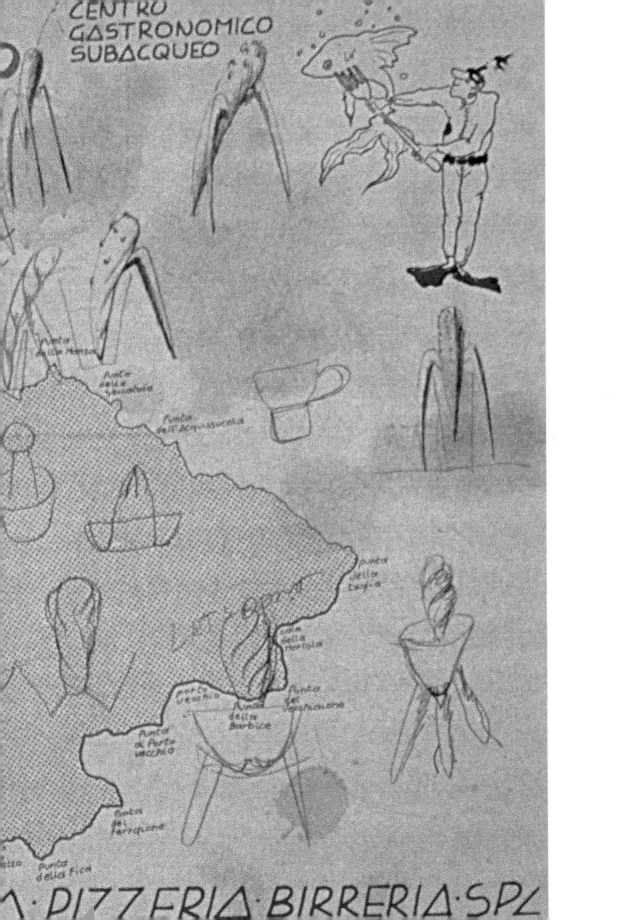

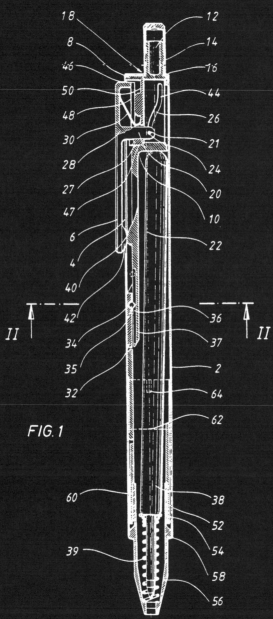

FIG. 1

Since its launch in 1990, the Lamy Swift capless rollerball pen has demonstrated itself commercially accountable to its manufacturer. The first capless rollerball to incorporate a retracting safety feature to avoid inkstains, this landmark in late twentieth-century pen design, it provides ammunition for the modernist argument that innovation and traditional core values can coexist in any given object. Despite its svelte proportions, the Swift feels surprisingly weighty in the hand. Its satin-effect nickel-palladium-coated shaft, embellished only by a tiny black Lamy logo near the base and a thin set of pitted indentations designed to aid grip near the nib, exemplifies German design understatement. Its inventive retractable pocket clip that folds flush with the barrel at the press of a button adds to an overall sense of quiet efficiency and sleek control. Designer Wolfgang Fabian qualified as a goldsmith before studying industrial design. Working as a freelance for Lamy, he came up with the disappearing clip as a way of indicating whether the pen was safe to place in a pocket or not. A push of the tip simultaneously exposes the rollerball nib and retracts the clip in one seamless movement. This design innovation was in response to the recently refined Lamy M66 refill cartridge used in the Swift; while it offered a smooth and capacious flow of ink, there was clearly potential for leaks. With Fabian's practical as well as elegant solution, the Swift user can confidently carry the retracted pen in a shirt pocket. An independent family company based in Heidelberg, Lamy first forged its reputation in 1966 with the launch of the Bauhaus-styled Lamy 2000 fountain pen designed by Gerd A Müller. The Lamy Swift embodies the Bauhaus philosophy and, more importantly perhaps, it enforces the notion that modern design can add value to a time-tested tool without undermining its integrity.

893

Lamy Swift (1990)

Wolfgang Fabian (1943–)

Lamy 1990 to present

LAMY

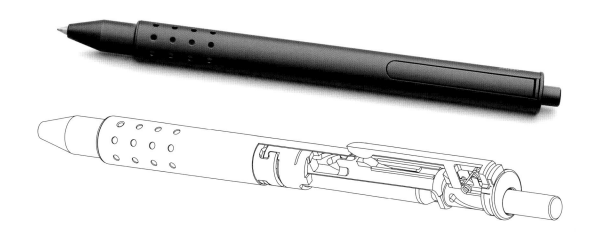

We've remodeled the most important parts of your kitchen.

We've remodeled the peeler. We've remodeled the garlic press, the can opener and the wooden spoon. And we didn't stop there. Any kitchen tools that weren't comfortable or easy to use were fair game. The idea isn't to make the old tools obsolete, it's to make them better. If we can't make them better, we don't make them at all. Pick up OXO Good Grips® and you'll feel what we mean. They're easy to hold, easy to use and easy to love. In fact, they might just change the way you feel about your kitchen.

OXO GOOD GRIPS

For information call 1-800-545-4411

'Why do ordinary kitchen tools hurt your hands?' This question prompted Sam Farber's development of a series of easy-to-use kitchen tools, Good Grips. His wife, Betsey, suffered from arthritis in her hands and had difficulty in using conventional kitchen tools. Farber, a Harvard graduate entrepreneur, first established COPCO, a kitchen design company in the 1960s, after which OXO International was founded in 1989 as his second venture. This company's philosophy, based on ideas of universal design, expresses a desire to create products that can be easily used by people of all types of abilities, sizes or ages. Farber initially approached the New York-based industrial design company, Smart Design, to develop a range of products. After extensive research into ergonomic requirements for general users, professional chefs and arthritis sufferers, the company fulfilled the brief by producing a range of affordable, comfortable, high-quality and good-looking kitchen products. Smart Design began their research by interviewing consumers and chefs, and by examining and observing the effects of ageing. From these studies, the company divided the movements of the hand and wrist into three categories: twisting and turning, pushing and pulling, and squeezing. The designs for the scoop and peeler fell into the first category, the graters and knives into the second and the garlic press and scissors into the third. Among the first fifteen Good Grips products launched in 1990, the vegetable peeler exemplifies the brand. As its name implies, the key to the product lies in its handle. It is made from Santoprene, a polypropylene plastic/rubber that is soft and flexible and prevents slippage. It is also durable and dishwasher-safe. With its patented flexible fins, inspired by bicycle handlebars, the handle fits comfortably into the hand, no matter what the size, age or ability of the user. The stainless-steel blade was designed with great care to minimize the effort required for peeling. Manufactured by a Japanese company that also produces samurai swords, the blade swivels and glides through the skins of fruit and vegetable with ease. The Good Grip tools have won many major design prizes and, while they are part of the design collection of New York's Museum of Modern Art, they have also been recognized by the Arthritis Foundation. Today OXO manufactures around 500 products based on the same principles. Every year it introduces more than fifty new products, each an innovative solution to the problems experienced by users engaged in everyday tasks. The products that fulfilled a design brief originally intended for a minor demographic, now meet the demands of a wider public.

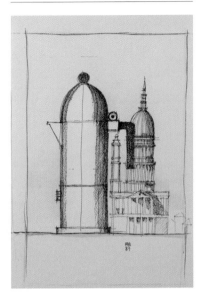

To architect Aldo Rossi objects were small buildings. The La Cupola coffee maker is deceptively simple, composed of Rossi's standard components: building blocks of geometric elements such as cones, cubes, spheres and pyramids, which he would reassemble in multifarious ways, depending on the context and the emotion he wanted to communicate. The coffee maker, comprised of two aluminium cylinders topped by a dome, is an iconic piece that was successful both in achieving Rossi's aim of making something where 'use and decoration are one', and in making something for true mass production. It followed in the wake of Rossi's Milan Triennale 1985 exhibition, where he constructed a huge model where architecture and oversized coffee makers like miniature buildings combined to create a new domestic landscape. Commissioned by Alessi to design a coffee maker, Rossi researched the theme of brewing and serving coffee, making polaroids and drawings of traditional coffee pots, with his design next to them. Reminiscent of Morandi's endless studies of form, Rossi's quest was for something as emotional and archetypal as the classic enamel coffee jug. Something, in his own words, that could be so 'laconic' (brief, terse, concise) that it would become private and domestic in perpetuity. In manufacturing terms it was simply a new interpretation of the classical aluminium coffee maker. La Cupola is made of cast aluminium, like the classic Bialetti original, and is then hand polished. The boiler has a thick-flanged aluminium base to guarantee even heat distribution and to protect the body from the flame or heat source. It is finished with a polyamide handle attached to the body and a polyamide knob, in pale blue or black, to top off the cupola. Rossi was at the height of his powers when he was commissioned to design this piece. An architect who has been claimed by both Modernists and Postmodernists as one of their own, he has produced work of lasting significance.

Claimed by Olympus to be the best-selling camera in the world today, with sales of more than 22 million, the Olympus μ (or Mju) range of cameras is a good example of a competent original design evolving to meet new demands and incorporate new technology. The Mju (called Stylus or Stylus Epic in the United States) was introduced in 1991 as a simple auto-focus point-and-shoot camera. The black polycarbonate casing was streamlined and rounded, making the camera compact and lightweight. New variants and models were introduced almost immediately, including date backs and alternative body finishes. A second series with a f/2.8-wide aperture lens, compared to the f/3.5 standard, zoom and panoramic models, later appeared. Both the first and second series Mju cameras were also produced in limited editions of 50,000 and 65,000 respectively, in addition to the standard production cameras. A third series of Mju cameras launched in 2002 developed the range further with new styling and enhanced performance. The all-weather body was reduced in size and new auto-focus and metering was designed to improve amateur photography success rates. At a time when the rise of the digital camera has transformed photography, the sales figures and longevity of this range of cameras prove that good design and continued technical improvement can keep a traditional camera one-step ahead and in favour with the public.

Most of Jasper Morrison's projects reveal a great interest in sculpture, not so much in an unlimited artistic way but in terms of a strong sense of volume, mass, proportion and space perception. Unlike that of many industrial designers, his work shows a preoccupation with basic polarizations such as light and heavy, open and closed, and positive and negative spaces. The Three Sofa de Luxe is such a piece. Its soft physical presence within a geometric block of foam and textile creates a negative form reminiscent of a lying silhouette of a stylized human figure. This furniture 'floats' on four short, thin metal legs, which creates an impression of lightness that corresponds with the open shape of the figurative top line of the sofa. The effect suggests a small, intimate landscape, creating an instantly recognizable and memorable product. A piece with such a strong identity makes a dramatic statement in the home, and one that many consumers choose to identify themselves with. What sets the design apart from traditional sofas is its dual purpose as a sofa and a daybed. The design's 'cut-out' image dominates the piece, and yet seems to perform no practical purpose. The viewer is both confused and challenged to adapt a new way of thinking about the use of a sofa. The turn of the twenty-first century saw a revived interest in the sofa, and a large group of designers created all kinds of more or less spectacular 'sofa landscapes', which ignored for the most part economic and social considerations in favour of creating more bombastic and monumental pieces. In this context, Jasper Morrison's simple Three Sofa de Luxe was re-evaluated and confirmed as a successful design.

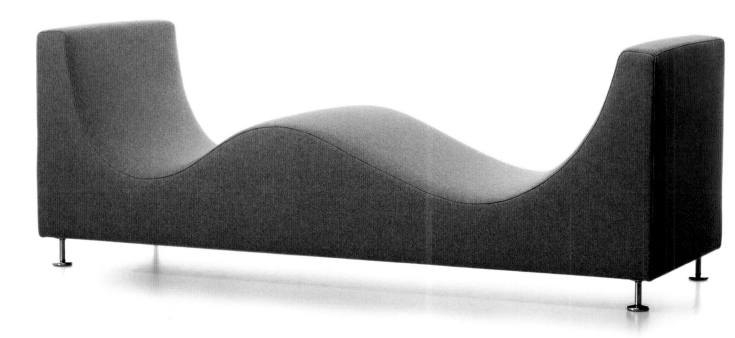

897

Three Sofa de Luxe (1991)
Jasper Morrison (1959–)
Cappellini 1992 to present

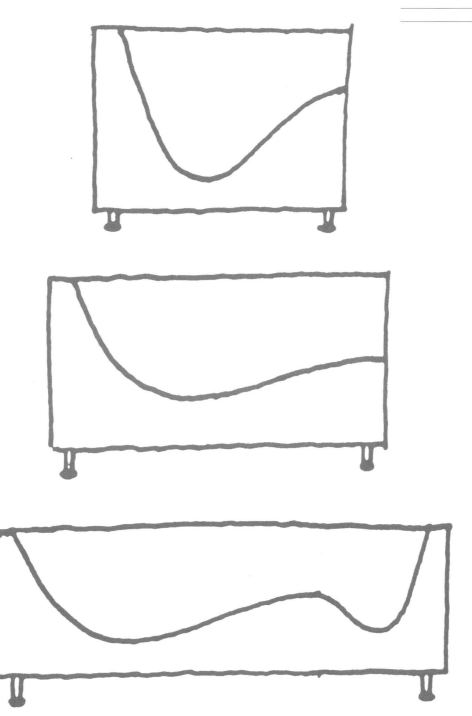

Miss Sissi Table Lamp is a cute, almost cartoon-like study of a table lamp. All its components – shade, stem and base – are made from the same material, a polycarbonate plastic, and it comes in a range of translucent candy colours. The fake stitching detail up the side of the lamp adds to its self-conscious sense of kitsch, while the name 'Miss Sissi' conjures up a typically Starck-esque mixture of references, from boudoir to burlesque by way of Betty Boop. Starck wanted to produce a lamp that was everybody's 'idea' of what a lamp should be. Miss Sissi was created partly in reaction to 'intelligent', highly engineered and complex designs such as Richard Sapper's Tizio lamp, which graced the desk of almost every architect and designer at that time, and partly to produce an inexpensive product that could bring a simple kind of pleasure to its owner. Miss Sissi became an instant success and went on to gain something of a cult status. It appeared on the market around the same time as Alessi's colourful plastic objects, which included pieces designed by Starck, and can be seen to share the same childlike qualities that Alessi's Family Follows Fiction series relied on. These drew on ideas from child psychoanalysts D W Winnicott and Franco Fornari, which centred on our subconscious desire for objects that remind us of our childhood. This was a particularly effective marketing tool in the early 1990s when, at a time of economic recession, the idea of expensive and over-styled 'designer' objects was fast becoming anathema. Starck is known for providing 'narratives' for his products, through stylistic references as well as the witty and character-led names he gives them, and Miss Sissi is no exception. Miss Sissi's packaging earned her a special place in Starck's oeuvre: she came in a cardboard box that mirrored exactly the kind that would house a beautiful doll.

Philippe Starck

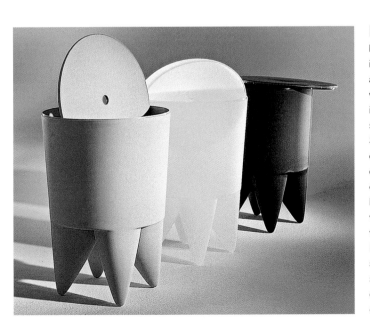

It may look a little straightforward and a lot like a cartoon cow's udder, but the Bubu Stool is actually an extremely versatile design. Produced using injection-moulded polypropylene, it is light, easily transportable (both by the user and the manufacturer), can be used either indoors or outdoors and comes in a variety of opaque and translucent colours. Although notionally a stool, the Bubu is also a table and a flexible storage container. The 'seat' lifts up to reveal a space that can be used for everything from cooling drinks to housing plants. Starck describes the shape of his product as an upside-down crown, encouraging, as he does with many of his designs, a sculptural reading of the object that opens up its comic and cartoonish possibilities. 'I dream that it will create an emotional bond between itself and the person who uses it, that it will become a social and cultural flag,' says Starck, getting typically carried away while presumably picturing the social message provided by the behind of the working man perched on top of this plastic coronet. Metaphors aside, it is the Bubu's relatively low cost and multi-functionality that have made it a popular success. Indeed, it is perhaps the perfect example of Starck at his best: practical, stylish, inexpensive and a little weird. Originally sold by France's 3 Suisses mail-order company, it has been manufactured by XO since 1991 and sells in quantities of around 40,000 per year.

Flores Box (1992)
Enzo Mari (1932–)
Danese 1992 to present

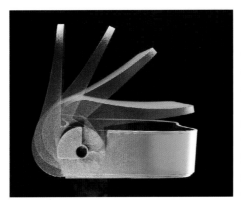

No less than 80 per cent of the objects Enzo Mari created are still actively listed in sales catalogues. Craftsmanship, a perfect eye for aesthetics and a disdain for the short-lived objects of consumerist society characterize Mari's work. Trained as a theoretician, the self-made designer would gain fame for both his theoretical work and for his products, which include office and table accessories, furniture, games, toys, graphics, and research in three-dimensional space and visual communication. Mari himself describes his philosophy as one of 'rational design'. The outcome of each design project should be beautiful, while performing its function efficiently. A good example of this is the Flores Box. Made out of semi-transparent technopolymer, the box uses all the characteristics of this relatively young material. Until the middle of the twentieth-century plastics were used only to imitate natural materials. But technology has brought polymers to such a sophisticated level of formal and structural evolution that today's plastics are not only very practical, sturdy and resistant, but are also of great beauty. They can take on many shapes, from the most straightforward to the most articulated, their skin can resemble translucent glass and the material can be produced in many colours. Flores Box incorporates all of these qualities. The tiny box, which comes in blue, green, orange and 'neutral', not only functions perfectly, but its soft and smooth curves also look and feel delicate. Like Mari's other designs in plastic, Flores Box played a decisive role in persuading the public that plastic products are not necessarily cheap and tacky. The multi-talented designer wrote many books on aesthetics, design and perception and his designs are exhibited in collections and museums all over the world. He was been awarded the Compasso d'Oro three times: in 1967 for his research on design, in 1979 for his Delfina chair for Driade and in 1987 for the Tonietta chair produced by Zanotta.

The ultra-modern hand-held PalmPilot, with its easy-to-use buttons, stylus, 'large' LCD screen and 'Graffiti' software was a revelation when launched in 1996. A beautiful object in its own right, it was effectively worn like jewellery, like a modern-day pocket watch protected within the owner's clothing. Designed with the assistance of only thirty employees and a relatively limited budget, the PalmPilot achieved huge critical acclaim, becoming one of the best-selling personal computing products of all time (over 1 million units were shipped within the first eighteen months). While other manufacturers were attempting to gain the upper hand in an emerging market, their offerings were significantly lacking: Apple Newtons were of almost brick-sized proportions while Psion Organizer's fiddly QWERTY keyboards were more akin to toy laptops. Jeff Hawkins, who set up Palm Computing in 1992, focused development on two key insights gleaned from his passion for neurobiology and cognitive theory. Firstly, he applied auto-associative memory to temporal data, effectively simplifying data entry to a bare minimum of stylus strokes, which were then recognized by the handwriting 'pattern-recognition' 'Graffiti' software. Secondly, he used intelligent systems that do not just act, they also anticipate (like humans), speeding up information input and retrieval. Quick and intuitive interactions therefore allowed for easy interfacing with the PC back at home, keeping the user in touch and networked to their digital world. Several incarnations and refinements followed, offering even more features through 'convergence' of other technologies (such as sound recording, MP3 player, Bluetooth wireless connection, etc). From a broader perspective, the PalmPilot was an object that people would choose to 'wear' on a regular basis, akin to a watch, a wallet or a mobile phone. Switching from the bulging 1980s personal organizer, the Filofax, to the minimal 1990s PalmPilot 'personal digital assistant' implied that the earlier autonomous individual had been superseded by a globally connected one. In a more chaotic world, where information overload is ever present, owning and using a PalmPilot implies that a busy professional schedule is being handled efficiently and successfully, the Protestant work ethic being polished to perfection.

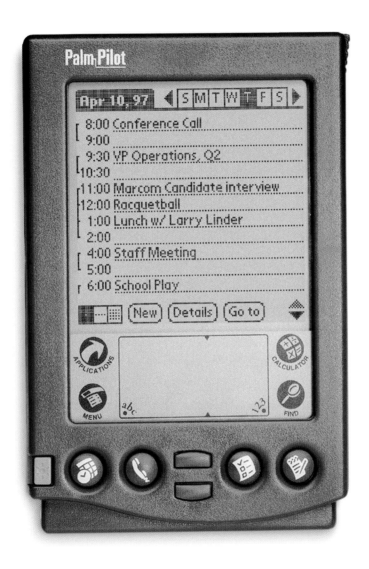

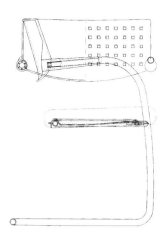

Perhaps the secret to the success of the Visavis chair is its timelessness. Based on simple geometries and well-used materials, every element is clearly formed and easily comprehended. The cantilevered metal frame clearly refers to chairs by Marcel Breuer and others of the 1920s, and so it is part of a Modernist continuum spanning seven decades, while the moulded plastic seat back brings the chair up to date. It has balance and elegance without ostentation. The pierced square motif in the back recalls Viennese Secessionist design and is the chair's only decoration. It is the work of the Italian architect and designer Antonio Citterio with the German designer Glen Oliver Löw. Since 1990 the pair have designed many successful chairs for Vitra, including this chair. Citterio's style is a quiet Modernism based on simple forms, muted colour palettes and highly engineered structures. His designs complement rather than compete with the interiors where they are placed. The manufacturer offers numerous variations of material and finish that transform the design for different interiors. The metal frame is available in matt or polished chrome, or painted black. The seat can be covered in fabric or leather, and the polypropylene integrated arm- and backrest can include cushioning and upholstery. There is even a version with a folding table for seminar rooms. Although the Visavis chair was designed for use as a conference chair, it offers a great degree of comfort and is equally suited to the home. In 1998 Vitra introduced Visasoft, a fully upholstered variant of the chair. A further variant with four legs on castors is called Visaroll, and Visacom is a fully upholstered version for waiting and visiting areas. The family of chairs has been a Vitra bestseller. Unlike more eccentric designs, the basis of the Visavis chair's success may actually be its neutrality and its ability to harmonize with any interior.

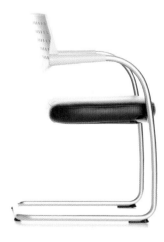

902
Visavis (1992)
Antonio Citterio (1950–)
Glen Oliver Löw (1959–)
Vitra 1992 to present

Trained as a typographer and graphic designer, German designer Ingo Maurer has developed lighting design as his specialization. A recurrent theme in his work is a fascination for the bare light bulb, which he often combines with lightweight materials like paper and feathers. In doing so Maurer underlines the illusive, immaterial nature of his objects. This is especially true for the Lucellino lamp, which derives its name from the Italian words *luce* ('light') and *uccellino* ('little bird') and seems to refer to both. But Lucellino's ethereal and humorous design overrides any literal association. A special incandescent light bulb is coupled with small hand-crafted wings, made of real goose feathers. Copper wire supports the wings and a cheerful accent from a red electric cord completes the design. The lamp is available in wall sconce and table lamp versions. Functional as it may be, it strikes primarily as a true piece of art, which appeals beyond practicality. On a more psychological level the object plays with light–heartedness, with humour and with the untouchable transient wave of light, which seems to be on the verge of making a daring escape into the sky. Not surprisingly, Ingo Maurer is often considered an outsider in the smooth design world. He likes to add fun, poetry and provocation to design. His approach to the design field is that of an artist; his designs have a strong aesthetic, emotional and seemingly universal appeal. Their reputation has scattered them throughout the world, where the designer works for many international companies. Apart from working on tiny pieces Maurer also has larger commissions, such as the recent 40-metre-long sculpture made of light for the Lester B Pearson International Airport in Toronto.

903

Lucellino (1992)
Ingo Maurer (1932–)
Ingo Maurer 1992 to present

On its release in 1992, the ThinkPad put IBM at the forefront of the new portable computer market. It is still considered to be one of the most successful products in computing history. The desires and needs of the consumer market of the early 1990s were in part a reaction to the overtly commercial, playful and sometimes brash aesthetic of the 1980s. As a result, the ThinkPad is a study in sleek and subtle design that offered movable technology for the progressive and busy individual. The product's name, apparently derived from standard-issue notebooks used by IBM employees that were stamped simply with the word 'Think', also identified the new target customer as one who valued spontaneous thought and creativity within the business world. IBM has a history of commissioning refreshingly experimental products, which may have attracted the talented industrial design Richard Sapper to join the company as chief consultant for product design in 1980. A multiple Compasso d'Oro winner, German-born Sapper is most famous for his work with Italian legend Marco Zanuso on such classics as the 1960 Child's Stacking Chair and 1967 Grillo Telephone. Sapper best summed up the purpose of the ThinkPad: 'The computer should work properly and shouldn't invade your life […] We don't think the computer should be shouting, 'Here I am!' As a result his famous and mostly unchanged design is an appealing mixture of function and refinement. Based on the black-lacquered Japanese bento lunchbox, the ThinkPad's simple black casing is made desirable by its subtle quality and attention to detail. The linear casing features bevelled edges to make it seem slighter, and the only interruption to its unembellished jet casing is a diminutive red, blue and green IBM logo in one corner. Originally a comparatively hefty 3 kg (6.5 lb) the ThinkPad, like all laptop design, has become lighter and lighter, with the 2002 ThinkPad X30 weighing in at a mere 1.6 kg (3.5 lb). Other innovations and design additions over the years include the famously unsuccessful 'butterfly' keyboard, which unfolded from within the ThinkPad to a full desktop size. Designed by engineer John Karidis in 1995, this received a lot of customer complaints but still found its way into the permanent design collection of The Museum of Modern Art in New York, as has Sapper's 1992 original.

The cross-shaped cabinet designed by Thomas Eriksson is a first-aid box which combines a few languages. First of all the red colour, sign and symbol of the cross naturally refers to the international Red Cross help organization. Apart from that the Red Cross Cabinet speaks of the natural language of function; the simple box is well suited to contain all necessary items for first aid. Like the other works of the Swedish designer/architect, which comprises furniture, lighting and architecture design, the box advocates the usage of internationally well-known images. We live in a rapidly changing world in which cultures, religions, markets and lifestyles influence one another constantly. Design has turned into a cultural mixture of different influences and, no matter whether we look at Brazilian or German design, we gradually seem to share some general values about quality. Within this framework Swedish design has gained a favourable reputation over the years. But unlike design from countries like Italy and Germany, this reputation is not so much caused by some specific national imagery and technique, rooted in the nation's history, but more by the way designers have understood their profession. Like they did a century ago the Swedes continue to establish a firm relation between the use of natural materials like pale-coloured pine, linear forms and simple shapes and last, but certainly not least, rationality. The combination leads to the non-standardized grace, elegance and beauty of plain Swedish design. What is interesting about Thomas Eriksson's work is the way he mixes the Swedish approach to design with globally familiar symbols. His designs can be found not only in Swedish-based companies like Scandinavian Airlines (SAS), IKEA and Hästens, but also in the collections of international companies and museums like Cappellini and The Museum of Modern Art in New York.

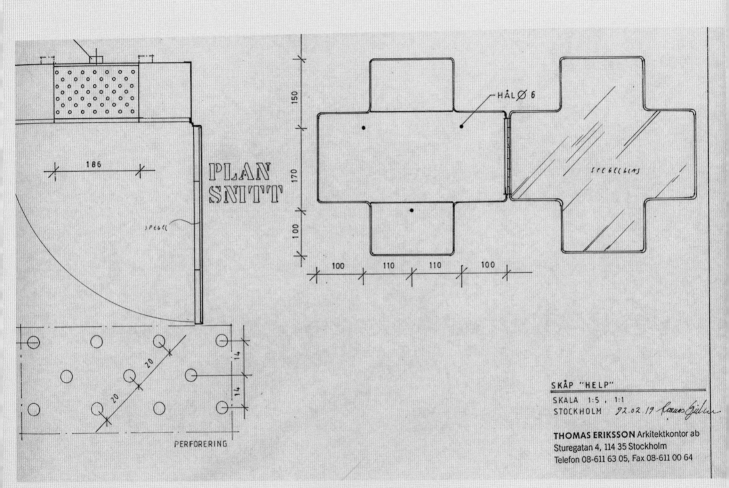

PLAN
SNITT

SPEGEL

186

20
20
20

14

14

PERFORERING

150

170

100

100   110   110   100

HÅL Ø 6

SPEGEL(GLAS)

SKÅP "HELP"

SKALA 1:5 , 1:1
STOCKHOLM   92.02.19

THOMAS ERIKSSON Arkitektkontor ab
Sturegatan 4, 114 35 Stockholm
Telefon 08-611 63 05, Fax 08-611 00 64

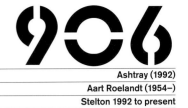

906

Ashtray (1992)
Aart Roelandt (1954–)
Stelton 1992 to present

In re-imagining the traditional open ashtray form as a closed container, complete with tip-up lid, Aart Roelandt's Ashtray for Stelton is, in effect, an 'ashtray for non-smokers', as the sight and smell of cigarettes disappears under the lid. This timely symbol for our increasingly smoke-free culture allows both smokers and non-smokers to share the same environments. The design for the satin-polished stainless-steel ashtray was arrived at by serendipity rather than by design, according to Aart Roelandt, a graduate of the Academy of Industrial Design in Eindhoven, Netherlands. While experimenting with a system of boxes with self-closing swivel-top lids, Roelandt was struck by how the box would be ideal as an ashtray as it closed automatically and could therefore 'enclose the nasty odours and the sight of cremated cigarettes', according to the non-smoking designer. In addition, an unexpected yet happy discovery was made that the ashtray removes the need to extinguish a cigarette, because once the laser-cut lid is closed the oxygen inside is either used or replaced by smoke, which in turn extinguishes the cigarette. Stelton, the renowned Danish manufacturers of contemporary classic stainless-steel hollowware, decided to invest in Roelandt's ashtray design, as its innovation and pared-down simplicity clearly chimed perfectly with the Stelton philosophy. The ashtray is constructed by taking sheets of stainless steel, forging these into tubes and milling the cylinder-shaped container. Finally the laser-cut lid is incorporated and both pieces are hand polished. Ultimately, as well as being a simple, elegant and timeless design, the ashtray is also extremely durable and easy to clean, which has prompted Aart Roelandt, the only non-Danish designer representing Stelton, to suggest that ex-smokers can use the well-rinsed box for sugar. As a result of its impeccable design credentials the multifunctional ashtray is currently being sold in more than seventy countries and figures prominently on Stelton's best-sellers list.

The Brera lamp demonstrates Achille Castiglioni's long experience with Functionalism, modernity and design fashion, an experience that finally allowed him to create a very modest and simple suspended lamp in opaline glass. A thin thread of stainless-steel wire hangs from the ceiling, suspending a milky-white glass oval. The quality of light corresponds to the accuracy of the glass shape. When it is switched off it resembles a Brancusi sculpture, but a fine, glimmering translucent body of light appears when it is switched on. The light 'floats' into the room and at the same time the small 'light sculpture' stays as a visual centre of energy. The Brera lamp demonstrates an outstanding beauty and is an exciting industrial product using the most advanced technology. The often-cited mantra of 'less is more' applies more to this brilliant Castiglioni light object than to any other lamp. Castiglioni's design looks rather technical, comprising a steel wire and a glass ball, and is reduced to the minimum instead of being invested with too many design elements and materials. There is nothing too romantic or associative about this product. The glass quality and shape are somehow reminiscent of classical kitchen lamps of the 1950s, and the hanging wire was typically used in the 1970s and 1980s for highly industrial lighting fixtures. For all that, this light object has a surprisingly basic elegance that is characteristic of most of Castiglioni's designs. It is definitely one of the elements that allow us to easily identify his products.

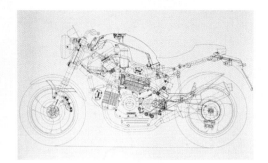

The Ducati Monster M900

brought with it a flood of so-called 'naked' bikes aimed directly at the growing cruising market. It started with young suburbanite bikers in Pasadena, a Los Angeles suburb, in the late 1980s. Miguel Galluzzi, arriving there from Argentina to study automotive design at the Art Center College of Design, drew inspiration from the way local kids grunged-up their unremarkable Japanese sport bikes. Junking the fairings and unnecessary bodywork, they turned them into naked street rockets. Galluzzi understood that this was grunge-biking at its most sexy and hip, and that it perfectly mirrored the music, clothes and attitude of the emerging Quentin Tarantino era in southern California. Galluzzi was not employed by Ducati to start a revolution, but working overtime, he assembled a concept bike from parts of other Ducatis. The result is a light and compact bike weighting just about 185 kg (408 lb), which is an advantage in manageability in particular for women. It has no bodywork and its only overt style is its bulbous gas tank. The race success of the Ducati brand guaranteed its pedigree, of course, but the company's development efforts at that time were directed to an emerging road-going version of a pure racing bike. Ducati took a major gamble, however, and introduced the M900 at the Cologne motorcycle show in September 1992. Initially Ducati planned a limited edition run, but the bike was a huge hit and became the company's bestseller over the next decade, predicted to continue in production for many years to come. The M900 was nicknamed the Monster by Galluzzi himself: 'It was never the Italian version, *Il mostro*, as some people think. I always called it a monster.'

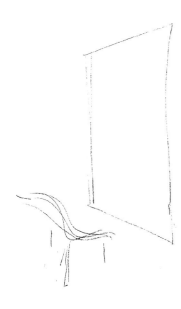

The work of Maarten van Severen rewards careful contemplation. A closer look reveals painstaking attention to detail, materials and forms. In this chair the designer has striven to conceal every joint, so the chair is comprised only of planes intersecting lines. The plane of the seat and back tapers almost imperceptibly, but sufficiently to release it from pure geometry into something more organic. The front legs are not vertical, but subtly raked to give the chair added stability. They are flat extensions of the frame inside the chair, whereas the round back legs appear to be temporarily placed there to support the sweep of the seat. This is minimalist design at its most sublime. Van Severen began making furniture in Ghent in the late 1980s. He is not concerned with ornament or decoration, and favours self-coloured and natural materials like beech plywood, aluminium, steel and latterly, acrylic. These have an innate purity and elegance that complement his staid, geometric forms. His designs appear to be artfully balanced compositions of shapes and materials, pared to their most fundamental elements. In this sense his work is comparable to the furniture designed by the American sculptor, Donald Judd. Chair No. 2 is from a series of designs exploring the same reductive ideas. Early versions in aluminium and pale beech plywood were made by van Severen himself, but production was subsequently adopted by Belgian manufacturer Top Mouton. The Swiss furniture giant, Vitra, has also successfully translated the design into polyurethane foam, in eight mostly muted shades of grey, green and red. Whereas van Severen's originals are resolutely anti-industrial, Vitra's highly engineered stackable versions embrace industrial production and include springs embedded in the chair back for comfort. Van Severen has resisted the 'minimalist' tag that is often ascribed to his furniture, preferring to view his work as 'maximalist' in recognition of the almost obsessive attention to detail that goes into its development. Nevertheless, his pure, utilitarian furniture is recognizably part of a trend towards spare and restrained minimalist design associated with 1990s architects such as John Pawson and Claudio Silvestrin.

9O9

Chair No. 2 (1992)
Maarten van Severen (1956–2005)
Maarten van Severen Meubelen
1992 to 1999
Top Mouton 1999 to present
Vitra 1999 to present

David Lewis

This music system, comprising CD player, tape player and FM radio, is one of a long line of products designed by David Lewis for Bang & Olufsen since the mid-1960s. A British designer, trained at the Central School of Arts and Crafts, London, David Lewis has been based in Denmark ever since he was hired by Bang & Olufsen early in his career to work on audio and video equipment alongside such famous names as Jacob Jensen and Henning Moldenhawer. In this and all his other work for the company he maintains a tradition of innovative, uncompromising design and a relentless attention to detail. While other hi-fi companies struggle to update models several times a year, the BeoSound Century is still part of the Bang & Olufsen range over ten years after it was introduced. It pre-empted several trends that have since been taken up by more mainstream companies. In line with Lewis's dislike of 'black box' design for high-tech goods, the BeoSound Century has always been available in six colours: green, silver, blue, red, black and yellow. The materials and forms are reminiscent of many other Bang & Olufsen products, where primary shapes, symmetry, aluminium and acrylic dominate to great effect. The controls, of which there are many, have been rationalized for ease of use, through a matrix of LEDs, which illuminate the functions available in any particular mode. The unit's slim-line form makes it suitable for wall mounting, for which a special stand is available to complement the more familiar table-top stand. While not compatible with the networked capability of the Beolink system, it may be controlled using the sculptural Beo4 remote control, also designed by Lewis. In 1994 the BeoSound Century won both the iF (Industrie Forum) Best of Category Award and the Danish Design Centre's IP prize.

Aldo Rossi

Aldo Rossi's Momento wristwatch was the first watch to be manufactured by the Italian design company Alessi. Momento, like all Rossi's designs, is highly original and shaped around a bare geometrical form, in this case the circle. The watch is composed of a double steel case, within which an inner case encloses the movement and dial, and is mounted on an outer case. The inner case can be removed and reinserted easily, making it possible to use it as both a wristwatch and pocket watch. Rossi, one of the most influential architects of the postwar era, immeasurably enriched the world of design with his imaginative ideas and sense of fun, which Alessi recognized as mirroring its own approach to domestic design. Momento is astonishing in its simplicity and confirms Rossi as a leading exponent of Neo-Rationalism. The watch's changeable elements for different usage offer an alternative to the technological and functional emphasis of Modernism, and also reveal Rossi's reductionalist approach to design. Rossi died tragically in a boating accident, but will always be remembered as one of the great masters of accessible, practical and fun design that became synonymous with Alessi, and for creating products that epitomized European Postmodernism of the late 1980s.

When writer Ellen Levy enlisted architect and designer Ali Tayar to create a modernist Manhattan loft space, little did she know that one of its elements would turn out to be an award-winning mass-seller. The cool elegance of the aluminium shelving bracket that took her name became a hit with discerning individuals and office and retail designers alike after it won an award from *ID* magazine and featured in The Museum of Modern Art's 'Mutant Materials in Contemporary Design' show in 1995. Tayar took inspiration from his early mentor, Jean Prouvé, a mid-century pioneer in prefabrication who had also worked in extruded aluminium. When a search for an appropriate shelving system to accompany the loft's prefabricated elements drew a blank, Tayar realized he would need something bespoke, and so began the process that ultimately produced the prototype for the brackets. It was this prototype that was used in Levy's loft. Although Tayar confronts mass-production issues in all his designs, it was not until after the brackets were installed in Levy's loft that the idea of manufacturing them took root. In 1993 Tayar founded Parallel Design Partnership. Its first product was a parallel ruler for architects, which turned out to be a bad move, as not only was the profession facing a slump but its practitioners were increasingly adopting CAD-based methods at the expense of traditional drawing tools. At a friend's suggestion, Tayar fixed on Ellen's Brackets as a suitable alternative. The original design needed modification, however. The prototype was in milled aluminium and, to be viable, the brackets would need to be extruded aluminium. Working with engineer Attila Rona, Tayar made incremental alterations which eventually yielded the production design. The unbroken line of the surface supporting the shelf had been broken, and the closed holes for the steel rods attaching the bracket to its wall-mounted track were replaced with a rounded lip fulfilling the same function. But the graceful yet incisive lines of the original were fully intact. The brackets were an immediate success. They featured in new Aveda beauty salons and became available for consumers first through a New York-based and then a national retailer. A horizontal version with a different track and simplified bracket was launched and both it and the vertical version continue to sell well.

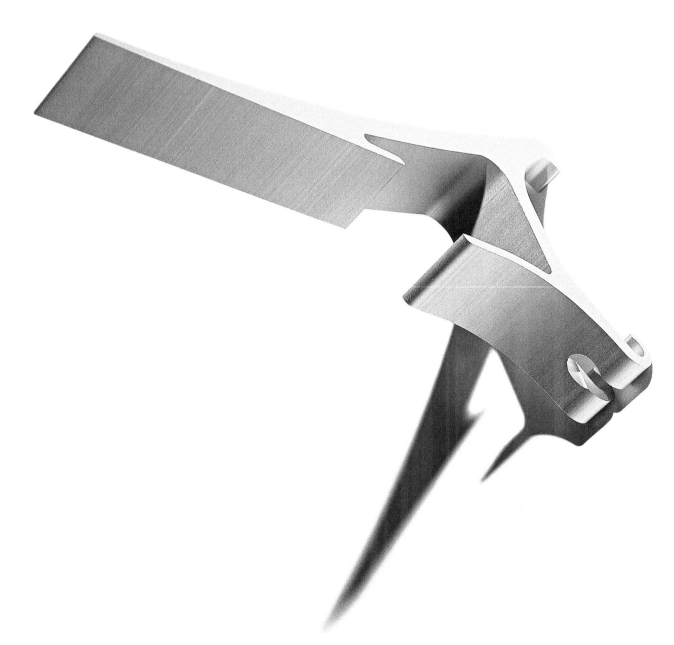

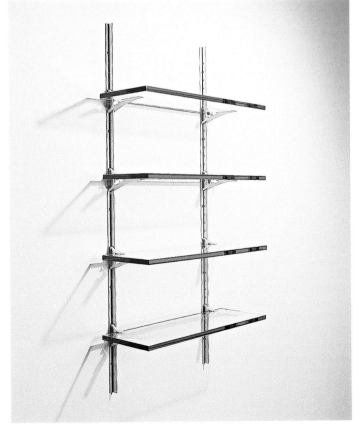

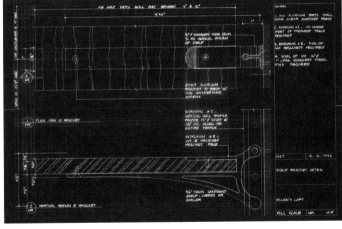

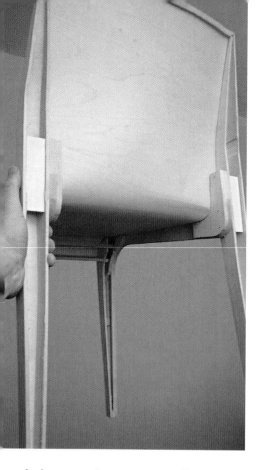

Laleggera is an unusually lightweight
stacking chair, constructed of a heartwood frame to
which two thin layers of veneer are applied, with the
hollow between them injected with polyurethane
resin. The chair exploits the potential of veneer, a
material (usually wood) used to cover a less distinguished material underneath. While the heartwood
frame alone provides sufficient strength to carry the
weight of a person, the polyurethane prevents the
chair from caving in, a technique borrowed from the
construction of the wings of gliders. The chair's frame,
of maple or ash heartwood, can be venaLeggera is an
unusually lightweight stacking chair, constructed from
a heartwood frame to which two thin layers of veneer
are applied, and the hollow between them injected
with polyurethane resin. The chair exploits the potential
of veneer, a material (usually wood) used to cover a
less distinguished material underneath. While the
heartwood frame alone provides sufficient strength
to carry the weight of a person, the polyurethane
prevents the chair from caving in, a technique
borrowed from the construction of the wings of
gliders. The chair's frame, of maple or ash heartwood,
can be veneered with a number of woods, including
maple, ash, cherry or wengé, or is finished with a coat
of paint in a wide range of colours. In effect, it can be
seen as an updating of the Modernist dictum 'truth to
materials'. Neither overtly proclaiming its technology,
nor trying to disguise it, the LaLeggera suggests we
are comfortable with the notion of marrying old and

new without feeling bound to make a self-conscious
statement about it. The Italian architect and designer,
Riccardo Blumer, has made a career out of exploring
the qualities of light and lightness. He likes the idea
of lightness for its own sake, and commented, 'it has
more things to say.' The LaLeggera Chair owes much
to its elegant predecessor, Gio Ponti's ultra-light
Superleggera Chair of 1957. The chair is named in
homage to Ponti's design Blumer borrowed the word
'leggera', meaning light, agile and nimble, as a compliment to its older progenitor. While the Superleggera
weighs an astonishing 1,750 g (61.25 oz) the
LaLeggera is a little heavier, but still a featherweight
at 2,390 g (83.65 oz). The LaLeggera Chair won the
Compasso d'Oro prize in 1998, much to the surprise
of Alias who, while wholeheartedly behind the project,
had not envisaged a level of demand that would
require the setting up of a special production plant.
The judges said, 'The most stimulating element of the
project is the juxtaposition of the traditional materials
on the outside and typically modern materials on the
inside….The combination of these materials efficiently
redefines the design problems involved in achieving a
good balance between image and technology.' eered
with a number of woods, including maple, ash, cherry
or wengé, or is finished with a coat of paint in a wide
range of colours. In effect, it can be seen as an
updating of the Modernist dictum 'truth to materials':
neither overtly proclaiming its technology, nor trying to
disguise it, the Lalagerra suggests we are comfortable

with the notion of marrying old and new without
feeling bound to make a self-conscious statement
about it. The Italian architect and designer Riccardo
Blumer has made a career out of exploring the
qualities of light and lightness. He likes the idea of
lightness for its own sake. 'It has more things to say,'
he says. The Lalaggera Chair owes much to its
elegant predecessor, Gio Ponti's ultra-light
Superleggera Chair of 1957. Named in homage to
Ponti's design, Blumer borrowed the word 'leggera',
meaning light, agile and nimble, as a compliment to its
older progenitor. While the Superleggera weighs in at
an astonishing 1,750 grams the Lalaggera is a little
heavier, but still a featherweight at 2,390 grams. The
Lalalggera Chair won the Compasso d'Oro prize in
1998, much to the surprise of Alias who, while wholeheartedly behind the project, had not envisaged a
level of demand that would require the setting up of a
special production plant. The judges said, 'The most
stimulating element of the project is the juxtaposition
of the traditional materials on the outside and typically
modern materials on the inside….The combination of
these materials efficiently redefines the design
problems involved in achieving a good balance
between image and technology.'

Riccardo Blumer

Chandelier 85 Lamps is Rody Graumans' only contribution to Droog Design and among the group's first pieces. The Chandelier 85 Lamps formed part of Graumans' final exam at the Utrecht Art Academy. After his graduation in 1993 he became a product designer, covering a wide range of projects from interior design to jewellery. Droog Design, founded in 1993, has become an extensive collection of products, projects, exhibitions and statements, curated by designer Gijs Bakker and art historian Renny Ramakers. They have chosen the products for this collection because of a comparable attitude in concept, simplicity and wit. What started as an international platform for young, unconventional Dutch designers has now become for the outsider, rightly or wrongly, synonymous with contemporary Dutch design. Graumans' Chandelier 85 Lamps is one of the very few objects in the Droog collection that is a real, sellable consumer product. Many other Droog items have remained as single prototypes or in expensive limited editions. The Chandelier 85 Lamps is as simple as can be. It comprises eighty-five 15-watt bulbs, eighty-five black plastic sockets and eighty-five equal lengths of black electric wire, which are gathered together by as many plastic connectors as necessary to assemble all loose ends. The multitude of bulbs defines the elegant profile and provides a witty echo of a Louis XVI chandelier. With this design Graumans, and with him many other Droog participants, has introduced a sense of fun into Dutch design, which has for decades been dominated by a Calvinistic, sober aesthetic approach. The simplicity of the chandelier is comparable to the modernist lighting by the De Stijl architect, Gerrit Rietveld, in that both use hardly anything more than bulbs, sockets and wire. Rietveld uses them in a very well considered, constructive way, whereas the young and open-minded Graumans just lets things happen, with the outcome generated by the idea itself. The result is sublime.

The Mobil storage system was conceived for the modern home and the flexible workspace, and is one of several significant designs produced by Antonio Citterio and Glen Oliver Löw since they began collaborating in 1987. The name Mobil underlines the product's essential character as a unit that is light and easy to move and serves many functions. A tubular steel frame supports containers and drawers of semi-transparent plastic that can be positioned vertically or horizontally in two- or three-level columns, with or without handles and wheels. Particular attention is paid to the material, a metacrylate plastic, which has a satin-like effect, and the sixteen different colour schemes, including orange, smoke grey and lime green. The flexibility of the units and the possibility of customization have made Mobil a commercial success. In 1994 the design won the prestigious Italian industrial design prize, the Compasso d'Oro. Mobil can also be found in the permanent design collection at The Museum of Modern Art in New York. Technically Mobil fits in with Kartell's policy of striving for constant, creative experimentation with low-cost plastic materials. Its appeal validates the use of plastic within both the domestic and office environment. Mobil's multifunctionality is a hallmark of Antonio Citterio's furniture and product design output. A proponent of rational design, Citterio specializes in products that are flexible enough to adapt to the changing needs of the office or home, typified by his office systems for Vitra.

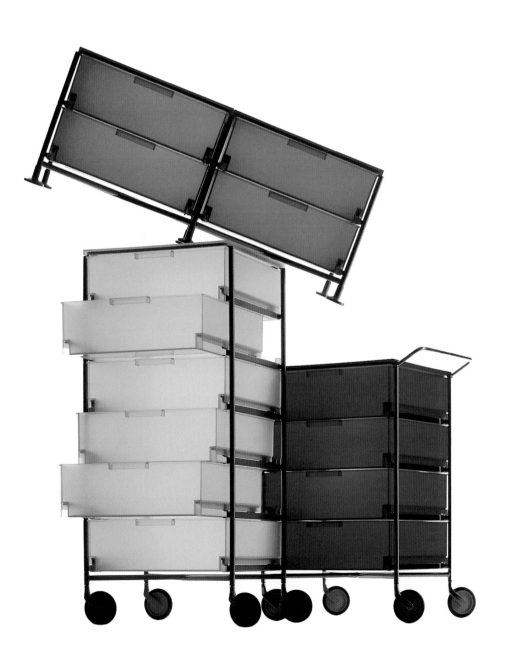

Morten Kjelstrup & Allan Østgaard

Among Scandinavian designers the creation of furniture specifically for children has usually been brought on by parenthood. Alvar Aalto, Hans Wegner and Nanna Ditzel designed suites for children, but with the exception of school furniture, sales of the various models have often been quite limited. IKEA's Mammut range was to change that. Excluding the high-chair, the usual approach to designing furniture for children is simply to scale down furniture for adults. This method works up to a point, but does not take into account the fact that a child's body is different in its proportions from an adult one, nor the different functional requirements of children's furniture. Both Wegner and Ditzel were wise to these factors. So, too, were Morten Kjelstrup, an architect, and Allan Østgaard, a fashion designer, which partly helps to explain the robust proportions of the Mammut Child Chair and the sturdy plastic from which it is made. Where Kjelstrup and Østgaard really moved the subject on was in creating furniture not intended for an adult's aesthetic preferences but instead for the world of childhood fantasy. Kjelstrup and Østgaard took their lead from cartoons on children's TV, and had a helping hand colouring in their designs from their own children. The deliberately gawky and brightly

coloured forms that are the result are immensely popular with children, appealing to them through their imaginations and encouraging use through play. Crucially though, the choice of IKEA as manufacturer – probably the only firm large enough to fully realize the project – has kept the Mammut cheap enough to appeal to the average adult's pocket. The chair was originally presented to IKEA in 1993, and made available to the public that very same year. In 1994, the Mammut Child Chair was given the prestigious award of "Furniture of the Year" in Sweden, establishing its success and popularity.

James Dyson

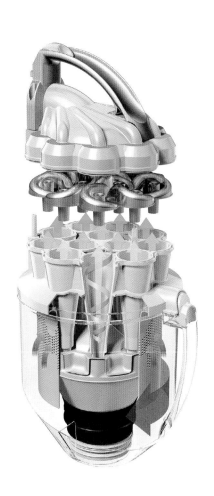

The launch of the DC01 in 1993 was testament to one man's vision and tenacity in the face of the professional short-sightedness of countless marketing men, venture capitalists, bankers, manufacturers, toolmakers and retailers. Its subsequent success in the British and overseas markets was simply down to the fact that the DC01 was peerless in its ability to do what vacuum cleaners are supposed to do: suck up dirt. Despite being twice the price of its competitors and enjoying barely any advertising, the DC01 quickly outshone its rivals, becoming the best-selling model in the UK, by volume, in under five years. Before the Dual Cyclone all vacuum cleaners had had bags or filters that tended to clog with fine dust particles, swiftly reducing their power at the business end of the device. Inspired by the cyclonic filter that he had seen at a local sawmill, James Dyson set about adapting the principles and shrinking the scale to that of a domestic, portable device. Undaunted by almost universal scorn from the industry, he set about perfecting and building the machine himself. From an initial cardboard mock-up taped to an old Hoover upright, via 5,127 prototypes and a very brief Rotork incarnation (the Cyclon), the fully-fledged version was released to the Japanese marked as the 'G-Force,' in 1986. This lilac and pink version became an unlikely hi-tech status symbol in the country that invented that market niche. Following this success, Dyson went on to produce the DC01 in the UK using his own name as the brand, expanding the range in 1995 with the cylinder version DC02. With its faintly constructivist aesthetic and bold colour scheme, Dyson made no concession to prevailing taste in consumer durables. His desire to stand out from the competition by expressing the engineering and functional integrity of the device through its styling found favour with a market that had not seen anything remotely new in vacuum cleaner design for decades. This helped tap into a whole new market traditionally unassociated with domestic chores but hugely influential in purchasing power: men. Dyson managed to turn conventional marketing wisdom on its head and quickly had a huge hit on his hands. As well as winning numerous awards, the designer's seemingly inexhaustible determination has led to his name becoming shorthand for a particular approach to innovation, entering the language much in the same way as 'Hoover' did forty years earlier and acknowledged by the 'Doing a Dyson' exhibition at the Design Museum, London, in October 1996.

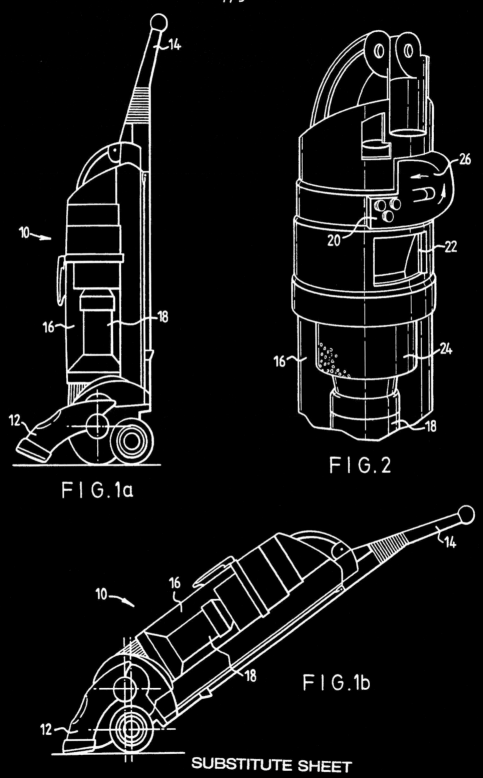

FIG.1a

FIG.2

FIG.1b

The elegant wind turbine, engineered and constructed by the Nordtank Energy Group in conjunction with Mecal Applied Mechanics, elevated the previously functional wind turbine to that of a dynamic sculptural intervention in the landscape. Designed by Jacob Jensen, most famous for his role as chief designer with the leading consumer electronics manufacturer Bang & Olufsen from 1964 to 1985, the Nordtank 1,5MW Wind Turbine displayed his ability to craft elegant functional design solutions in the field of mechanical structures, as well as electronic consumer products. His diverse portfolio of design work has been awarded over 100 international design awards, with the Nordtank Turbine being recognized by Germany's Industrie Forum Design through the award of the highly prestigious IF Product Design Award in 1997. The Nordtank Wind Turbine was first installed in 1995 at the Tjaereborg testing site, near the city of Esbjerg in Denmark. The original model had a 60 metre rotor diameter (197 ft) and two 750kW generators in parallel. It weighed a colossal 193 tons, and was one of the largest wind turbines designed at that time. There was extensive wind tunnel testing and structural finite analysis and the design was gradually fine tuned, which subsequently aided its progression into mass production. The innovative turbine design currently manufactured by NEG Micon is now in commercial service not only in Germany, but also in the Netherlands and Spain. It now features an enlarged rotor, which stretches to some 64 m (210 ft) in diameter. This design provides both sustainable and clean energy, having a low ambient noise-pollution level because of its systematic and considered design. Jacob Jensen's design has become a case study, and the commercial template for the emerging alternative energy industry.

Traditionally, the notion of a bookshelf made up of anything other than horizontal supporting planes was inconceivable. At least, that was before architecturally trained Ron Arad dreamt up the idea of a flexible, snaking alternative that would distort the order of shelving as it had previously been known. The now famous London-based designer had spent much of the 1980s and early 1990s creating one-off workshop designs made from salvaged materials. The Book Worm Bookcase was one of them, born out of Arad's ongoing experiments with sheet steel from which it was originally made. Kartell, the pioneering Italian manufacturer of contemporary plastic household items, took on the design in 1994, recognizing that the concept design could be produced using an extruded flexible thermoplastic polymer. A year later the company was able to create a colourful mass-market alternative without jeopardizing the shelf's toughness, stability and functionality that had been achieved by the original steel counterpart. Positive consumer response to this playful and organic shelving alternative took immediate effect and the company was soon supplying Book Worm in a variety of colours as well as three different lengths. Refreshingly, the configuration of the shape is entirely up to the purchaser, giving a mass-produced item a certain sculptural individualism that would prove to be a unique selling point for the manufacturer. Each bookend is fixed to the wall and can tolerate a load of around 10 kg (22 lbs) on each support. Introduced by a company that has never shied away from the new, Book Worm has rapidly established its place as a recognizable icon of its time in many shops, homes and offices across the world. The product was a redefinition of shelving that successfully reinforced the reputations of both Arad and Kartell as innovators, not followers.

The LC95A is a chaise longue made of a single sheet of aluminium which curves in on itself like a spiral. The strength and suppleness of the aluminium allows a flexibility that affords the sitter great comfort while at the same time the thinness of the aluminium sheet gives the chair a gravity-defying elegance which enhances its simple beauty. The design of the LC95A (LCA stands for Low Chair Aluminium) arose almost by chance. By taking a leftover piece of aluminium and folding it over itself, the form of a low chair became apparent. Van Severen was intrigued by whether it would be possible to use this simple device to design a chair that was sturdy enough to hold a person's weight and still be comfortable. He solved the question by using a long thin sheet of aluminium, only 5 mm (0.2 in) thick, and connecting the two ends with a special rubber, achieving the correct tension and bend. Van Severen studied architecture before turning his attention to interior and furniture design in 1986. His first piece was a table, and four years later, he began to create designs specifically for chairs, working in aluminium, Bakelite, plywood, and polyester. The LC95A, like many of his designs, remained a one-off until Kartell approached van Severen to produce a plastic version of the chair. Using a transparent acrylic plastic called Metacryl, and a much thicker plate of 10 mm (0.4 in), the chair was successfully translated into a more commercial product and became available in bright colours such as yellow, orange, sky blue or clear. While this version of the chair was perhaps more user- and market-friendly, it lacks the pared-down elegance as the original design. As van Severen points out, in its transparent plastic state the LCP, Low Chair Plastic, takes on a completely different appearance: where the aluminium version is more like a 'graphic' object that draws its form in space, the transparent version creates more of a mass, taking up volume in its environment.

920

LC95A, Low Chair Aluminium (1993–5)
Maarten van Severen (1956–2005)
Maarten van Severen Meubelen
1996 to 1999
TM, division Top Mouton 1999 to present

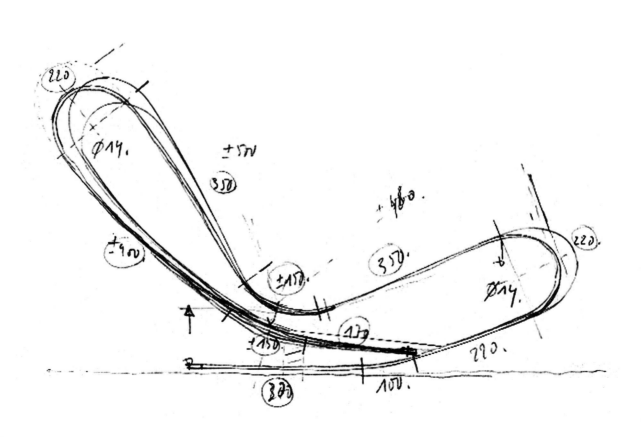

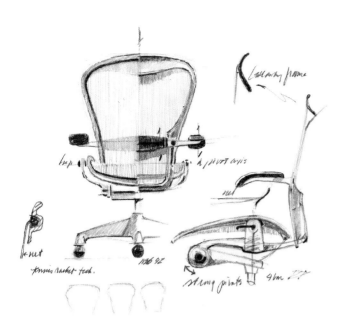

Combining pioneering ergonomics,

new materials and distinctive looks, the Aeron rethought the office chair. Inspired by the human form, the chair's biomorphic design, without upholstery or padding, creates a radical new design approach. Constructed from advanced materials such as die-cast glass reinforced polyester for the frame, polyurethane foam for the pads and recycled aluminium for the legs, the chair's distinctive black Pellide webbing seat structure is durable and supportive, while the mesh elements allow air to circulate around the body. Leading office furniture manufacturers Herman Miller asked Don Chadwick and William Stumpf to design a totally new kind of office chair. Through the innovative adoption of a user-centred approach, extensively researching what an office chair really ought to be with ergonomists and orthopaedic specialists, the designers created a chair that answered the questions that other manufacturers had failed to ask. The design actively dealt with the postural health problems associated with comfort, acknowledging that people often sit incorrectly and lead sedentary working lives. Featuring a sophisticated suspension system, the chair distributes the user's weight evenly over the seat and back, conforming to individual body shapes, and minimizing pressure on the spine and muscles. The design aimed to fit all people well, rather than merely accommodating them, and as such is available in three sizes, like a personalized tool. A logical series of knobs and levers allowed users to adjust the seat height, tilt tension and range, forward tilt, arm height, arm width, arm angle, lumbar depth and lumbar height, facilitating a customized, perfect posture for the user. The Aeron has sold millions since it was introduced in 1994, becoming an emblem of the dot-com boom, symbolizing the 1990s' caring non-hierarchical office environment. Designed for disassembly and recycling, the design reflects a growing concern for environmental issues.

Aeron Chair (1994)
Donald T Chadwick (1936–)
William Stumpf (1936–)
Herman Miller 1994 to present

Soft Urn (1994)
Hella Jongerius (1963–)
JongeriusLab 1994 to present

Soft Urn is part of the early Droog Design collection, featuring conceptual products by young Dutch designers. Soft Urn is a good example of this conceptual approach to design; beyond its plain functionality the vase has a story to tell. The product, which comes in many colours, deals with the relationship between old and new, and between craft and industrial production. At first sight it appears to have the familiar shape of a hand-moulded antique urn, made of clay. Jongerius says, 'Why would I design yet another new form for a vase? The age-old, round-bellied urn functions perfectly.' Jongerius appropriated the archetypal form to inject it with a new structure. A closer look not only reveals the opposing quality of the fabric – soft, strong, thin rubber instead of hard, fragile, thick ceramics – but also the seams and marks of an industrial casting process. The seemingly unique piece proves to be a serial product. The visible marks of fabrication, deliberate faults in the manufacturing process and accidental residues are an essential part of the vase, and are in fact essential to most of Jongerius's work. Instead of polishing away all the unevenness of the surface as the industry has been doing for years, thereby equating beauty with smoothness and perfection, imperfection has become part of the charm and content of her products. As craft is always an essential part of the design process, Jongerius chooses to emphasize it without denying the advantages of modern technologies. In combining old and new techniques her work questions an outdated order of priority between materials and techniques, between beauty and decoration. The imperfections of the skin become new ornaments and the material of Soft Urn suits its purpose even better than ceramics: the rubber will never break.

When it was first

launched, the Smart Car was a surprising sight on the streets because it hardly resembled a typical car, but it was to transform ideas of how to negotiate urban mobility. It was the result of the high ideals of Nicolas Hayek, CEO of Swatch, who wanted to produce an affordable and, most importantly, environmentally friendly alternative to the average car. In 1994 Hayek established a joint venture with Daimler-Benz, after initially approaching Volkswagen. The young Harald Belker, upon leaving his first job at Porsche, Germany, for Daimler-Benz, began working with a team to develop Hayek's idea. The Smart City-Coupé, a two-seater, was premiered in 1997 at the IAA in Frankfurt, the prestigious International Motor Show.

Production began immediately after in 1998 at a purpose-built factory called Smartville in Hambach, France. The car was designed with ecology in mind, and therefore is constructed by synthetic preassembled modules, attached to a rigid integral body frame. The Smart ecology policy is focused on energy efficiency, using sustainable raw materials and recycling its used components. The car also uses powder-coating, a more environmentally friendly method of painting, that uses 40 per cent less energy with no solvent emissions. The Smart design team limited the speed to 135 kph (84 mph), as they believed that this was the best balance between safety and usability, but this also made Smart the most efficient petrol car on the road. Initially, consumer reception

was lukewarm, and sales were lower than the 1998 forecast of 200,000 predicted by Hayek. The public felt it was slightly too expensive compared to most four-seater cars, and the technology did not offer anything particularly new. As only 20,000 were sold, Swatch decided to pull out of the venture, but they seem to have acted too quickly, since sales of the car and the growth of its models have since exploded. The Smart Car, now owned by Daimler-Chrysler, is ideal for negotiating cities weighed down by traffic and for squeezing into minute parking spaces. Interestingly enough, Harald Belker's later work was the antithesis of the Smart Car, as he went on to design the Batmobile for the Batman movies, among numerous other flamboyant designs for the silver screen.

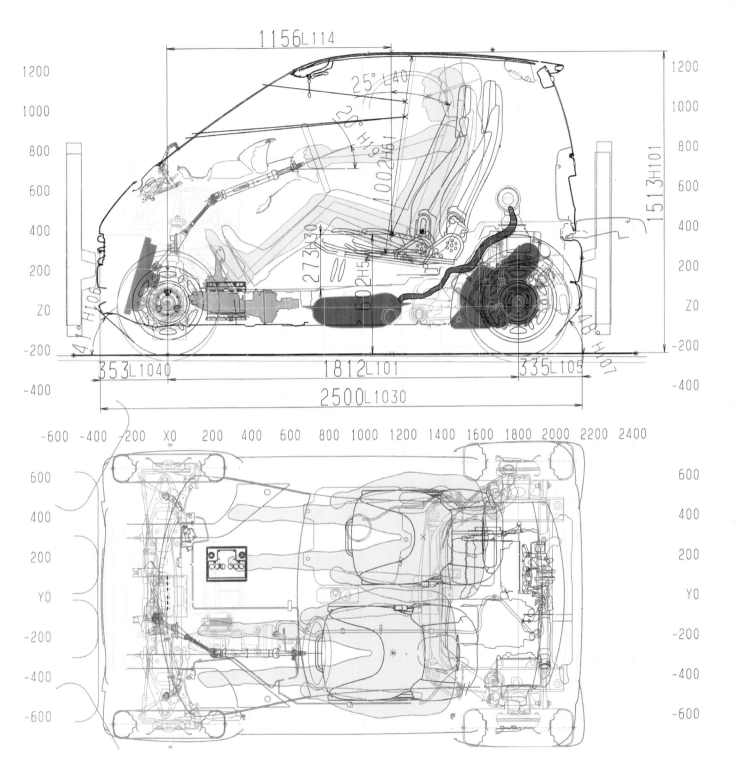

Italian designer

Alberto Meda

Alberto Meda became involved in design following an encounter with Giulio Castelli of Kartell in 1973, which led to his becoming production manager at Kartell and began his fascination with the merging of design and engineering disciplines that underpins all his work. Meda's attention to technical aspects and quality of materials signifies a remarkable design approach, in which objects are viewed initially from the inside, as if the design had the task of, in Meda's words, 'liberating the intelligence contained in things… because each object and the material from which it is made inherently contains its own cultural and technological background.' Meda's motto for design is 'less forms, more ideas'. The Bigframe chair is typical of Meda's ideology in its use of state-of-the-art materials in ways that are stunning as well as being structurally sound. The Bigframe chair follows on from his 1987 sculptural Light Light Chair, which used a honeycomb core and a matrix of carbon fibre to achieve strength and lightness. The Bigframe uses tubular polished aluminium for the frame and polyester mesh for the seat and back. The use of mesh provides an element of extreme comfort that is not usually achieved in non-upholstered seat design. With the Bigframe chair Meda accomplished a combination of ergonomic sophistication with a visual coherence that demonstrates his engineering background. The chair epitomizes Meda's approach to design through its innovative use of contemporary materials and technologies, and the reduction of its components. It clearly illustrates Meda's fascination with the apparent paradox of uncomplicated designs that are technically advanced yet organic in nature.

Wine consumption and connoisseurship have become worldwide preoccupations since the 1970s, and with them came a growth in the development of wine accessories and related products. The role of the designer has similarly realized new dimensions in the second half of the twentieth century, and has played a primary role in identifying and defining new product needs. Since he opened his Office for Design in London in 1986, Jasper Morrison has become one of the world's most influential designers. His office has re-envisioned products ranging from ceramics and kitchen appliances to exhibitions, architecture and the Hanover Tram. In 1994 he was commissioned by the Italian manufacturer Magis to design a bottle rack. Morrison's ready-to-assemble solution is simply called Bottle. It has interlocking tabs that function as feet or stabilizing devices and allow the user to create a storage system that can sit on a shelf or table or be stacked into a wall-sized structure. Its clean lines and structural stability permit the owner to create space for storing beverages that escapes the conventional idea of the dusty wine cellar. Each modular piece consists of two injection-moulded polypropylene units with openings for six bottles and curved elliptical supports that both cradle individual bottles and provide the structural integrity required for the system to become a stacked wall. The pieces are joined by anodized aluminium tubes, and are available in clear or blue versions. In many ways this, like most of Morrison's work, is an exercise in limits: colour, materials, form and organizational possibilities come together to create an elegantly controlled aesthetic impact. Still available from Magis, Bottle is a fine example of the stylistic vocabulary and simplicity that was the goal of many designers at the end of the twentieth century.

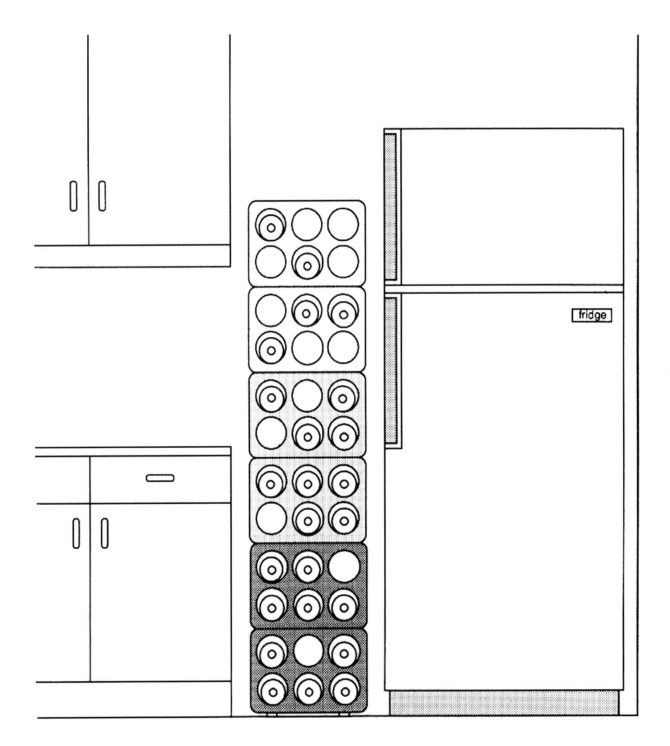

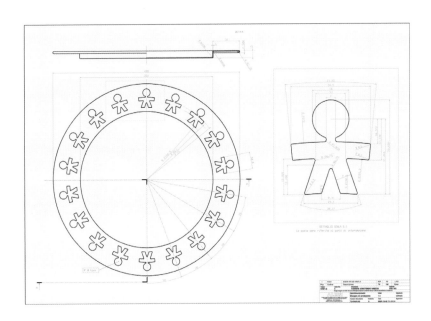

Girotondo, the name in Italian for the children's nursery rhyme 'ring-ring roses', is a group of objects decorated with a perforated man motif resembling the paper-chain shapes children cut out with scissors. The first in the line of 61 products was a simple stainless-steel tray introduced in 1994. Much to Alessi's surprise it became an instant best-seller and the little men soon invaded other products, appearing on everything from chopping boards to napkin holders, photo frames to keyrings, bookmarks, candles and jewellery. The playful, cartoon-like quality of the Girotondo line marked a seismic shift in the Alessi product range, and in product design in the 1990s generally. The 'designer' label had been hit hard by the recession of the late 1980s and Alberto Alessi rightly identified a need for a quieter, more thoughtful approach to design. More astutely, he also knew that his products must address a younger market. Drawing from the work of psychoanalysts D W Winnicott and Franco Fornari, both of whom put forward the view that we are drawn to objects that we have some emotional, mostly subconscious, connection with, Alessi reasoned that the key to successful product design was to tap into childhood memories to encourage an emotive involvement. King-Kong was the *nomme de guerre* of two young Florentine architects, Stefano Giovannoni and Guido Venturini, who were introduced to Alberto Alessi by Alessandro Mendini. The freshness of their quirky, playful designs acted as a catalyst to Alessi's new line of thinking and led directly to the setting up of the 'Family Follows Fiction' workshop of 1991 to 1993, which was responsible for the more colourful, humorous and mostly plastic output that characterized Alessi products in the 1990s. Alessi said: 'The authoritativeness, lucidity and impact of the products that had been made until then did not quite satisfy our most delicate, tender, intimate and affective demands. We needed new sensorial experiences, and new materials to represent our thoughts.' Although the King-Kong partnership has now split up, both designers have since designed products independently for Alessi.

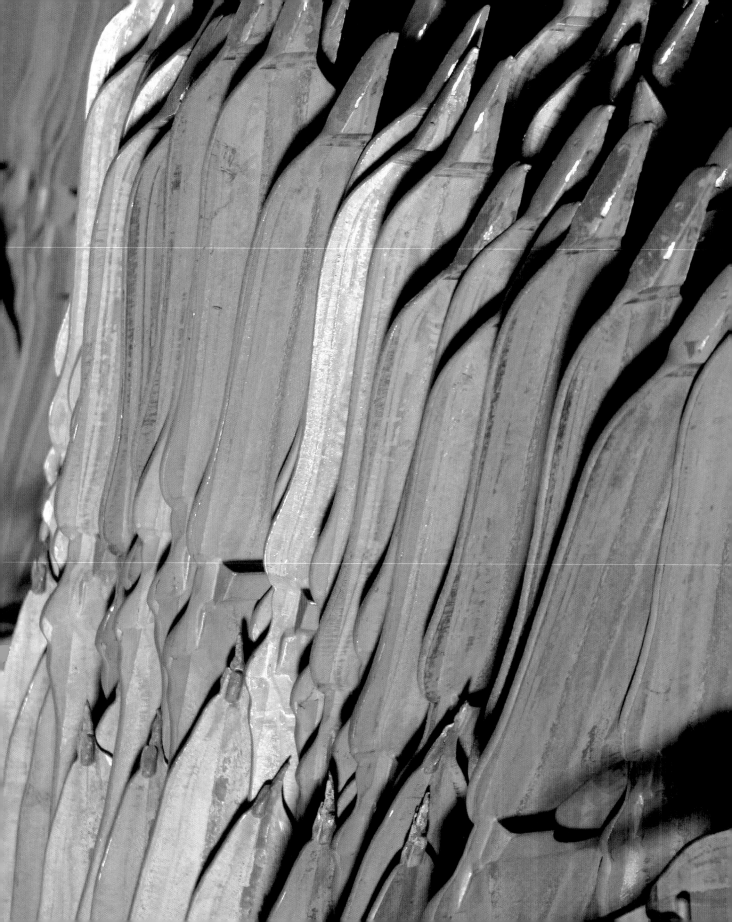

The Kappa collection comprises three sizes of chef's knife designed to perform all general kitchen duties. The knives' smooth surfaces and classic form make them essential items of kitchen equipment for the professional or keen amateur. The Kappa range has been produced in Solingen, Germany, by the firm of Güde since 1994. Established in the first decade of the twentieth century, the company remains in the control of the Güde family, now in its fourth generation. Their knives are handmade in small numbers, using unique methods developed by the Güde family. The Kappa range is exceptional in that the blade and handle are formed from a single piece of high carbon-chromium-vanadium stainless steel. The knives are hot-drop forged before being ice-hardened, then hand-ground and polished. The seamless surface makes these knives very hygienic and suitable for the dishwasher. Traditional in form, the design is the result of many decades of refinement. There are twenty-five different items in the Kappa collection, within the three sizes, and each is designed for a specific purpose. These include knives for cutting meat, vegetables and cheese, plus a fork, spoon and bottle opener. Some of the knives have wavy serrations on the edge of the blade, an innovation developed by Franz Güde to maintain a sharp edge for longer. The knives are prized by professional chefs for their extremely sharp blades and beautiful balance. Their solid construction makes them very tough and gives a reassuring heaviness not found in knives with hollow or wooden handles. The Güde company's desire to concentrate on quality and craftsmanship without compromise has resulted in the retention of a valuable tradition and a superb knife.

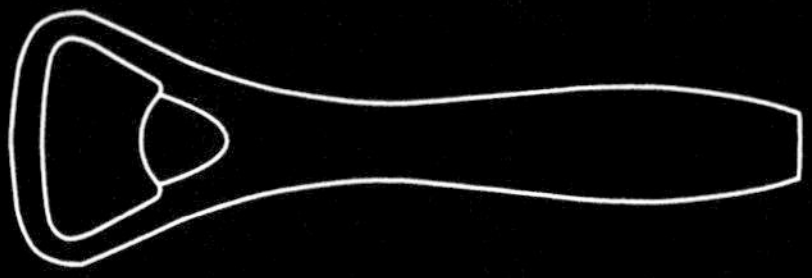

Kapselheber
bottle opener

0090/00

Schälmesser
bird´s beak

0703/06

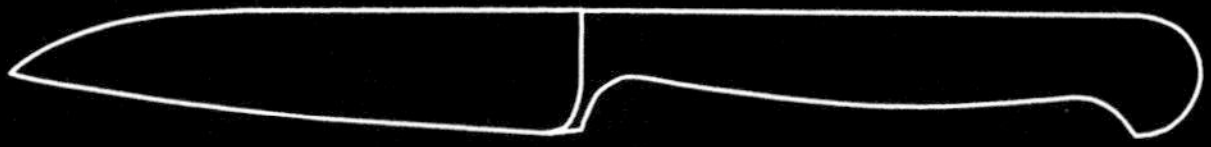

Gemüsemesser
paring knife

0701/09

Buntschneidemesser
decorating knife

0704/09

Spickmesser
office knife

0764/10

Spickmesser
office knife

0764/13

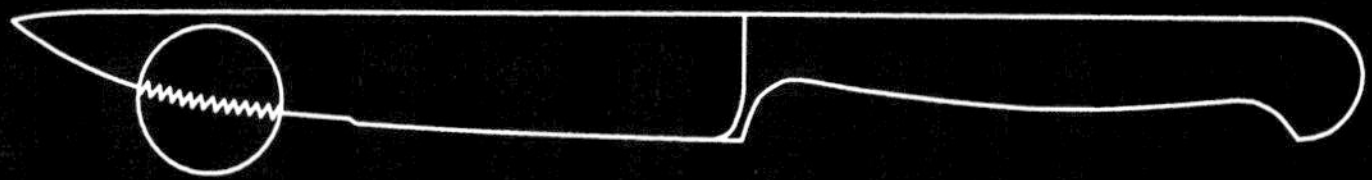

Steakmesser
steak knife

0313/12

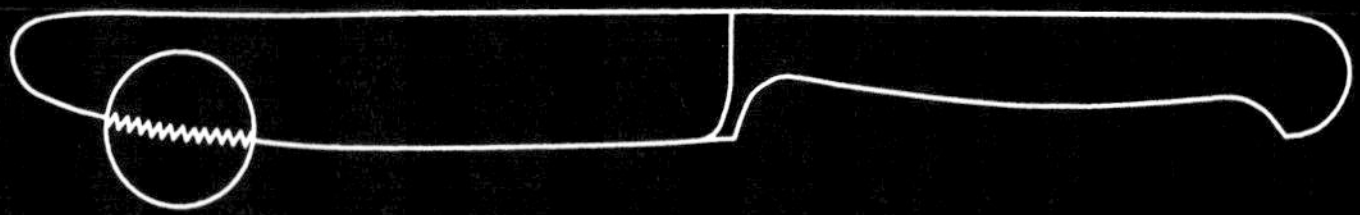

Tafelmesser
table knife

0314/12

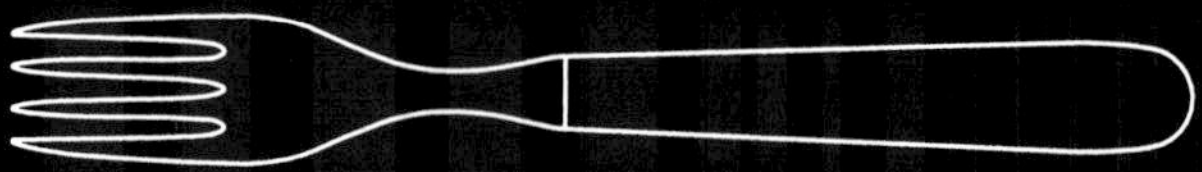

Steakgabel
steak fork

0013

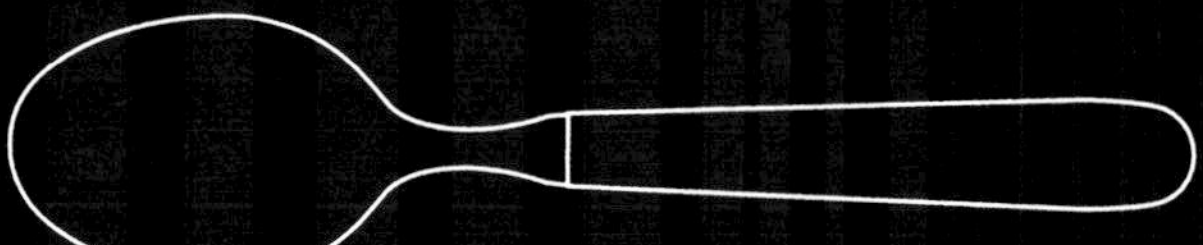

Tafellöffel
table spoon

0012/09

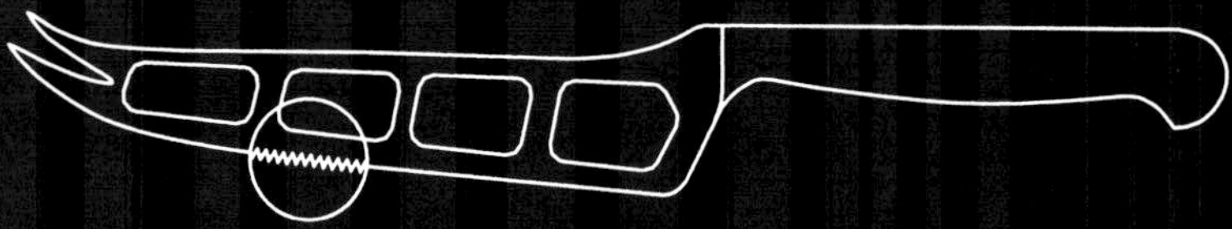

Käsemesser
cheese knife

0290/15

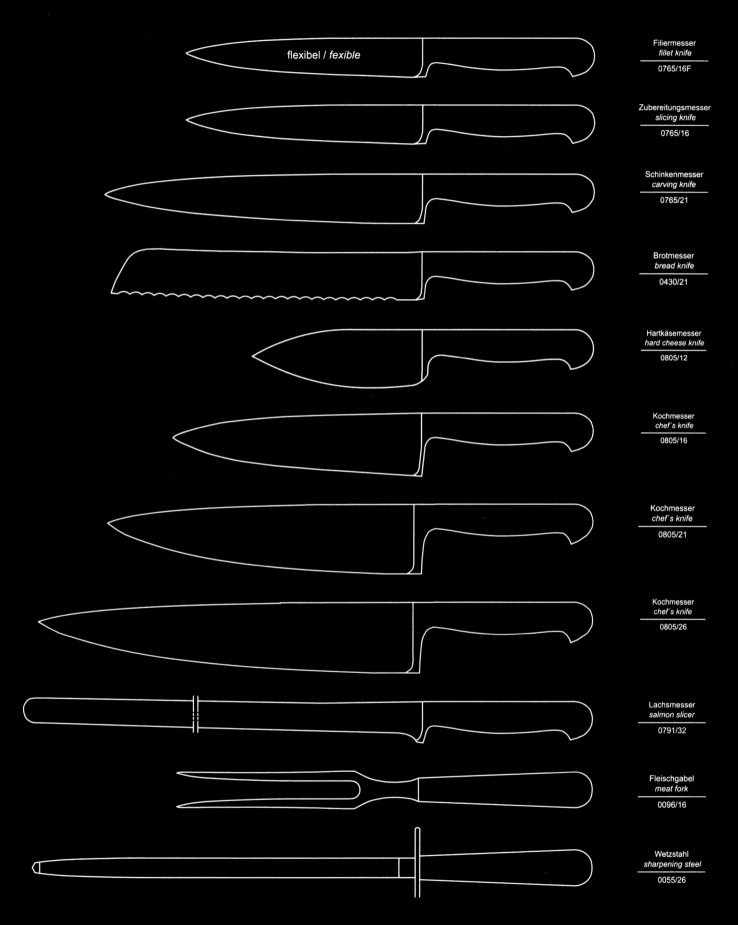

flexibel / *fexible*

Filiermesser
fillet knife

0765/16F

Zubereitungsmesser
slicing knife

0765/16

Schinkenmesser
carving knife

0765/21

Brotmesser
bread knife

0430/21

Hartkäsemesser
hard cheese knife

0805/12

Kochmesser
chef´s knife

0805/16

Kochmesser
chef´s knife

0805/21

Kochmesser
chef´s knife

0805/26

Lachsmesser
salmon slicer

0791/32

Fleischgabel
meat fork

0096/16

Wetzstahl
sharpening steel

0055/26

James Irvine's JI1 Sofa Bed, designed in 1994, perfectly illustrates his ability as an industrial designer to shed preconceptions and to consider the needs of the end consumer. The 1990s witnessed an emerging trend towards multi-purpose and modular furniture within the domestic interior. Versatile modular furnishings provided urban homes with overlapping zones of public and private space. Movable dividers and modular furniture allowed those spaces to open onto each other as necessary. Materials formerly used in industry and for leisure entered the home because they were sleek, low-maintenance and functional. The value of a piece of furniture was also derived from

the ingenuity and beauty of its design: imaginative, eye-catching, practical, portable and perfectly scaled for the sleek urban home. In Irvine's design the sofa bed's seating is made up of an MDF base supported on lacquered steel legs. The seat is made of high-density foam and polyurethane covered with a wool fabric. The ingenuity of the design becomes evident when the sofa is easily transformed into a bed by simply lowering the backrest. James Irvine studied furniture design at at the Royal College of Art in London, graduating in 1984. Since then he has been based in Milan, working with the Olivetti design studio until 1993 and as a partner of Sottsass Associates until 1997. In 1988 he lived in Tokyo and worked in the Toshiba design studio. Today Irvine's studio designs industrial products for companies as wide-ranging as Canon, Artemide and Whirlpool. Irvine has described his aim as wanting to create products that people wish to own because they really want them and not because someone has told them that they are a failure if they do not own them: 'I think of the end consumer and I do not design for the smoke-screen which is put up by many manufacturers. Too many manufacturers look at each other to decide what to do rather than thinking about Joe Bloggs.'

'**The connections** were resolved in the clearest manner, using elementary methods of construction, employing the material as supplied by industry.' The images accompanying this description were of a pair of tables that used iron strips for structure and employed simple bends for material junctions. The description was written for Frate and Cugino, a pair of tables designed by Enzo Mari for Driade in the 1970s. When Konstantin Grcic designed the Mono Tables he was in the process of examining Enzo Mari's simplicity of solutions as found in these designs and others. This was part of a larger reflection by Grcic on the vicissitudes of batch production, materials and finishes. He was not pursuing solutions for definitive forms, but rather seeking a process that married batch production with simplicity of materials and construction, to deliver high quality products economically. SCP, a manufacturer and retail store, has produced some of the earliest works of a collection of now well-known designers, including Grcic. While his earlier works for SCP were predominantly of wood and relied on more obviously archetypal forms, the Mono Tables were different. They were an intentional move away from wood and towards metal. They were his first work creating a purposeful 'family' of products. While they offered a vague outline of use, their forms

were not prescriptive. They were the intended result of an approach in which the aesthetics of form were a mere by-product of the choice of materials, production methods and desired simplicity. The result is a series of intentionally utilitarian surfaces born from varied folds of monochromatic, powder-coated sheet metal. Each top joins its solitary column along a folded matching plane to allow a simple, welded connection. In turn, each of these four columns stands bolted to single-footed attention, lending an idiosyncratic detail that Grcic still amuses in today. The tables have only ever been produced in their signature matt grey – the only colour Grcic ever imagined. His penchant for casual mobility works for both the users and the designer's own use of the tables, as they can be arranged in a numerous ways, and can be used for numerous items and can be even stored in various locations.

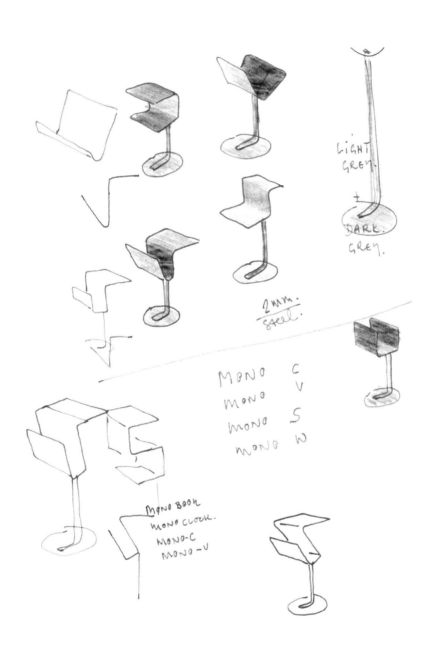

LIGHT GREY.
+
DARK. GREY.

2MM. steel.

MONO   C
MONO   V
MONO   S
MONO   W

MONO BOOK
MONO CLOCK.
MONO-C
MONO-V

It would seem impossible to improve upon something as simple, inexpensive and brutally functional as a rubber band. Indeed, bands made of vulcanized rubber and designed to fasten bundles of stationary were first patented in 1845 by Perry and Company of London, and they have changed little ever since. But the X-Shaped Rubber Band, produced by Läufer, proves that design is often at its best when deployed to rethink the kind of standard, everyday objects we generally take for granted. In this regard it is, as The Museum of Modern Art, New York, describes it, a 'humble masterpiece', which earned it a place in the Museum's permanent collection. The X-Shaped Rubber Band actually looks more like an H-shape when it is loose in its box. Essentially it is a standard, extra-wide rubber band with two strips cut out of its centre and two narrow bridges of rubber between the gaps. Stretched and spread into a cross or X-shape it performs a function that would normally require two rubber bands, and acts more like a cradle than a restraint to those bundles of paper or computer disks. But although its various colours and variation on a seemingly fixed product make the X-Shaped Rubber Band seem incredibly new, part of its beauty lies in the way in which it performs essentially the same function as the traditional piece of string with which parcels are fastened. Indeed, because the rubber band is essentially H-shaped, when stretched into an X-shape it is distorted in exactly the same way as a single piece of string is when used to fasten a rectangular box. The success of this product lies in the fact that it looks as though it has always been there.

X-Shaped Rubber Bands (1995)
Läufer Design Team
Läufer 1995 to present

931

Genie of the Lamp (1995)
Wally with Germán Frers (1941–)
Wally 1995 to present

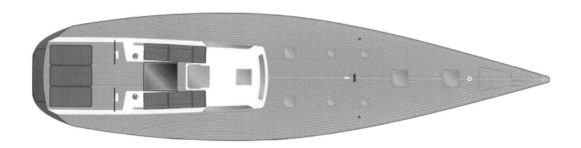

When Luca Bassani began life as a boat-builder, he did not anticipate ushering in
a new era in sailing. At the beginning of the 1990s, however, he introduced an entirely new
sailing philosophy – the solo maxi yacht - a yacht without a large crew. The most representative boat of this genre is the Wally 80 'Genie of the Lamp', the first 24 m (80 ft) solo
boat, launched in 1995. The advanced design concepts and technology behind the Genie of
the Lamp were developed to make cruising sail yachts more comfortable, faster and easier
to handle with a small crew, and they mark a turning-point in the history of yacht design.
Interpreted by cruising and racing boat designer Germán Frers, the new rules of simplicity,
high performance with minimum effort, striking lines with great comfort and luxury, and
innovative technology simplified the manoeuvring and handling and improved the quality of
sailing. Because people spend a lot of time on deck while cruising, the team designed an
'easy' deck, free from dangerous obstacles. As on all Wally yachts, the running rigging lines
on Genie of the Lamp run under the deck, leaving plenty of space to walk safely around.

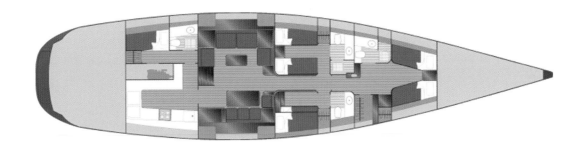

The mainsail and jib sheets are led inside the spars and sheeted by hydraulic rams located in easily accessible areas. The mainsail and jib sheets trimming buttons are positioned in the twin helm stations, next to the steering wheels and together with the navigation instruments, to allow the helmsman to sail the yacht alone and to avoid any interference with the social areas. The lifting keel system, which is controlled by a push-button arrangement, provides two keel positions to reduce the draught when anchoring in shallow waters, for motoring, for sailing downwind in light weather or for increasing the lift while sailing upwind. Interior designer Tommaso Spadolini created a comfortable layout with elegant decoration without exceeding the weight limits required for a high-performance cruising yacht. The spacious saloon is located in the area of maximum beam. There are three double cabins where guests can rest, away from where the captain and crew operate. Interiors are constructed in advanced composite carbon fibre and foam cores, veneered by varnished or natural teak, keeping weight to a minimum.

The Aprilia Moto 6.5,

the work of the product designer Philippe Starck, might have become the bike of the century if only it had achieved its first imperative and won the acceptance of motorcycle riders. Instead, although it failed commercially and was never even imported into the important US market, the Aprilia Moto 6.5 has become something of a cult, both among designers, and among enthusiasts and collectors. Aprilia's decision to look completely outside the narrow world of motorcycle designers to Philippe Starck, a man known more for his boutique hotels and quirky household objects than for any expertise in the automotive world, was an eccentric one. So there was little surprise that Starck created a motorcycle that was both championed and rejected by the motorcycle world. What is most surprising is that Starck's design was one of the best all-round motorcycles of the 1990s. It was certainly one of the leading motorcycles in an important new niche for motorcycle design, the suburban motorcycle, with handling and engine characteristics that made it both easy to use in city traffic, and fast enough for the short, quick, motorway excursions for both the daily commuter and the weekend tourist. The design is replete with standout details. First among them is the marvellous Rotax engine, used by several other manufactures, including BMW, but rendered by Starck in a monotone grey to match the frame and the plastic body parts. The ovoid shape Starck created to integrate the frame and engine is unique to this Aprilia. And with a gesture to Henry Ford, the bike was available in only two colour schemes: grey with a yellow tank, or black with a grey tank. The Moto 6.5 had a brief but luminous production life and is now a sought-after collector's piece – helped, no doubt, by its inclusion in the Guggenheim Museum's landmark exhibition 'The Art of the Motorcycle'.

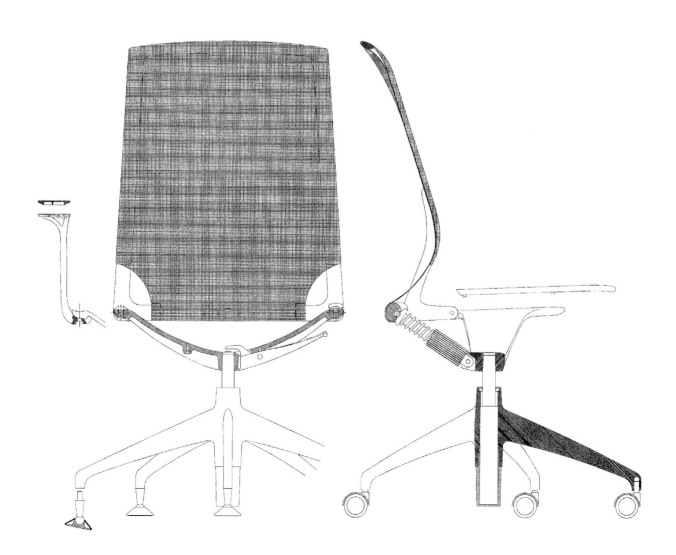

This was planned to be a match made in heaven – one of the world's greatest designers working with one of the most creative, and sensitive, manufacturers, Vitra. The collaboration did not disappoint. The Meda Chair, designed by Alberto Meda in 1996, has the refined looks one would expect, is simple to use and is extremely comfortable. Like the Vitra Chair AC1 that Vitra manufactured eight years previously, the Meda has an uncluttered appearance, keeping mechanisms and levers to a bare minimum. According to Vitra, a 'synchronous process is set in motion when the user moves – without the usual synchronous mechanism.' Two pivots at the side allow the back to drop, which, at the same time, changes the shape of the seat. The process is controlled by a pair of springs (one spiral, the other pneumatic) that are located between the back of the chair and the bridge, underneath the seat. The height, meanwhile, can be adjusted by pressing a button below the right armrest, and the lever on the other side fixes its position. Upholstery is stretched and supported across the frame, giving the chair a pleasant sense of elasticity. There are several versions of the chair, the Meda, Meda 2 and Meda 2 XL (which all have a five-star, die-cast polished aluminium base) as well as a conference version that completes the range. Beautiful without being obviously engineered, or conspicuously high tech, it is neither aggressive nor overtly male and remains one of the great office chairs.

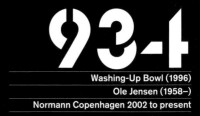

93-4

Washing-Up Bowl (1996)
Ole Jensen (1958–)
Normann Copenhagen 2002 to present

The rubber Washing-Up Bowl by Ole Jensen was initially designed to protect fragile glasses and porcelain from the hard and unfriendly surface of the stainless-steel sink. The flexibility of the rubber allowed it to contain objects of any shape and size and today the bowl may be found being used as a foot bath, as an ice bucket, wine cooler and even for cleaning the tables at The Museum of Modern Art in New York. Jensen started thinking about a bowl that would adapt to any shape while one day washing his own dishes and noticed in frustration that his sink could not accommodate unusually shaped objects. He set about making a prototype out of a flexible material on a potter's wheel, achieving a handcrafted character in both its production method and style. The bowl was now both flexible, durable and, accompanied by a washing-up brush made of Chinese pig bristles glued onto a wooden handle. It was first exhibited at City of Culture Copenhagen Kulturby 96, then shown at the Danish Arts Foundation and the Danish Craft Organization. The innocent rubber bowl then lay in the designer's ceramic workshop for a few years, until it was brought into the Danish Crafts Collection, and subsequently exhibited at the Ambiente International lifestyle fair, 2001, in Frankfurt. One more year and one more display at the Ambiente triggered a sudden surge in demand. Jensen immediately began a production run of 500 bowls by hand while simultaneously experiencing problems with acquiring the right materials, losing money, and seeking suitable sub-contractors. But demand continued to grow. Normann Copenhagen had seen the bowl at the Ambiente and decided to start producing it in 2002, also by hand. Initially encountering similar problems with the materials, the company invested in a very expensive mould and now uses santoprene, an artificial rubber. It also produces the hog-and-wood bristle brush, a touch which prevents the bowl from appearing too modern and carries a sense of traditional Danish domestic ware to the forty or so countries where it is distributed. Although among the most expensive of washing-up bowls, Jensen is pleased with its multi-purpose profile, each bowl embedded with its user's character.

Ginevra (1996)
Ettore Sottsass (1917–)
Alessi 1996 to 2001, 2003 to present

The simple, seductive form

of the Ginevra crystal decanter creates an object of great beauty, with its shape reflecting the luxury of its purpose: the art of drinking. But it is also remarkable in that it is the final piece in the tableware range designed by Ettore Sottsass for Alessi, a range that spans four decades and represents so many of the designer's innovative, often radical and always influential ideas. The Ginevra decanter and the accompanying glass range were originally introduced by Alessi in 1996, but production had been fraught with difficulties and high costs. The range has since been redesigned and re-engineered to suit production needs, and was finally reintroduced in 2003. The elegantly attenuated decanter, shaped like a beautiful unadulterated bottle, was the final missing link in the 'beautiful table' design philosophy of the designer. Sottsass has always pursued the conceptual route in his designs, and the idea of the 'beautiful table' is not simply an aesthetic consideration; it is more about the ritual act of sharing, the notion of showing awareness, respect and care about the whole occasion of eating. The Sottsass tableware ranges, produced by Alessi, bring many different characters and personalities to the 'beautiful table', from the earliest 5070 Condiment Set of 1978, with its stylistic nod to the postmodern design language that Sottsass effectively helped create, to the Ginevra glassware, characterized by pure, pared-down and utilitarian yet beautiful lines. The Ginevra decanter is one of the most elegant and essential players in this 'beautiful table' ensemble. Ettore Sottsass has maintained that a 'beautiful table', where everything is clean and neat, and all the tableware is carefully laid in its proper place, invokes a feeling of engagement, participation, even communion, with the Ginevra decanter a suitably sociable late guest.

The Nokia 5100 mobile phone's success lies in its timely introduction into an aspiring and expanding market for telecommunications. Slim-line, lightweight and inexpensive, the phone was designed with consumer tastes in mind rather than as a reflection of its technological function. A fashion-focused device, it promoted a lifestyle attitude to mobile communications. Previously, the mobile phone was a luxurious service and handsets expensive chunks of clunky technology. All that changed with the advent of cheap mobile network deals and the emerging teenage consumer market. Nokia cornered the economy end of the mobile handset market with the 5100, itself an evolution in the systematic design process of Design Director Frank Nuovo towards miniaturization, a trend started with the Nokia 2110 model. Chunkiness was replaced by smooth corners, edges and sculpted buttons. The black and white LCD screen was large enough to display scrolling menus and a modal screen function activated by hard keys that made for easy access to telephone address books and SMS messaging. The power-on button was moved from the function key area to the top of the phone. The slim-line battery of 170 g (6 oz) – although slightly heavier than the previous Nokia 2110 one (105 g/3.7 oz) – is still a crucial detail in making the 5100 a truly pocked-sized product. But the real clincher that set the design apart was a front face removable graphic cover. Nuovo's design allowed the front plastic cover to easily unclip, thus spawning the concept of customer personalization. Thousands of producers jumped on the bandwagon, creating multicoloured designs for the phone, from simple colour choices to Donald Duck-themed ones. In market terms, the popularity of removable covers allowed Nokia to surpass in sales competitors such as Ericsson and Motorola, proving that the decorative and fun element was more enticing to the telecommunications audience than the promise of technical advancement.

The TGV Duplex passenger train, which made its inaugural Paris–Lyon journey in 1996, is a bold yet unequivocally expedient feat of design engineering. Responding to the need to increase passenger capacity on busy train lines, French industrial designer Roger Tallon took the unprecedented step of designing the first high-performance double-decker train. The TGV (*train à grande vitesse*) Duplex high-speed train for the SNCF French rail company belongs to the fourth generation of high-speed trains: after the TGV Sud-Est of 1981, the Atlantique of 1988 and the Réseau of 1993. The high-speed lines connecting Paris to other French cities and neighbouring European destinations were reaching saturation point when the decision was made to explore the possibility of a model with greater passenger capacity than the existing TGV rolling stock, such as the Atlantique and Réseau, also designed by Roger Tallon. The option of a longer or wider train would have undoubtedly created a knock-on effect for signalling and braking systems. Therefore Tallon investigated the idea of creating a higher model. As a result, the TGV Duplex has seating on two levels, allowing for 510 seats, eclipsing the capacity of other models such as the Réseau, with its 377 seats. In design terms, the Duplex's innovation lies in the extruded aluminium construction, which is extremely lightweight; the strict requirement of a 17-ton axle load limit made it essential to reduce weight wherever possible. The aerodynamic, streamlined nose and the improvement in the gap between trailers meant that the Duplex could cruise at a speed of 300 kph (186 mph) and experience only 4 per cent more drag than a single-level TGV. With transport, and particularly car-related pollution, being one of the key areas of concern for the future of global environmental well-being, the fully electric TGV Duplex is seen as an exemplar in terms of providing a solution to environmentally sustainable transport systems. As well as being responsible for relatively low pollution levels, it is also safe and extremely comfortable. And since it is moreover one of the fastest trains in the world, it is one of the most thrilling ways to get from A to B.

937

TGV Duplex (1996)
Roger Tallon (1929–)
Alsthom/Bombardier 1996 to present

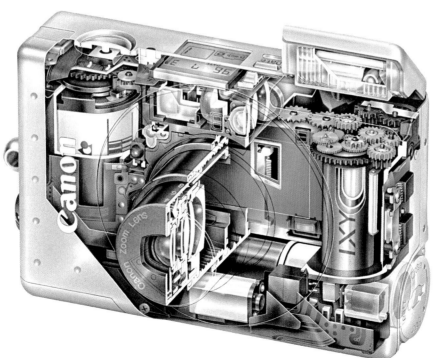

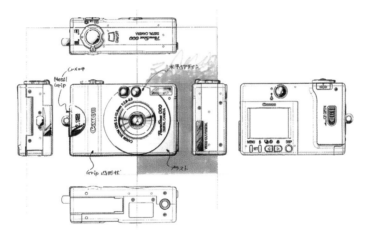

The Canon Ixus called the Elph in the United States and Ixy in Japan was launched in 1996 and immediately became a 'must-have' fashion accessory thanks to the camera's stylish design and an innovative advertising campaign. The camera was made from stainless-steel alloy with rounded corners and incorporated a pop-up flash and zoom lens that extended when switched on. The camera was truly pocket-sized and was the smallest camera with a zoom lens when launched. The LCD screen on the top of the camera offered a means of dating the photographs and showed the status of the camera. The Ixus was one of the first cameras made to take a new film format, Advanced Photo System (APS), which was developed jointly by Canon, Eastman Kodak, Fuji, Minolta and Nikon and launched in 1996. The film cartridge, which was 30 per cent smaller than conventional 35-mm cassettes, allowed smaller cameras to be made and offered a range of information to be recorded on a magnetic strip on the film. APS permitted photographs to be taken in different formats, notably a panoramic format, on the same film. The APS format was ultimately short-lived, with several of the founding companies discontinuing APS camera manufacture by 2004. However, the Ixus kick-started interest in the new APS format and by early 1997 the Ixus represented 19 per cent of all APS cameras sold. In September 1997 Canon introduced a gold version of the Ixus in an edition of 30,000, to commemorate the sixtieth anniversary of Canon's founding. Other variants closely resembling the original design followed, including a digital Ixus. The Ixus was important in raising Canon's profile with the public and received several design prizes and awards from the photographic press.

With the establishment of Produzione Privata in 1990 Michele De Lucchi added yet another strand to his already varied oeuvre. It seems a paradox that the very same person who, in the 1980s, designed that strong statement that is the First Chair and who lists among his clients multinationals such as Deutsche Bank and Olivetti, would come up with the idea of creating a line of designs to be produced solely by traditional craftsmanship. Acquatinta is the purest example of Produzione Privata's glass workshop. In the 1980s and 1990s there had been numerous collaborations between lighting distributors and Murano's master glass blowers, so the idea of employing hand-crafted production methods was not a new one. But De Lucchi was not interested in revitalizing older craft traditions to give them a more contemporary image. Instead he wanted to get back to the root and key principles of hand manufacturing. Experimenting with new techniques, using, in his words, 'hands and mind', he created a unique piece each time. Designed in collaboration with Alberto Nason, the Acquatinta pendant lamp is revolutionary not as the reworking of a traditional shape, but for the irony of featuring a transparent lampshade in its original version. Over time, many different versions have been realized, incorporating and playing with the possibilities that the transparency of the Murano blown glass provides. Other finishes include sand-blasted, opaque, etched and mirrored. Acquatinta, along with its wood moulds, is today rightly part of the permanent design collection at the Pompidou Centre in Paris, testimony to the fact that a timeless piece can be made with minimal means.

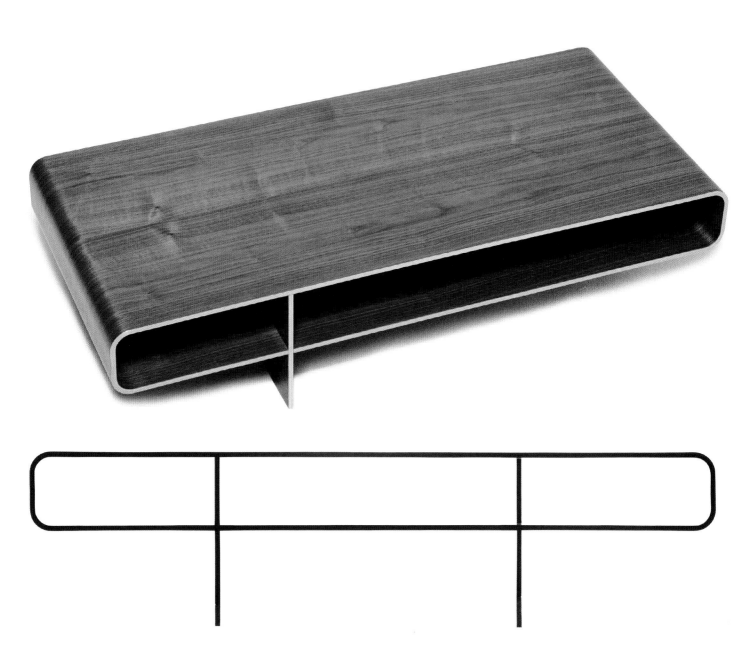

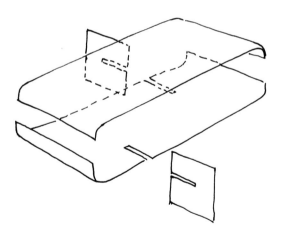

The Loop Coffee Table, a laminated table, was the first piece of furniture designed by Edward Barber (1969–) and Jay Osgerby (1969–) under the aegis of their new partnership, Barber Osgerby, founded in 1996. Originally designed as part of an architectural project for a London wine bar, the table quickly took on a life of its own. British manufacturer Isokon Plus was the first to put the Loop into mass production. Founded as Isokon in 1935 by Jack Pritchard, with the appointment of Walter Gropius as controller of design and Marcel Breuer as designer, Isokon Plus was particularly known for its fine crafting of products. The first piece to be added to the Isokon range since the 1950s, the Loop carries on this tradition, even being produced by some of the same machines. In 1998 the table was also incorporated into the range of the Italian manufacturer, Cappellini. The use of laminated pressed plywood for the structure and, more importantly, the exterior finish of the product revives old production methods. Pressure-formed ply is created by gluing and stacking several sheets of plywood, then inserting them into a mould where the application of pressure and heat forms and dries the sheets into the shape of the final object, This technique had long since faded from popularity, and the use of ply relegated to hidden interior structures. Despite being considered a return to an old material and manufacturing process, the design is unquestionably new. The designers' preoccupation with each plane, each joint and each detail marries performance with unadorned beauty. The sparing use of materials and purposeful elimination of the superfluous translates into a clarity of form and illuminates a design language that speaks effortlessly and lucidly. The illusion from nearly every angle that the table rests lightly on a single leg, nearly floating in space, is created by the play of lines, intersections and curves which superimpose a simple, graphic elegance on to this pure structure.

Above all, avant-garde designer Tom Dixon is a craftsman who focuses on new applications of traditional and modern materials and forms. He created the company Eurolounge in the 1990s to make design and crafted, industrialized artefacts more affordable. The first object Eurolounge produced was Jack Light, so-called for its resemblance to the children's toy of the same name. The object, which is available in red, blue and white, grew out of Dixon's desire both to make lamps in an industrial way and to make lighting multi-functional. The Jack Light gives off a spherical light, can be stacked into a high pile and, as it stands on the floor, can be used as a stool or, when needed, support a tabletop. All these possibilities are the result of intense research into plastic manufacturing techniques. Dixon discovered that by using a rotary moulding technique a range of products could be created more cheaply without losing quality, a complete new concept at the time. The Jack Light would define Dixon's career, earning him the Millennium mark in the UK. Some of Dixon's other most famous products include the S Chair, Bird Lounge Chair and the Pylon Chair. He works with many high-end Italian furniture, lighting and glass companies such as Cappellini and Moroso, received an OBE for services to the British design community and in 1998 was appointed International Head of Design at Habitat.

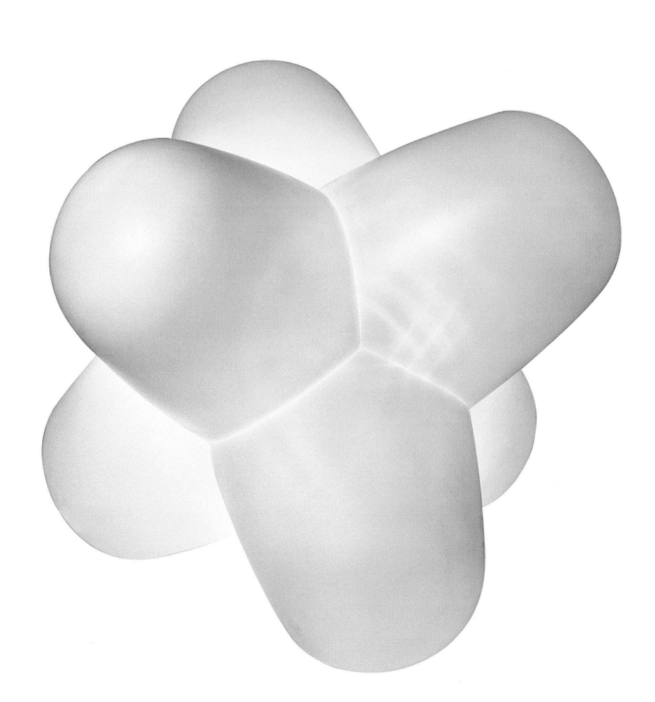

From the outset, MUJI has been associated with simple, basic products in a pure design. The Polypropylene Stand File Box is a straightforward, functional product, practically a 'non-design' item without any sophisticated details, made from translucent polypropylene. It is what MUJI calls a core product as part of a larger office range in the same material. Today it is still a major product within the family of containers and boxes produced by the company. Like all the products in the line, the box is extremely simple; minimalist in shape, light and translucent in material and modest in the best sense. The shapes and sizes of the products are linked with economical, functional and visual aspects. With this product MUJI, as a company, represents the whole philosophy of a manufacturer of archetypes. In MUJI's language there is little space for shallow fashion in its products. In every way, the box is an everyday product; its construction is suited to industrial production methods, making it easy to produce in high volume, and thus inexpensive to buy. When MUJI started this product line in 1996 the use of polypropylene was at its peak, and the translucent, matt-finish surfaces had conquered the world. MUJI was not interested in inventing something new but instead used this elegant and light material to develop a range of practical basics with the aim of satisfying a wide group of consumers interested in a long-term and mobile container system and functional aesthetics at a reasonable price. The File Box does not have the appeal of the avant-garde, but charms us by its very utilitarian nature. It is an intelligent product for everyday use without the attitude of a bourgeois design project.

Belgian designer Maarten van Severen initially trained at the Architectuurinstituut Sint-Lucas in Ghent in the 1970s before embarking on a career in design. After working in various studios practising interior and furniture design, van Severen set up a workshop for limited and semi-industrial furniture in 1987. Early furniture editions, particularly his steel and aluminium tables, established his reputation on an international level. Working with design companies like Vitra, Edra and BULO also gave van Severen access to materials and production techniques, and considerable public exposure of his work. Alongside furniture design, van Severen was also involved in interior architectural projects. Since 2003, he worked with Rem Koolhaas on seating design for the Porto concert hall in Portugal, and a modern shelving system for the Seattle Public Library, which opened in Autumn 2004. Another important product of van Severen's industrial design work was the U-Line lamp created for the firm Light in 1996–7. With his Low Chair Aluminium (1993–5), van Severen became recognized for his refined and minimalist designs, and this design focus is clearly demonstrated in the U-Line. The simplicity and linearity of form enhances the beauty and elegance of the lamp. As a functional light it is structurally perfect, producing maximum light with minimal casing, fixtures and wirework. Using industrial materials in the U-Line, van Severen created a simplified and minimalist object capable of mass reproduction without loss of form, structure or beauty. With his knowledge and understanding of space and our relationship to, and use of, objects within space, Martin van Severen worked outside the sphere of traditional industry, and his individual approach gained recognition in the international design world. Designed as pieces of micro-architecture, van Severen's products work to combine usefulness with understated and uncomplicated design. Many pieces of van Severen's interior architecture have been showcased around the world, including exhibitions at the Carnegie Art Museum, in Pittsburgh, Pennsylvania, the Industrie Forum Design in Hanover, and the Salon du Meuble in Paris.

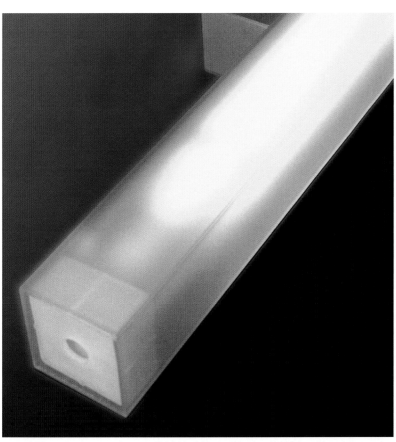

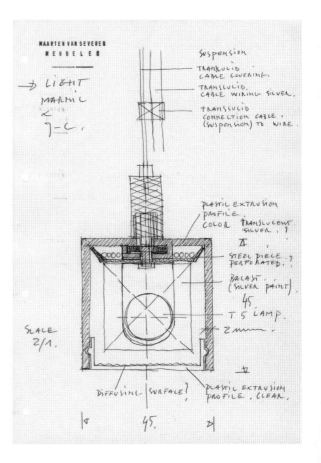

The Motorola StarTAC Wearable Cellular Phone, weighing just 88 g (3 oz), was about the size of a contemporary pager in 1996, and was feather-light in comparison to earlier mobile phones, which weighed no less than 850 g (1 lb 14 oz). This cellular phone set the standard for all future mainstream phones, and was the smallest, lightest and therefore most portable of its kind available on the market. Motorola, often perceived as the first company that began producing mobile phones, nicknamed the StarTAC the phone that was 'ready-to-wear'. It was designed to be worn as a piece of jewellery would be – around the neck or clipped to a belt. By using communications equipment as an item to be worn, Motorola set a new standard by appealing to the fashion sensibility of the consumer. It was developed from the tiny MicroTAC handset designed in 1989, which had a flip-lid mouthpiece that became an inspiration for the StarTAC, which had a similar flip cover extended over the length of the phone itself. It came equipped with a headset for hands-free operation, making it a completely wearable object. One of its unique features was that it could have two batteries that could be attached simultaneously. They were carried on the flip cover, allowing a talk time of sixty minutes or more, with an additional, slim battery at the base of the phone. The 'piggy-back' battery at the base, a lithium ion battery, allowed for ninety minutes, giving an enormous total time of 180 minutes. There were three printed circuit boards compacted into the base portion of the phone, creating even weight distribution between the boards, battery and the exterior packaging of 82 cubic centimetres (5 cubic inches). Both the design industry and the public were astounded by it, and it was deservedly given a silver medal at the Industrial Design Excellence Award by the Industrial Designers Society of America in 1996.

The Knotted Chair is a design that provokes a complex range of reactions, thoughts and responses. Visually it can confuse one into misunderstanding the material and technique of production, and users are often wary about the chair's ability to support their bulk. The lightness of the design in both transparency and weight will always bring a sense of awe. The finely knotted outline of the small four-legged chair is made from inspire rope twisted round a carbon core. The carefully handcrafted form is impregnated with resin and hung within a frame to harden; its final shape relies on gravity. The Knotted Chair is a highly individualistic design that marries an inventive use of craft with both modern materials and strong ideals: 'a hammock with legs, frozen in space'. It is a design that reflects a highly personal perspective on the creation of modern objects and furniture. It communicates in a refreshing new language, whereby the processes of industrialization and commerce become secondary to the importance of invention and communicatory design. Marcel Wanders became a prominent force as part of the highly influential Dutch collective Droog. In 1993 the group launched their first exhibition of high- and low-tech designs that had – and continue to have – a profound effect on international design. Using a mixture of existing products, materials and processes, fused with creative, forward-thinking media and typographies, a wide cross-section of furniture and household products was designed. The Knotted Chair was launched in 1996 as part of the Droog collection of that year. Wanders continues to communicate similar messages through his own collection and designs for Moooi, Cappellini and a host of international producers inspired by his individualistic approach: 'I want to give my designs visual, auditory and kinaesthetic information in order to be interesting to a wide group'.

Harri Koskinen is now a leading designer for iittala and Hackman, but one of his most famous designs was created while he was still a student at the University of Art and Design in Helsinki. The Block Lamp, a lamp composed of two heavy, hand-cast glass blocks, resembles a block of ice. It was the result of a technical exercise in which Koskinen explored the difficulties of casting an object in glass. In the finished piece the encased light bulb appears to be suspended in air. The two sections of glass undergo a lengthy cooling or annealing process in order to avoid cracking when exposed to high temperatures, and the bulb shape within is created by sand-blasting, leaving a matt surface. Light is provided by the 25-watt bulb, which emits a soft, diffused light. Many see the lamp as a continuation of the Finnish glasswork tradition that was established during the 1950s and 1960s by Timo Sarpaneva and Tapio Wirkkala, who created glassware and vases that carried the properties of ice. As ice is a large component of the Finnish environment, this connection could be easily made. But for Koskinen, the lamp is not intended to represent a block of ice. It stands only for itself, or a block of glass. Koskinen received immediate recognition for this piece, which won the Excellent Swedish Design Award in 1998, and was put into production by Design House Stockholm that same year. The Block Lamp is compatible with other Design House Stockholm products, which reflect traditional Nordic themes and use natural materials and colours. This lamp follows in the Finnish design tradition, reflecting the natural environment, but also retains an element of beauty, and is thus both an object of function and art.

Top

Sideview

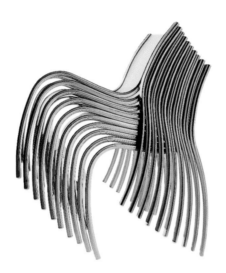

The FPE chair is a lightweight stacking chair with a revolutionary production technique. Designed by Ron Arad for Kartell, the FPE is about making a chair on an industrial scale, simplifying the problems of manufacture by removing any excess material and processes to create a soft, sinuous and sensuous solution. The translucent lightweight chair is available in white and grey as well as vibrant red, yellow and blue, enabling the chair to live comfortably indoors or outside. Two double-barrelled aluminium extrusions are cut to a staggered length. An injection-moulded translucent polypropylene sheet is slotted into the extrusions. The metal and plastic are then bent together in a single piece to form the FPE's distinctive profile, the unique process causing the extrusions to 'bite'

the plastic, automatically bonding the plastic membrane which makes up the seat and back in place without any adhesives or fixings. Each extrusion is partially split to provide a back as well as front leg. The cost of the industrial manufacture of plastic and metal components is driven by the size of the tooling. The FPE's almost flat aluminium extrusions and injection-moulded sheet reduce the amount of material required while dramatically lowering the cost of the tooling required. This minimalist approach is reflected in a pared down structure that remains flexible until the weight of the occupant sitting locks the seat, creating a stiff and rigid structure from the most minimal use of materials. Upon graduating from the Architectural Association, Israeli-born Arad founded his own

architectural design office/showroom 'One Off Ltd' in Covent Garden, London. Infused with the spirit of DIY, and faced with a stagnant furniture market and recession, Arad decided to 'go it alone', and become a maker as much as a designer. Having redefined contemporary design with his inventive and witty approach of recycling found objects, such as old Rover car seats and scaffolding, he has moved from a period producing bespoke objects in his workshop to embrace industrial mass manufacture with the FPE, going on to produce designs that are as much technologically playful and emotional as pragmatic and functional and forging a lasting collaboration with plastic furniture specialists Kartell.

The Cable Turtle is an award-winning design that tackles the small but significant issue of modern office and domestic life: the complex cable management of the ever-increasing multitude of electronic products we now use in contemporary life. It is designed to prevent unnecessarily long electrical cables from becoming entangled and unsightly. The Cable Turtle provides the perfect solution for handling electrical power supply, printer connections, excess mouse cables, keyboard cords and more, in any environment. Created by Dutch designer Jan Hoekstra, the Cable Turtle is a round shell with a polypropylene joint at its centre. The shell opens and the excess cable can be wound around the joint like a yo-yo. After gathering up the required length of cable, the user simply closes the flexible elastomer shell and aligns the ends of the cable with the lip-like openings on either side, enabling the cable to exit neatly from the pliable, doughnut-like form. The design is available in two sizes: the small Cable Turtle holds about 1.8 m of electrical cable, while the giant variant can hold up to three cords, or significantly longer lengths of single cable up to 5 m long. The device is designed to handle up to a 1,000W load per turtle safely. The Cable Turtle's tactile form has a beguiling, playful quality that rejects traditional conservative office design, and adds a welcome dose of humour to the solving of a humble problem. Manufactured from recycled plastic and available in nine eye-catching colours, including blue, lime-green, black, orange, grey, red and brown, the simple and intuitive object has been recognized as a contemporary design classic, most notably winning Germany's Good Design Award. It has been selected for inclusion in New York's Museum of Modern Art's permanent design collection.

9·48

Cable Turtle (1997)
Jan Hoekstra (1964–)
FLEX/the INNOVATIONLAB
Cleverline 1997 to present

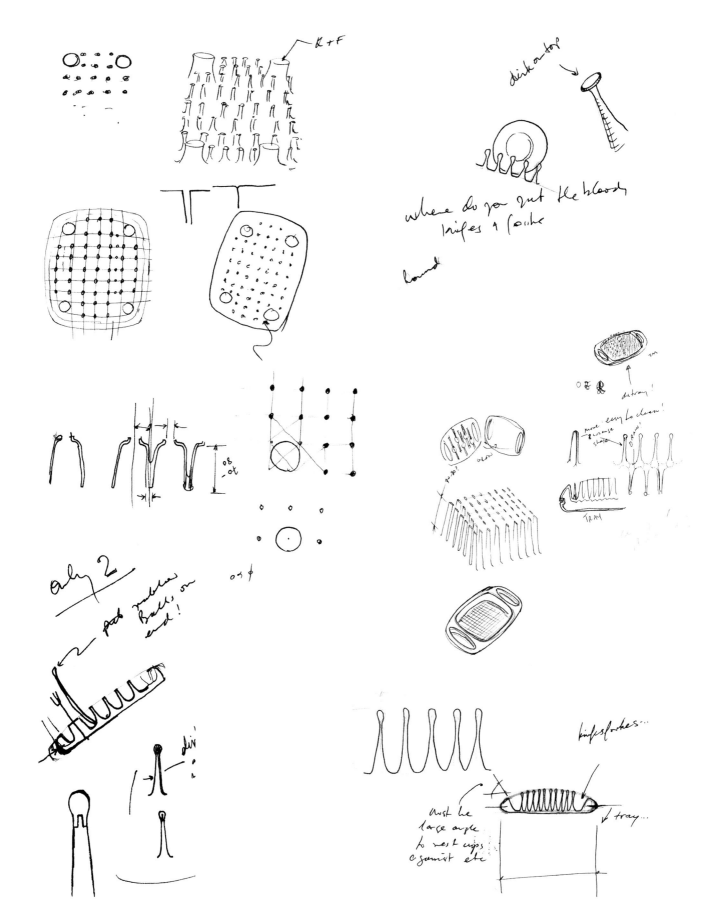

K + F

disk on top

where do you put the bloody
knifes & [forks]
board

only 2

put rubber
Balls on
end!

knifes forks...

must be
large angle
to nest cups
against etc

tray...

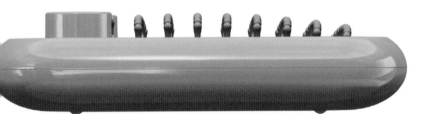

Marc Newson's Dish Doctor drainer for Magis is an example of Newson's characteristic design vision. Acknowledged internationally for his funky, futuristic, but technically rigorous approach to design, Newson has designed products ranging from a concept car and a doorstop to this dish drainer. Newson has created a unique family of objects that share this Australian-born designer's individual approach. Designed for twenty-first-century living, the brightly coloured plastic Dish Doctor was created for use in small kitchens. With its integral reservoir to collect water drips, it is ideal for use with small sinks and those without drainers. It is constructed in two pieces to allow the collected water to be easily poured away. From the relatively low-tech world of furniture design, Newson started experimenting with CAD software. Helped by Benjamin De Haan, who became his business partner, he went on to master the art of rapid prototyping technologies using computer-aided design, the Dish Doctor being one of the resulting products. As a designer his interest is not concerned purely with the exterior but also with the use and the relationship between design, science and nature. The Dish Doctor, with its bright colour and quirky form, has more of the look of a toy or game than an unassuming piece of kitchenware. The flexible pegs that hold the crockery in place are precisely designed in height and position to support any size of crockery safely in any direction. Gone is the regimented rack separating plates and saucers. The two integrated cutlery drainers save on space and keep the cutlery apart. The Dish Doctor is a radical rethink of the design of a humble domestic object. Newson's solution is a unique, and fun product that is a desirable object in its own right. As one of the outstanding industrial design innovators of his time, Newson is a maverick who has revamped design as the new commodity fetish.

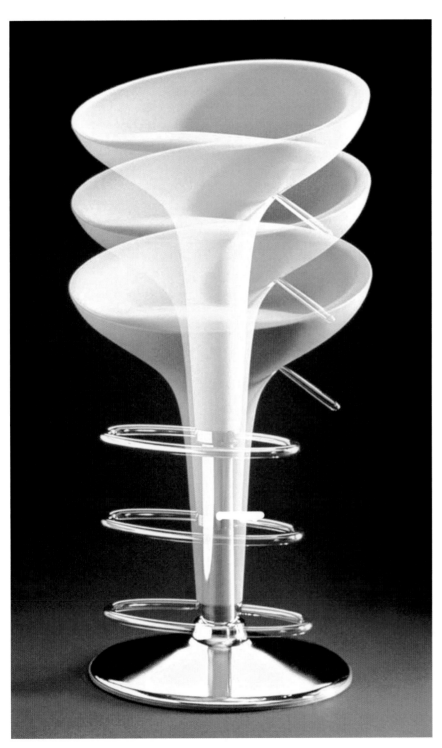

Of all typologies of furniture, chairs have the unique ability to symbolize a culture's defining elements. Thonet's Chair No.14, or Wegner's Y Chair fall into this category. Not only do they tell us about style, but they also give us clues about conviviality, and attitudes about the body and gender, industry and environment. Beyond the singularity of their designs, the status of these chairs has been secured by the number of units sold and the variety of applications that have been devised for their use. Introduced in 1997, on the cusp of a new millennium, Milan-based designer Stefano Giovannoni's Bombo Stool has quickly become an icon of that pivotal era. At a point in which all eyes were looking to the future, hearts and psyches were nostalgic for what was about to become the past. The Bombo Stool owes some of its success to the fact that it combined retro styling with youth-culture-orientated functionality and contemporary technology. The Bombo Stool established its reputation in trendy public venues such as bars, restaurants and salons, where its adjustable height and range of fifteen colours gave it a versatility that made it applicable for users of all ages. The ergonomic design of its seat and footrest also meant it offered a welcome relief from the standard office stool at a time when work environments were being rethought. The stool's curvaceous form mimics the shape of a standard wine glass. Its bowl-like seat, with lever to adjust its height, is balanced on a tapering stem, and opens out into a wide round base. The allure of the Bombo Stool lies in its combination of Art Deco detailing inherent in the combination of injection-moulded ABS plastic and chromed steel trim, and the contemporary technology of its German gas-lift mechanism. Since its introduction, the Bombo Stool has spawned a family of furnishings including the Bombo Chair, the Bombo Table and Al Bombo, a polished aluminium version of the original.

MV Agusta F4 Serie Oro (1997)
Massimo Tamburini (1943–)
MV Agusta 1997 to present

**Massimo Tamburini with a prototype of the
MV Agusta F4**

Massimo Tamburini is, simply, the *capo di tutti i capi* (the boss of the boss) of motorcycle design. Tamburini's first signature designs were seen in the 1980s at Bimota, his own design works producing high-end and expensive sport bikes ('ta' in 'Bimota' is for Tamburini). It was during his time at Bimota that he collaborated with Claudio Castiglioni, boss of Cagiva, who had bought not only Ducati, but also the rights to the name of MV Agusta, perhaps the most glorious name in Italian motorcycle history. Together, Tamburini and Castiglioni made several interesting machines for Cagiva, but it was the Ducati 916, introduced in 1994, that brought Tamburini international acclaim. The story might stop right there, so successful has the 916 been for Ducati. Nor is it an exaggeration to say that the 916 rightly belongs in any top five list of 'greatest-ever' motorcycles. But no sooner had the 916 led the world in design, and in many, many race victories, than Tamburini and Castiglioni moved the mark forwards again. Castiglioni had sold Ducati and fled Bologna returning to the Cagiva headquarters on the lake at Varese. He owned the MV Agusta marque, the mythical name that carried riders like the formidable Giacomo Agostini. So it was natural that he should turn to Tamburini for a completely new sports-bike. The MV F4 is the result, and from the moment it made its first appearance, at the Milan motor show in 1997, its reputation has been secure. With a mastery of sculpted, wrap-around bodywork first seen on Bimotas and on the Cagiva Paso, and returning to the classic grey and red colour scheme of MV Agusta's golden years, the F4 looks as good as a motorcycle can look. But it is not just a question of style. The engine, designed in collaboration with Ferrari, features a cassette gearbox that allows the rider to swap gear ratios with relative ease. And the chassis, a miracle of welded CrMO tubes, gives it the best road manners of perhaps any sports-bike ever designed, thus leading to its enormous impact on motorcycle design.

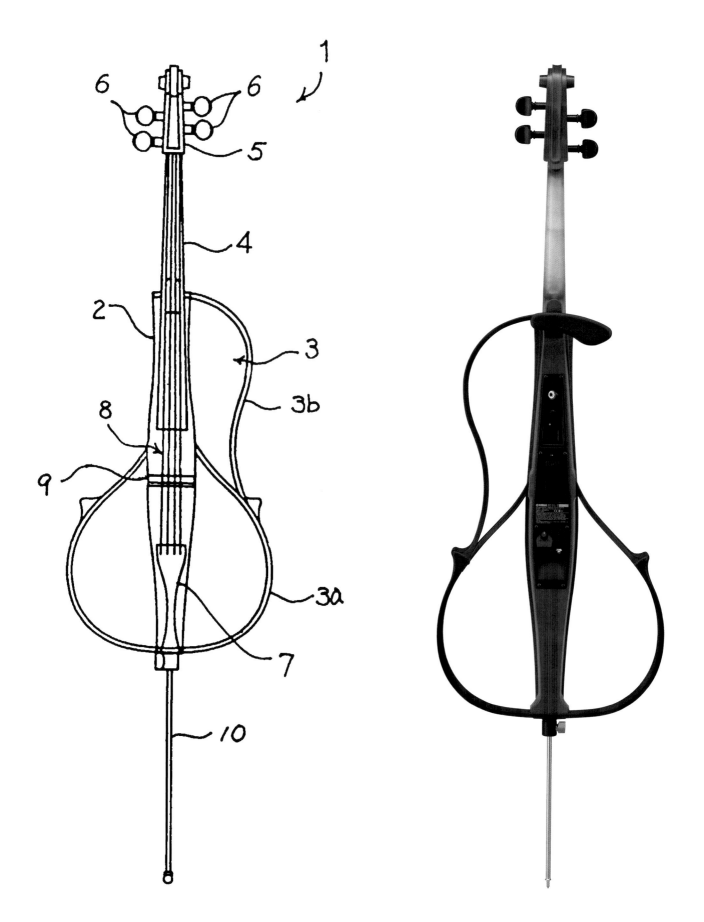

The cello is one of the mainstays of any classical music group, from string quartet to concert orchestra. The rich bass sound, with its resonating loud, deep tone, is the foundation for any musical score. The cello is also a large instrument and is rather awkward to carry. In 1997, after thorough consultations with cellists, the designers at Yamaha developed their first Silent Cello, an electronic alternative that achieved the same natural warmth and feel of the original acoustic instrument. The benefits of the Silent Cello for the musician included the ability to practise with no sound restrictions, the reduced size and weight of the instrument and added functions for different styles of music. The design of the Silent Cello does not reject its traditional acoustic counterpart, but pays homage to it: the seductive curves of the cello are evoked, despite there being no need for the shape which serves to resonate the sound. The key components are crafted in high-quality woods, including maple, spruce and ebony, in keeping with the tradition of classical instrument making. The sound it produces is generated electronically, yet in keeping with the philosophy of Yamaha – working to the highest standards of audio production. In contrast to the instrument's skeletal appearance the sound is warm and full-bodied, with most of the characteristics and nuances found in any acoustic cello. Further, it is able to place the sound in acoustic environments without requiring any external processing equipment, since it is all done internally. By using headphones, the cello can be played in any environment and, with its slim proportions, is easily transported because of its the ability to be broken down to fit into a compact case.

Yamaha Silent Cello Model N. SVC100K
(1997)
Yamaha Design Team
Yamaha 1998 to present

Silver/Felt Bracelet (1997)
Pia Wallén (1957–)
Pia Wallén AB 1997 to present

Stockholm-based designer Pia Wallén's sterling silver and felt bracelet was essentially born out of a direct response to the cold Swedish winters. The bracelet's 100 per cent wool lining was designed to insulate the skin against sub-zero temperatures. Yet the bracelet also demonstrates Wallén's concern for combining unusual and contrasting materials in a harmonious way. The 4 by 6 cm (1.6 by 2.4 in) bracelet embodies Wallén's concept of 'unpossible combinations', in this case sterling silver and industrial felt, which, according to tradition, should not form natural bedfellows. In terms of material hierarchy, silver is considered to occupy a nobler position, with the utilitarian felt playing a lowlier, proletarian role. Wallén's bracelet, however, unites the two democratically as a single product, and both materials, in equal measure, provide beauty. In addition, the application of an organic, natural material such as felt to Wallén's pure, contemporary jewellery provides a powerful connection and continuity with the Scandinavian craft tradition. Indeed, Wallén's unique and contemporary take on the application of traditional materials led to a commission, in 1992, to design the Felt Programme for the Progetto Oggetto collection by Cappellini. The influential Milanese furniture company was keen to tap into the 'new functionalist' cultural *zeitgeist* at the time, and the type of ordinary and extraordinary utilitarian design as pioneered by Wallén fitted its criteria perfectly. Pia Wallén's bracelet set a precedent in terms of successfully exploring unusual material juxtapositions and, in doing so, also challenged our perception of jewels and jewellery and their intrinsic value. The 'utilitarian with a twist' ideology also successfully chimed in with the back-to-basics mantra of the 1990s. And such is the 'noughties' demand for Wallén's unique mix of precious and natural, hi-fi and low-fidelity creations that the designer, who studied fashion at the Beckman School of Design in Stockholm, has extended her sterling silver/felt collection to encompass rings, hair decorations and pins.

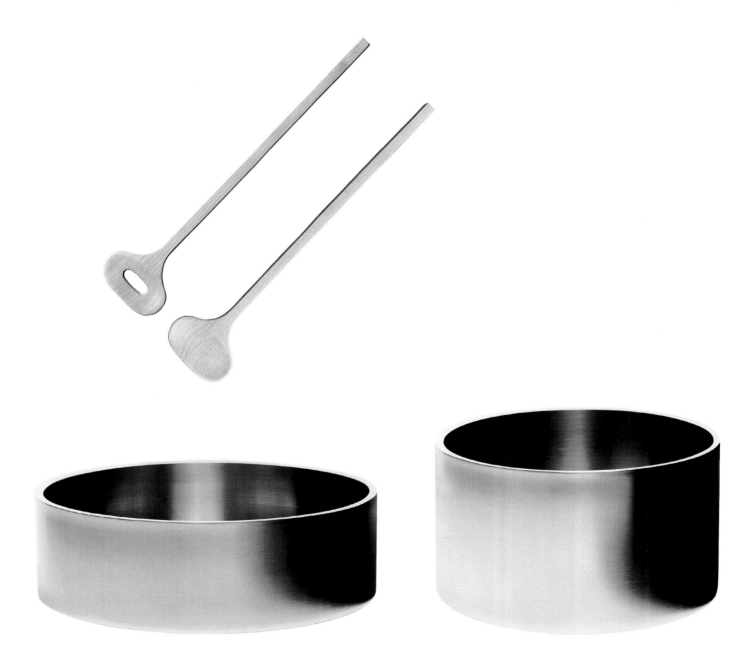

Carina Seth Andersson

Scandinavian design has long been concerned with balancing out chilly northern landscapes with warm, human-centred objects – whether cheery textiles, good lighting or comfortable, body-hugging furniture. The Stockholm-based designer Carina Seth Andersson has continued this tradition in a set of serving bowls and utensils originally created for Finnish housewares company Hackman in 1997. Rather than resort to the expected idioms of 'classic' Scandinavian design, however – what could be called the 'teak trap' – she presents something a little harder and much cooler. In order to accommodate both hot and cold food, Seth Andersson designed her bowls out of two layers of stainless steel; the pocket of air that rests between the layers keeps salads cool and pasta hot while enabling comfortable handling no matter what the temperature of the contents. The double-thick walls and matt-brushed surface provide both the low-slung 10 × 34 cm (4 × 13.4 in) and the taller 14 × 26 cm (5.5 × 10.25 in) bowls a distinctly sleek silhouette. At this point, one might think that Seth Andersson has eschewed the Scandinavian wood tradition altogether, but then she presents a set of blonde birch utensils. In an elegant nod to this classic Swedish modernist wood, Seth Andersson has created two sinuous serving tools with oblong heads – one gently scooped out, the other incorporating a lozenge-shaped slat. The birch utensils converse with the stainless-steel bowls in a dialogue of opposites: metal/wood, cold/warm, thick/thin. One design element that remains hidden from sight speaks volumes about Seth Andersson's control of details and may just reveal a sly sense of humour. Even though the birch utensils look delicate in comparison with the bowls, they are actually shot through with steel for strength and stability.

95-4

Bowls and Salad Cutlery (1997)
Carina Seth Andersson (1965–)
Hackman 1997 to present

Precision manufacturing and dynamic curved forms come together in the highly distinctive work of Marc Newson. This combination is visible even in the relatively mundane context of a flashlight. Newson's Apollo Torch was created for the celebrated Italian manufacturer Flos, associated since its foundation in 1962 with innovators such as the Castiglioni brothers. It was another Flos alumnus, Philippe Starck, who recommended Newson to the company in the early 1990s just as Newson was becoming recognized in Europe. Flos had already launched an edition of Newson's Helice Lamp in 1993 when it decided to produce the Apollo Torch seven years later. By that time Newson had become more entrenched in Italy, moving on from an initial association with furniture manufacturer Cappellini to work with others such as Magis and Alessi. Newson's Italian experience marked a fascinating coming together of his self-made talent with the European tradition of design and manufacture that he had admired but had not previously been involved in. In Italy he was surprised to discover that manufacturers were as involved in furniture design as the designers themselves, who in many cases were architects whose concepts needed refinement. This resulted in extremely high standards of workmanship but potentially difficult relationships between manufacturers and designers such as Newson, who liked to retain full control from design to production. If this tension existed, the Apollo betrays none of it. Its sleek form, presented in milled aluminium, is an exercise in cool futurism that acknowledges the designer's love of space-age iconography, made more obvious still by its name. Its lines were made even cleaner by a head-rotating on-off mechanism, doing away with the need for the push button found on the Maglite, the Apollo's apparent inspiration. Like its predecessor, this futuristic variation on the theme also featured a spare bulb in its base.

955

Apollo Torch (1997)
Marc Newson (1962–)
Flos 2000 to present

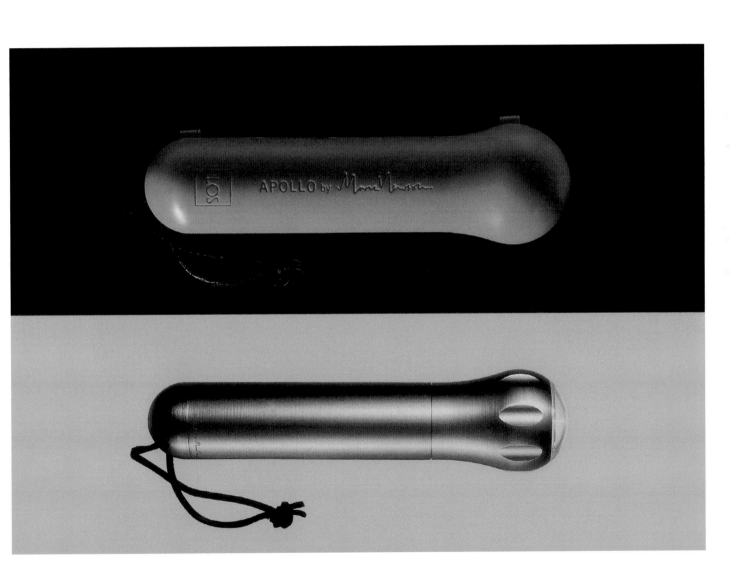

Tower of Tom Vacs, Milan, 1997

In 1997 *Domus* magazine invited Ron Arad to create an eye-catching sculpture for a prestigious site in central Milan for the annual Furniture Fair. The commission enabled Arad to develop a design he had been considering and to make a tower of sixty-seven stacked chairs. His design concept was for a single curl of material to create a continuous seat and back. The chair is detailed with ripples that both articulate the surface and strengthen it. The ripples are close together on the sides, effectively reinforcing and narrowing the form where stress is greatest. On the seat and back the ripples are more open. The Tom Vac chair has proved to be one of Arad's most adaptable designs, perhaps because of the simplicity of the form. Unlike most chairs it has been successfully rendered in different materials. As a mass-produced chair it has been a commercial success and one-off versions of the chair have proved popular with the top-end collectors' market. The chairs in the *Domus* tower were made of vacuum-formed aluminium, which is one source of their name. The other is the photographer friend of Arad's, Tom Vack. In a few early examples Arad deliberately left the metal untrimmed, so the ripples of the chair are framed within a square. Arad always perceived the Tom Vac as a mass-produced chair and today Vitra manufactures it in polypropylene with a variety of leg configurations. One version, with wooden rockers, is a deliberate homage to the Eameses' **DAR** rocking armchair from 1950. The version with stainless-steel legs can be stacked. There is even a version produced in clear acrylic. In 1997 Arad produced an edition of twenty Pic Chairs which lacked the ripples of the production version but which were each unique objects incorporating **LED** lights, pigments and other media. The body of each Pic Chair was glass fibre and polyester. Arad also produced a limited edition, Tom Vac, from carbon fibre, which transformed the character of the chair again.

With its articulated, sinuous silhouette in a myriad of softly translucent pastels, and of course its low price tag, the Garbino wastepaper bin has sold more than two million since its launch by Umbra in 1997. The Garbino champions the very essence of its designer's self-proclaimed sense of sensual minimalism and his adrenalin-laden vision for the democratization of design. In the shadow of this success, however, remains a more subtle and fascinating tale of achievement. Household utilitarian goods have long been a low-margin, high-volume business. The invention of injection-moulded polypropylene allowed for high production runs, but carried with it a significant initial tooling cost. Manufacturers tended to rely on generic, long-established forms when launching products, differentiating them only by superficial restyling, new packaging or prominent promotion. In the face of these economic realities and even though feedback from initial focus groups was at best tepid, Umbra took a deep breath and pressed ahead with a product that bore little relation to existing designs. While the Garbino's unique shape appears asymmetrical from many angles, it is indeed perfectly symmetrical. Its body and base are each a uniform thickness and, despite its curves and varied profile, the bin is entirely devoid of sharp corners and undercuts. The combination of these design considerations allows an uninterrupted flow of resin during the injection process, uniform cooling and a simplified, symmetrical high-yield mould with markedly low wastage, a common manufacturing concern where undercuts can result in incomplete filling and where varied widths can cause imperfections from shrinkage during cooling. The uniformly tapered sides allow easy stacking of large quantities, reducing costs of transport and retail stocking, while the shallow curve of the interior base discourages sticking during stacking and allows Umbra to avoid the expense and waste of a lining tissue for each bin during shipment. Scratches from daily use are hard to see on the translucent matt exterior. The edgeless concave base permits easy cleaning, and its added thickness provides a lower centre of gravity and structural balance. The swooping rim, cut-out handle and curved profile have allowed the design to be patented and attempted counterfeits successfully prosecuted.

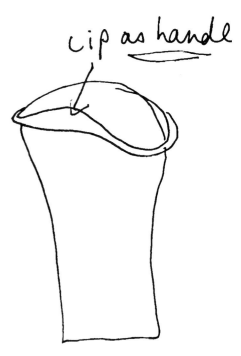

lip as handle

958

Wait (1997)
Matthew Hilton (1957–)
Authentics 1999 to present

This fully recyclable plastic chair by British talent Matthew Hilton marked a turning-point in his career, moving from high-value, low-volume furniture into the realm of affordable mass production. The chair is made from a single piece of injection-moulded polypropylene, incorporating strengthening ribs in the seat and back to give a stability that belies the naturally flexible properties of the light material. Engineering such a design to perfection took Hilton two years of development time, with his work split between his own low-tech design approach and the sophisticated equipment made available by his manufacturer, the German company, Authentics. The costs for tooling the moulds of any injection-moulded product are high but, once the expense of this initial investment has been swallowed, the subsequent unit costs are minimal due to the rapid production time, use of only one material and no hand labouring. Although it was launched in 1999 into a market already saturated with cheap plastic chairs that used the same production process, the stackable Wait chair quickly achieved classic status. Hilton and Authentics cleverly attained a price point that was more expensive than standard, crudely designed alternatives but much cheaper than other all-plastic 'designer' chairs. The Wait chair sidestepped the former through classic good design and avoided the status of the latter by deliberately dispensing with a fashionable avant-garde appearance. The result is an unobtrusive, good-looking, comfortable and affordable chair that is stackable, suitable for use indoors or out, and available in various translucent or solid colours. Hilton designs for the likes of SCP, who produce his iconic Balzac chair (1991), as well as European manufacturers such as Driade, Disform, Montis and XO. Shortly after the release of the Wait chair, Hilton took up a part-time position as head of furniture design at Habitat, where he would be able to continue developing mass-produced furniture at a price that most can afford.

Dahlström 98 is arguably the best and most expensive range of pots and pans on the market today. The Finnish manufacturer Hackman invited a number of influential designers, including Swedish-born Björn Dahlström, to develop for its Hackman Tools series an innovative range of cooking utensils that was both beautiful and durable. Part of Dahlström's brief was to use a manufacturing technique developed by Hackman to create long-lasting and durable products, called the 'sandwich' technique. A thick aluminium sheet is wedged between two thinner stainless-steel sheets, which are drawn together and shaped in a press. The sturdiness of steel combined with aluminium creates a high-performance material particularly noted for even heat distribution. A group of top chefs from Helsinki, Oslo and Stockholm were brought in to work directly with the Hackman specialists and engineers, contributing their professional expertise to the design process. The basic idea was to produce professional-quality oven-to-tableware pots that would also appeal to the domestic market. Function is the primary concern, with, for example, heavy cast iron used

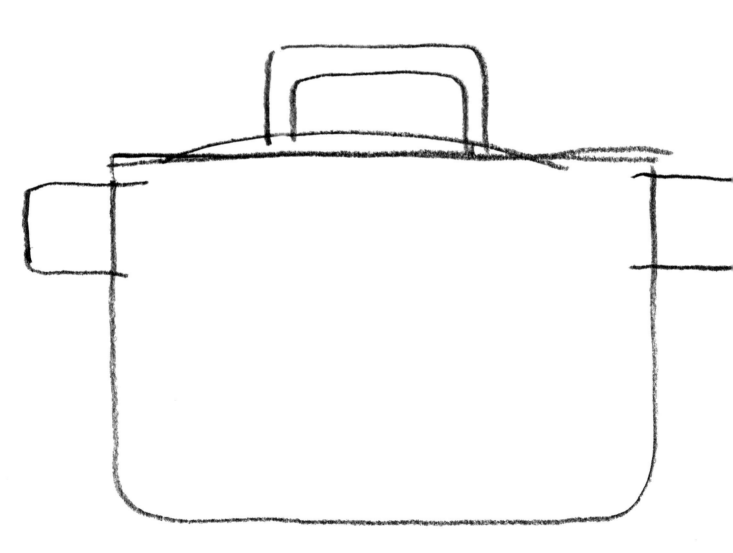

for frying and grill pans. Rather than the utensils competing with the food for attention, the simple form of the casserole pot, for example, and its understated, matt, brushed steel finish allow the food to be shown to its best advantage. Where a shiny, mirror surface shouts machine-made, the matt finish of the Dahlström 98 cookware has a more tactile, domestic feel. For the thick, hollow handles, Dahlström borrowed a technique typically used for producing cutlery in the Hackman factory, while his background in graphics is evident in the two-dimensional quality and strong silhouettes of the utensils. This elegant range surpasses the expectations of the original brief, and is realized as a beautiful object.

Dahlström 98 (1998)
Björn Dahlström (1957–)
Hackman 1998 to present

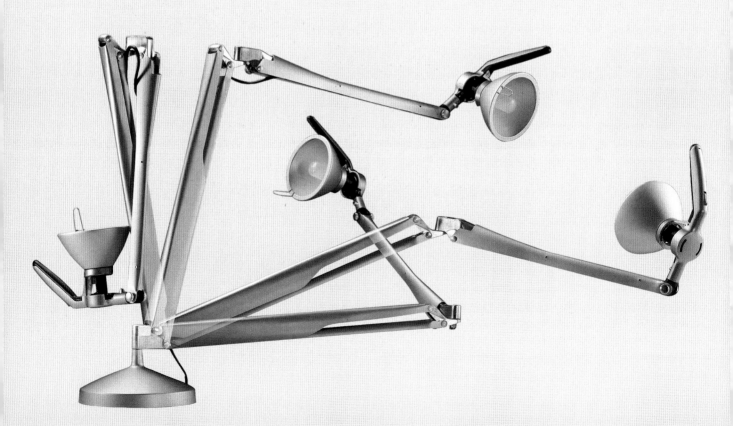

When it first appeared in 1998 the Fortebraccio was instantly considered a tour de force in lighting design, as it is quite simply one of the most versatile and flexible interior lighting systems in production. Designed by Alberto Meda and Paolo Rizzatto, possibly the most successful partnership in contemporary lighting design, the Fortebraccio was conceived more as a practical tool. In terms of its design, the idea was to make the light independent from the electric wiring, so the heads, arms and attachments are all designed for separate assembly, whereas the electrical parts are prewired to the heads. This effectively made it possible to substitute different light sources on the same arms, in much the same way as a screwdriver can accommodate different tips on the same grip. As a result a variety of 'different lamps' can be easily composed: for example, the two-armed table or floor lamp, the single-arm lamp, the spot with one head and its own attachment, or the floor lamp version. The central joint between the two articulated arms also has a vertical rotation axis that allows the outer arm to rotate on two planes, both horizontally and vertically. This permits the lamp to be moved easily into unusual positions. The head, which varies according to different halogen or incandescent bulbs (the table lamp is the first of its kind to incorporate a halogen bulb and no transformer that can be handled with total safety), is articulated via a safe and ergonomic polycarbonate grip for directing the light. Fortebraccio also has a universal attachment that means that it can be clamped straight on to tables, vertical walls or tilted planes because of its special articulated release at every 25-degree point. The model is named after the charismatic Norman knight William of Altavilla, known as Fortebraccio, who was renowned for his big nose. And like the knight, one of the main features of the Fortebraccio table lamp is its 'nose' or handle, which directs the light into different positions. Finally, in terms of construction, its use of moulded and pre-bent sheared and formed sheet-steel has helped to keep manufacturing costs down. So, all in all, the Fortebraccio is one of the most advanced and affordable lighting systems to emerge in recent years, and forms a perfect role model for the LucePlan manifesto dedicated to the 'constant search for simplicity as the solution to complexity'.

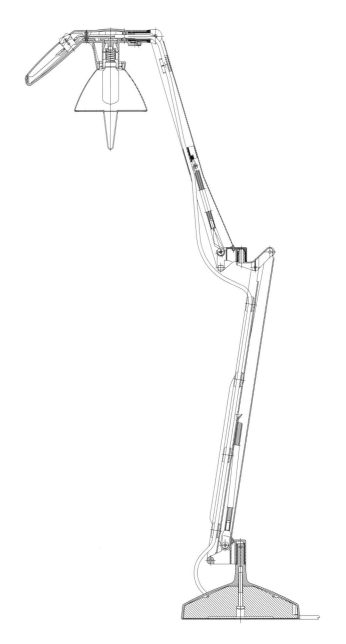

From the cook's knife to the teaspoon, every item in iittala's Citterio 98 range of flatware displays the same perfectly balanced proportions. With broad bases and slim central sections, the pieces achieve the considerable feat of being both heavyweight in performance and lightweight in looks. Designed by the prolific Italian architect and designer Antonio Citterio, with his German colleague Glen Oliver Löw, the range has been a best seller for iittala since it was introduced. Indeed, such has been the popularity of Citterio 98 that it rapidly became a symbol for 1990s design. Like many of the most successful modern designs, Citterio 98 is an update of an enduring archetype. In this case, Citterio and Löw looked at French café cutlery, the type that consists of thin steel knives, forks or spoons with additional wooden or plastic panels to lend weight to the handle. The duo observed the practical benefits of a heavy handle (it equals greater ease of use) but translated it into a product that is made solely from steel. Although the Citterio 98 range could be described as angular in appearance, each corner has been softened to create a dynamic yet tactile shape. To accentuate the softness of their design, Citterio and Löw insisted on using matt-brushed steel, giving the flatware a seductive, subtle appearance. Prizes have rained down upon the collection since its introduction, including awards from Germany, the United States, Italy and Finland – where the range is made. Unsurprisingly, iittala have encouraged Citterio and Löw to continue to expand the collection and as a result the range now includes far more than the original, simple table setting. Although Antonio Citterio has designed everything from showrooms to entire kitchen units, it is this range of knives, forks and spoons that has really stamped his name on the history of modern design.

Surely in the hundred or so years since the earliest opal pendant lights were turned on, designers should have exhausted this archetype long ago. But with his Glo-Ball series, Jasper Morrison revisits the hanging glass globe in a simplified, yet exciting interpretation. Launched in 1998, the Glo-Ball series has had tremendous commercial success. Morrison had actually begun to work on the idea five years earlier with Flos, with the objective of creating lighting that would meet the demands of any possible situation. To produce the characteristic soft, matted glow of the Glo-Ball, a clear glass core is dipped into a second molten white opal glass, in a process known as flashing, and then hand-blown into the striking, slightly flattened oval shape. A diffuse, uniform glow radiates from what appears to be an entirely flat surface, which refuses even the slightest reflection when seen from afar; a mirage achieved by exposing

the thin outer casing of opaline glass to acid to create a highly matt surface. Each of the lights in the Glo-Ball series possesses a calming anonymity that gives way only when noticed, and melds form into function. The Glo-Ball avoids the industrially perfect sphere in favour of something oddly more natural. The mechanisms that support each light disappear into its core unnoticed. Its soft, intensely uniform glow gives no hint that the light it radiates is of course not from its surface but merely another light bulb. It is this subtle reworking that makes the form the function. The series mirrors the very core of what Jasper Morrison has long been known for – an appreciation and respect for the past, a pursuit of honesty in form tempered by soul and an ability to uncover elegance previously hidden by an unnoticed edge.

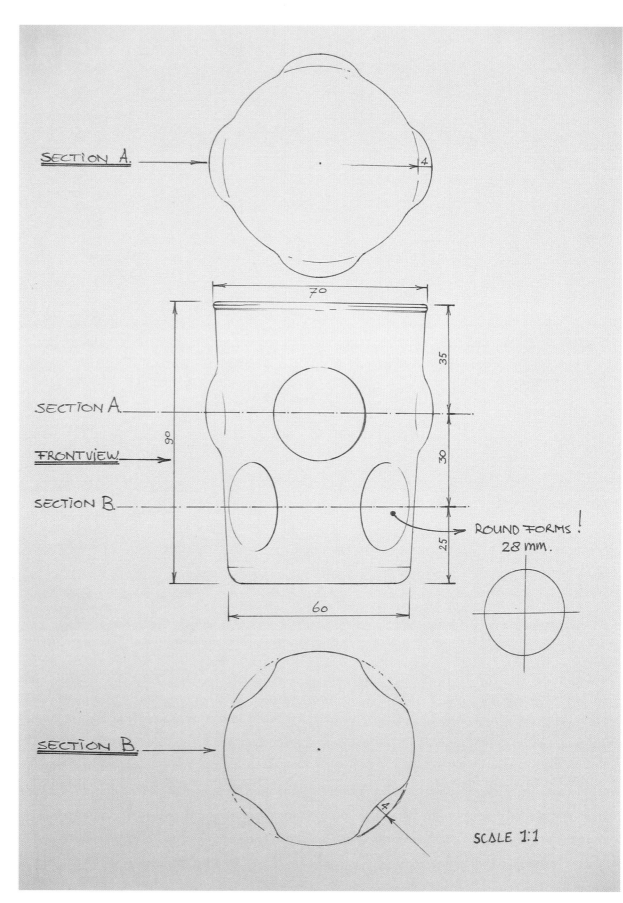

SECTION A.

SECTION A

FRONTVIEW

SECTION B

SECTION B.

70

35

90

30

25

60

4

4

ROUND FORMS !
28 mm.

SCALE 1:1

Optic Glass began life when designer Arnout Visser was asked by Dutch collective Droog Design to respond to its brief, 'The Inevitable Ornament'. Visser's interpretation of this was to look for ornamental possibilities embedded in the materiality of objects, rather than in applied decoration. When examining expensive camera equipment he discovered that the largest lenses were actually filled with liquid. This sparked the notion that if a drinking vessel could be shaped similarly, perhaps the drink could provide a magnifying effect. Starting with specially made, tall, smooth-sided tumblers in heat-resistant borosilicate glass, Visser heated the tumblers and concentrated blasts of air at the glass to morph the surface into a series of concave and convex areas. For production, a stubbier, off-the-shelf borosilicate glass provides the master, but the hand processing remains. The resulting glass is an uncommon mix of industrial design and craft. Once it is filled, light reflects and refracts through its undulating skin, providing a beautiful and intriguing effect. If used for alcohol a fresh and witty reading of the object becomes possible, with its form reflecting the user's possibly wobbly state of mind or vision. Optic Glass was presented by Droog in Milan in April 1998, along with other work in 'The Inevitable Ornament' collection from designers including Hella Jongerius, Richard Hutten and Marcel Wanders. The product is now made in Eastern Europe and has a couple of serendipitous features Visser had not predicted. The bumps allow the glasses to stack without jamming and also create a comfortable supporting grip. Beyond the regular consumer, both elderly and blind users have given positive reviews, highlighting its ergonomic characteristics. Visser has contributed many products to the Droog collection and has become known for his simple and elegant glass designs that often use the laws of physics as their starting point.

This chair is a sign of its times, combining the most advanced materials with a radical rethinking of office life. It was designed for business high-flyers and has a hard-edged appearance – and price tag – to match. Little wonder to find it starred with Tom Cruise in the futuristic thriller *Minority Report*. Designer Mario Bellini and furniture manufacturer Vitra have been at the forefront of design responses to changes in the workplace for two decades. In recent years the hierarchies of traditional office life have been replaced by open plans and 'hot desking'. Long working hours and seismic shifts in computing technology simultaneously brought home life and work life closer together. Less formal attitudes towards work and innovative technology mean workers are no longer tied to the keyboard. They can even recline, as they might do in front of the TV at home. These are the ideas that inspired this chair, which Mario Bellini designed with his son Claudio (1963–). The Ypsilon is so-named for the Y-shaped structure of the chair's back. The chair's chief feature is the adjustability of the back and headrest to an almost fully reclined posture, while still holding the head and shoulders in a position where a computer screen can be viewed. Every element of the chair is designed to support the body in the utmost comfort, not in order to relax, but to keep the worker at peak performance for long periods. The chair frames the sitter like an exo-skeleton: it is simultaneously anthropomorphic and robot-like. A special gel in the lumbar region 'remembers' the form of the shape of the sitter's back. The taut, translucent chair back was inspired in part by the wooden beaded mats used by cab drivers to ensure ventilation, and was designed for the same purpose. Vitra chairman Rolf Fehlbaum likens the back to Marcel Breuer's famous 1926 illustration of the chairs of the future, where people will sit on nothing but air. In this instance he believes the chair is so comfortable it cannot be felt: it is like sitting on air. Numerous critics have agreed and the chair has won prestigious prizes, including Best Product Design 2002 in Germany's Red Dot Design Award.

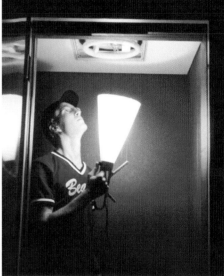

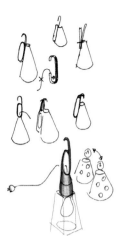

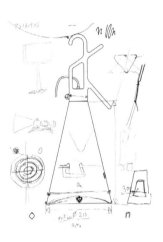

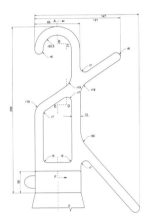

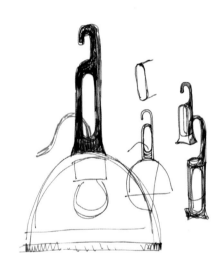

May Day, International Workers' Day, refers to the annual celebration of working class strength. The lamp of the same name by German designer Konstantin Grcic has the appeal of a plain security or utility lamp – a working lamp – but on closer look it reveals more elegance, more attention to detail than might be expected of a purely utilitarian lamp. In many interviews the designer underpins his conviction that a formal signature is not what design should be about. Nevertheless his stripped-down, functional designs are definitely recognizable. Most designs by Grcic, which range from cutlery, lighting and furniture to exhibition design, look familiar enough to be called archetypes,

almost universal shapes that could have been designed by anyone, except that all possess tiny little details that distinguish them from similar objects. His designs derive most often from the technical possibilities and impossibilities of materials and machines. Grcic has a solid background in Bauhaus design, and a similar practical-minded approach, but whereas Bauhaus designs were attempts to define an all-encompassing, sleek machine aesthetic, Grcic aims at objects that will work in any environment. His Minimalism belongs to contemporary, flexible ways of living. May Day Lamp was not designed for a fixed position. The design of the handle suggests there

are various ways of using the object: it can be suspended from a hook or held in the hand or it can be shifted around and put on a flat surface, where it will produce diffused light. There is a choice of four different colours (orange, blue, black and green) for the handle. The outer material is injection-moulded tapered opaline polypropylene diffuser. The light itself takes two different types of bulbs, and there is a push button switch on the handle itself. Once you start looking attentively at Grcic's seemingly plain designs, the clever elegance incorporated in all of them becomes apparent.

Sony's Aibo Robot pet signalled the arrival of a sci-fi futuristic promise. With its articulated limbs, shiny plastic coat and familiar behavioural interactions with its owner, the Aibo literally aims to replace the real thing. While there have been several robot companions for sci-fi film and television heroes, like Star Wars' R2D2 and Dr Who's K9, until the arrival of Aibo they only existed on our screens. Aibo is not meant as another 'labour-saving' device, but as, according to Sony, 'an autonomous robot that acts in response to external stimuli and its own judgment... capable of interacting and co-existing with people as a new form of robot entertainment.' Developed by Sony Digital Creative Laboratory and first introduced in 1999, the Aibo sold 3,000 units in its first twenty minutes of availability, confirming Sony's intuition that it was commercially viable. The name Aibo is derived from 'artificial intelligence' and 'robot', as well as meaning 'companion' in Japanese. It responds to voices, touch and owner's faces, while retaining some autonomy by emulating 'mood swings', 'hunger' and 'tiredness' and can then be recharged in its docking plinth. It is smart in that it records experience, allowing it to learn and develop its personality, enhancing emotional bonds with the owner over time. It can also communicate via a PC, using wireless LAN technology to read out emails and enabled website texts through its mouth-speaker. Along with multiple sensors on its back, stereo microphones in its ears, and a 'brain' based upon a 100Mhz 64 bit RISC processor with 16MB of memory, a choice of programme options allows the owner to shape its behaviour. Many versions have been developed up to 2004. The ERS-220A model is a robot visually differentiated from its predecessors by its aggressive, more futuristic look. Having no mouth, though, it can't bite. The ERS-7, however, is akin to a 'cuddly' puppy, with droopy ears and a friendly stance, and is complemented by a range of appropriate toys for it to play with. Essentially, these are domestic pets without the hassle of real-life mess, for an age when people work longer, less predictable hours and cannot commit to looking after real animals. 'Your true companion', as Sony puts it, modifies notions of friendship along with expectations of what emotively based products can be.

Aibo Robot (1999)
Hajime Sorayama (1947–)
Sony Design Team
Sony 1999 to present

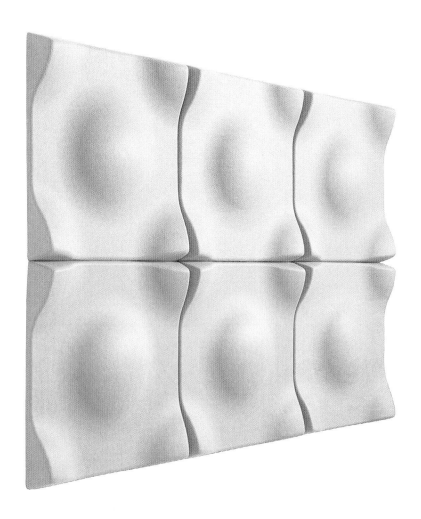

Acoustic design

has long been an element of architectural projects from concert halls to airports, while engineers dutifully ensure every conceivable sound resides in countless consumer electronics products. Yet, despite this breadth of attention devoted to enhancing and eliminating sound, acoustic products for interior environments were either customized or destined for the high-specification world of recording studios. Soundwave was a generic solution to a specific problem. The problem was posed by the new interior design for Helsinki restaurant Pravda, where large expanses of glass were going to create a cacophony of reflected sound. The solution was found by Teppo Asikainen – sound dampening panels in the form of three-dimensional wallpaper. He wanted a strong, visual identity and universal pattern that could be used over a broad expanse of wall and the result was Soundwave, an undulating swell across a sea of moulded wall panels, its modestly oversized scale creating a play of light and shadows. While the automotive industry had long used moulded polyester panels to absorb sound, as noise reduction is a critical element in the design, they had certainly never been designed to be noticed. Asikainen's use of this same material within the realm of mass-produced, design-sensitive consumer products was entirely novel. The prototype was created rather than engineered, and the thickness and softness of the commercial version had to be fine-tuned in collaboration with an acoustic laboratory. The initial 'Swell' motif was followed by a pattern called 'Scrunch', reminiscent of crumpled paper. The difference between these first two panels was primarily styling, but the range has grown to include a version of 'Swell' designed to diffuse rather than absorb sound as well as a newer panel design that absorbs an extended lower spectrum of sounds, the 'Swoop' (later renamed 'Luna'). Together these panels comprise the Soundwave acoustic system and offer an adaptable, Velcro-applied system of attractively designed, mass-produced panels that can be used in homes and offices just as easily as in studios and auditoriums. Originally launched in 2000 by the innovative Finnish design group, Snowcrash, the range is now produced by Offecct in Sweden and continues to evolve as new colours and textile finishes are added.

967

Soundwave (1999–2000)
Teppo Asikainen (1968–)
Snowcrash 2000 to 2003
Offecct 2003 to present

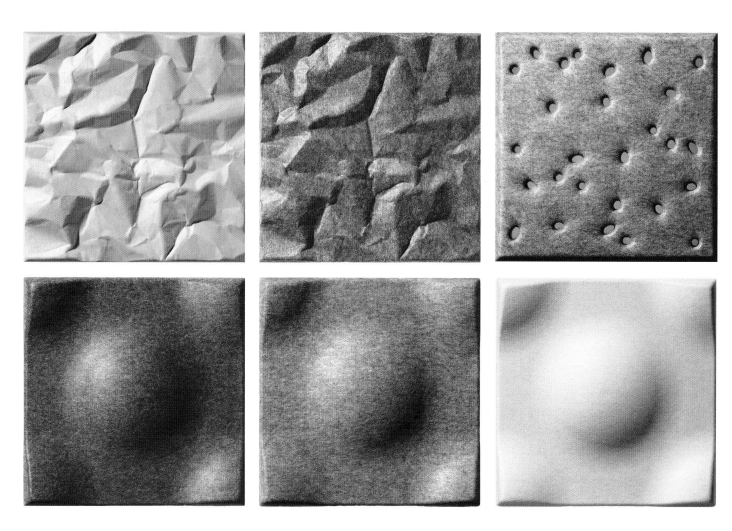

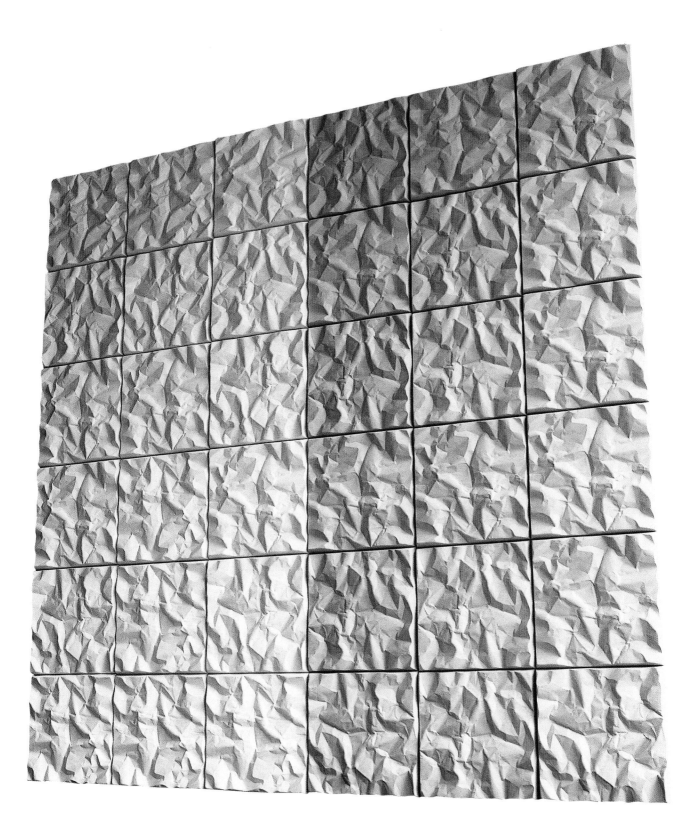

Through designing several smaller, equally successful plastic products for the Italian company, Magis, Jasper Morrison was introduced to a relatively new moulding technology and used it in the design of the Air-Chair. One interesting aspect of this chair, and why it is very cheap to produce, is the use of what is actually an evolution of regular plastic injection-moulding technology: gas-assisted injection moulding. The gas assistance means that the molten plastic is forced under pressure to the extremes of the mould, leaving voids in the thicker parts of the moulding. In this design this means that the 'frame' of the chair is effectively a series of tubes, therefore using little of the material, glass-reinforced polypropylene, and reducing its weight. It also means that a fully formed and finished, almost seamless chair can be produced in a matter of minutes. The efficiency of production means that the original Air-Chair retailed for less than £50, unusually inexpensive for a piece of well-designed, beautifully made Italian 'designer' furniture. The word 'designer', in this context, has little to do with what marketing departments mean by the term. It is a genuinely successful, simple, everyday chair; the type of design that Jasper Morrison is so good at. His designs combine utilitarianism with a level of subtle refinement, which means his beautifully simple solutions can sit happily in any environment, look good and work extremely well. The inevitable and immediate success of this indoor/outdoor, domestic/contract chair, which comes in a number of light colours, has led to the design of a whole family of other 'Air-' products: dining table, low table, TV/video table and, more recently, a folding chair.

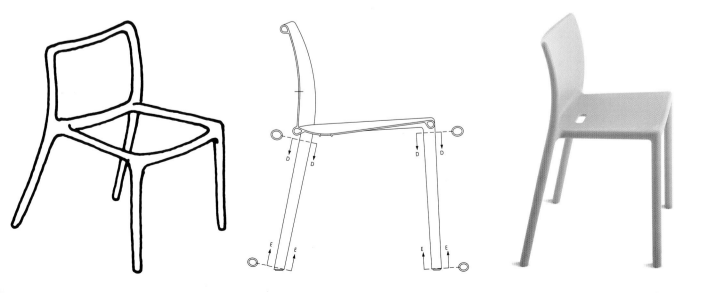

BGM
3

1. Pastorale siciliana
2. Tarantella napoletana
3. Il carnevale di Venezia
4. U cchiu' beddu diamanti
5. Gran valzer
6. Controdanza
7. Mi votu e mi rivotu -violin solo
8. La traviata -Preludio all' atto 1
9. Taormina···si bedda tu
10. Torna a Surriento
11. Passeggiando per Lipari
12. Mi votu e mi rivotu
13. Cavalleria rusticana-Intermezzo
14. Vitti' na crozza

MUJI
無印良品

MUJI, one of the most progressive companies in recent times, appears not to play by the same rules as typical manufacturers. The reasons are numerous, but the important factor is that it is not a manufacturer at all, but a retailer. It is reliant upon products with a combination of reasonable prices, honest materials and relevant functions for daily life. It does not bother itself with top-down marketing strategies nor incremental stylistic changes. These factors allowed MUJI and its key visionary, Masaaki Kanai, to notice the experiments that Naoto Fukasawa and IDEO Japan were making with their 'Without Thought' workshops. These workshops were focused on the belief that design could involve contemporary memories that emerged from actions or behaviour. These 'active memories' could then be applied to technologies with little history or with unsuccessful placement in daily life. Although Fukasawa had been experimenting with these ideas for many years, they had not yet reached the production stage. It was when MUJI saw a simple, wall-mounted CD player that operated on a similar principle to an extractor fan, that they felt able to contemplate production. Within a few months a programme was set up. The MUJI Wall Mounted CD Player is a complex product because it treads a fine line between artistic humour and authentic innovation. And it is this fine line that has resulted in such popular success. It easily graces the walls of children's bedrooms, while also looking calm and reserved in minimalist homes. Functionally, the product centres on a Sony Walkman CD module. Operationally, it has been reduced to minimal controls. Its on/off switch is a pull-cord, a highly original yet perfectly acceptable form of interaction for a wall-mounted object. There is no lid, nor a digital display, as both features are dictated by design rather than fundamental necessity. Fukasawa now helps to oversee MUJI's product catalogue and continues to produce designs that are tangential to what the market might expect. His criteria are rooted so deeply in the human condition that his products feel as though we have already lived with them previously.

The

Random Light demonstrates one of the mandates of good design – simple in appearance, complex in execution – but took three years to develop. Random by name and random by nature, the light 'just happened' according to its creator, Bertjan Pot. All the materials in the design – resin, fibreglass and balloons – were lying around in Pot's workspace, left over from a graduating project which had seen him trying to knit with the fibreglass. 'That didn't work very well,' Pot admits, 'the fibres kept breaking during the knitting. However, coiling the fibre around a big balloon in straight lines worked much better.' The light is a piece of classic craft design created with high-tech materials: epoxy and fibreglass, chromed steel and plastic. The fibreglass, soaked in resin, is coiled around the balloon, and the balloon is then removed through a hole in which the light bulb is later placed. The light certainly has an appeal and Marcel Wanders introduced it to the well-respected Dutch manufacturer Moooi, who then brought out around 2,000 in the first two years of its production. Random Lights are particularly popular with architects and designers. 'Architects love them because you can hang a room full of them and the space still looks open and light, even when the lights are off, because they are transparent,' says Pot. The play of light is especially effective due to the light being produced in three sizes: 50 cm, 85 cm, and 105 cm (20 in, 34 in and 42 in), which can be hung at different heights. Not satisfied with successfully using this technique for one product, Pot has challenged himself with the more complex follow-up of a hand-coiled chair. Pot first came to the notice of design aficionados as part of the duo Monkey Boys, which he founded in 1999 with Daniel White. For three years they created cleverly conceived lighting and furniture. Pot has also taught at the Rietveld Academy, Amsterdam, but since 2003 has worked independently.

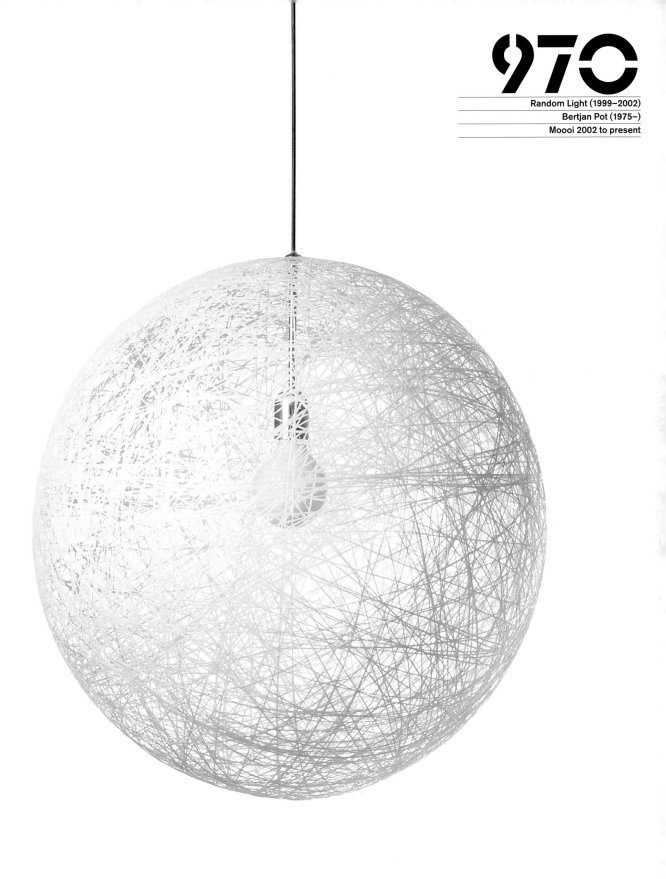

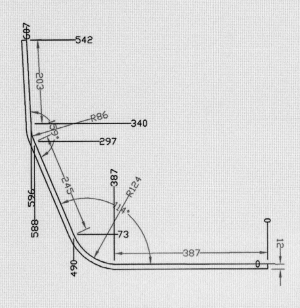

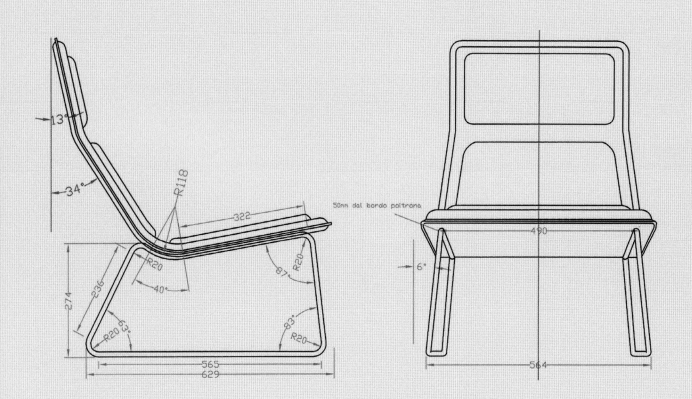

LOW PAD dimensioni generali

The Low Pad combines elegance and simplicity with cutting-edge production techniques. Its minimal styling and sinuous line give it a sense of weightlessness that owes much to the look of mid-twentieth-century modern design, while its moulded padding, gently rising from the seat and back to give comfort and support, gives it a sophisticated contemporary twist. Jasper Morrison openly acknowledges Poul Kjærholm's PK22 chair (1956) as the inspiration for the Low Pad. He had been an admirer of the PK22 for as long as he could remember, but, having owned and lived with one for a few years, had become aware that it wasn't the most comfortable of chairs. The initial idea for the Low Pad was to develop a comfortable low chair with as little volume and the same reduction of materials as Kjærholm's classic. Morrison recalls, 'The prototypes of our first drawings were not particularly exciting, consisting of more or less traditional upholstery on a wire frame base. After some refinement I still wasn't sure it really had anything going for it, but on my way back to London I noticed the profile of an airport bench, and that, combined with a memory of having seen some moulded leather forms, gave me the concept.' Morrison is known for his interest in new material technologies, and Cappellini was more than happy to encourage his experiments, helping him to source a company making car seats that had the skills and expertise to press leather. Morrison experimented with various shapes for the back of the chair, and finally settled on a in-plywood panel, with multi-density polyurethane foam moulded to the required profile, cut to shape, with leather or upholstery stitched over. The manufacturer's skills with upholstery were suited to Morrison's design, creating a balance between the shape and the finish. Stainless steel has been used for the two rectangular legs, while four rubber 'feet' sit under, at opposing ends.

The last decade of the twentieth century has shown hardly any true innovation in the production of glass tableware. Most producers rely on historically based designs or modernist design classics, which have been available for decades. Even a renowned factory like the Finnish producer iittala, which has always been very design-conscious, had more trust in re-editions of Aino Aalto, Tapio Wirkkala and Kaj Franck. Yet in 1999 iittala invited the Munich-based designer, Konstantin Grcic, to create a new range of glassware. Their collaboration led to an instant commercial and artistic success. His glasses for iittala are elegantly proportioned, tapered tumblers. In this design it is not only the outline of the glasses that is important, but also the precise definition of the thickness of the glass. The glasses have minimal adornment, with just one judiciously chosen line, which brings harmony to the range. The Relations set consists of three different tumblers, a carafe with a glass turned upside down as a stopper, a large tray and a low dish. It comes in two colours, brilliant white and smoky-grey. It is a truly versatile glassware range that is suitable for all kinds of drinks, from fresh juice to refreshing beer, ordinary milk to fancy cocktails. Grcic was interested in using a machine for pressed glass, and chose to rework the archetypal cone-shaped glass, adding a step on the inside wall in order to make a stacking glass. The glass could now be cleverly stacked, while keeping the outer wall flush by creating a thicker inner wall. Because the glasses are produced using a double-sectioned mould, the range can be produced in large quantities, and the step is the detail that can only be manufactured by pressing the glass. Grcic, who trained at the Royal College of Art, London, is one of the most significant innovators of design in recent years. He works for major design companies like Authentics, ClassiCon, Driade, Flos and Cappellini. Grcic is a designer who is able to reduce his designs to their utmost essence, advocating purity and elegance.

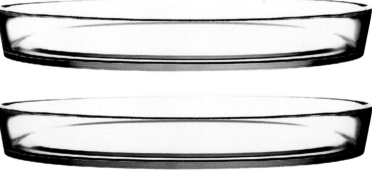

Werner Aisslinger lying on the 930 Soft lounge chair at the Salone del Mobile, Milan, 2000

The 930 Soft lounge chair has a base made of solid wire while the lounge cover is made from a soft polyurethane material called Gel, a material generally used in the medical field. The designed grid pattern gives stability and at the same time surprises the user with an exciting softness when lying on the chair. The overall impression of the lounge chair is one of lightness and elegance and its two materials – polished stainless-steel wire and translucent gel – emphasize this apparent fragility. The product proves that materials and technology, not typically used for the manufacture of a chair, combined with the discipline of designing a functional object can still allow for the creation of a piece of furniture with a recognizable identity. In many of his products Werner Aisslinger combines a rather basic design language with investigations into new materials and technologies. The chair owes its reputation to its unique and expressive shape rather than by number of sales. Gel is a costly material and means it will always be a luxury item, to be appreciated by collectors and destined to be a museum piece. This does not in any way detract from the value of the design itself. The challenge of creating a product for industrial production that incorporates the innovation of new materials is obvious. This chair is a typical product of its time, where the charm and value of synthetic material combined with new technologies allows the designer to develop an archetype with longevity without being influenced by mere transient fashions.

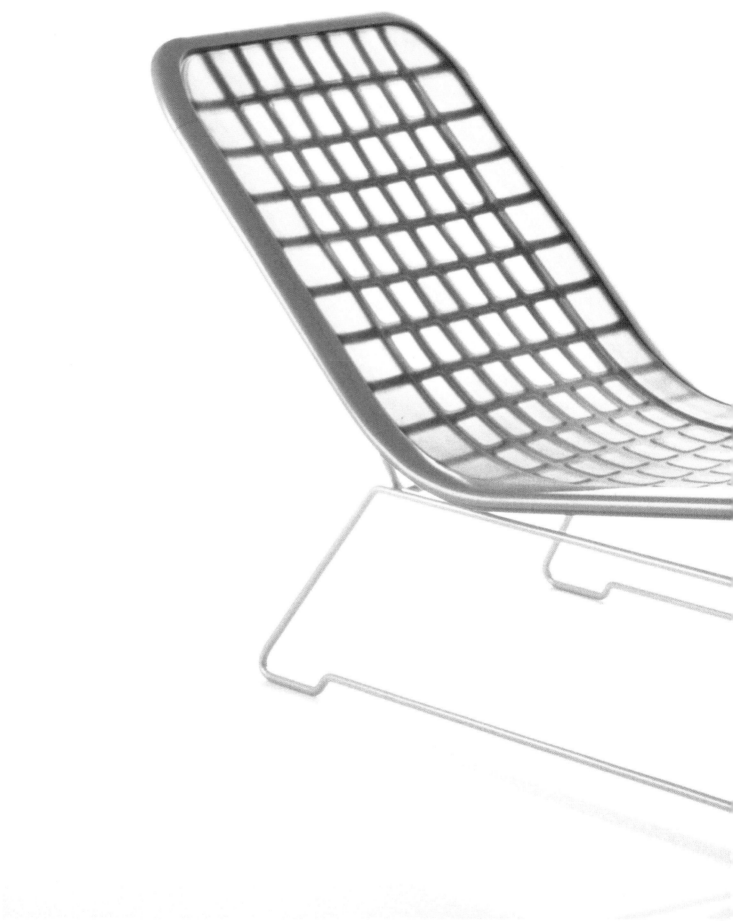

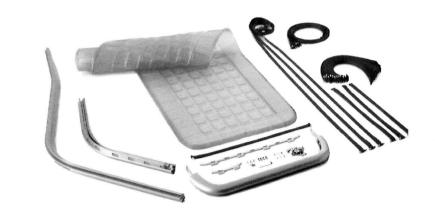

For over twenty years the design work of Antonio Citterio has contributed to the redefining and reshaping of design. Citterio's training and experience span many design disciplines and his work consistently epitomizes a combination of practicality with luxury. He employs sensuous and elegant lines, and the highest standards in finish and materials to produce understated classic designs. Citterio Collective Tools 2000 illustrate this perfectly. Designed for iittala, the 2000 collection was preceded by the Citterio 98 Collection, designed in collaboration with Glen Oliver Löw, and formed a complementary set of cooking and culinary utensils for the earlier flatware range. In keeping with iittala's ethos, the range acknowledges the core concept of practicality and beauty in design, and exemplifies an elegance and simplicity that belie the strength of its use. The Citterio Collective Tools 2000 set of tableware and utensils consists of serving spoon, a cake server, serving tongs, a bottle opener and more. Antonio Citterio has earned a reputation for his uncompromising design and craftsmanship, which contribute to the design being widely accepted as a modern classic. This set stands apart from others for several reasons, most immediately the individual form used in the design. Manufactured in matt-brushed 18/10 stainless steel, all the pieces share the same generous proportions and a design that fits easily into the hand. The hollow handle construction has a perfect balanced weight, again illustrating Citterio's dedication to harmony in form, material and function. Still in production today and widely available, the Citterio Tools Collective 2000 is a familiar mainstay in the permanent design collections of many American and European museums, including The Museum of Modern Art in New York, and the Architecture and Design Museum in Chicago, as well as being awarded the Design Plus Award in Frankfurt in 2001.

The manufacturer lapalma originally provided a modest brief for a simple, adjustable bar stool which gave way quickly under the intense observations of ergonomics and use that Shin Azumi brings to his industrial design projects. While bar stools varied in structure, Shin Azumi observed that each appeared unnecessarily rooted in common assumptions and suffered from a number of similar problems. Existing stools most often comprised a fixed footrest with a padded seat for comfort, on top of a column or simply appeared as a standard chair at a raised height. Many were difficult to mount or get down from, were uncomfortable and were even unstable. With the LEM bar stool Azumi set out to grasp the particular requirements of a bar stool that set it apart from its functionally similar cousin, the chair. He soon concluded that comfort and ease of use depended most importantly on the relationship between the seat and footrest. As his investigation continued, he sought a new structure that would both improve this form of seating by tackling what others had overlooked, and create a new visual identity. Expressing the essential co-dependence between seat and footrest became a guiding principle in the design. With a single, continuous loop of matt-chromed metal that first enclosed a plywood seat before dropping downward to form the footrest, the LEM uniquely linked seat with footrest. This elegant and simple relationship depended, however, upon a far less simple engineering challenge. The slim

rectangular tubes had to be bent into a loop across three dimensions and overlapping, compound curves without producing visible wrinkles. The eventual solution relied upon a new technology that had only recently been deployed for the first time by a manufacturer of luxury automobiles. Together the seat and footrest are mounted on a rotating and adjustable gas-sprung column, with each reaming fixed relative to the other regardless of the column height or direction of the seat. The use of beech plywood for the seat was chosen to balance the warmth of wood against the more industrial frame and base. These materials, in conjunction with the illusion of a static loop, when viewed at eye-level, merge into the highly comfortable LEM.

NL Architects were asked by Droog Design, an innovative editor of design ideas, to create a system of displaying products for the Paris store of Mandarina Duck, a fashionable label selling leather goods, luggage and clothes. NL Architects initially looked at the design of suitcases, most of which are equipped with a rubber strap in the soft interior, to hold or pack down the articles placed inside. Taking their cue from this idea, and influenced by the common sight of bicycles in Holland which are also equipped with a strap at the rear, the Dutch designers decided to reinvent this rubber binder, which led to 'Strap'. Pieter Bannenberg, of NL Architects, said that they began to research all bike stores, and found the strap to be manufactured by a variety of companies. After contacting a number of companies, they finally found one manufacturer who would provide just the rubber binder without the metal attachment that connects to the bicycle frame. NL Architects decided to rewrite the user's manual for the bicycle strap, and created a strap that could be featured on the walls of the Mandarina Duck store. Never before had the humble rubber band been adopted to be used on a wall, and NL Architects are adamant in their statement to say that they did not invent the strap, but simply took an archetype and 'changed reality a little'. Their design features a double strap made of a soft, stretchable type of latex, flexible enough for fastening while displaying different types of objects. The Strap, as a product, is essentially reinvented by the addition of two small screws, which are then fixed on to a wall. Strap is available in four colours, originally chosen and co-ordinated for the Mandarina Duck store by Droog Design. The simplicity of the design and the material chosen represent the essential value of the product. Strap is made using a press-casting technique, in which the fluid latex material is pressed between two steel moulds and, after undergoing a chemical reaction, is removed from the mould as an elastic material. Strap is an extraordinary design solution, but is perhaps too far ahead of its time, and was only produced in limited numbers. The fascination of this product is the combination of a materialized vision and the investment of little material.

Spring Chair (2000)
Ronan Bouroullec (1971–)
Erwan Bouroullec (1976–)
Cappellini 2000 to present

Erwan and Ronan Bouroullec

Since the mid-1990s a generation of young, influential French designers has emerged, with the brothers Ronan and Erwan Bouroullec among the most successful of this group. Their best-known work to date has been with Cappellini in Italy, and the Spring Chair, which was nominated for a prestigious Compasso d'Oro award in 2001, was the first chair they designed for the company. The Spring Chair is not a radical or particularly innovative form, but is nevertheless an elegant and refined design. The chair is constructed from a series of thin, moulded pads that connect together to create a delicate lounge chair, supported on fine metal glides. The head-rest is adjustable like a car or plane seat, and the foot-rest is set on a spring that responds to the movement of the sitter's legs. The chair is composed of a shell of wood and polyurethane, with high-resilience foam, wool and stainless steel. There are four versions: the armchair, the armchair and foot-rest, the armchair and head-rest, and finally the armchair, foot-rest, and head-rest. The idea of creating a lounge chair that is little more than a padded surface, lacking volume, can be traced to Eero Saarinen's Womb Chair of 1947. The segmented form of the Spring Chair also recalls the Eameses' reclining chair of 1956. More recently, Jasper Morrison has designed similar chairs and the Bouroullec brothers are happy to acknowledge a debt to him. In return Morrison describes their work as 'thoughtful and disciplined, with a real spirit and poetry'. Ronan Bouroullec studied furniture design at the Ecole Nationale Supérieure des Arts Décoratifs in Paris and Erwan initially joined Ronan to assist him. But soon the brothers were co-signing their designs. On occasion they present their work individually, as, for example Erwan's extraordinary Lit Clos Sleeping Cabin, a bed chamber on stilts he designed for Cappellini in 2000. Erwan describes their style as 'deliberately very simple with an element of humour'. The same spirit pervades work by some of their contemporaries and is characteristic of design of their generation.

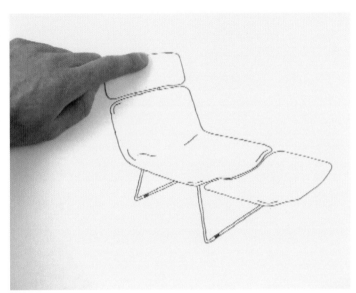
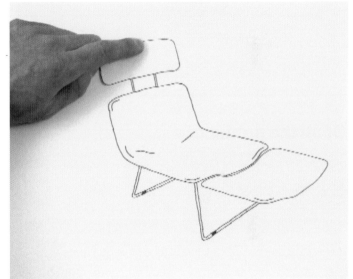

Of all the products he has designed, Jonathan Ive regards the sleek, silver PowerBook laptop computer as the one (along with the iPod) that he is most proud of. With its super-slick detailing, complete with friendly radiuses and a jewellery-like metallic keyboard, it's a product he never goes anywhere without. Originally made of titanium, but later replaced by a more scratch-resistant aluminium alloy, the casing leaves no doubt that this is a serious product for a serious user. Sophisticated in an understated manner, compared to previous Apple products, the PowerBook plays safe with a chromo-phobic and minimalist aesthetic, not unlike the designs of Braun's audio equipment of the late 1950s and early 1960s. Traditionally, serious electronic products have always been wrapped in black, white, various shades of grey or preferably silver, to emphasize and efficiency. This aesthetic suits the loyal Apple user, first hooked in the 1980s and 1990s, reflecting the inevitable 'grown-up' conservative values and aspirations that age brings. The PowerBook has over ten years of innovative Apple laptop designs to draw upon. The original grey machine of the early 1990s contained several new features, including an inverted

tracker ball mounted below the keyboard and an ergonomic palm rest. The PowerBook Duo literally docked into a corresponding desktop machine to become its brains, while the G3 version had a softer 'feminine' form with a clam-shell lid. The aluminium G4 plays it safe, with a cold 'masculine' style of rational technology and refined detailing. Originally only available in 12- and 17-inch versions – and strangely advertised using analogies with midgets and giants – a 15-inch model followed within a year. The G4 processor came with a choice between 40 and 60GB, 256 to 512MB of SDRAM

(Synchronous DRAM, a speed which runs at 133 MHz, much faster than conventional memory) along with built-in CD/DVD burning and Bluetooth functions. The 'OSX Panther' software delivers an impressive graphical front end based on a UNIX platform. Here translucent icons warp, when clicked, into brushed aluminium 'windows' mimicking the real product itself, indicating that inside and out are at one with each other. With a mix of refined traditionalism and obsessive attention to detail, the PowerBook radiates confidence to and from its owner, signifying their shared maturity.

The iPod MP3 player, along with Apple's iTunes software, represents 'joined-up-thinking' from an ever wiser company. It is effectively technology worn as jewellery, from a brand that really knows the effectiveness of holistic design. iPod is revolutionizing the way people download and listen to music, with a storage capacity of up to 10,000 songs housed in a lightweight, pocket-sized design. Its evolution has primarily concentrated on size reduction and alternative memory options (10Gb, 20Gb and 40Gb), with additional modes, such as recording of voice notes, games and retrieving phone numbers, reflecting the PDA market's obsession with technological 'convergence'. From the beginning Apple decided to outsource not only the manufacturing of the iPod, but also most of the internal design. With platform design from PortalPlayer (and contributions from other manufacturers), the battery from Sony and the hard drive from Toshiba, the result was faster and better than each could have probably created on their own. The 'touch wheel' makes scrolling through an entire music collection quick and easy, while the 'shuffle' mode allows for the ultimate personal jukebox experience. As a cheeky wink from CEO Steve Jobs to Bill Gates, the iPod also offers Windows PC-compatible software. Aligning itself alongside the iMac G4, eMac and iBook computers, the minimalist purity of the iPod reflects the material and spiritual angst that accompanies relentless technological advancement. A hesitant transference from one era to another is effectively softened by the retro reassuring 'colour' aesthetic of 1960s Futurism. White and shiny chrome continue to signify optimism and innovation over forty years later. Perhaps then, it is not such a surprise that the iPod's visual appearance, 'colour' and flush radial interface are almost identical to another seminal portable music device from over forty years ago: Dieter Rams's 1958 T3 pocket radio designed for Braun. The iPod Mini (2004), signalled the obsession with 'the now' and all tiny – it is even smaller, and available in gold, silver, blue, pink and green shiny anodized aluminium, the synthesis of the fruity iMac of the 1990s with the precious-tech PowerBook of the noughties. The lastest incarnation is the minute iShuffle (2005), playing 120 or 240 songs, in millions of different orders, always surprising its listener. What the following models and inventions are, will only be seen with time.

Advertisements, 2003

Wednesday Garland (2001)
Tord Boontje (1968–)
Habitat 2003 to present

Sometimes, the most seemingly simple idea changes the way we think about an everyday object. Tord Boontje's Wednesday Garland is one such example. The humble light shade has always been a favourite object for new designers to stamp their mark, and many have attempted to present it in a new and imaginative way. The Wednesday Garland, however, is exceptional and transforms the light shade into a piece of art, one that not so much shades the light as dresses it. Born in Enschede in the Netherlands, Boontje studied industrial design at the Eindhoven Design Academy before moving to London in 1992 to study at the Royal College of Art, returning there as a design tutor in 2002. Boontje's style has been described as techno-romanticism. Taking inspiration from the richness and sensuality of hand-crafted design from previous centuries, he uses computer technology to produce intricate works in modern materials that are suitable for mass-market consumption. The influence of nature, particularly the way trees filter light in a forest, is evident throughout his work, as is his love of fashion and his admiration for designers such as Martin Margiela. Having worked with Alexander McQueen and confessing to a fascination with seventeenth-century embroidery, it is not surprising that a sartorial quality pervades many of his mysterious and beautiful designs. Originally known as the Wednesday Light when it was designed in 2001, the piece is designed to be attached to the cord above a hanging light bulb and draped around the bulb itself. Essentially 150 cm in length, the metal flower garland can be safely wrapped around the bare bulb and arranged according to preference. Originally made from stainless steel, it was changed to acid-etched brass when it was adapted for production by Habitat in 2003, and named 'Garland'. The garland displays a soft, organic appearance despite being made of metal, with an intricate design photographically etched on to the various flowers and leaves. Whereas previously a design brief for mass production had emphasized the need to avoid superfluous detail, or even decoration, the Wednesday Garland successfully celebrates it, reinforcing Boontje's idea that, because of the technology available today, contemporary manufacturers can now incorporate detailed and ornate patterns that had previously been unthinkable for mass-produced items. The Wednesday Garland marks a progression in product design, looking at improvements in materials and computer technology and imaginatively applying them to the mass-production process.

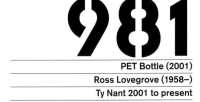

Mineral water has become a fashionable accessory for health-conscious urban dwellers across the world. Competing water brands became all too aware that the packaging of this natural fluid would have a marked effect on attracting different target markets. While selling essentially the same liquid, the water brands soon discovered that their brand appearance, coupled with the quality and appearance of their bottle design, could considerably alter the price perception of their product. Bottles emerged on to the market in all sorts of shapes, colours, and sizes, in plastic or glass. When the phenomenon had really caught on, marketing directors were stumped as to where to progress from there. Ty Nant is a Welsh water brand that enjoyed early success when it launched its elegant signature cobalt-blue glass bottle in 1989. This award-winning, trademarked bottle proved an instant hit and is served at top venues around the world. At the turn of the millennium Ty Nant's directors were eager to offer their product to a larger trade sector, that of the impulse and retail sector, leading grocers and stylish premises including clubs, cafés and sandwich bars. The company knew it had to introduce innovative packaging within the growing plastic bottle market that would have the same impact as its premium glass predecessor. The difficult task was allocated to internationally renowned Welsh-born designer Ross Lovegrove. The result comes in the form of the blow-moulded asymmetrical PET Bottle that was specifically designed to mimic the fluidity of water. Lovegrove based his studies and final model on foam sculptures. The production tool was a singular form, in two halves, from which tests were done to see how uniting the halves would create a whole bottle shape that would not show the non-linear seams. The production tools were created from aluminium in three sizes: 50cl, 100cl and 150cl. The ripple-effect packaging, made from PolyEthylene Terepthalate (PET), manages to refract light and colour in the same manner as surface reflections on water. By default, the shape instantly communicates the bottle's contents, allowing Ty Nant to keep labelling to a minimum. This design is perfectly aligned with Lovegrove's futuristic, organic and minimal design approach.

The Segway Human Transporter is the first electric-powered transport machine that balances itself and is designed to carry one individual at a time. Segway's design team came up with this unique 'people-carrier', perhaps as an answer to crowded buses, traffic jams and stuffy underground railway systems. Dean Kamen (1951–), president of DEKA Research and Development in the United States and founder of Segway LLC, had earlier designed the iBOT, a wheelchair that can climb stairs as well as prop itself up on to two wheels to bring the user into an upright position. The Segway HT stemmed from the balancing technology Kamen had developed for this earlier product. The Segway HT, intended for use on the pavement, has no braking system and a maximum speed of 19 kph (12 mph). The rider, or driver, controls the direction and can stop the movement by simply turning a mechanism on the handlebar. The rider can also control these factors simply by shifting his or her weight. The scooter consists of an in-built computer, five gyroscopes and a disc mounted on a base that allows the axis to turn freely in numerous directions while retaining its orientation. Kamen and his team developed ground-breaking technology which they called 'dynamic stabilization', meaning that it enables the self-balancing ability to respond immediately to the movement of the body. Therefore, the tilt sensors and gyroscopes monitor the body's centre of gravity at a rate of about 100 times a second – when the user leans forward the Segway HT moves forward. The economics of the Segway HT were also considered when it was designed: it requires only one battery, which costs 10 US cents, and lasts for 24 km (15 m). The vehicle weighs 30 kg (65 lb) and is believed to be harmless if it runs over any toes. It easily adapts to various surfaces – pavement, grass, and gravel – and is no wider than the average adult's shoulders, and no longer than a big shoe. Its high cost of $3,000–$5,000 has perhaps been the cause of slow sales. The initial forecasts were that it would sell between 50,000 and 100,000 units in the first year alone, but after twenty-one months only 6,000 had been sold. As it is such a unique way of carrying people, presumably we shall simply have to wait to become accustomed to this great design.

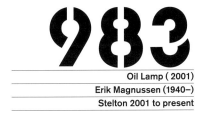

Oil Lamp (2001)
Erik Magnussen (1940–)
Stelton 2001 to present

Erik Magnussen's stainless-steel and borosilicate-glass Oil Lamp for Stelton is a contemporary table lamp that not only embodies the Danish design ethos of elegantly crafted forms, but also addresses increasingly important energy-efficient solutions to suit the new eco-aware culture. In design terms, the small but perfectly formed lamp can be adapted for both indoor and outdoor use and, indeed, emergency lighting. When the lamp is filled it can burn for approximately forty hours. The durable fibreglass wick has almost eternal life and the lamp itself is low-maintenance, as it is both easy to fill and clean. The Oil Lamp is a worthy addition to Magnussen's Stelton range, which includes the now iconic vacuum jug with rocker stopper created in 1977

shortly after the designer joined the company; it is currently one of the company's biggest sellers. Indeed, Magnussen's Stelton collection essentially picks up the legacy of the designer's predecessor at the company, Arne Jacobsen, both in terms of offering a softer, humanistic take on Modernism and in the same deep understanding of the symbiotic relationship between design and the industrial process. The rational yet sensual forms of Jacobsen's Cylinda-Line stainless-steel hollowware range for Stelton, 1967, are similarly present in Magnussen's Oil Lamp. The Oil Lamp has already become an essential table decoration in many discerning homes and restaurants around the world. Whereas undoubtedly the

beautifully pure and simple Scandinavian form is a part of the product's huge appeal, the lamp should also be seen against the current backdrop of growing ecological awareness, with its concerns for future energy sources, and the desire to seek more ethically relevant products. In this context the lamp makes perfect sense in terms of its minimal use of energy and low-maintenance design manifesto. It is in other words an exemplar of stylish sustainability.

Erik Magnussen

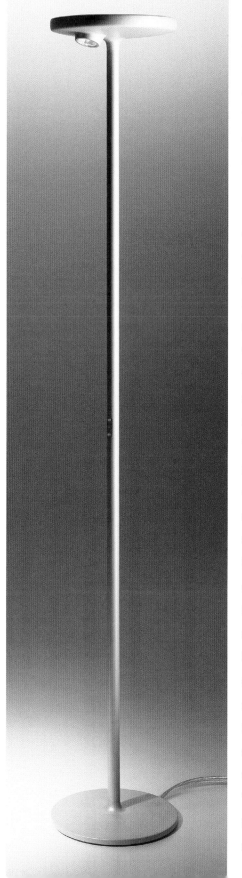

ø cm 30

cm 185

ø cm 30

The One-Two seems at first glance to be a classic uplighter, shedding a stream of soft light upwards into any space. Constructed in grey-painted aluminium, the light has a slender stem topped with a curvaceous mushroom shade. The design has been honed down to a minimal, organic form, giving it a misleadingly simple appearance. However, in typical Irvine fashion, this sparsely elegant design has a twist. Inset on the underside of the lamp's shade is a single halogen light. The floor-standing halogen light therefore functions as both an up- and a down-lighter. This means that the One-Two provides an indirect flood in order to light an entire space and a movable, directional under-light, which can function as a traditional reading light. This double emission allows for the possibility of using a focused light source without reverting to the harshness of a bright overhead light. The One-Two continues in a long tradition of Italian innovation in functional, chic and quirky design. Designer James Irvine studied at Kingston University and the Royal College of Art, both in London. In 1984 he settled in Milan where he now runs his own studio. Irvine is one of a school of UK designers, which includes Jasper Morrison and Michael Young, who combine innovative uses of products with a sophisticated minimalist aesthetic. The One-Two floor lamp was designed in 2001 and is manufactured by the Italian design company, Artemide.

The glory of Harley-Davidson lies in continuity, as much as any brilliance of design, at least it has until now. For over 100 years Harley-Davidson has produced various bikes, built around signature engine designs. The bike designs themselves never strayed far from a definitive Harley-Davidson style, but the engines did, and eventually garnered nicknames: the Knucklehead, the Panhead, the Evolution and so on. From these engines flowed all the design decisions. That is not to say that design theory plays no part in the development of one of the great brands of our time. Harley-Davidson design chief, Willie G Davidson, is the man who, more than anyone else, has created the look, the feel, the sound and the spirit of the Harley-Davidson brand in the modern era. Davidson, too, has overcome seismic shifts in the motorcycle world as he developed his vision. One of those shifts was the ageing of the Harley-Davidson demographic. Towards the end of the twentieth century the average age of a devoted rider was careening towards the late forties. Willie G, as he is known to a devoted legion of Harley-Davidson lovers, had to find a younger and wider audience, and he had to do it without alienating his base: the weekend rebels who have become central to the outsider myth of Harley-Davidson ownership. His answer was to assemble the best young engineering and design team ever to work at the motorcycle company. With it, he created unquestionably his greatest work, the VRSCA V-Rod. He started with the engine, as all new Harley-Davidsons do. Water-cooled, which was a new application, and with technical input from Porsche, the new engine was powerful and sophisticated. Around it Willie G and his team composed a chassis that, while staying true to long-held rubrics of Harley-Davidson as the all-American cruiser, looked to a high-tech world well into the twenty-first century. This is the muscle-cruiser that is to twenty-first-century bikes what the Corvette was to an earlier generation. It has made its mark with confidence, and it presages an exciting new direction for the most venerable motorcycle name of all.

985

In the late 1990s Sharp began to explore designs for a new flat-screen liquid crystal display television (LCD TV) that would target the anticipated high-growth market of LCD TVs for the home. While Sharp had long been a world leader in the development and commercialization of LCD products, stretching back to the 1973 launch of the world's first LCD calculator, the company had been unable to develop a new design that would champion its move from the business market to the home market. In a break with past product development, Sharp took the uncharacteristic step of inviting an outside designer to help create a new line of televisions. Between 1998 and the launch of the new range in 2001, Toshiyuki Kita worked with Sharp on a design that would avoid stereotypes. He sought a new face and image for the television a form that was aesthetically pleasing, even when switched off. The resulting Aquos C1 abandoned the cold, rigid geometry of high tech. In its stead, Kita pursued a form and a function which also had a 'soul'. This more feminine take on technology is more organic, even anthropomorphic; its face is sharply distinguished by a pair of symmetrical speakers balanced almost decoratively below the screen, while both are held suspended on top of a softly curved crescent moon-shaped base. The multitude of connections and relays are cleanly grouped and hidden behind an easily removable cover, and the entire ensemble can be easily picked up and carried about. The success of this new design was immediate. It catapulted Sharp into lead position as maker of LCD TVs for the home. The design attracted worldwide attention from industry glossies to mainstream media like the *Financial Times* and *AdWeek*. The Aquos C1 touched a new market for televisions that cut across gender and introduced 'design' in place of the black box.

When the young French designers Ronan and Erwan Bouroullec started to design a new office system for Vitra in January 2001, they focused on the idea of a big table. It was to be a spacious workspace, with generous proportions; something with larger dimensions than a solitary desk, which can belong to one person at a time. The idea of a table with flexible workspace for more than one person came from very homely origins: memories of the large family table. Joyn is an innovative furniture system where parts of a large tabletop can be fixed on to a central supporting beam, which rests on two trestles. This works with an ingenious 'click' system that requires no screws. Power and telecommunications run within a high-capacity central channel that acts like a raised floor. Wiring can be simply laid into the channel, linking all desktop office utilities. Joyn aspires to the same flexibility which the mobile phone and the laptop permit. The office itself achieves a dynamic state, constantly adjusting to changing demands. 'Our office is not "playful" in the literal sense of the word, but its flexibility gives a certain suppleness and simplicity. It leaves room for movement', said Ronan Bouroullec in an interview. Joyn is an open system that embraces the diversity of the workplace and encourages communication between people, networking, and interaction by breaking down the physical barriers between them. It does not impose a specific method. Joyn can be used in many ways, from individual work to teamwork and conferences, with minimal means. Additional and adjustable elements, like screens and blotters, called micro-architecture, can create areas for seclusion and specialized tasks. As nothing is fixed, work areas simply contract and expand to meet immediate needs.

Joyn Office System (2001)
Ronan Bouroullec (1971–)
Erwan Bouroullec (1976–)
Vitra 2002 to present

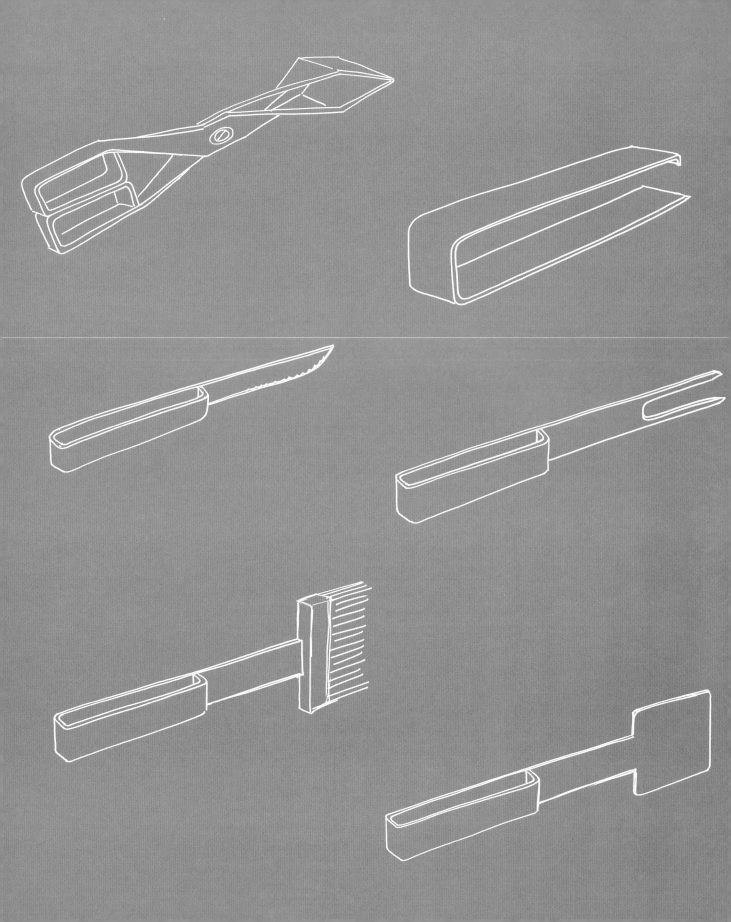

The most striking feature of the Hackman Outdoor Cooking Tools range is its scale. These oversized utensils could be straight out of *Alice in Wonderland* for the twenty-first century. The broad, flat chrome elements that make up each item accentuate this sense of scale, while emphasizing the practical purpose for which they were designed. Practicality and design have been a core concept of the Hackman cooking and tableware products ever since their inception, and are the guiding principle in the creation of the Outdoor Cooking Tools designed by Harri Koskinen in 2002. In addition to a high standard of design, the innovative use of materials and product development, as well as environmental friendliness sets this range apart from other sets of barbecue tools. The core ideologies underpinning Finnish design are the promotion of functional and ergonomic qualities, and that design must also pay attention to ecological factors. Koskinen's Outdoor Cooking Tools maintain this tradition. Graduating in 1994 from the University of Art and Design, in Helsinki, Koskinen became a designer for Hackman in 1998. His work pays homage to the Finnish design tradition and represents the new generation of Scandinavian product designers making an impact on the international design scene. The Outdoor Cooking Tools range includes a pair of tongs, spatula, carving fork and brush and clearly reflects the designer's Finnish origin: the design concisely combines simplicity with style. Balance is the key in form, and the design allows each piece to be put down on the table without dirtying the surface of the tool or the table. The use of stainless steel makes each piece durable and easy to clean. Produced as part of the Hackman division of iittala, the barbecue set exemplifies the relaxed Finnish culture of dining indoors and out, without compromising style. Koskinen's Outdoor Cooking Tools work well and look as good in the kitchen as in the garden.

Maarten van Severen first sketched
the early version of his chaise longue, CHL95, in
1994, when he was still producing each piece in his
own workshop. The initial glass-fibre resin shell
prototype was followed by two further prototypes in
1995, which gradually refined the support system
and angle of recline. The resulting reinforced

polyester lounge chair is both strange and familiar,
and the very hallmark of its maker – the material is
neither adorned nor co-opted to be anything other
than itself by sight or by touch. The perceptively
thin surface imparts a sense of lightness to the
occupant, and both chair and person remain
intimately connected to ground and earth. With

CHL98, developed in collaboration with Vitra and
launched as the MVS Chaise in 2002, van Severen
created an entirely new chaise longue. While the
shape draws heavily on the earlier version, its
composition and finish are fresh. The surface
material of polyurethane suspended by steel trim
introduces flexibility and colour. Polyurethane was a

revelation for van Severen, as it offered comfort without sacrifice. While comfort was always a component of this architect-trained designer's work, it was never the dominant prerequisite. Finding a material that did not require an artificial cover or superficially applied colour, despite the burdens of mass production, allowed for an authenticity in the

use of materials in the same tradition as van Severen's other works. In profile, the striking originality of MVS Chaise materializes. Gone is the reliance of earlier prototypes on the presumptively obvious need for a set of four legs. In their place floats a chair on a single leg. With only the slightest shift in weight, the occupant pivots from reclining to

fully resting. The uneasy anticipation of precarious balance proves entirely unfounded; the comfort is remarkable and carefree. Van Severen's uncompromising poetry of form sets him apart, and the MVS Chaise, which marries industry, unadorned materiality and sculptural beauty, embodies his unique language.

Bang & Olufsen had never produced a plasma television until the BeoVision 5, but when it decided to go into this expanding market the company characteristically pulled no punches. Aimed at the luxury market, the BeoVision 5 cost almost £13,000 when it was introduced in 2002. It comes with a massive 105 cm (42 in) screen that sits directly above a speaker of the same proportions and which is then encased in a beautiful aluminium frame that is available in a range of colours. The thinking behind the set, the brainchild of Bang & Olufsen's chief designer, David Lewis, was that while the enormous screen and speaker system could be hung from the wall like a picture, it should also be more flexible. The BeoVision 5 can be fitted into a cabinet, casually lent against the wall, or even placed on a motorized stand that turns to face the viewer. It allows the room to be configured in any way, as opposed to being dictated by the position of the screen. To enhance picture quality the Active Picture Format Optimization function reads the transmission signal and adjusts it to ensure the best possible format, while the Automatic Picture Control sensors monitor the amount of light in the room and change the brightness, colour and contrast to match. Unlike the majority of TVs available today, the BeoVision 5 has an element of craft in its manufacturing process. Each product is hand-assembled by six people in the Bang & Olufsen factory, which takes much time and great precision as there are more than 1,000 components.

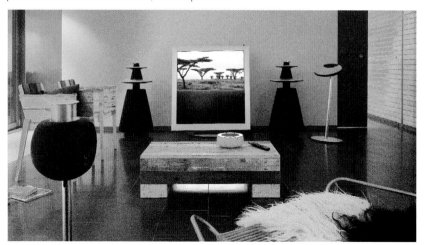

The visual impact of the Kyocera KYOTOP Series of knives is stunning. With their black blades and wooden handles, they embody an uncompromising juxtaposition of traditional Japanese Minimalism with high-tech innovation at its most sophisticated. As high-quality kitchen items, the Kyocera KYOTOP knives belong to a heritage firmly rooted in invention and innovation. Founded in 1959, the Kyocera Corporation specialized in investigating the potential of zirconia ceramics as a group of materials with unique physical and electrical properties. By optimizing its technologies, the company progressively expanded its product line to produce a variety of materials, components, finished products and integrated systems, while continuing to explore further applications and uses from 1984 onwards. All Kyocera knives are produced with either black or white blades, but it is only the KYOTOP series that is made with the black blade. The blade of the KYOTOP knife is made from the same ceramic material as the other Kyocera knives but has a further stage in the manufacturing process. The blade is pressed under high pressure in a process called Hot Isostatic Pressing (HIP), which allows the blade to be moulded and fired concurrently. The process uses a carbon mould, which stains the blade its characteristic black colour. The Kyocera ceramic-blade knife ranges are favourites with chefs world-wide, but are also popular in the domestic market due mainly to their individual and stylish appearance. With black wooden handles and black blades, the knives stand out from the competition in terms of both style and performance. The ceramic blade does not rust, and is claimed not to chip or pit and to hold its original sharpness longer than its steel counterpart. The ceramic blade is lightweight compared to steel, and provides a smoother surface, making it possible to slice through most foods effortlessly. The zirconia ceramic blades are reputed to be almost as hard as diamonds and, although in reality the blades are susceptible to chips, the overall high performance and the lightness of the knife seem to outweigh this. Added to this, the sharpness of the blade still out-performs its steel counterparts. The knives, from the outset, were models of style and achievement, and continue to ensure Kyocera's position at the forefront of the professional and domestic market. The range is now also available in white ceramic, which, although less dramatic-looking, has aided the transition into the domestic kitchen.

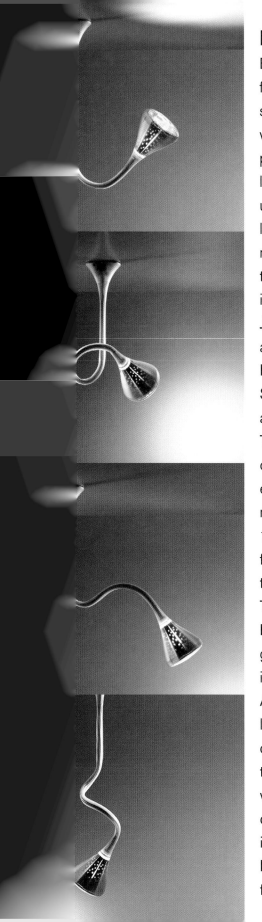

Most ceiling lights both hang and shine straight down. But the Pipe Sospensione lamp transforms tradition by its extremely flexible and adjustable steel tube that ends in a polygonal cone-shaped diffuser, with a polycarbonate lens, focusing the beam of light with great intensity. The aluminium diffuser, covered in a transparent platinic silicone sheath, is micro-perforated, so countless sparkles of light emerge from the sides of the lamp, embellishing its otherwise utilitarian appearance and turning it into a fairytale-like object. The lamp can be used for various purposes and environments, and even mimics octopus-like tentacles when grouped together. Mid-priced, the Pipe lamp is a highly desirable solution for a spotlight that serves its purpose while seeming stunningly ethereal at the same time. Jacques Herzog and Pierre de Meuron, two of the most celebrated architects in the international scene, designed and first used the Pipe lamp for their 1999–2004 Helvetica Patria office in St Gallen, Switzerland. They further developed this flexible pipe in a design for a computer monitor in the 2000–2003 Prada Epicentre in Aoyama, Tokyo, converting the dull grey box into a somewhat retro yet futuristic object. The work of Herzog & de Meuron is eclectic, experimental and extremely outspoken. Innovation comes from extensive research in materials, decorations and volumes. Both men were born in Basel in 1950, with nearly parallel careers, attending the same schools and forming an architectural firm in 1978. The two architects were chosen to share the highly prestigious Pritzker Architecture prize in 2001. Their most prominent project has been the conversion of the giant Bankside power plant along the River Thames in London to the glorious Tate Modern. Their way of working, a permanent search for innovation and excellence, led them to collaborate together with Artemide. Founded in 1959, Artemide is a world leader in innovative lighting design, defining new needs and introducing new concepts in collaboration with outstanding designers. The Pipe lamp is a product that combines the performance characteristics of a dark/light emission with the functional and aesthetic values of a flexible arm and reflection cone. Although the Pipe Sospensione lamp is a relatively new design, its potency and success have granted it immediate status of superiority. It was awarded the prestigious Compasso d'Oro prize in 2004 for its flexible, thin and elegant appearance.

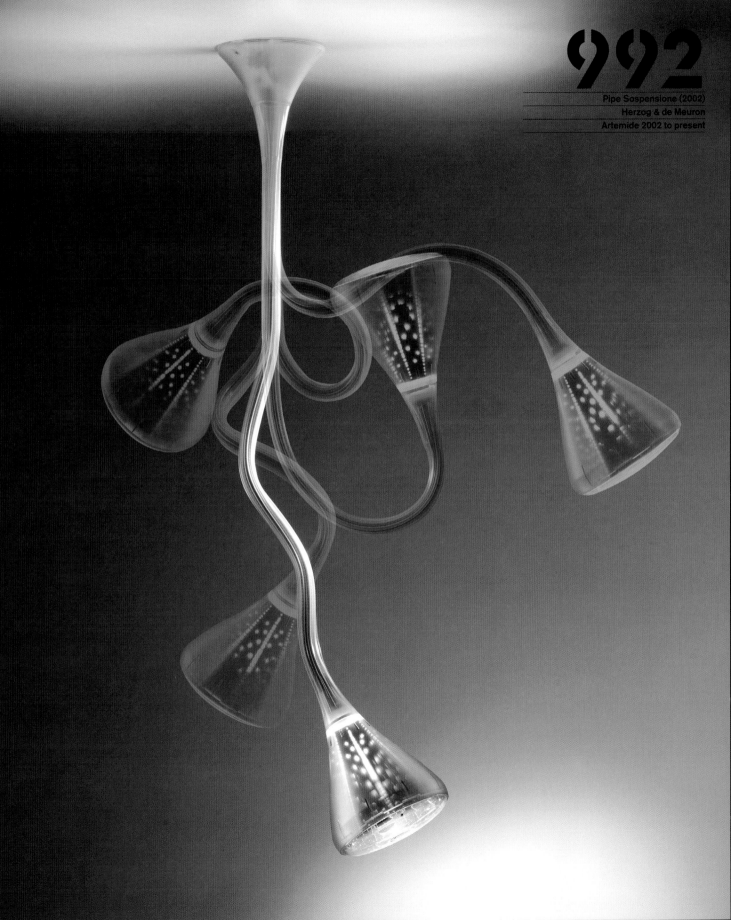

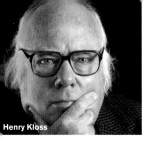
Henry Kloss

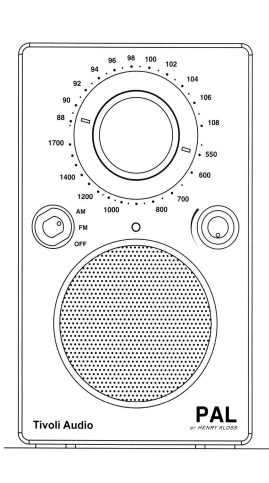

The PAL (Portable Audio Laboratory) is a small portable and rechargeable AM-FM radio. The PAL was the last project that Henry Kloss, the engineer, was working on before he passed away. It is based on the Model One Radio, another acclaimed product by Tivoli Audio, a company set up by Kloss's long-time associate Tom DeVesto . But it is different from the Model One in its material, as it is made out of a special waterproof plastic. The PAL produces a good sound, surprisingly so from such a little box measuring only 15.88 cm (6.25 in) high, 9.37 cm (3.67 in) wide and 9.86 cm (3.88 in) deep. It can also be connected to any audio device, or MP3 player such as the Apple iPod or a laptop, either through an auxiliary input or wirelessly via the iTrip FM transmitter. To ensure the length of the playback, the PAL comes with an environmentally friendly NiMH battery pack, which fully charges in just three hours and provides the system with sixteen hours of autonomy. The PAL, and now the iPAL, have cleverly assured themselves as the perfect component to the iPod, and while it comes in many colours, it is the sleek, white and silver look which is its aesthetic companion. But its success lies in its ability to tune to stations accurately and quickly, using the innovative AM/FM tuner, equipped with an Automatic Frequency Control that locks on to the centre of each station, avoiding any distortion. For its understated class and high performance, the iPAL is the culminating achievement of Kloss's long career. Kloss already had several notable innovations behind him. In the 1950s he pioneered smaller, bookshelf speakers with the manufacturer Acoustic Research, and in 1967, at the helm of Advent, he signalled a new era in hi-fi technology, launching one of the first cassette decks to incorporate Dolby noise reduction technology to limit tape hiss. He also invented the projection television and produced a new range of resolutely retro radios in the late 1990s.

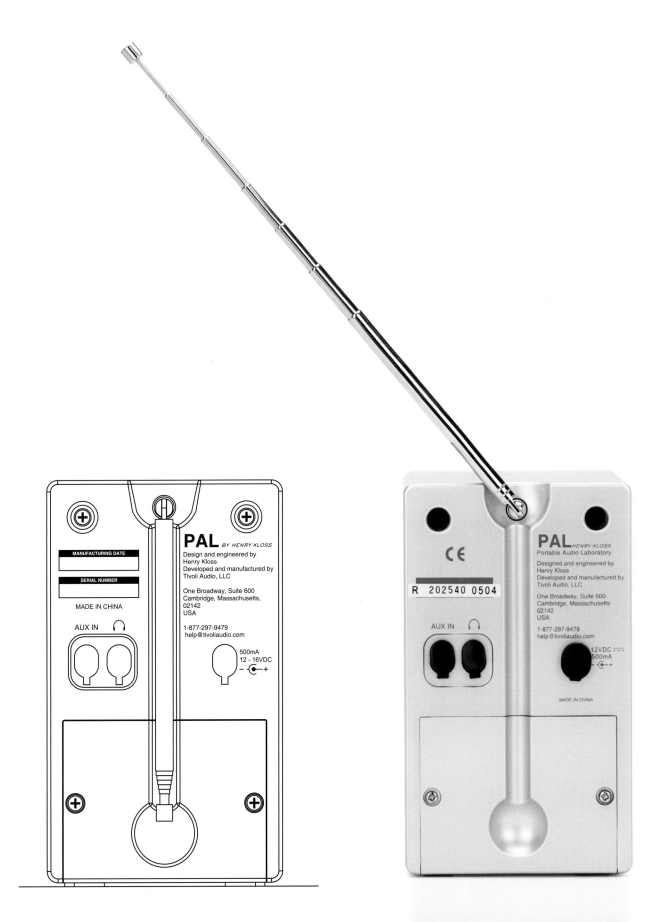

Philippe Starck

While Philippe Starck did not study science, he has said it is the only thing that interests him and is what motivates him to understand everything that surrounds him. Starck had been using Oregon Scientific weather station equipment in his various homes for years, but it was the fortuitous notice of his name on various orders to the company that eventually led to this collaboration. In a potentially dizzying array of functions, and calibrations on the back, Starck produced a rigorously organized, icon-driven display. This clock was not the first to incorporate displays of current and predicted weather conditions for Oregon, but it was the first to package them for mass consumption and personal use rather than the executive's desk. The Time & Weather clock, which comes in three sizes, is a triumph over button-laden, high-tech gadgetry in favour of thoughtful structure, grouping and communication of information and function. Through a series of permanently displayed read-outs that are each compartmentalized and visually distinct, a compendium of information is immediately available: the weather; current indoor and outdoor temperatures; the day and date in any of five languages; humidity, expressed both numerically and through a comfort level of wet, normal and dry; high, medium and low tides together with eight phases of the moon. The list goes on. In accessing this information or adjusting the various readings according to its location, the clock incorporates more hidden technology: a continuously updated clock synchronized to a standard time signal embedded within ordinary radio signals; an exchange of information with various sensors by wireless communication; seven alternative melodies, each available to wake you with a crescendo of sound; and a projector to beam the current time on to darkened ceilings or walls. Despite the obvious absence of dials and buttons, adjustments can be made by simple navigation through touch across a grid of flexible polymer with raised icons indicating function. The clock has attracted enormous sales since its launch, reaching far beyond that nebulous category of the 'design-conscious buyer'. Starck's unusual box, striking colours and stylized graphic design bear witness to his enduring ability to transform overlooked everyday objects and information into desirable commodities.

995

Beolab 5 (2003)
David Lewis (1939–)
Bang & Olufsen 2003 to present

The truly ground-breaking

Beolab 5 Loudspeakers, developed and produced by Danish electronics specialists Bang & Olufsen, are so technologically revolutionary and unprecedented in design terms that they have been described as being more sci-fi than hi-fi. Designed by David Lewis, chief designer at Bang & Olufsen, the Beolab 5, with its conical base and three ellipse discs on top, is a radical departure from the existing box-shaped loudspeaker design. Yet this is not simply a case of design for design's sake. Instead, the unusual form underlines the new technology embodied within, which is essentially a combination of Sausalito Audio Works' 'Acoustic Lens Technology', a system that took twenty years to develop, and the Adaptive Base Control System. The Acoustic Lens Technology, located in the ellipses, delivers the sound from treble and mid-range at a 180-degree angle in the horizontal plane and thus is radically different from conventional speakers, which aim their sound away from themselves and towards the listener. The Adaptive Bass Control functions by effectively 'listening' to the ambient sound within a room. This is achieved by pressing a button on top of each speaker, which sends out test sound waves measuring the room's bass properties and consequently adjusts its output in accordance with the loudspeaker's position. In design terms the cone shape of the speaker emerged by placing the bass unit at the base of the speaker and directing it downwards. The acoustic lenses then appear to almost float at the top of the speaker, thereby providing a light and elegant counterbalance. Had the Beolab 5, which comprises four speaker units, been designed using conventional methods it would have resembled a large cupboard or small wardrobe. However, Bang & Olufsen's pioneering compact ICE power technology has allowed the designer to reduce the speakers' size considerably. This system succeeds in achieving 90 per cent output power, whereas conventional analogue amplifiers convert only on average 10 per cent of their power to actual output to the speaker units, with the remaining 90 per cent wasted as heat. Consequently, Beolab 5 is currently the most compact, visually exciting and, in terms of sonic performance, the most faultless loudspeaker system in the world, and as a result it has helped position Bang & Olufsen at the leading edge of global audio visual technology.

Chair_One is manufactured by the Italian firm, Magis, typically associated with producing plastic products, and being slightly adventurous, but is the creation of the German designer, Konstantin Grcic, who trained in England. In many ways the chair is a hybrid of the different characteristics of these three different nations, with its initial impression of being uncompromising and cold, while simultaneously offering surprising comfort. The design is significant because it is the world's first die-cast aluminium chair-shell. Die-casting is an industrialized version of the much more basic sand-casting process. But, instead of pouring molten alloy into a void created in sand, the alloy is introduced or 'tooled', often under pressure, into high-precision, expensive and often very complex stainless-steel tools. This combination of pressure feeding with the precise and highly finished mould is what produces such a high-quality final product. Using this process to form a chair shell is interesting because cast aluminium has been common in furniture manufacturing since the middle of the twentieth century. English designer Ernest Race created the first cast-aluminium furniture components in 1945 to form the legs of his BA Chair. The next and more lasting use of die-casting occurred in the USA during the 1950s and was employed for components such as the four- and five-star swivel bases of chairs, from designers such as Charles and Ray Eames and Eero Saarinen. Grcic's design now uses the casting process not only to form the legs, but the seat and back as well, therefore utilizing an old process to create a new chair. Cast aluminium has since become a staple of the furniture industry, yet a closer relative to Chair_One is the Victorian cast-iron garden chair. Aside from the differences in material and weight, the most apparent difference between the two is the uncompromisingly digital, or computerized, form of this chair. Its spare, linear structure looks like something from the cult sci-fi film *Tron*, yet it is ergonomically determined and perfectly embraces the shape of the body. It forms part of a collection called Family_One, which consists of this regular four-legged version, with polished rectangular sections, aluminium legs intended for indoor or outdoor use, as well as tables and bar stools. There is also a dedicated public seating version of the chair, using a very similar geometric die-cast shell, but mounted on a conical cast-concrete base, as well as a beam-mounted version, which uses the same conical concrete base.

Konstantin Grcic

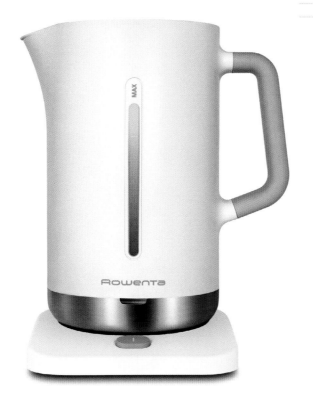

The modern kitchen evolved over the last century from an area of hidden activity into a room in which to gather and even show off. Unlike furniture that endures or overlooked objects that are anonymous, however, the modern kitchen appliance has long been promoted and purchased anew with each rising trend and fashionable innovation. Manufacturers have relied on marketing and styling both to distinguish their products and to ensure a respectfully short life. The consumer has been taken on a journey through streamlined speed, psychedelic pop culture, disposable consumerism and excessive self-expressionism, each innovation conspicuously displayed with a new knob, matching light and measurable dial. The Jasper Morrison Brunch Set, including kettle, coffee maker and toaster, by the German premium home appliance manufacturer, Rowenta, is different. Here surface and structure merge as the basis of communication, with subtle gestures and inviting curves. No one notices the absence of the on/off switch incorporated within the base, as the kettle switches off after boiling. This cordless automatic kettle, with a concealed, polished stainless-steel heating element, is as dignified in its use as in its appearance. The notion of concealment is carried on to the coffee maker, which has an all-in-one concept with the combined storage for the paper filters, the filter itself and the serving spoon. The 'Aromalock' lid seals in the aroma, as well as the temperature, while the stainless-steel Thermo jug has a double wall for insulation. The generous curves make cleaning easier. The last item in the set is the toaster with its large slot for chunkier pieces of bread. The silent efficiency of an optic sensor relegates to the past the need to adjust it for thin, thick or frozen bread. There is a useful warming plate for heating croissants or bread rolls, and the instructions are situated on the front of the toaster, instead of the usual side location. It is a mistake to tag these clean lines with a misleading label, whether it be Minimalism, Modernism or Functionalism. While others have toyed with similar endeavours, none has achieved such warm modesty and timeless typology. The Brunch Set is of course a 'designed object' and no doubt will often be bought as such, but its lasting success will be as kettle, coffee maker and toaster, nothing more, nothing less.

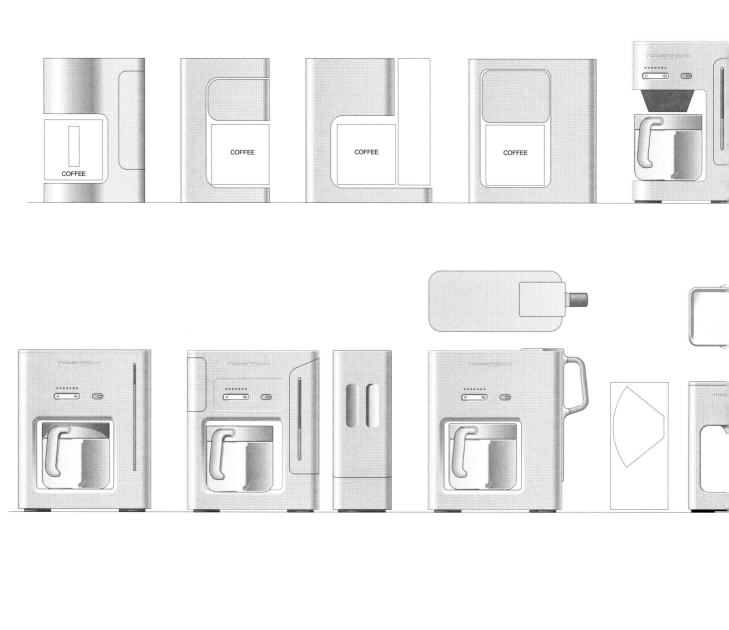

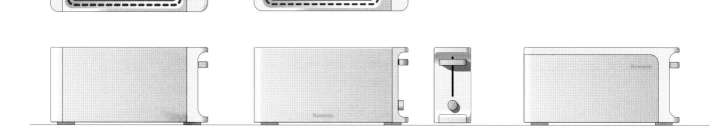

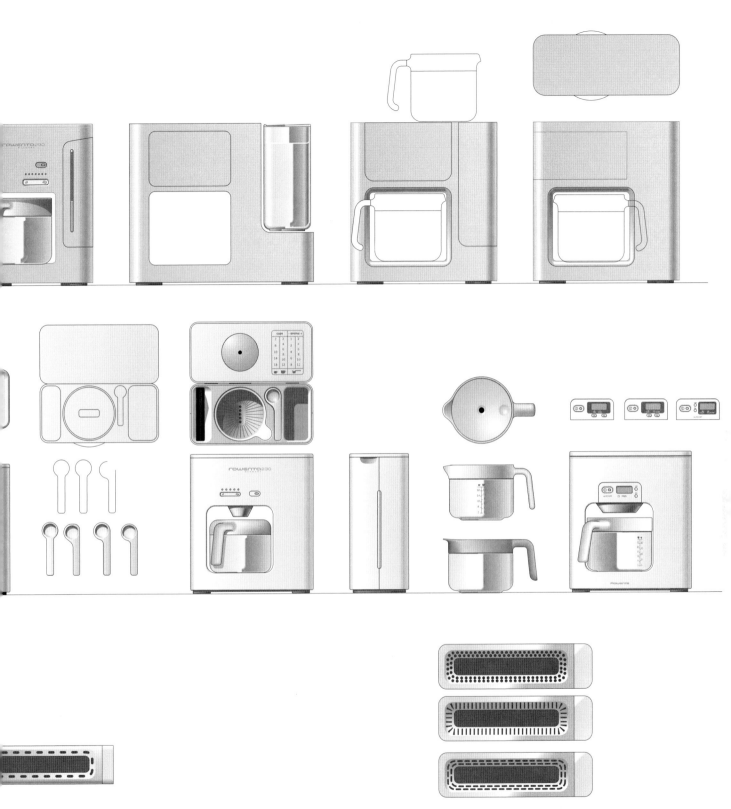

Where did the computer go? The computer is in the display, proclaimed Apple's marketing campaign for the iMac G5, in September 2004. A translucent white plastic box, roughly 5 cm (2 in) thick surrounds either a 17 or 20 inches LCD display and encloses up to a 2.0 GHz, G5 processor. Behind, a one-piece anodized aluminium pedestal is screwed to the case, making the computer lean slightly forwards and allowing the screen to be adjusted by tilting the whole base-unit. With the addition of wireless technology, the power wire is the only cable; all the rest, keyboard, mouse, Internet and mobile connection can all be linked through the AirPort Extreme Card that comes as standard. What makes this computer a home wizard is the width of the display: with the 20 inch model it is easy to read two browser windows side-by-side. Unfortunately for many fashion-conscious professionals, the sleek design comes with a price, as the iMac G5, despite the easy accessibility to the base-unit (just lean the display on a flat top and unscrew three Phillips screws), has very little that can be customized. Unlike similar computers with the same characteristics (namely, the PowerMac G5) the only expandability of this computer is in the doubling of the RAM, which comes normally in just 256 MB. As its sister system not only has the possibility of adding eight slots of RAM but a second internal hard drive, it can not be ignored by those who use the computer to its full potential. The idea of anchoring the design of the iMac G5 to the iPod was a clever stunt from Apple's marketing division. By doing so, it created a powerful identity, and was able to win over those PC users who, at the time, had fallen under the spell of the sleek lines of this famous mp3 player. But above all these factors, the idea of the computer – with its several separate components – has been transformed into a unified system for the first time, established within a beautiful design of a translucent, thin rectangle that sits elegantly, appearing only as a screen.

998

iMac G5 (2004)
Apple Design Team
Apple Computer 2004 to present

Since the mid-nineties Edward Barber (1969–) and Jay Osgerby (1969–) have produced a string of beautiful, rational pieces of furniture, predominantly created from plywood. Although it still contains the pair's characteristic style – the eye is drawn to, and fascinated by, the pure edges of all their products – the Lunar bathroom range, introduced by German manufacturer Authentics in 2004, is something of a departure. Until this point the designers had been mainly working at the top end of the market. However, Lunar brought them to address a brief from Authentics to design a full range of bathroom fittings. When Barber Osgerby began their research, they noticed that there was no full collection for the bathroom available on the market. They found that there were different styles for such items as the toilet brush, or the

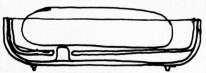 soap dish, but nothing that brought all the styles together in unified way. Made from ABS, the collection consists of a toothbrush tumbler, soap dish, a container with lid for cotton buds, waste-bin and toilet brush. On the outside each product has a clean, clinical look. However, inside there is an unexpected flash of colour that, apart from making them look rather fetching, helps hide dirt or dust. The real joy of this range, though, is in its simplicity and the stark contrasts of colour between the interior and exterior, and it was the designers' ambition to create a range that could be unified with a dash of colour. The range comes in combinations of white with red, light blue, dark blue, grey, orange, beige, or green. As ever, it is the details that are of the utmost importance. Lunar's bin, for example, eschews the conventional swing top for a solution that is more playful and practical. A hole cut in the lid means that rubbish is largely concealed. The Lunar range is what good product design should be about – honesty, detail, and innovation. The collection is one that is intended to grow, with additions to the variety of items and colour palette.

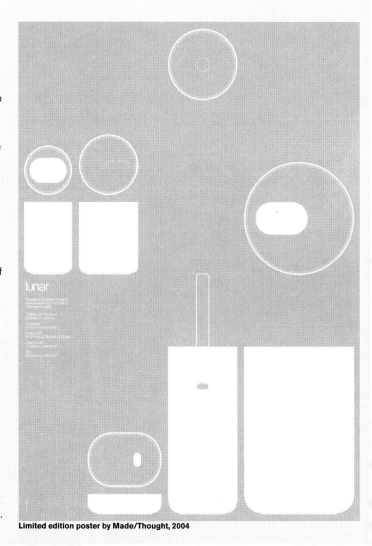

Limited edition poster by Made/Thought, 2004

index of products

designers

designers

designers

1663
Household Scissors, Zhang Xiaoquan **001**

1700s
Arare Teapot, Designer Unknown **002**

1730
Sheep Shears, Designer Unknown **003**

1760s
Sack-Back Windsor Chair, Designer Unknown **004**

1766
Jigsaw Puzzle, John Spilsbury **005**

1783
Hot Air Balloon, Joseph de Montgolfier, Etienne de
    Montgolfier **006**

1796
Traditional White China, Josiah Wedgwood & Sons **007**

1825
Garden Chair and Bench for Potsdam, Karl Friedrich
    Schinkel **008**

c.1825
Le Parfait Jars, Designer Unknown **009**

c.1830
Galvanized Metal Dustbin, Designer Unknown **010**

1837
Gifts, Friedrich Froebel **011**

1840
Hurricane Lantern, Designer Unknown **012**

1842
Pocket Measuring Tape, James Chesterman **013**

1849
Safety Pin, Walter Hunt **014**

1850s
Jacks, Designer Unknown **015**
Clothes Peg, Designer Unknown **016**
Moleskine Notebook, Designer Unknown **017**
Textile Garden Folding Chair, Designer Unknown **018**
Scissors, Designer Unknown **019**

c.1855
Tripolina, Joseph Beverly Fenby **020**

1855
Colman's Mustard Tin, Colman's of Norwich **021**

1856
Lobmeyr Crystal Drinking Set, Ludwig Lobmeyr **022**

1859
Chair No. 14, Michael Thonet **023**

1860s
Shaker Slat Back Chair, Brother Robert Wagan **024**
Folding Ruler, Designer Unknown **025**
English Park Bench, Designer Unknown **026**

1861
Yale Cylinder Lock, Linus Yale Jr **027**

1866
Key-Opening Can, J Osterhoudt **028**
Damenstock, Michael Thonet **029**

1868
Remington No. 1, Christopher Latham Sholes,
    Carlos Glidden **030**
Tabasco Bottle, Edmund McIlhenny **031**

1869
ABC Blocks, John Wesley Hyatt **032**

1870s
Waribashi Chopsticks, Designer Unknown **033**

c.1873
Sugar Bowl, Christopher Dresser **034**

1874
Peugeot Pepper Mill, Jean-Frédéric Peugeot,
    Jean-Pierre Peugeot **035**

1878
Toast Rack, Christopher Dresser **036**

1879
National Standard Pillar Box, Post Office
    Engineering Department **037**
Type Edison Lamp, Thomas Alva Edison **038**

Corkscrew, Peter Holmblad **774**
4875 Chair, Carlo Bartoli **775**
Rubik's Cube®, Ernö Rubik **776**
Banco Catalano, Óscar Tusquets Blanca, Lluís Clotet **777**
VW Golf A1, Giorgetto Giugiaro **778**
Chambord Coffee Maker, Carsten Jørgensen **779**
Vertebra Chair, Emilio Ambasz, Giancarlo Piretti **780**

1975
Kickstool, Wedo Design Team **781**
Brompton Folding Bicycle, Andrew Ritchie **782**
Papillona Lamp, Afra Scarpa, Tobia Scarpa **783**
Tratto Pen, Design Group Italia **784**

1976
Uni-Tray, Riki Watanabe **785**
Suomi Table Service, Timo Sarpaneva **786**
Kryptonite K4, Michael Zane, Peter Zane **787**
Ashtray, Anna Castelli Ferrieri **788**
Sonora, Vico Magistretti **789**
Glass Chair and Collection, Shiro Kuramata **790**

1977
Nuvola Rossa, Vico Magistretti **791**
Cricket Maxi Lighter, Cricket Design Team **792**
Vacuum Jug, Erik Magnussen **793**
Atollo 233/D, Vico Magistretti **794**
Telephone Model F78, Henning Andreasen **795**
Cab, Mario Bellini **796**
Atari Joystick CX40, Atari Design Team **797**
9090 Espresso Coffee Maker, Richard Sapper **798**

1978
Proust Chair, Alessandro Mendini **799**
Billy Shelf, IKEA of Sweden **800**
ET 44 Pocket Calculator, Dieter Rams, Dietrich Lubs **801**
A'dammer, Aldo van den Nieuwelaar **802**
Mattia Esse, Enrico Contreas **803**
Frisbi, Achille Castiglioni **804**
5070 Condiment Set, Ettore Sottsass **805**
Gacela (part of Clásica collection),
    Joan Casas y Ortínez **806**

1979
Maglite, Anthony Maglica **807**
Boston Shaker, Ettore Sottsass **808**
Balans Variable Stool, Peter Opsvik **809**
Absolut Vodka, Carlsson & Broman **810**
Headphone Stereo Walkman, TPS-L2 Sony
    Design Team **811**

1980
Post-it ® Notes, Spencer Silver, Art Fry **812**
Dúplex, Javier Mariscal **813**
Praxis 35, Mario Bellini **814**
Parola, Gae Aulenti **815**
Wink, Toshiyuki Kita **816**
Panda, Giorgetto Giugiaro **817**
Tavolo con ruote, Gae Aulenti **818**
Acetoliere, Achille Castiglioni **819**
Grob 102 Standard Astir III, Grob-Werke
    Design Team **820**
La Conica Coffee Maker, Aldo Rossi **821**

1981
Callimaco Lamp, Ettore Sottsass **822**
Commodore C64, Commodore Design Team **823**
Sinclair ZX81, Sir Clive Sinclair **824**

1982
Durabeam Torch, Nick Butler, BIB Consultants
    for Duracell **825**
18-8 Stainless Steel Flatware, Sori Yanagi **826**
Chair, Donald Judd **827**
MR30 Stabmixer, Ludwig Littmann **828**
Voltes V Transformer, Kouzin Ohno **829**
Costes Chair, Philippe Starck **830**
Renault Espace I, Matra Design Team, Renault
    Design Team **831**
LOMO-Compact-Automate, Mikhail Holomyansky **832**
Global Knife, Komin Yamada **833**
Philips Compact Disc, Philips/Sony Design Team **834**
Croma & Piuma, Makio Hasuike **835**
First Chair, Michele De Lucchi **836**

1983
PST (Pocket Survival Tool), Timothy S Leatherman **837**
Streamliner, Ulf Hanses **838**
Lightning TRS, Rollerblade Design Team **839**
Swatch 1st Collection, Swatch Lab **840**
9091 Kettle, Richard Sapper **841**

1984
Can Family, Hansjerg Maier-Aichen **842**
Apple Macintosh, Hartmut Esslinger, frogdesign **843**
Sheraton Chair, 664 Robert Venturi **844**
Gespanntes Regal, Wolfgang Laubersheimer **845**
Ya Ya Ho, Ingo Maurer & Team **846**

1985
Pasta Set, Massimo Morozzi **847**

Kappa Knives, Dr Karl-Peter Born **927**
JI1 Sofa Bed, James Irvine **928**

1995
Mono Tables, Konstantin Grcic **929**
X-Shaped Rubber Bands, Läufer Design Team **930**
Genie of the Lamp, Wally with Germán Frers **931**
Aprilia Moto 6.5, Philippe Starck **932**

1996
Meda Chair, Alberto Meda **933**
Washing-Up Bowl, Ole Jensen **934**
Ginevra, Ettore Sottsass **935**
Nokia 5100, Frank Nuovo, Nokia Design Team **936**
TGV Duplex, Roger Tallon **937**
Canon Ixus, Yasushi Shiotani **938**
Aquatinta, Michele De Lucchi, Alberto Nason **939**
Loop Coffee Table, Barber Osgerby **940**
Jack Light, Tom Dixon **941**
Polypropylene Stand File Box, MUJI Design Team **942**
U-Line, Maarten van Severen **943**
Motorola StarTAC Wearable Cellular Phone, Motorola
    Design Team **944**
Knotted Chair, Marcel Wanders, Droog Design **945**
The Block Lamp, Harri Koskinen **946**

1997
Fantastic Plastic Elastic, Ron Arad **947**
Cable Turtle, Jan Hoekstra, FLEX/the INNOVATIONLAB
    948
Dish Doctor, Marc Newson **949**
Bombo Stool, Stefano Giovannoni **950**
MV Agusta F4 Serie Oro, Massimo Tamburini **951**
Yamaha Silent Cello Model N. SVC100K,
    Yamaha Design Team **952**
Silver/Felt Bracelet, Pia Wallén **953**
Bowls and Salad Cutlery, Carina Seth Andersson **954**
Apollo Torch, Marc Newson **955**
Tom Vac, Ron Arad **956**
Garbino, Karim Rashid **957**
Wait, Matthew Hilton **958**

1998
Dahlström 98, Björn Dahlström **959**
Fortebraccio, Alberto Meda, Paolo Rizzatto **960**
Citterio 98, Antonio Citterio, Glen Oliver Löw **961**
Glo-Ball, Jasper Morrison **962**
Optic Glass, Arnout Visser **963**
Ypsilon, Mario Bellini **964**
May Day Lamp, Konstantin Grcic **965**

1999
Aibo Robot, Hajime Sorayama, Sony Design Team **966**
Soundwave, Teppo Asikainen **967**
Air-Chair, Jasper Morrison **968**
Wall-Mounted CD Player, Naoto Fukasawa **969**
Random Light, Bertjan Pot **970**
Low Pad, Jasper Morrison **971**
Relations Glasses, Konstantin Grcic **972**
930 Soft, Werner Aisslinger **973**

2000
Citterio Collective Tools 2000, Antonio Citterio,
    Glen Oliver Löw **974**
LEM, Shin Azumi **975**
Strap, NL Architects **976**
Spring Chair, Ronan Bouroullec, Erwan Bouroullec **977**

2001
PowerBook G4, Jonathan Ive, Apple Design Team **978**
iPod, Jonathan Ive, Apple Design Team **979**
Wednesday Garland, Tord Boontje **980**
PET Bottle, Ross Lovegrove **981**
Segway Human Transporter, Segway Design Team **982**
Oil Lamp, Erik Magnussen **983**
One-Two, James Irvine **984**
V-Rod, Willie G Davidson **985**
Aquos C1, Toshiyuki Kita **986**
Joyn Office System, Ronan Bouroullec,
    Erwan Bouroullec **987**

2002
Outdoor Cooking Tools, Harri Koskinen **988**
MVS Chaise, Maarten van Severen **989**
BeoVision 5, David Lewis **990**
Kyocera KYOTOP Series, Kyocera Corporation Design
    Team **991**
Pipe Sospensione, Herzog & de Meuron **992**
PAL Henry Kloss, Tom DeVesto **993**

2003
Time & Weather, Philippe Starck **994**
Beolab 5, David Lewis **995**
Chair_One, Konstantin Grcic **996**
Brunch Set, Jasper Morrison **997**

2004
iMac G5, Apple Design Team **998**
Lunar, Barber Osgerby **999**

Texts were written by the following (the numbers refer to the relevant product entries):

Simon Alderson 051, 056, 084, 109, 115, 121, 147, 175, 184, 185, 186, 198, 216 223, 399, 494, 515, 559, 587, 602, 604, 651, 708, 729, 807, 811, 858, 874, 876, 945

Ralph Ball 023, 157, 307, 311, 372, 408, 526, 509, 546, 608, 631, 844

Edward Barber 001, 025, 302, 342, 355, 398, 572

Lis Bogdan 289, 321, 352, 386, 572, 574, 710, 732, 746, 796

Annabelle Campbell 044, 065, 110, 122, 151, 159, 160, 201, 246, 273, 306, 319, 323, 382, 385, 390, 404, 463, 492, 495, 531, 536, 567, 589, 629, 646, 647, 656, 664, 671, 673, 687, 765, 777, 779, 790, 798, 805, 833, 849, 850, 884, 888, 892, 911, 924, 925, 949, 974, 984, 988, 991

Claire Catterall 454, 704, 722, 726, 736, 740, 750, 755, 773, 793, 799, 809, 821, 827, 830, 842, 857, 860, 866, 913, 920, 926, 959, 971

Daniel Charny / Roberto Feo 103, 108, 224, 247, 422, 559, 593, 599, 812, 864

Andrea Codrington 014, 015, 029, 069, 071, 088, 131, 217, 244, 247, 267, 285, 286, 288, 314, 341, 358, 402, 413, 481, 488, 506, 521, 553, 609, 658, 707, 723, 905

Louise-Anne Comeau / Geoffrey Monge 130, 235, 251, 347, 400, 586, 679, 689, 791, 827, 834, 887, 929, 962, 940, 951, 957, 975, 986, 989, 994, 997

Alberto Cossu 105, 190, 234, 281, 340, 407, 447, 669, 674, 739, 803, 931

Ilse Crawford 009, 048, 150, 154, 275, 375, 457, 469, 504, 563, 745, 895

Kevin Davies 061, 111, 198, 205, 206, 207, 208, 211, 243, 250, 282, 330, 331, 364, 378, 383, 420, 423, 438, 460, 483, 498, 500, 513, 519, 552, 561, 579, 612, 645, 694, 737, 743, 774, 786, 916

Jan Dekker 008, 046, 050, 076, 078, 080, 099, 141, 143, 168, 270, 284, 292, 353, 361, 377, 388, 426, 429, 432, 499, 518, 520, 524, 542, 575, 615, 713, 763, 886, 912, 955, 993

John Dunnigan 035, 254, 262, 274, 371, 418, 505, 534, 597, 881

Caroline Ednie 039, 040, 077, 086, 090, 112, 253, 272, 296, 363, 434, 449, 458, 459, 527, 548, 570, 573, 582, 594, 636, 659, 660, 666, 698, 715, 717, 758, 767, 771, 772, 783, 800, 802, 824, 825, 838, 845, 867, 872, 882, 891, 906, 935, 937, 953, 960, 983, 995

Aline Ferrari 010, 013, 019, 089, 169, 256, 335, 387, 442, 490, 868, 939, 998

Max Fraser 022, 072, 085, 142, 188, 204, 381, 405, 428, 444, 508, 555, 596, 626, 675, 709, 711, 738, 770, 788, 808, 847, 853, 863, 919, 958, 981

Richard Garnier 114, 162, 203, 213

Charles Gates 215, 351, 431, 516, 532, 535, 537, 640, 718, 795

Laura Giacalone 003, 446, 648

Grant Gibson 016, 047, 054, 060, 067, 117, 125, 129, 194, 236, 288, 304, 325, 354, 445, 594, 614, 618, 697, 730, 735, 756, 859, 873, 875, 883, 990, 933, 999

Anna Goodall 012, 028, 056, 095, 097, 158, 303, 412, 501, 502, 623, 630, 753, 820, 904

Katy Djunn 063, 140, 164, 189, 219, 220, 239, 312, 327, 585, 688, 841

Ultan Guilfoyle 092, 113, 133, 137, 231, 279, 298, 310, 316, 360, 410, 510, 493, 533, 547, 571, 569, 577, 591, 653, 677, 685, 701, 705, 761, 851, 880, 908, 932, 951, 985

Roo Gunzi 087, 237, 336, 368, 379, 389, 468, 889, 943

Bruce Hannah 011, 074, 278, 301, 411, 436, 451, 616, 780

Sam Hecht 479, 632, 637, 734, 969

Albert Hill 124, 305, 401, 409, 440, 453, 471, 475, 491, 525, 541, 556, 568, 617, 620, 633, 693, 869, 961